AF580056

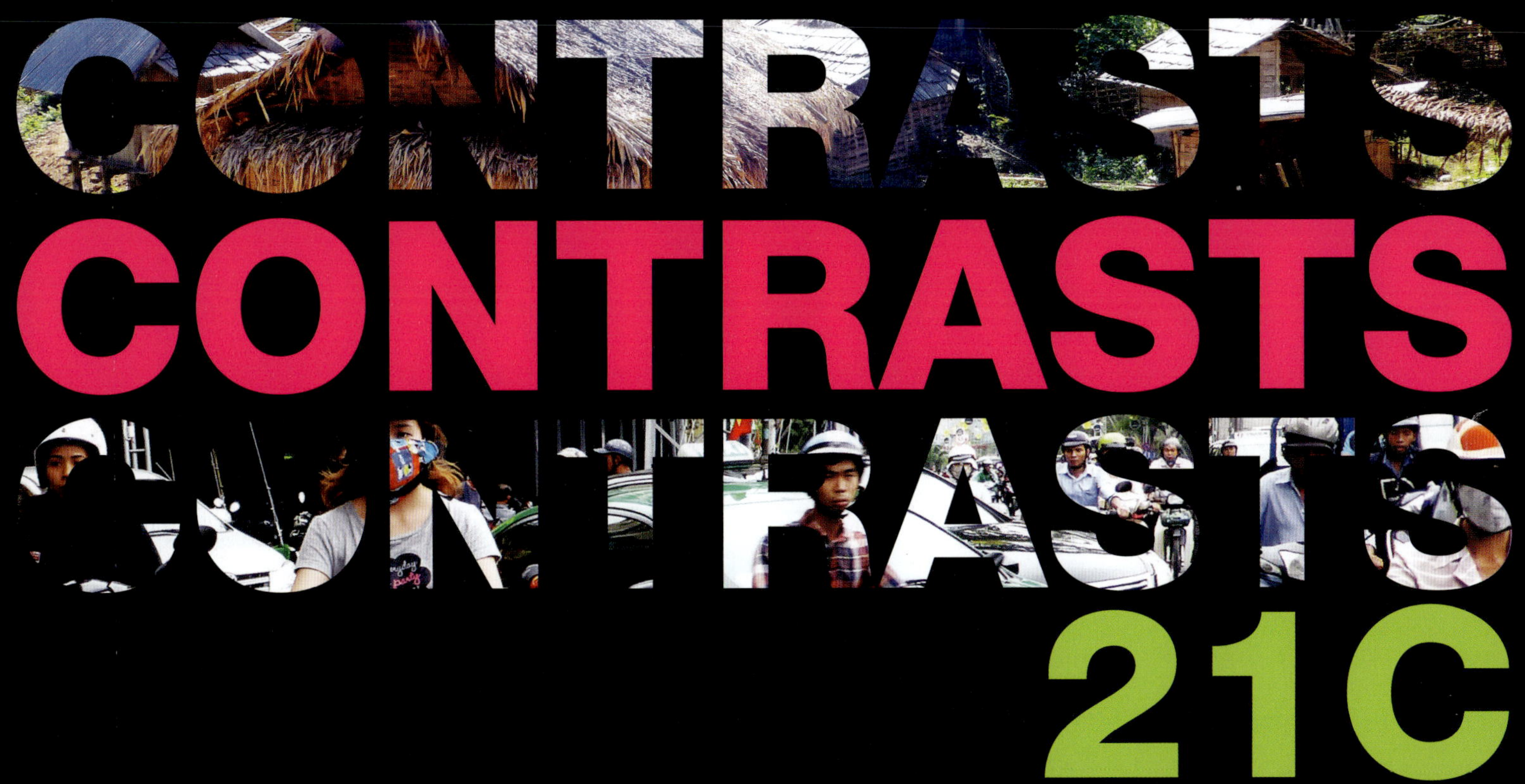
CONTRASTS
CONTRASTS
CONTRASTS
21C

CONTRASTS 21C

People & Places
Vietnam, Laos & Cambodia

A Photo Essay

BILL CAPLAN

First published in 2018 by Green Frigate Books

Green Frigate is an imprint of Libri Publishing

ISBN: 978-1-911451-04-4

A CIP catalogue record for this book is available from The British Library

Book and cover design by the author and Carnegie Book Production

Printed in the USA by Versa Press

Libri Publishing
Brunel House
Volunteer Way
Faringdon
Oxfordshire

Dedicated to the peoples of
Vietnam, Laos and Cambodia.

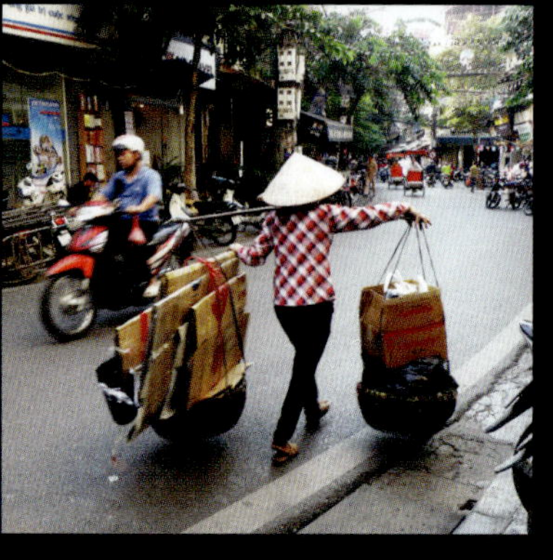

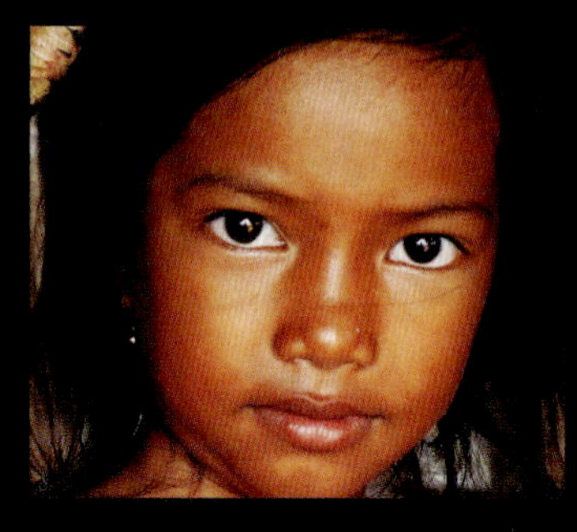

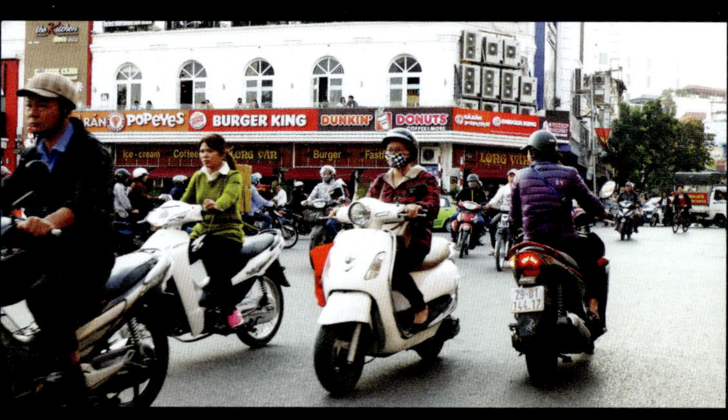
POPEYES
BURGER KING
DUNKIN'
DONUTS
Ice-cream
Burger

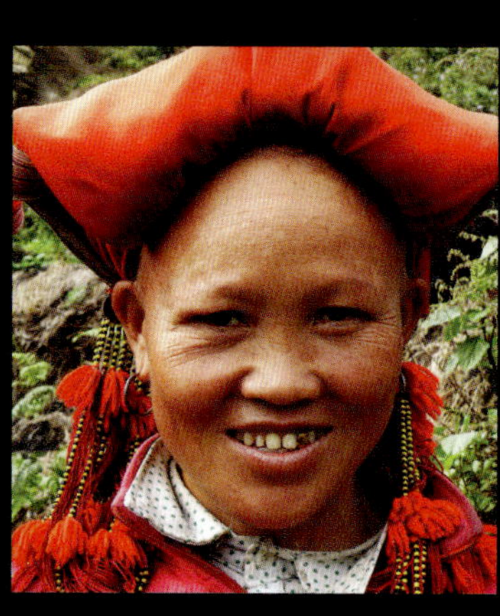

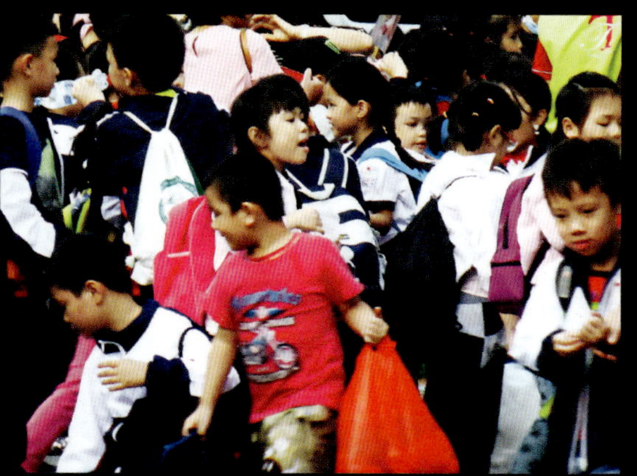

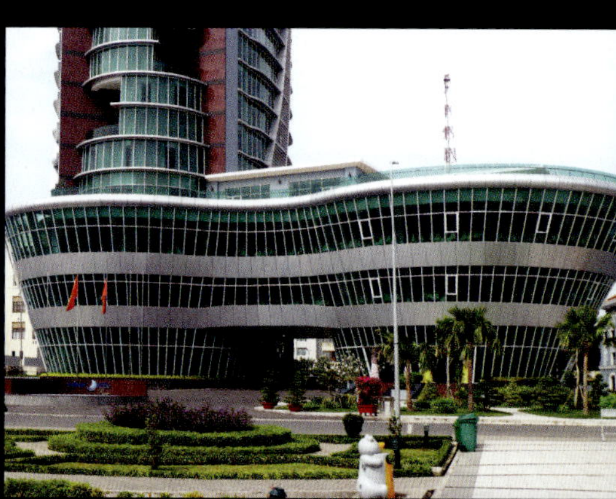

Contents

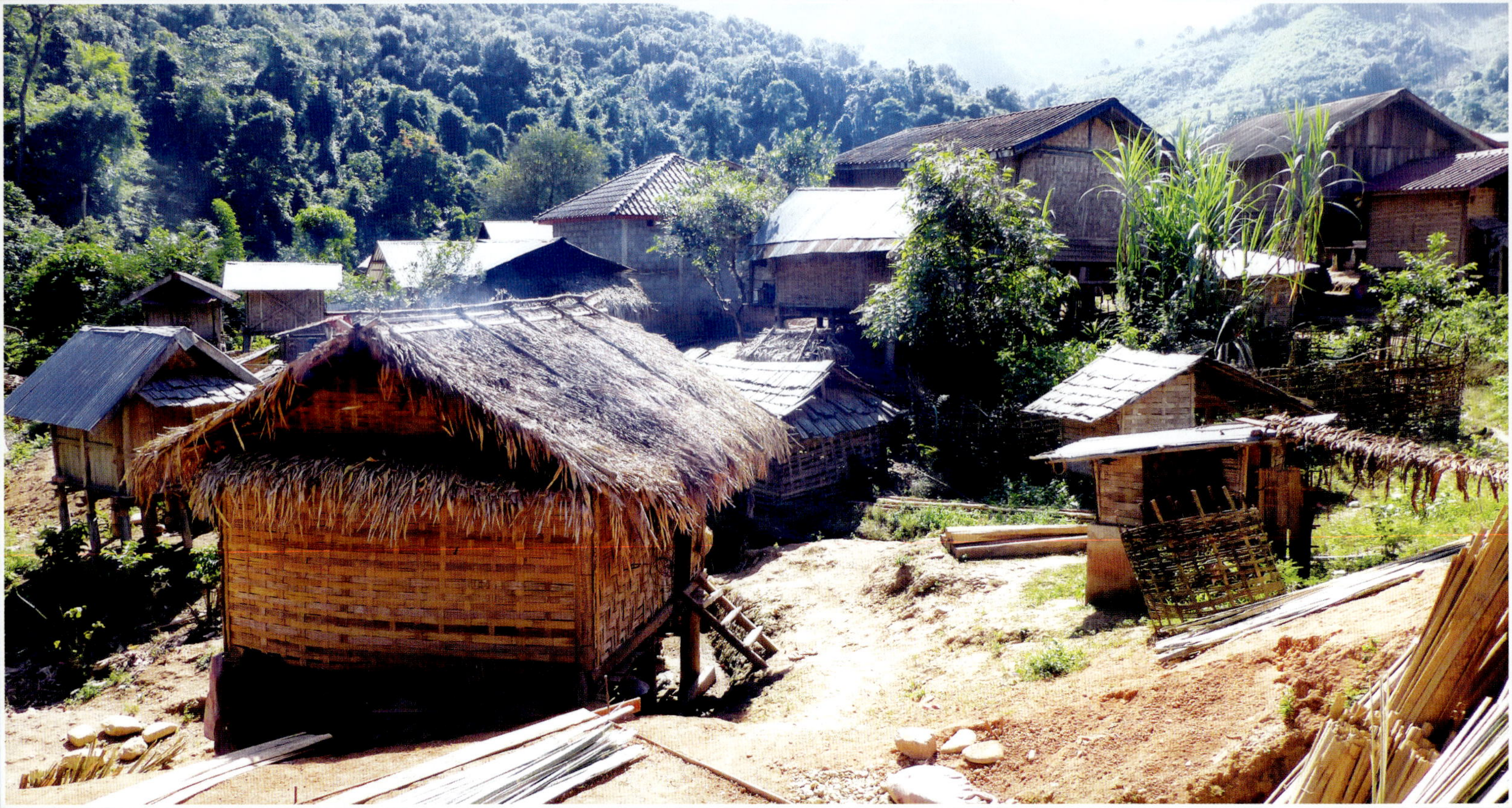

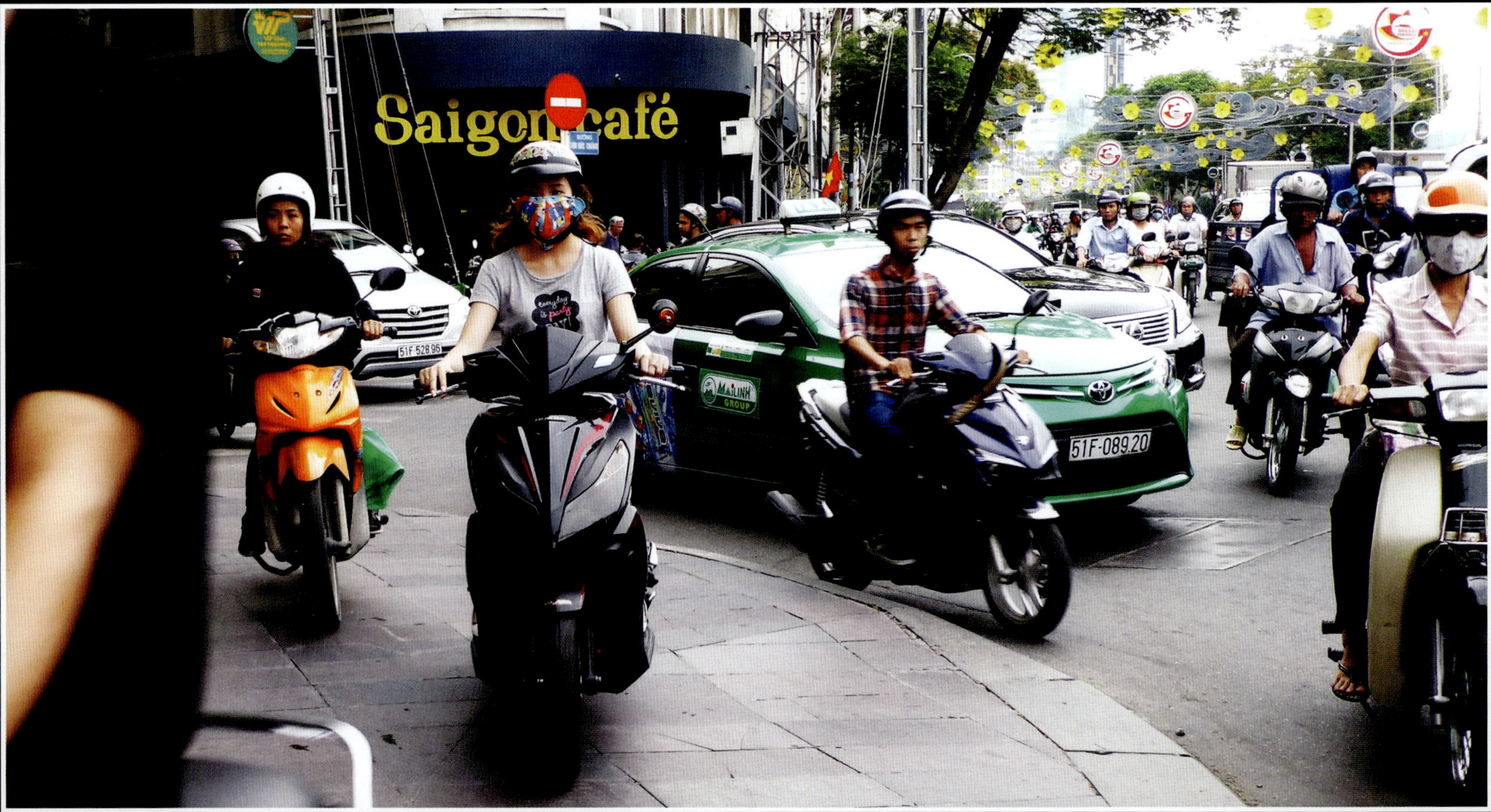
Saigon café
MAILINH GROUP
51F-089.20

Preface

Over the last millennium, an array of ethnic peoples migrated south from China to safer havens in Vietnam, Laos and Cambodia only to be dispersed by those who governed, wars and widespread discrimination. Minority groups settled predominantly in the mountainous terrain just south of the Chinese border while the ethnic majority in each country populated rural areas in the central lowlands and the banks of the Mekong and Red rivers. Lands of stunning beauty, these mountains, central highlands and river deltas are now home to a rich diversity of cultures.

Rural communities in Vietnam, Laos and Cambodia are generally small. They function outside the mainstream economy. Life, though tightly knit by family, ethnicity and tradition, is arduous; challenged by the impoverishing conditions of subsistence farming and foraging. Families lacking land to cultivate or water to fish or farm have few options apart from laboring, often for foreign companies that lease government territory. Although these leases fund each nation's treasury and often include foreign-built roads, railways and dams which facilitate development, many such leaseholds deplete future resources or pollute, to the detriment of the environment and its sustainability. Many have 20- to 30-year terms. Though still minimal, access to education, health services and paved roads is expanding, triaged from the restricted funds available.

While foreign investment in tourism nurtures the germination and growth of small business and service providers, this too brings environmental impacts and cultural intrusions. An increasing exposure to outsiders, travel and the lure of city life beckons the young, stressing families and shrinking village populations. The result is an admixture of ancient tradition and present-day reality. Progress for the rural peoples of Vietnam, Laos and Cambodia brings consequences to their customary existence.

To visitors from the developed world, lifestyle disparities between the urban and rural areas might seem a 21st-century anomaly, yet they are the norm for tens of millions of people and their communities throughout Southeast Asia. The Lao People's Democratic Republic and Cambodia register among the United Nations "List of Least Developed Countries". Although Vietnam has taken significant strides in economic development, a large portion of its ethnic minority and rural poor rely on subsistence farming and foraging from the land and waters. Inadequate food storage, cooking, health and hygiene conditions often prevail in all three of these countries.

In my prior book ***Buildings Are for People*** (Libri Publishing UK 2016), addressed to architects and planners, I remarked that we journeyed from "adapting" to the environment to "creating" our environment. No longer building the proverbial "primitive hut" for human shelter, our dwellings have evolved from creations of nature to creations of science. Yet in these areas of Southeast Asia, many communities are still rooted in "adapting to the environment"; where in 2017, shelters created from nature still constitute most or all of the built environment; where the primitive architecture of human shelter and husbandry is sustainable by default – dependent on local or foraged materials and reuse. One's lens and perspective quickly alter.

Living off the land or water is a family or community affair that relies on an ability to farm rice, to gather sustenance from the forests, rivers, ponds or paddies, or to trap or farm fish. While difficult, it inculcates resourcefulness and ingenuity. Aspirations for food security, healthcare, transportation, education and living in peaceful communities provide an impetus to yield more, to earn more, to have more.

The built environment there, however wanting, is often innovative, optimizing re-use and constructed from local materials. At the same time, this inherent sustainability is offset by practices such as the open air burning of trash and agricultural waste, causing extreme air pollution. In rural Vietnam, Laos and Cambodia, the architecture of people's lives and the architecture of their shelter is the "architecture of necessity". The toils of daily life are borne with dignity and pride, and endured with the joys of family, community and celebration; endured with an eye toward the future. To the visitor, a geniality belies the hardship.

From linear villages lining roadsides and shorelines, to small hamlets and large cities, this is a story best experienced by exploration, best told through its images – the people – their faces, their eyes and often their smiles; and their environs – these most incredible places. It is a story of 21st-century contrasts, told here in a photojournalistic essay that hopes to bring attention to the cultural diversity of this region, and its challenges.

The author's proceeds from the publication of this book will be donated to assist youth and educational organizations in this region.

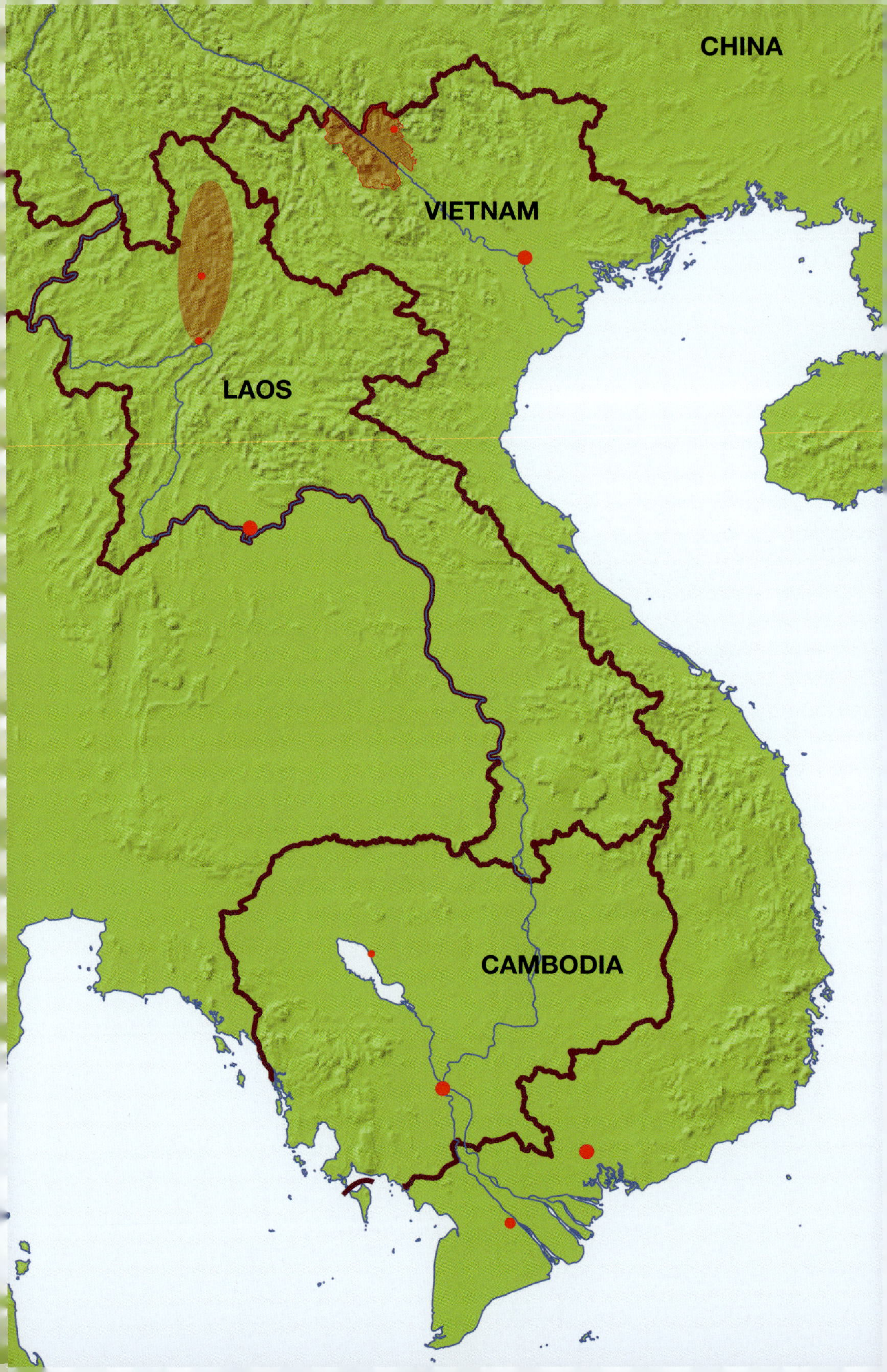
CHINA
VIETNAM
LAOS
CAMBODIA

and these most incredible places.

Contrasts in this 21st century.

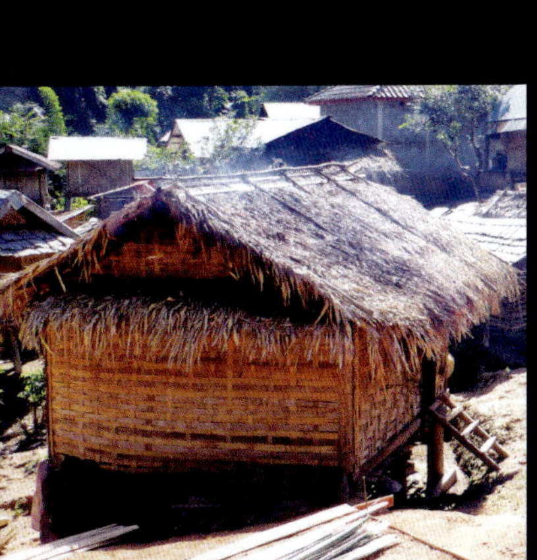

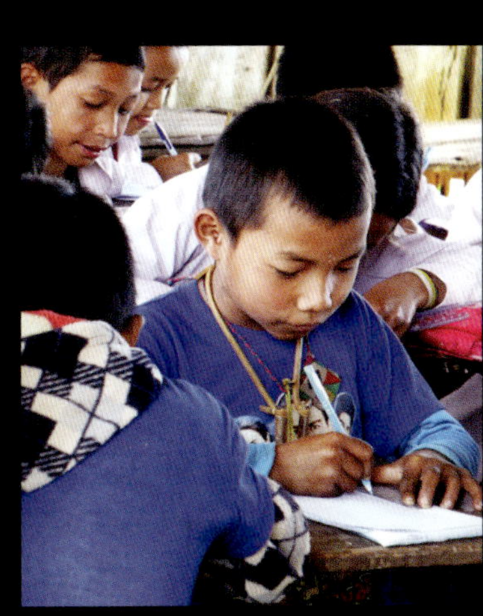

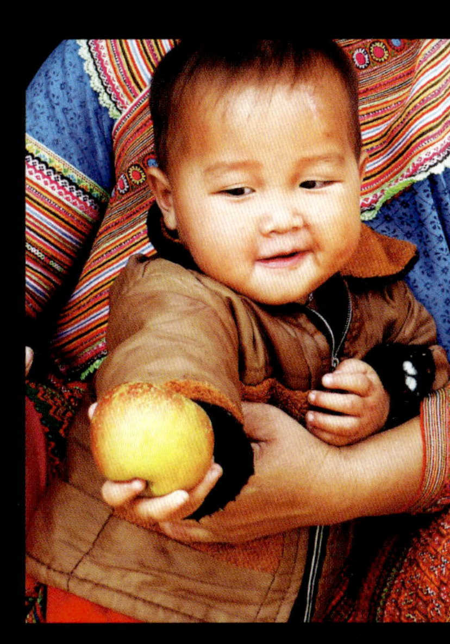

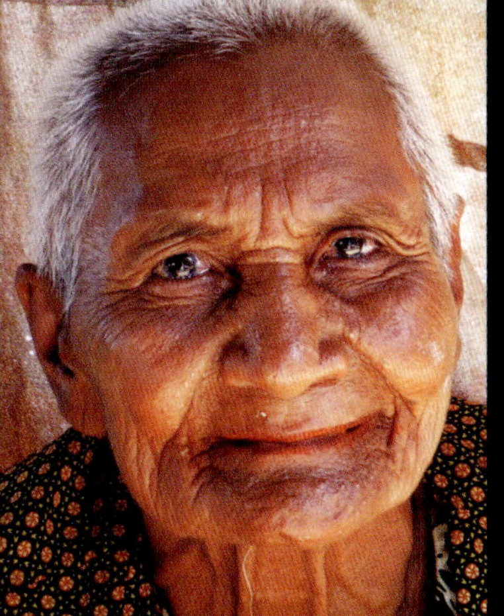

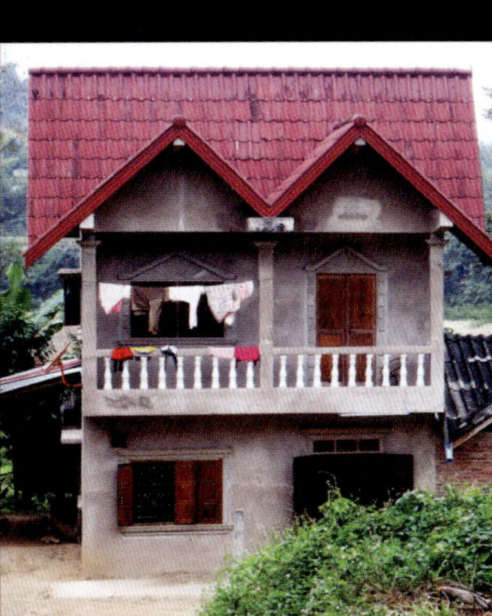

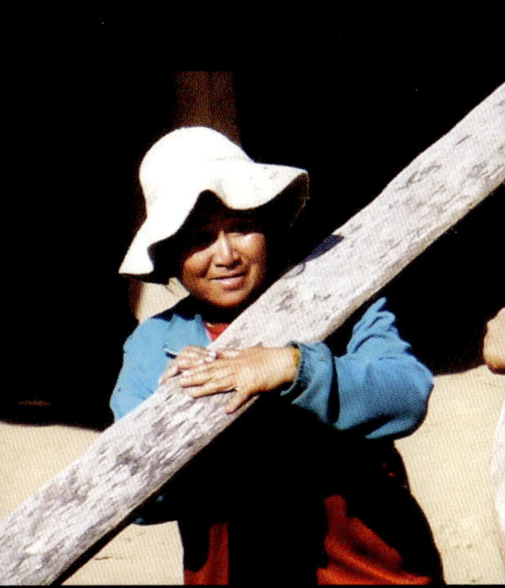

ONE

In the mountains of northwest Vietnam

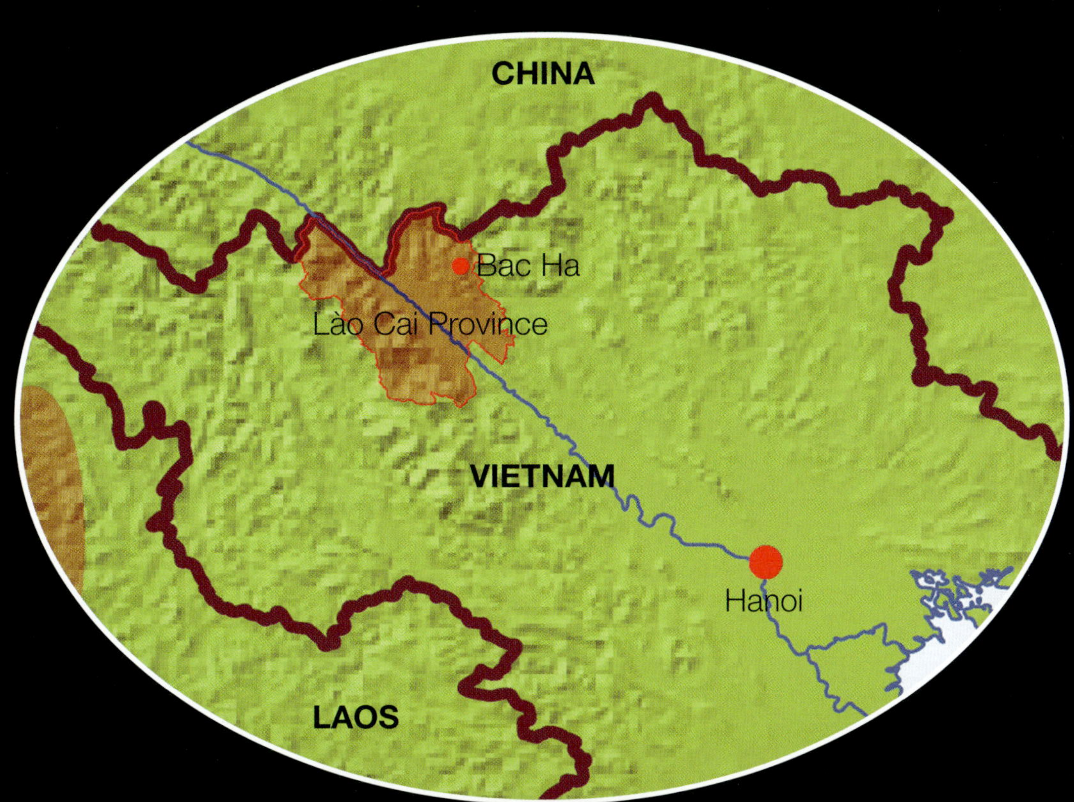

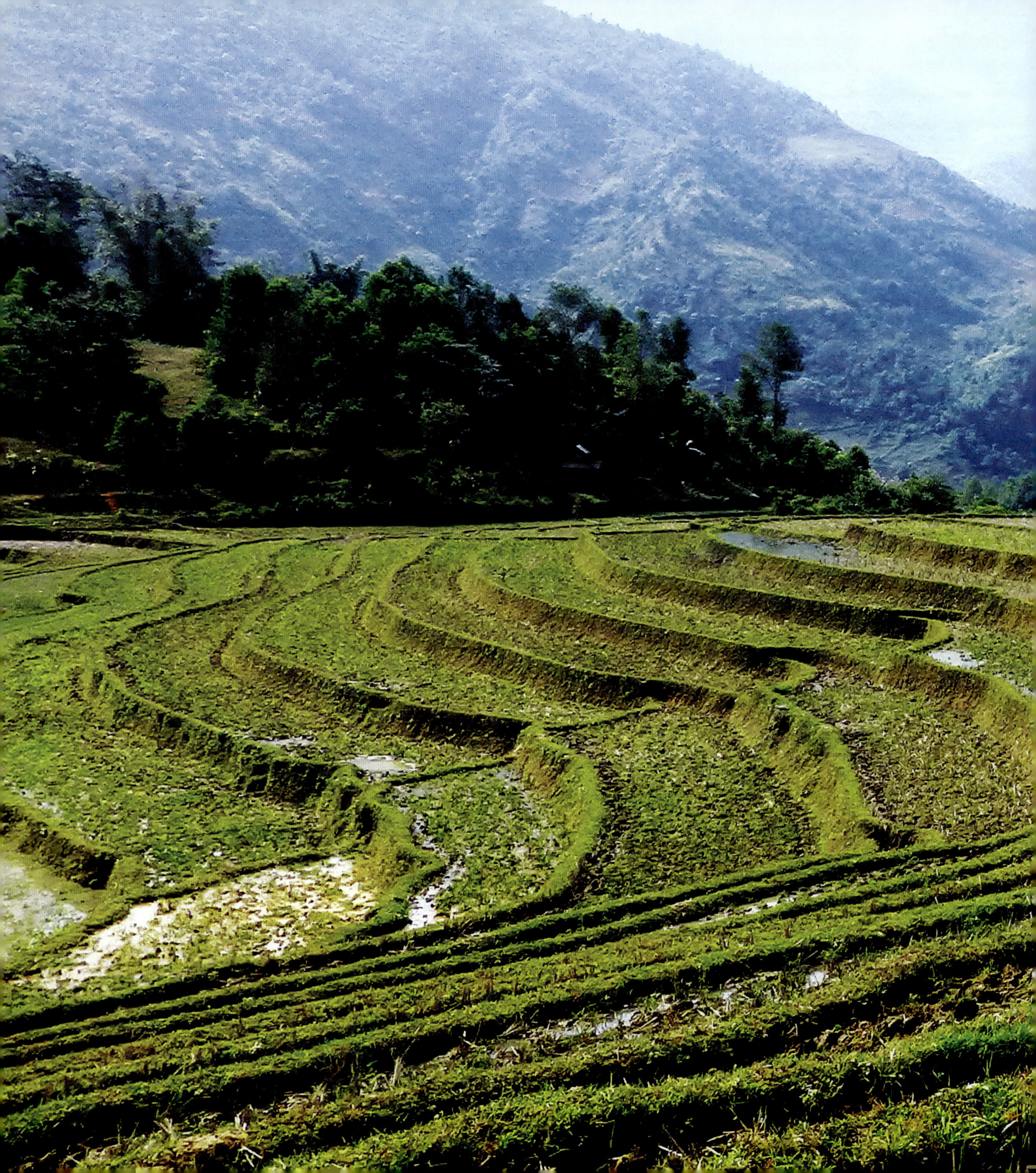

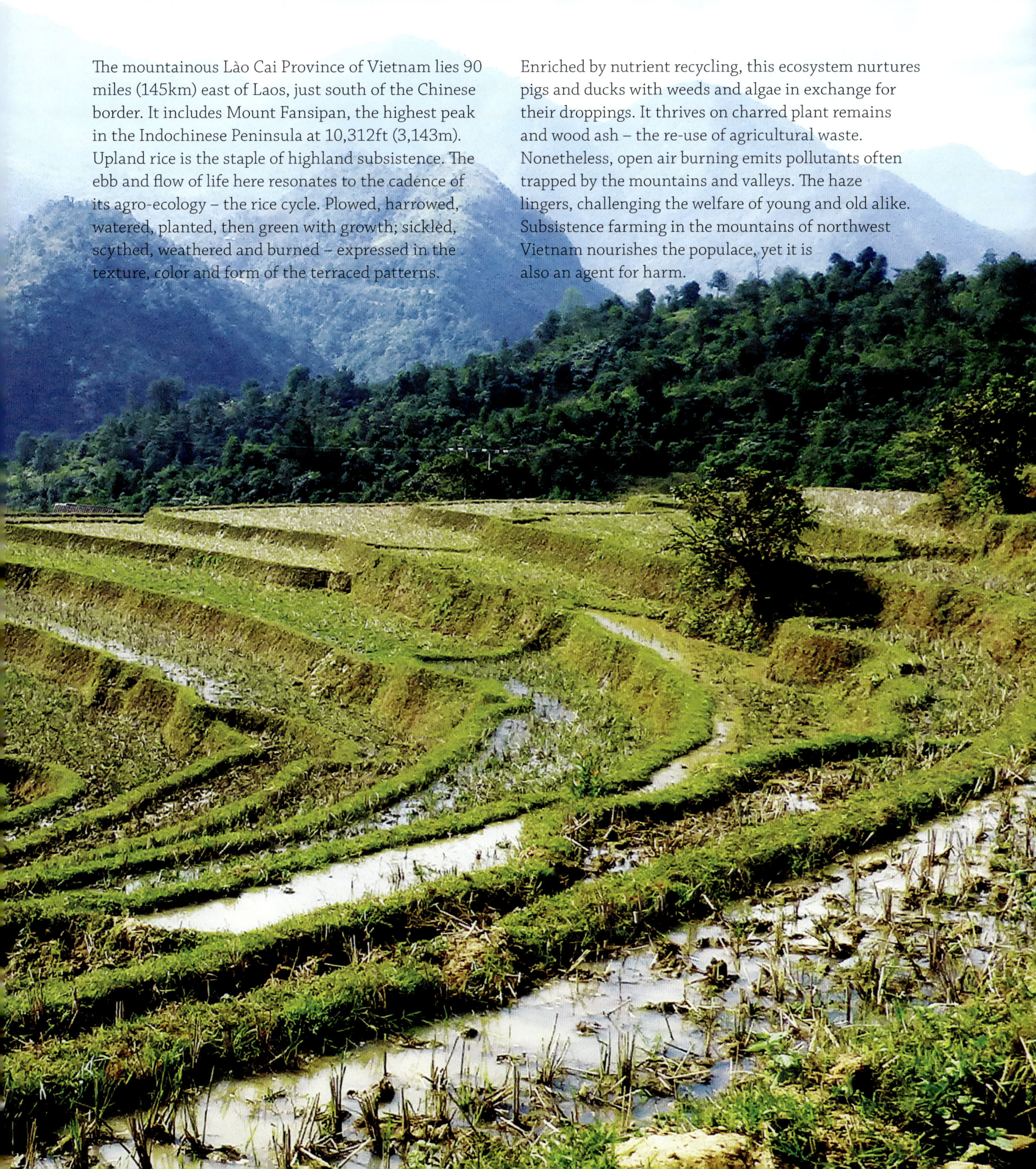

The mountainous Lào Cai Province of Vietnam lies 90 miles (145km) east of Laos, just south of the Chinese border. It includes Mount Fansipan, the highest peak in the Indochinese Peninsula at 10,312ft (3,143m). Upland rice is the staple of highland subsistence. The ebb and flow of life here resonates to the cadence of its agro-ecology – the rice cycle. Plowed, harrowed, watered, planted, then green with growth; sickled, scythed, weathered and burned – expressed in the texture, color and form of the terraced patterns.

Enriched by nutrient recycling, this ecosystem nurtures pigs and ducks with weeds and algae in exchange for their droppings. It thrives on charred plant remains and wood ash – the re-use of agricultural waste. Nonetheless, open air burning emits pollutants often trapped by the mountains and valleys. The haze lingers, challenging the welfare of young and old alike. Subsistence farming in the mountains of northwest Vietnam nourishes the populace, yet it is also an agent for harm.

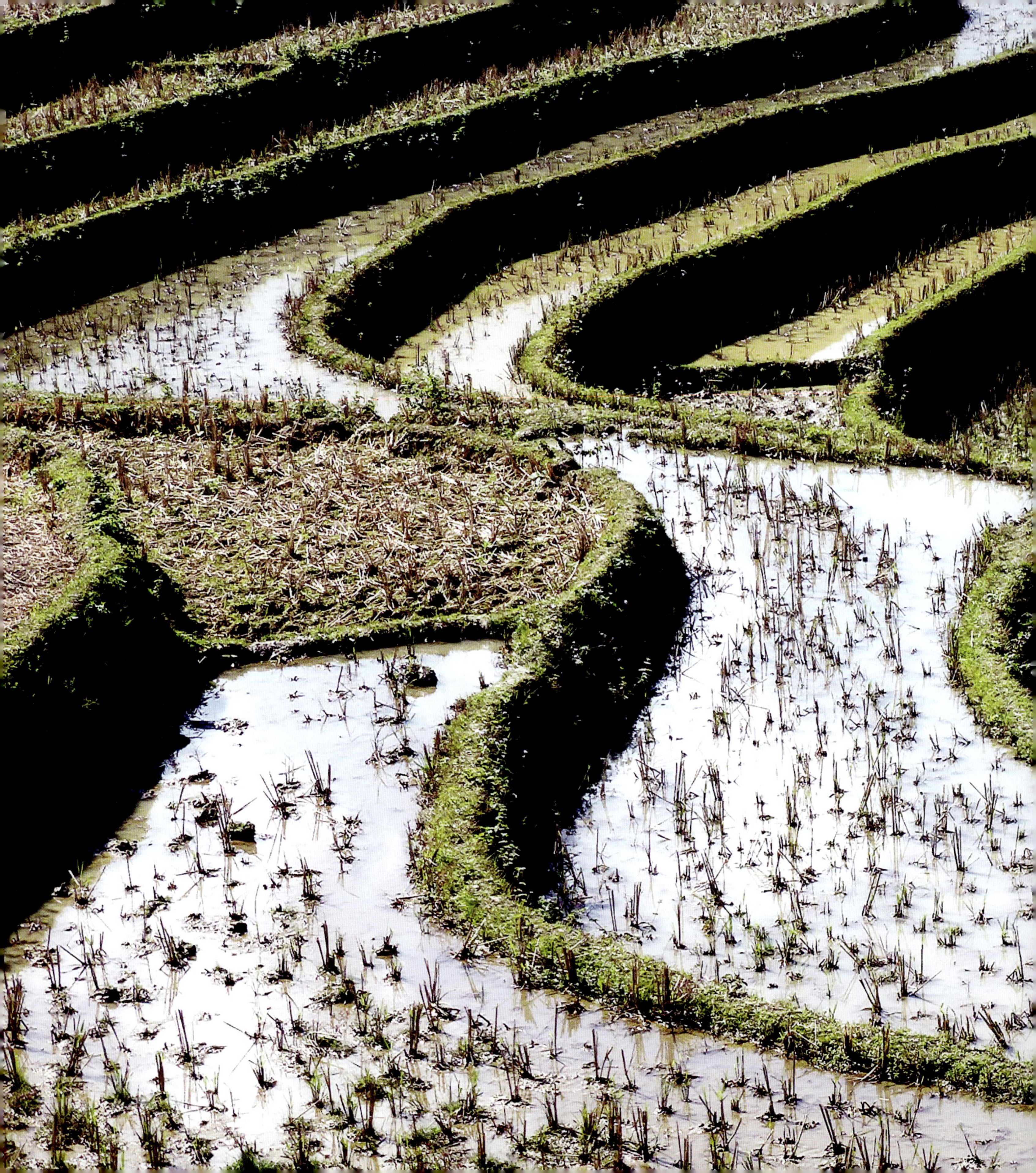

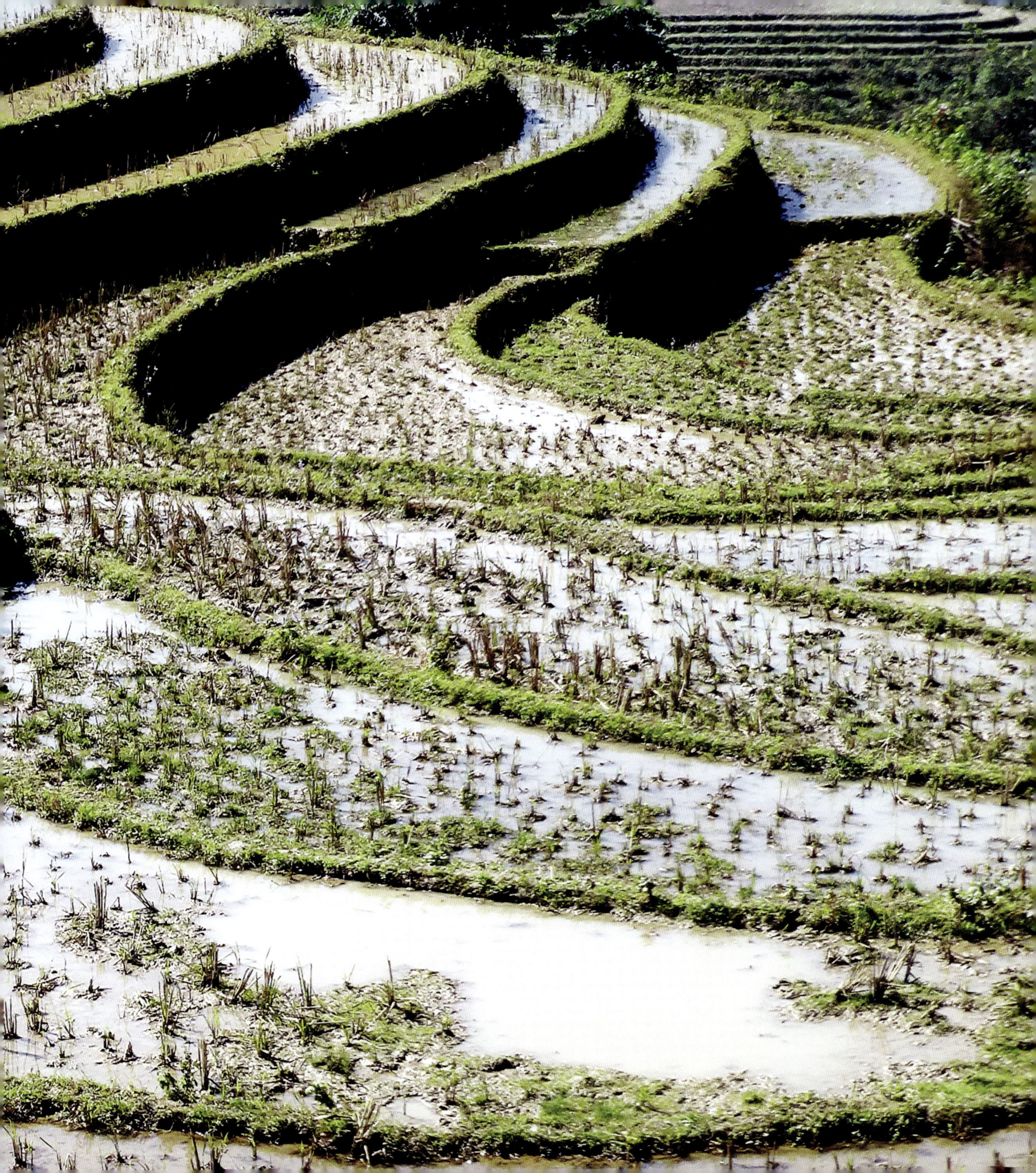

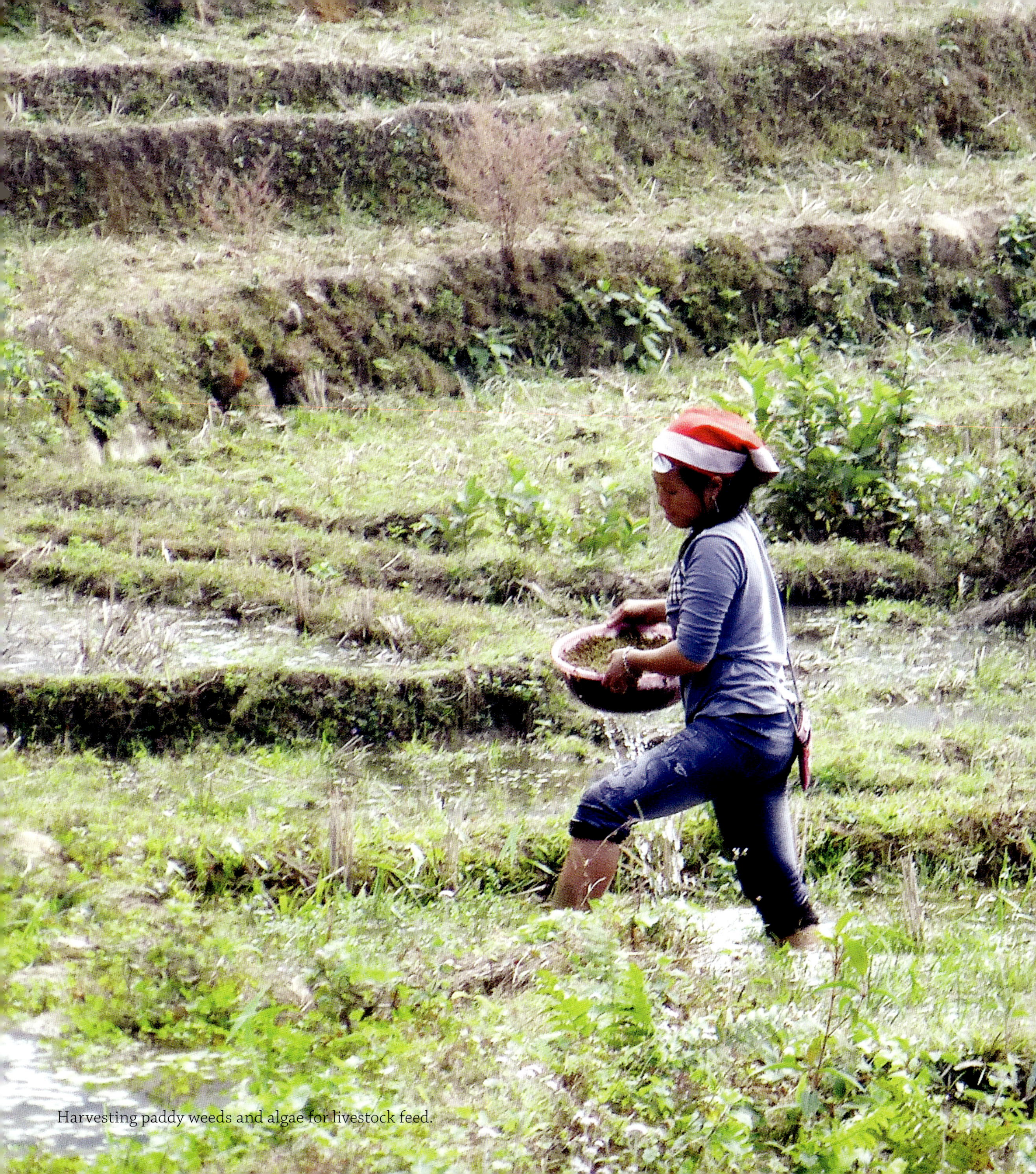
Harvesting paddy weeds and algae for livestock feed.

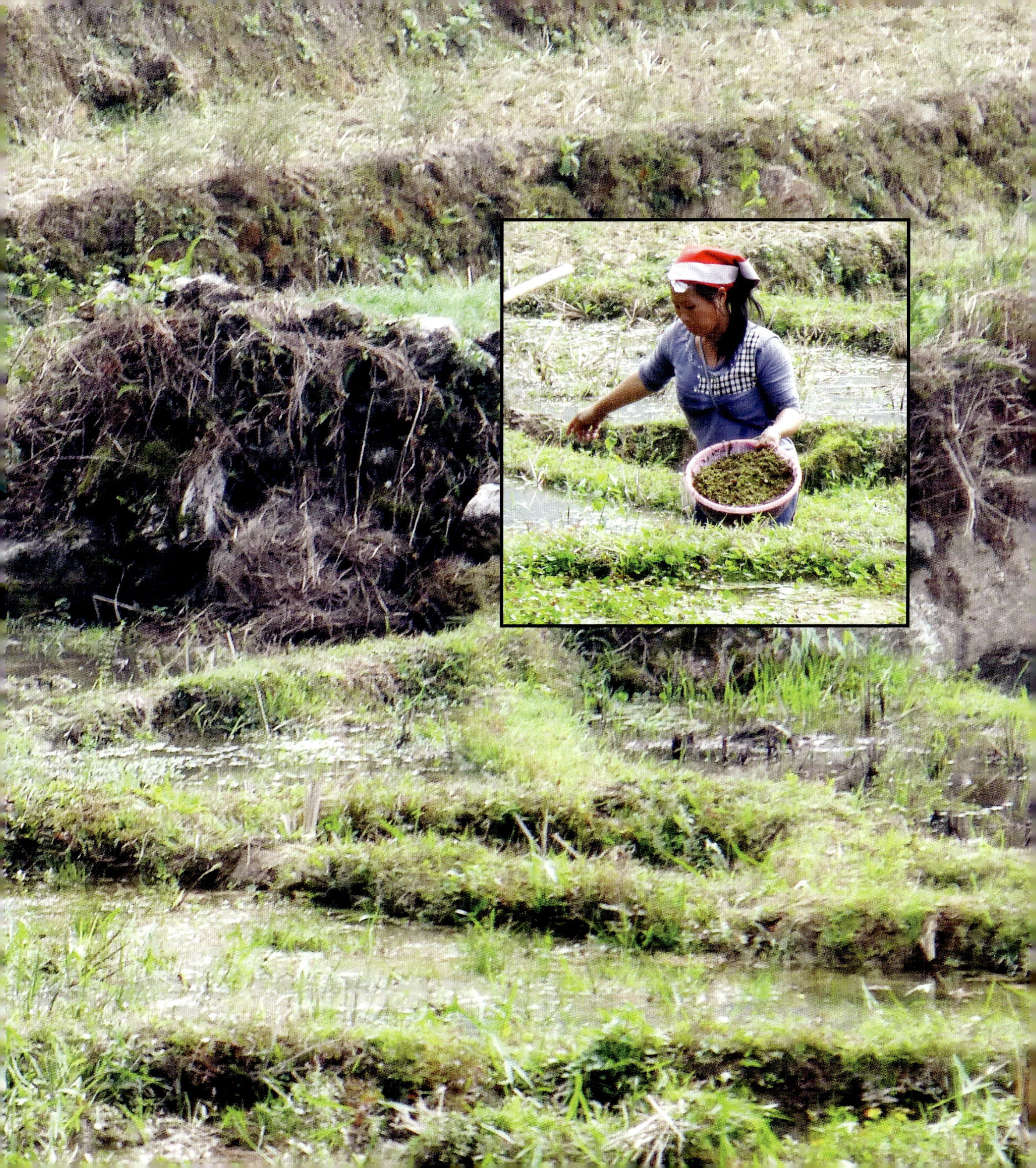

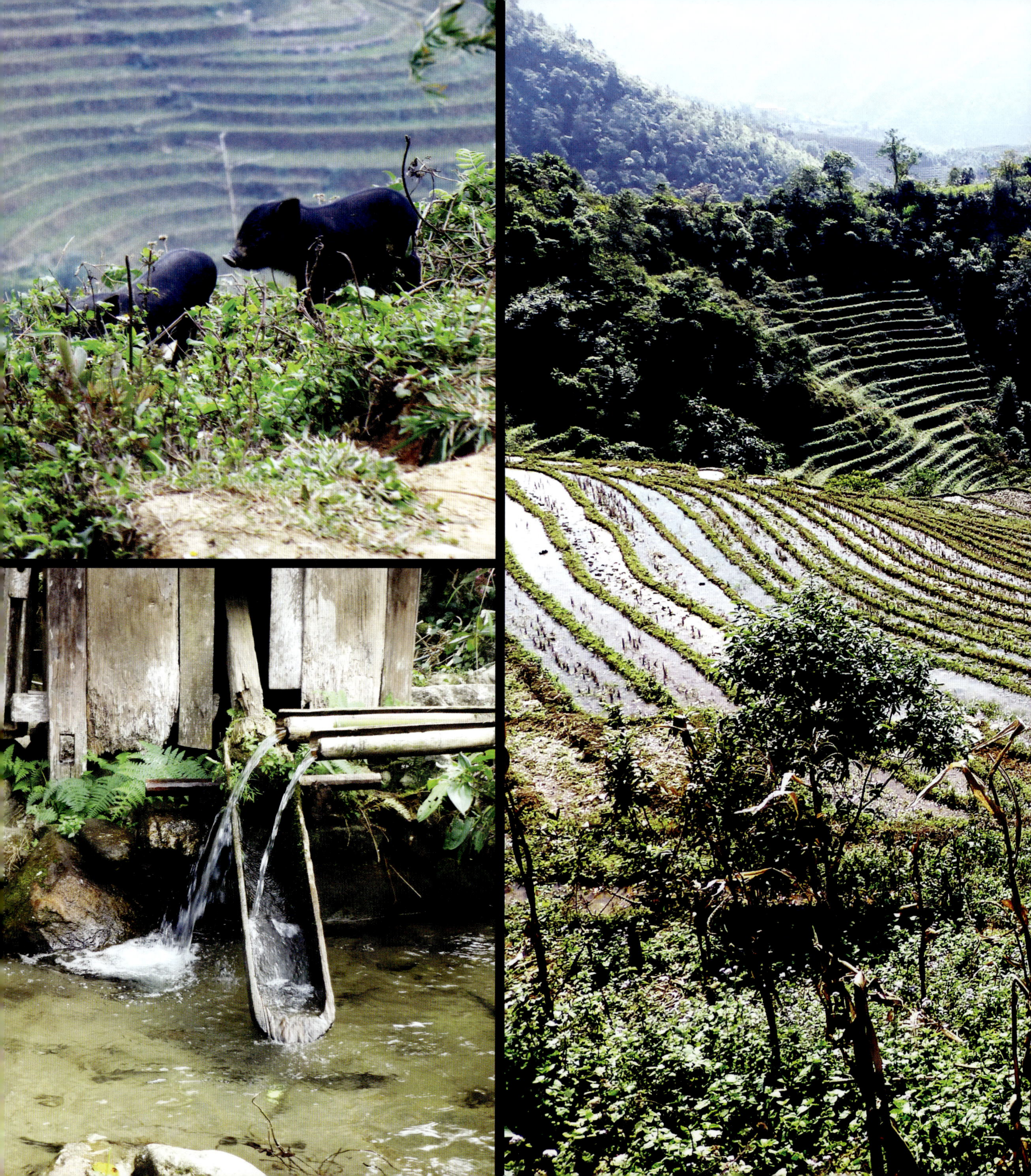

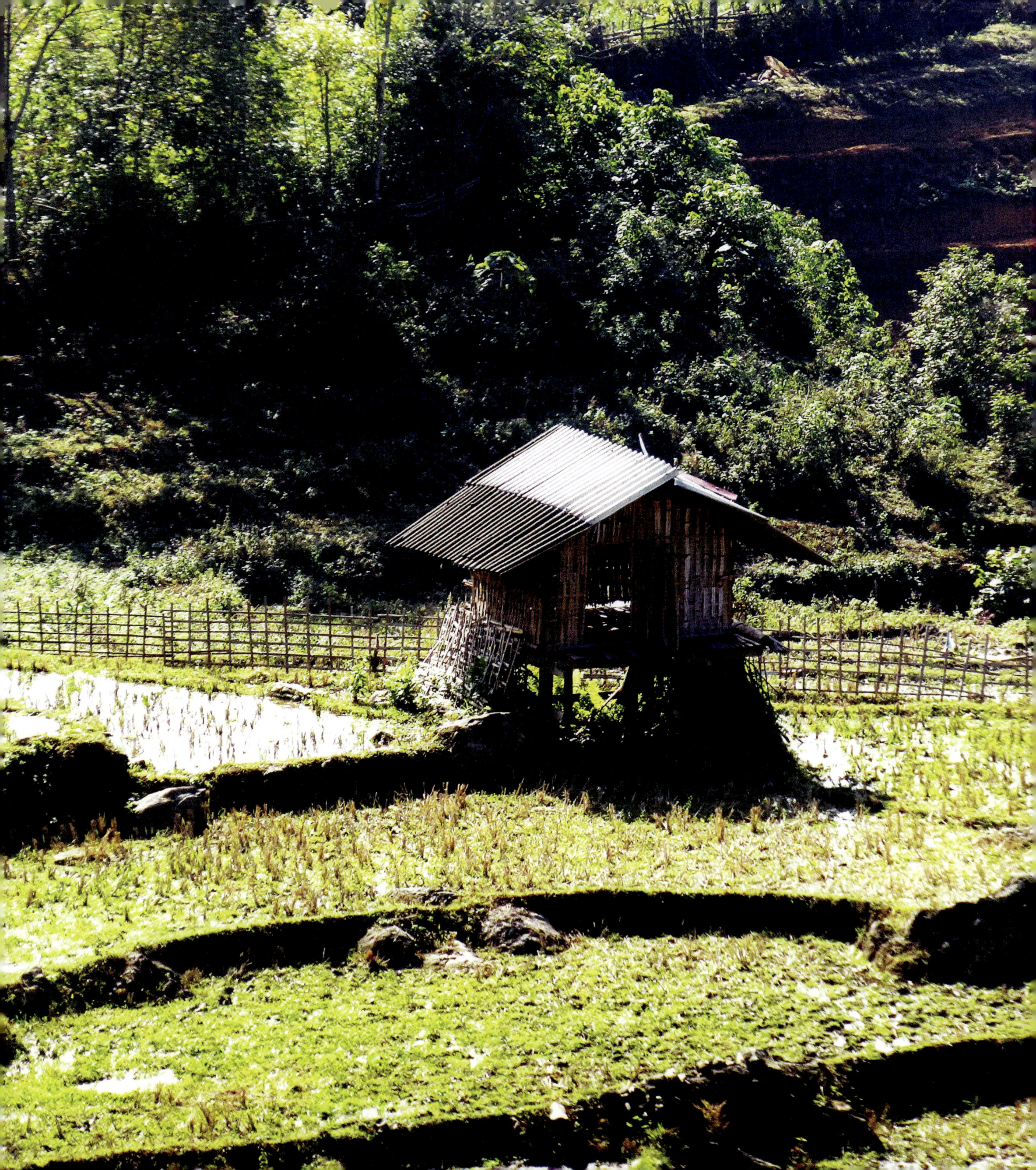

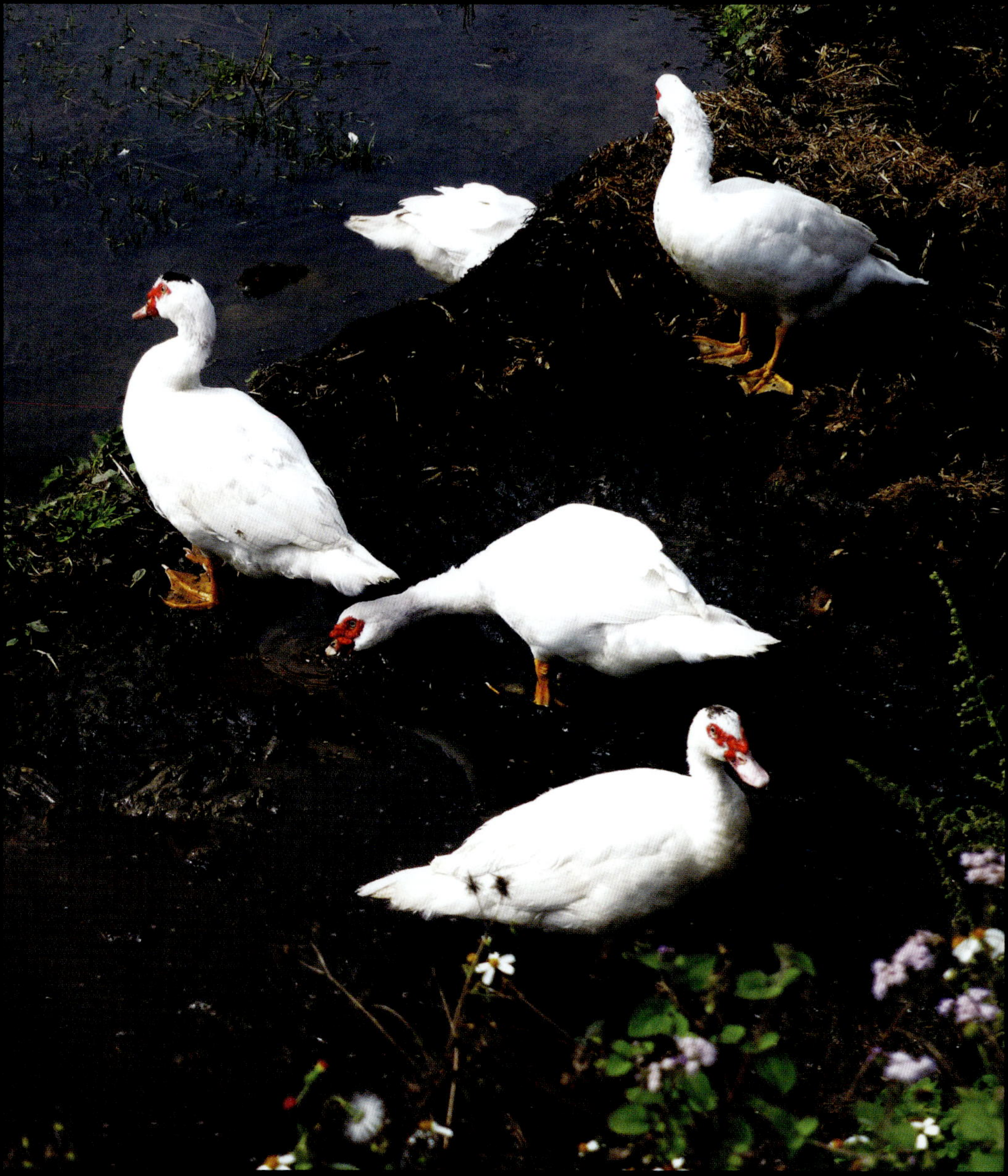

Ducks feed and fertilize.

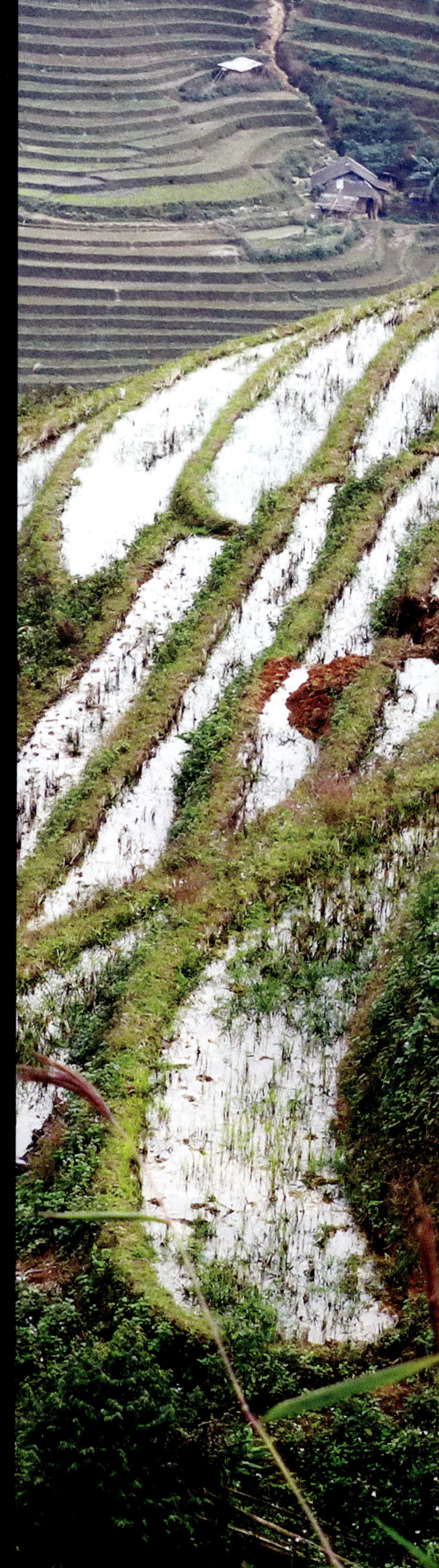

Cabbage planted on the rice terraces off-season.

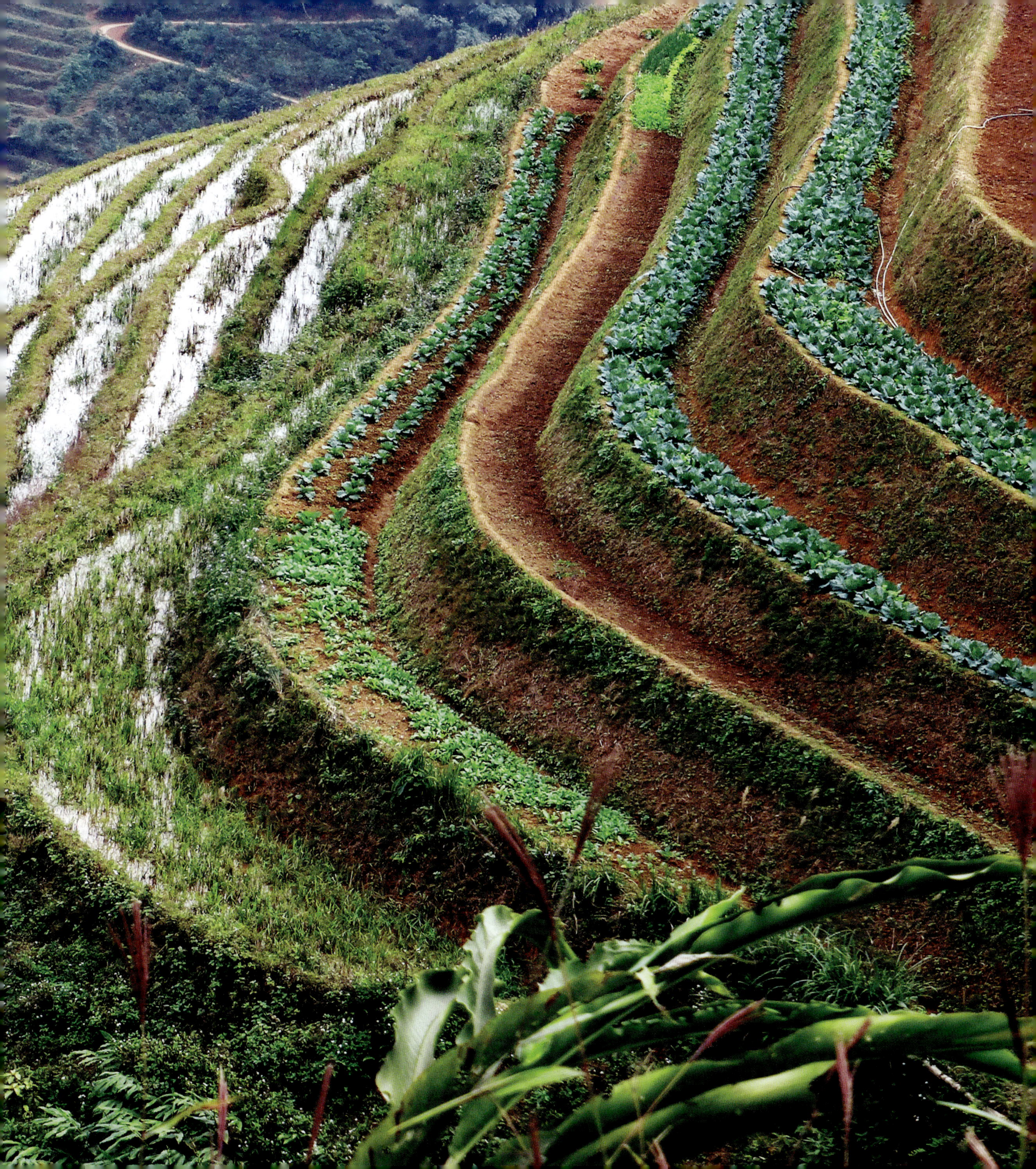

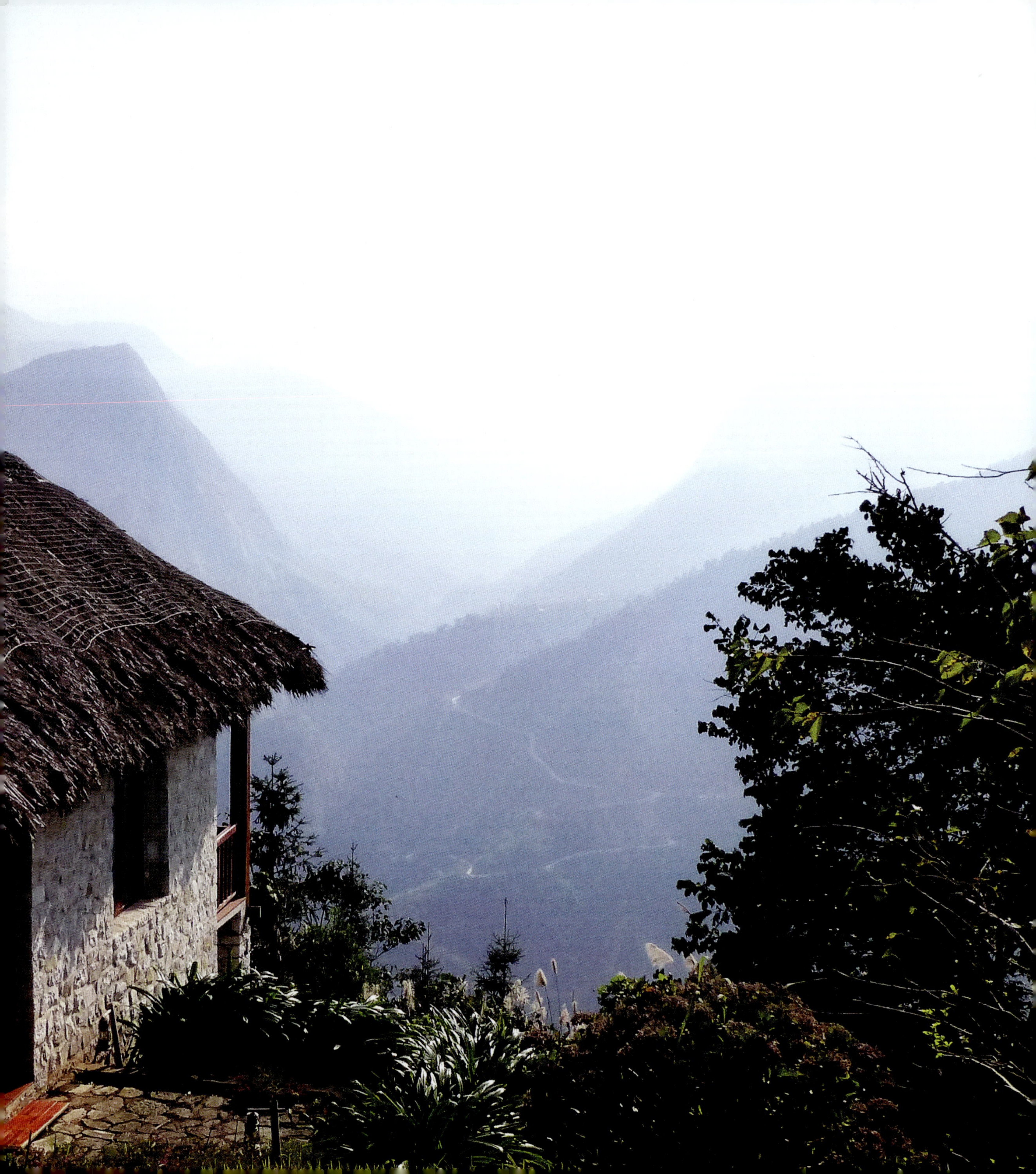

The mountainous province of Lào Cai hosts the popular trekking area Hoàng Liên National Park, home of high-peaked Mount Fansipan. Now only a day's drive from Hanoi, these mountain highlands are still a world apart from Vietnam's urban areas.

An expressway from Hanoi that opened in 2014 reduced the driving time to 5½ hours, encouraging investment in tourist accommodations and an influx of tourist spending. Although a significant boost to the local economy, the resulting commercialization strains rural life. New employment opportunities are available at tourist lodges, and for independent tour guides, drivers and craft sellers like the Red Dao ladies in the photographs that follow. Nevertheless, most families in Vietnam's highlands are bound to farming, and face trials and tribulations challenging their traditions along with tourism's benefits.

The Vietnamese government recognizes 54 ethnic groups – 53 are minorities. While ethnic minorities comprise only fourteen percent of Vietnam's population, they constitute an overwhelming majority of the people settled in the vast Northern mountains and Central highlands.

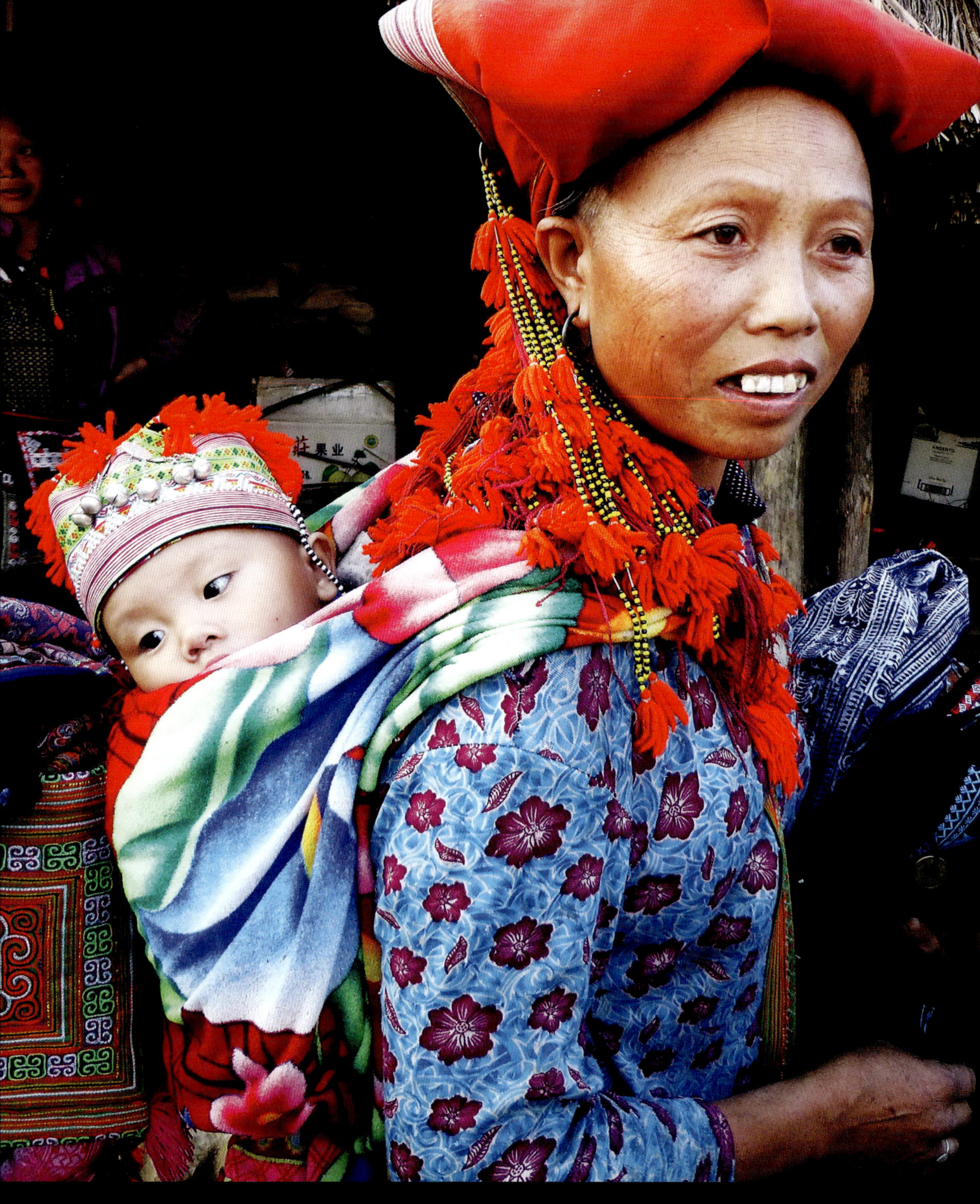

Red Dao ethnic minority in Lào Cai.

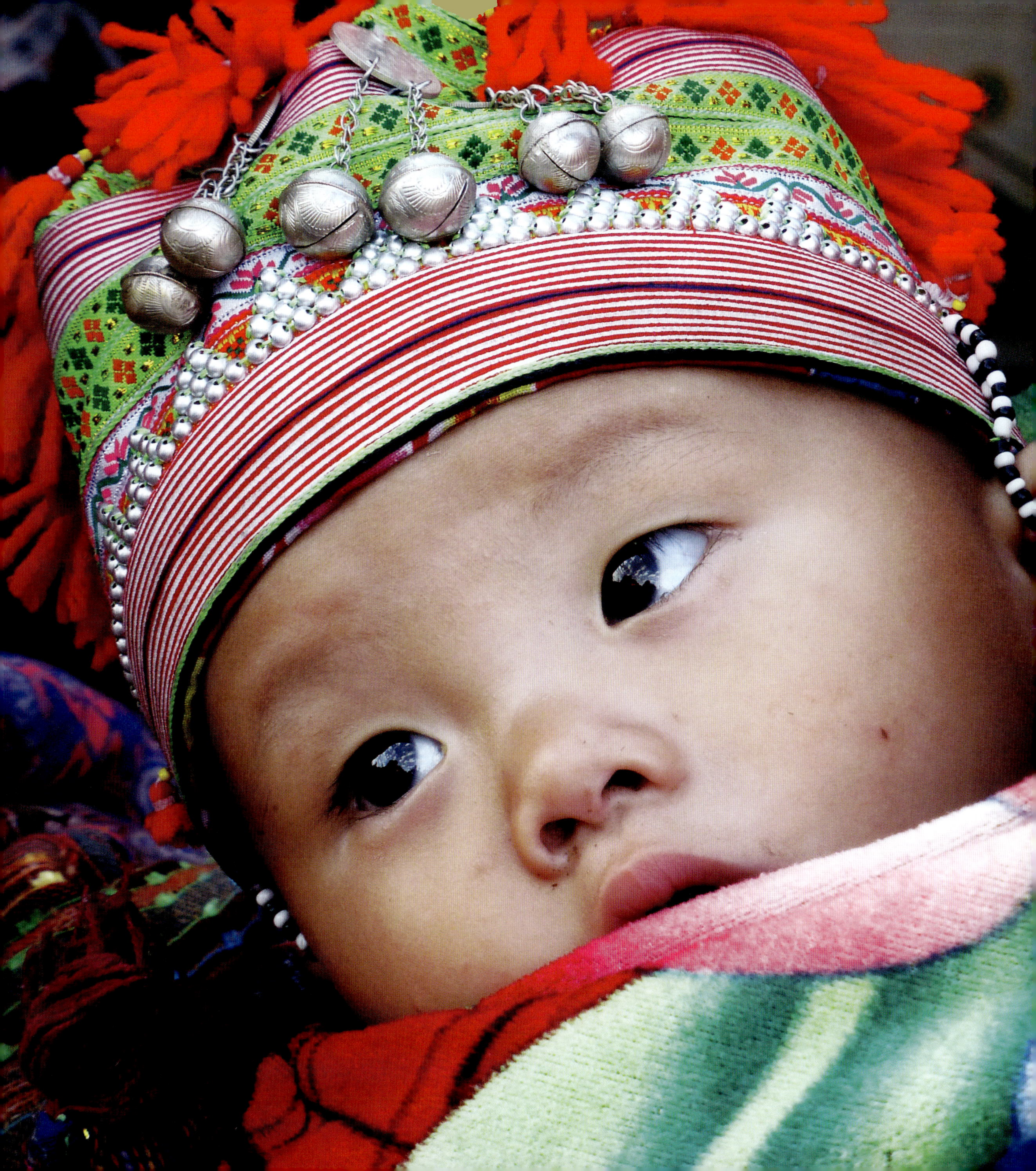

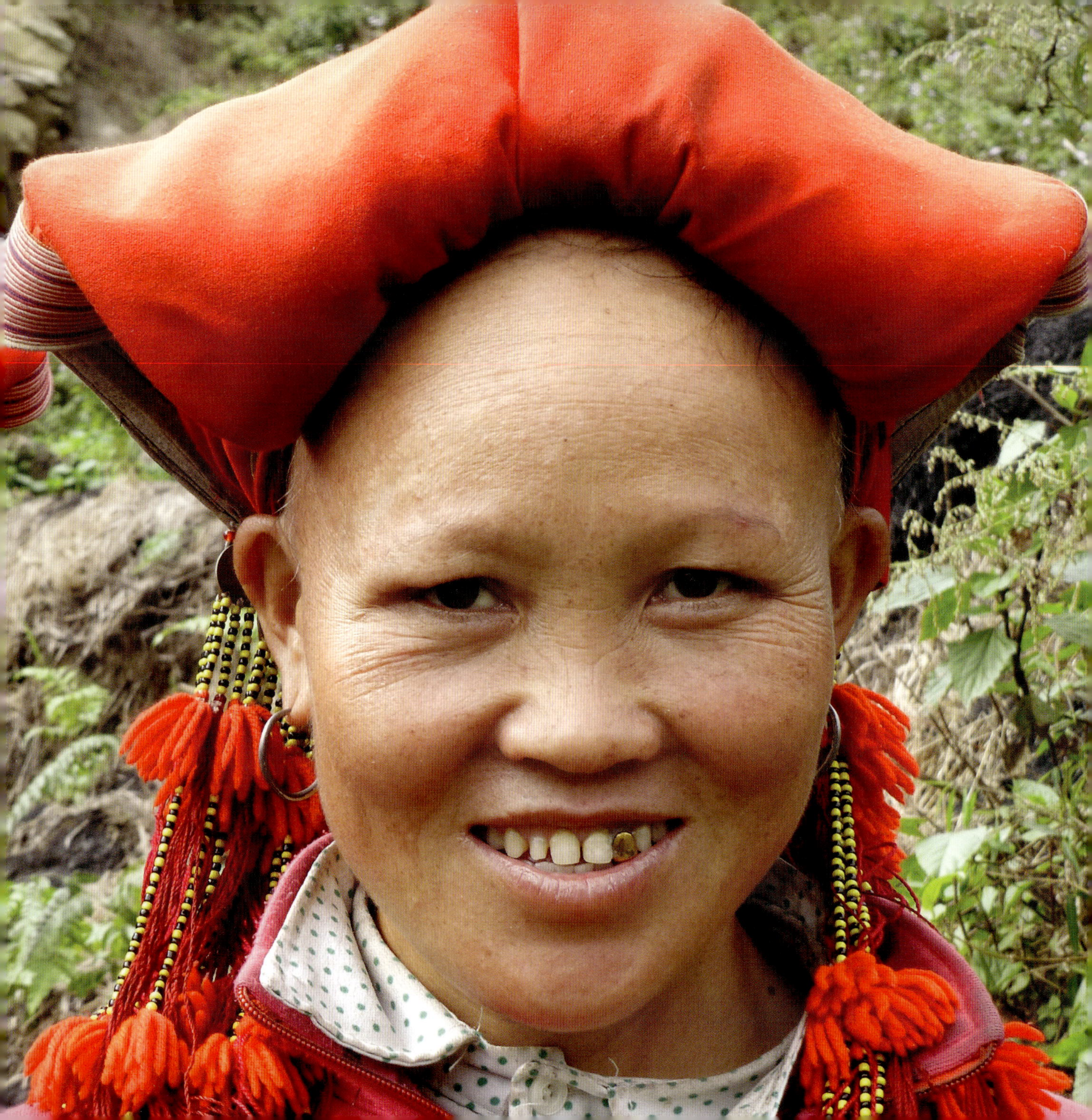

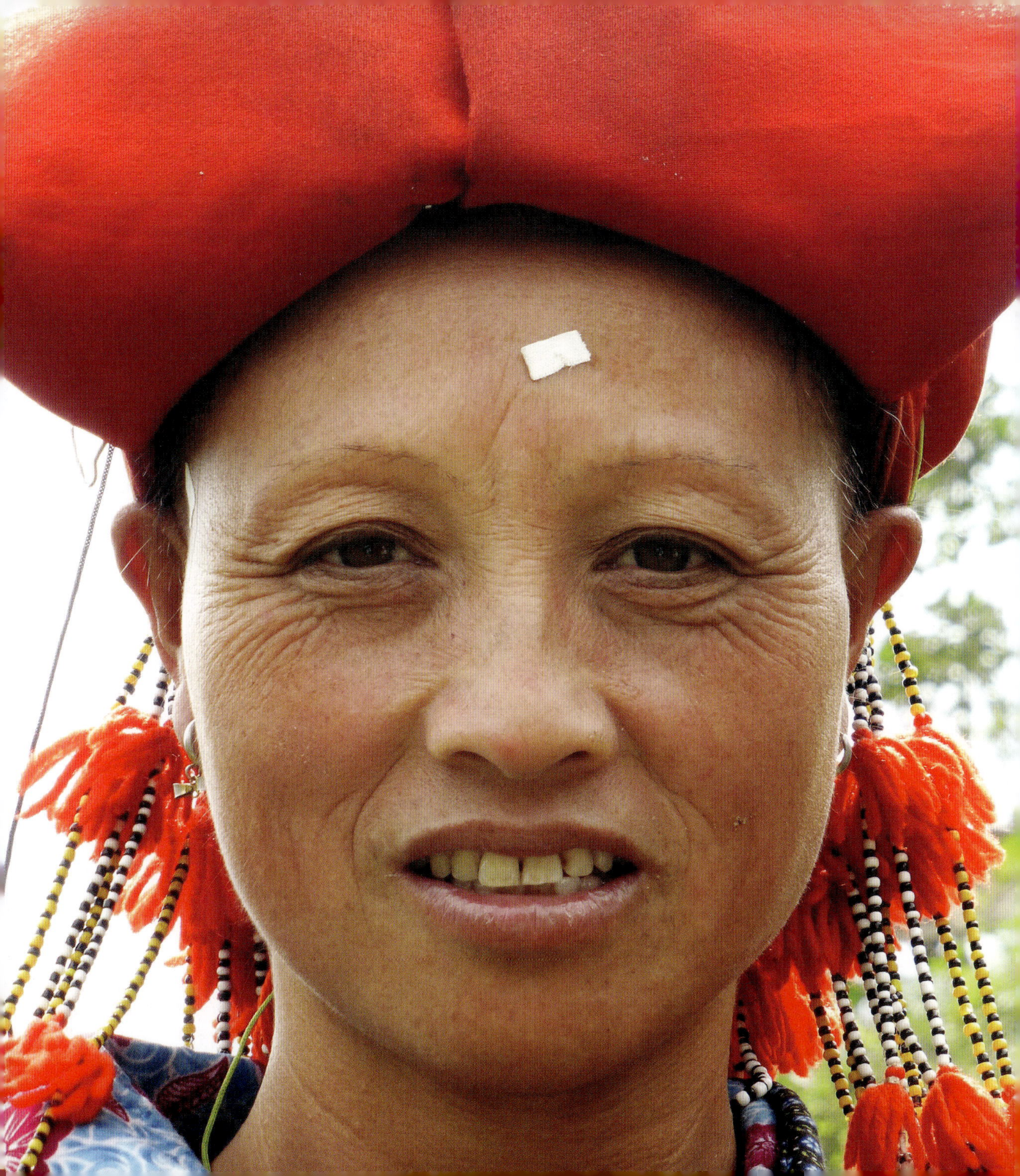

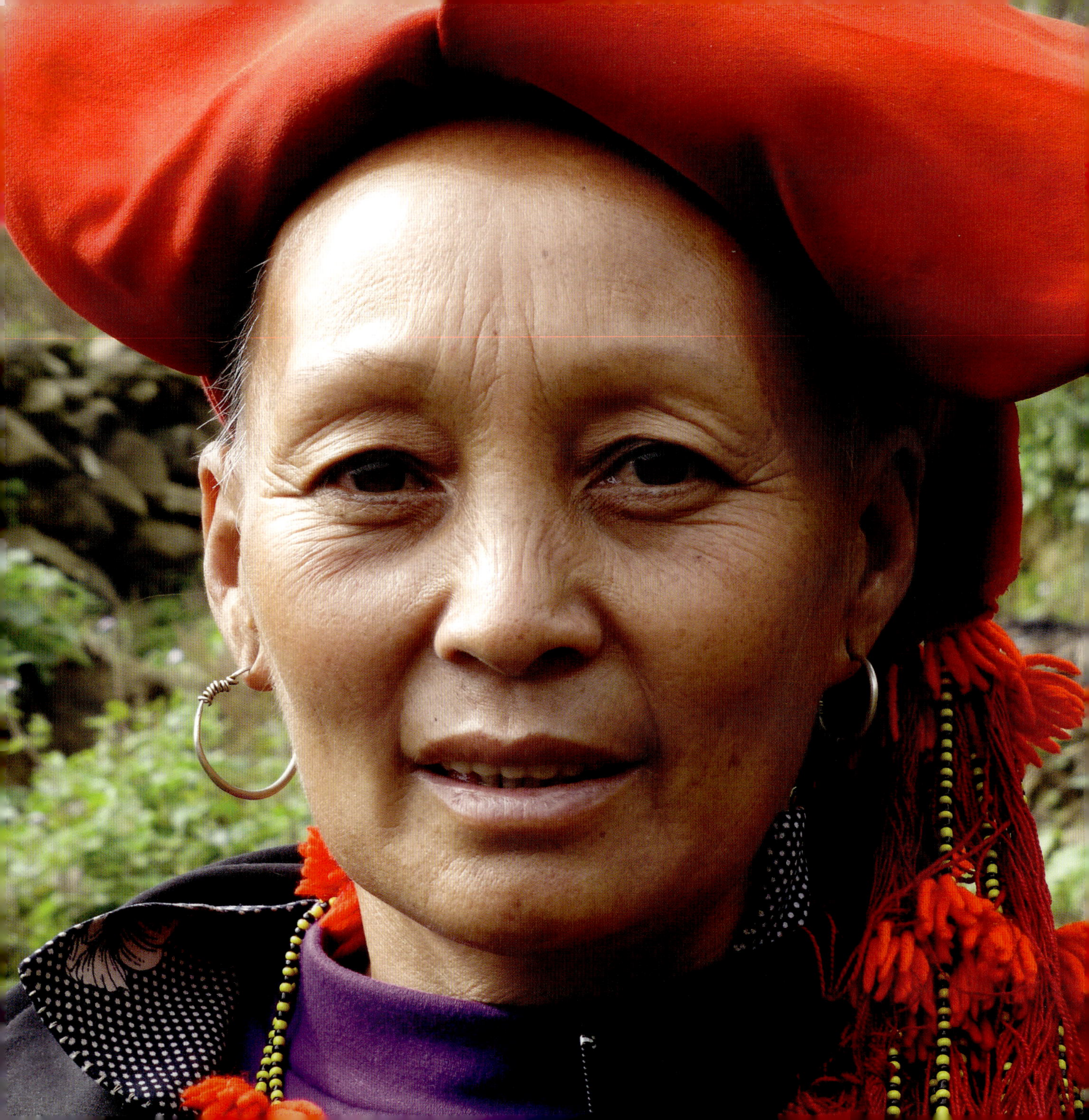

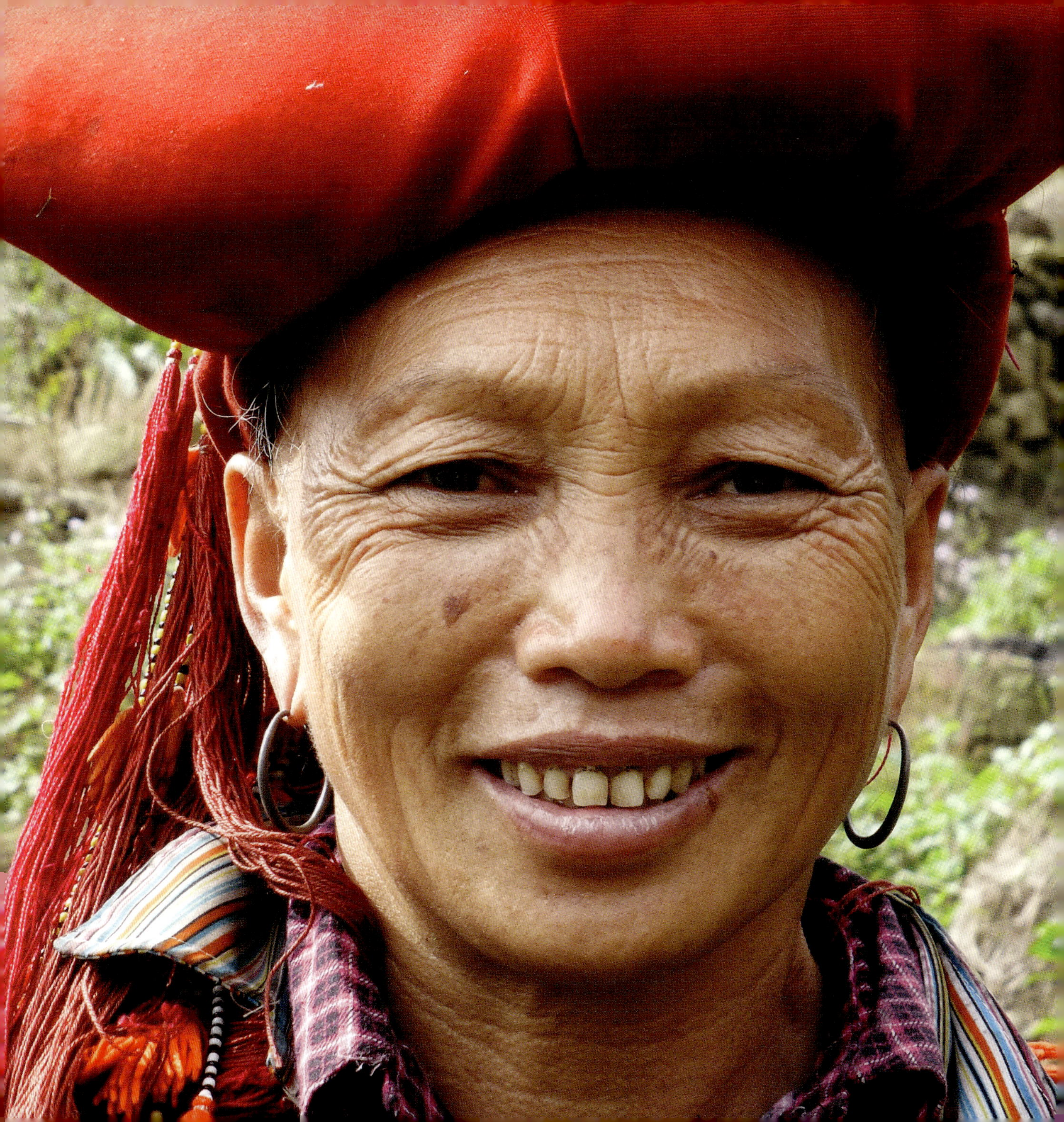

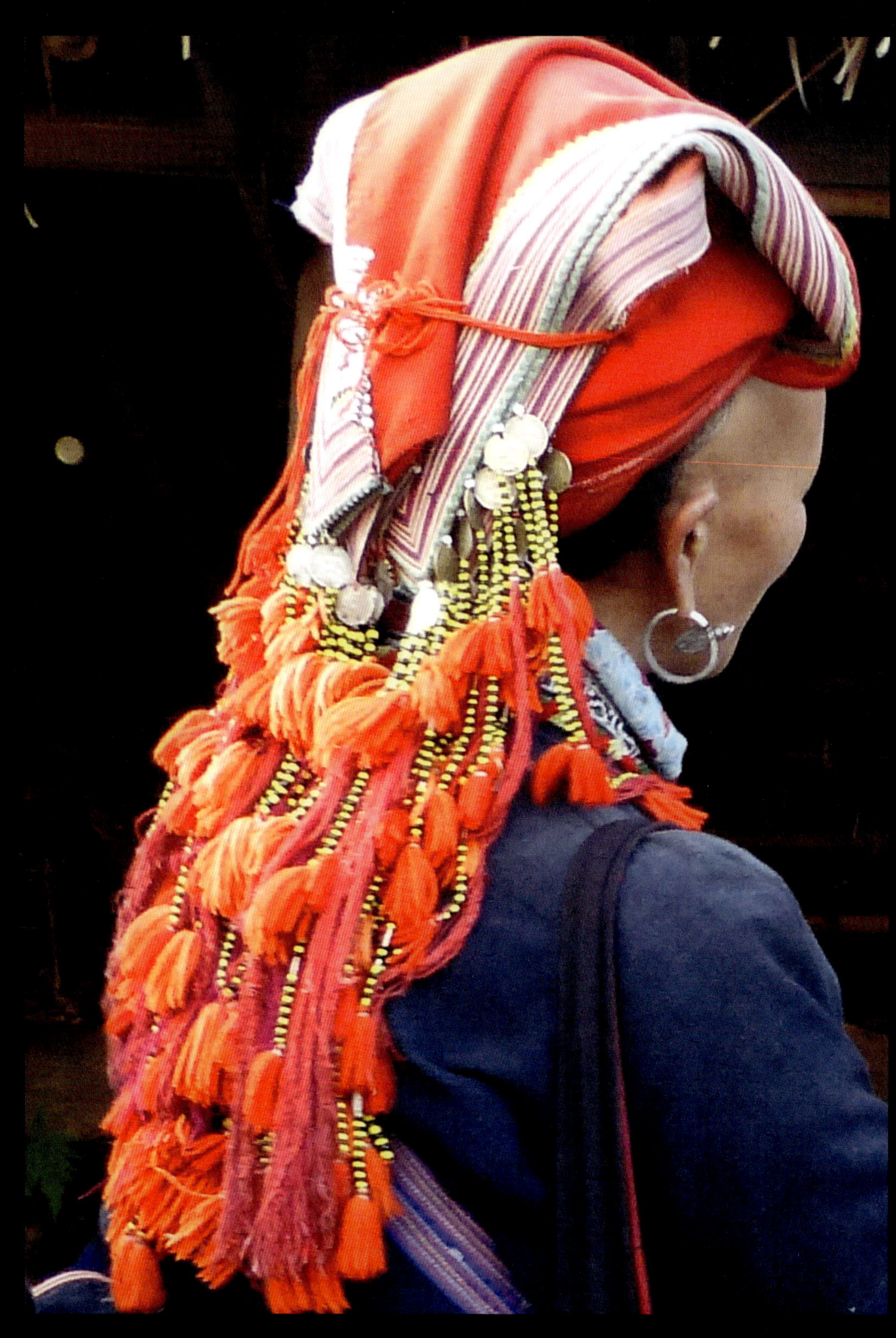

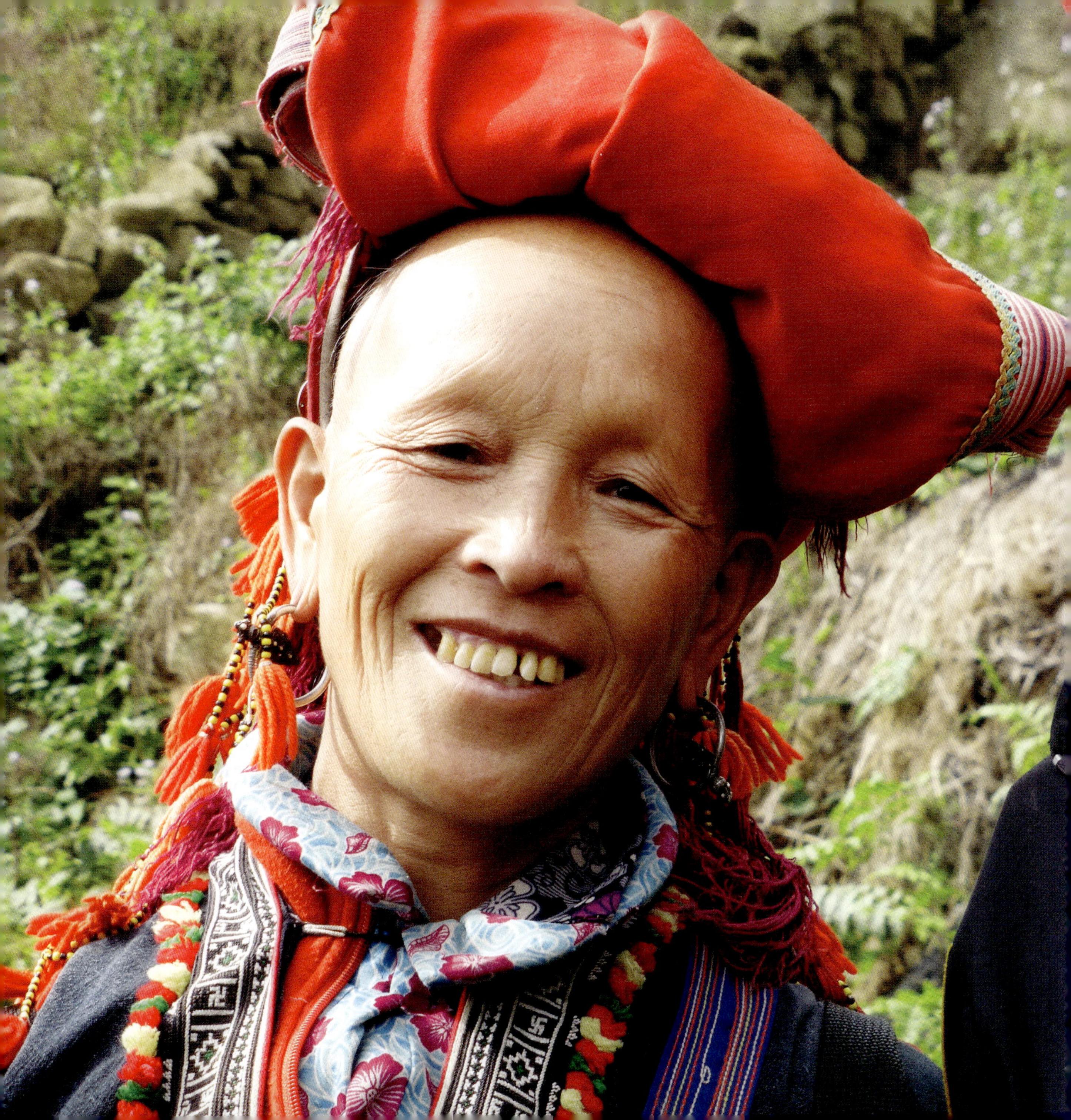

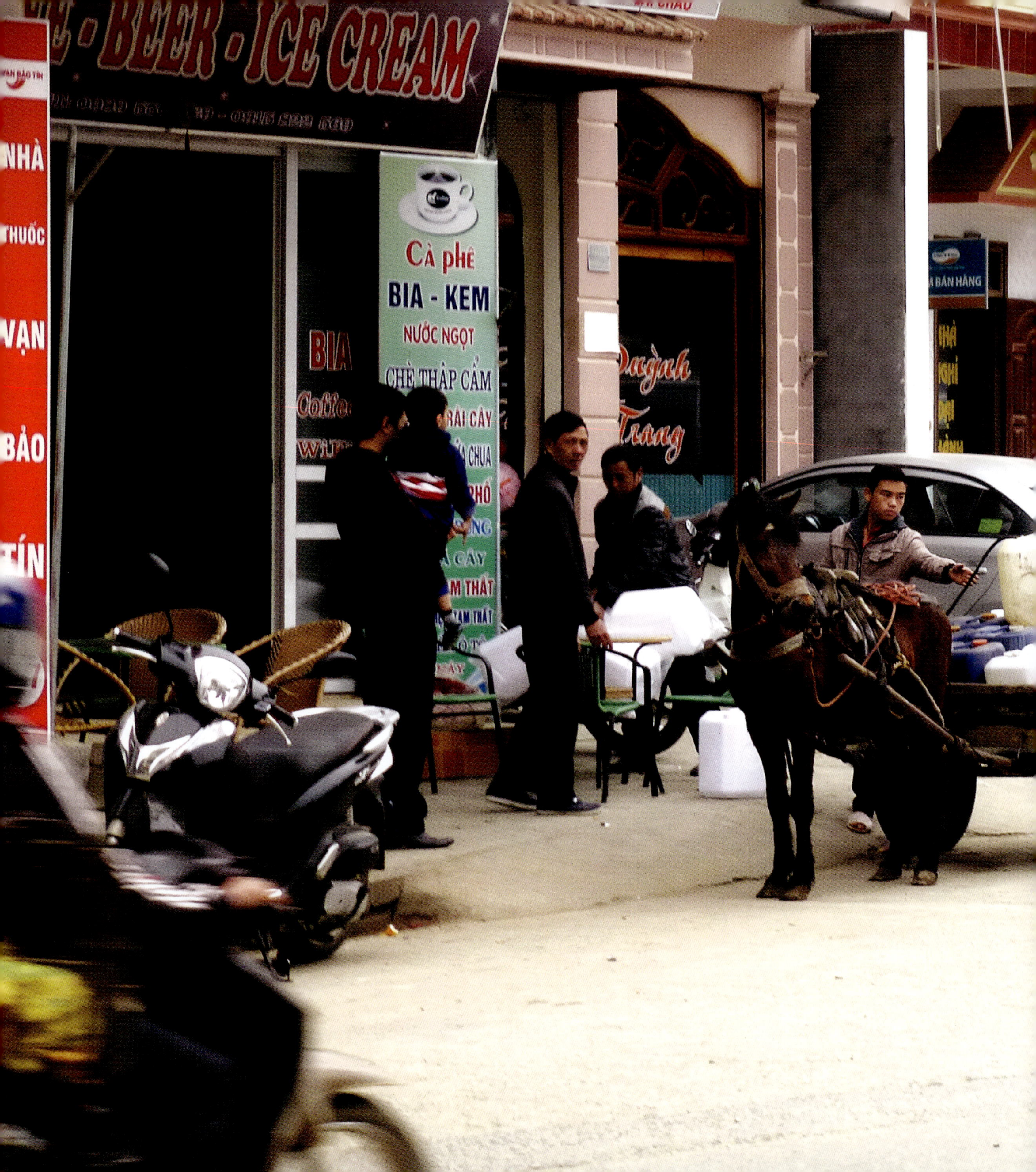
BEER - ICE CREAM
Cà phê
BIA - KEM
NƯỚC NGỌT
CHÈ THẬP CẨM
BIA
NHÀ
THUỐC
VẠN
BẢO
TÍN

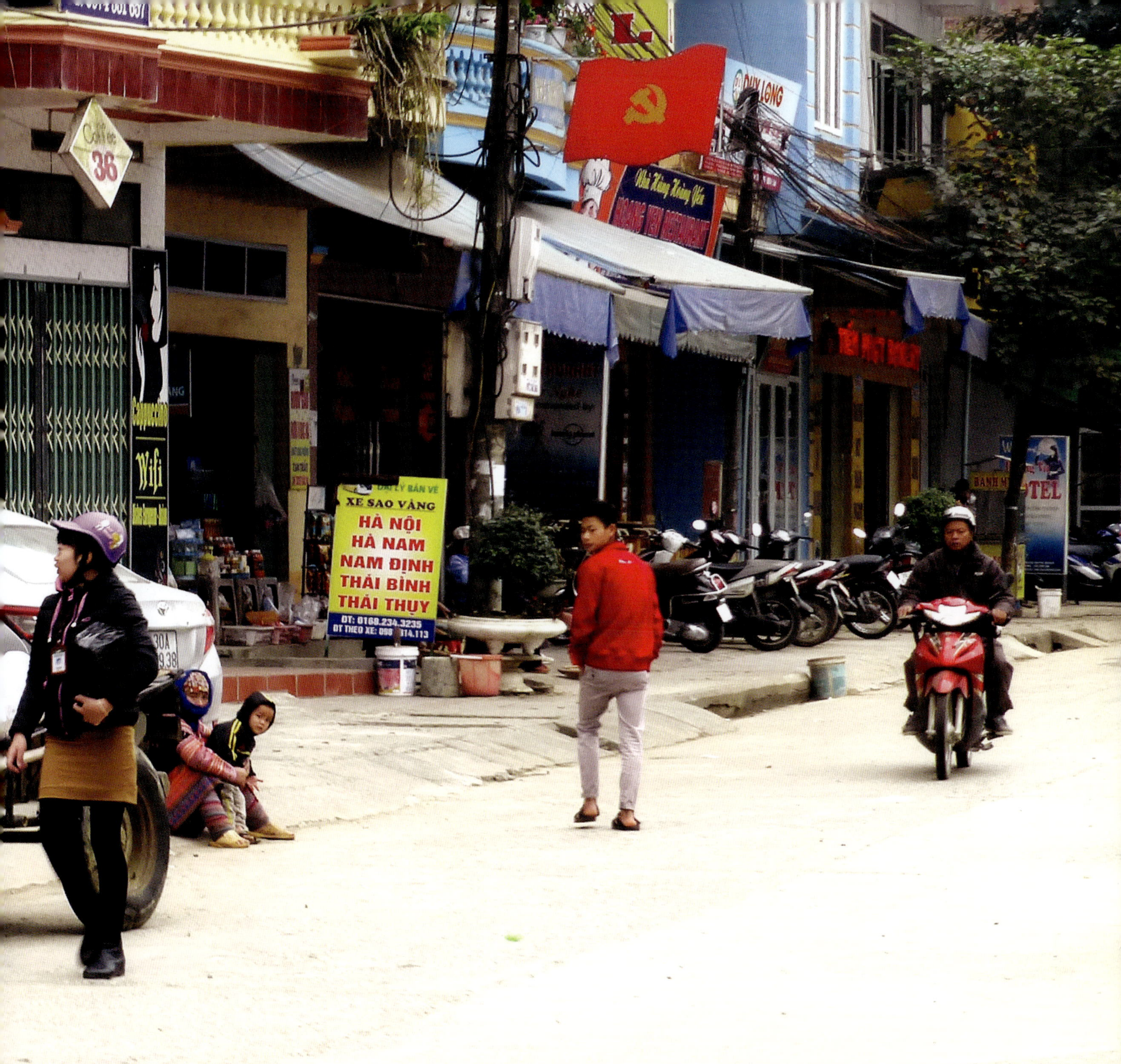

The town of Bac Ha sits only 40 miles (65 km) from the Chinese border-crossing at Lào Cai city, the capital of Lào Cai Province. Its Sunday market is a gathering place for Flower Hmong, Phu La, Black Dao, Tay, Nung and other ethnic groups. Bring your water buffalo or whatever you have to barter or sell. Or just come to buy or socialize, dressed in your finest.

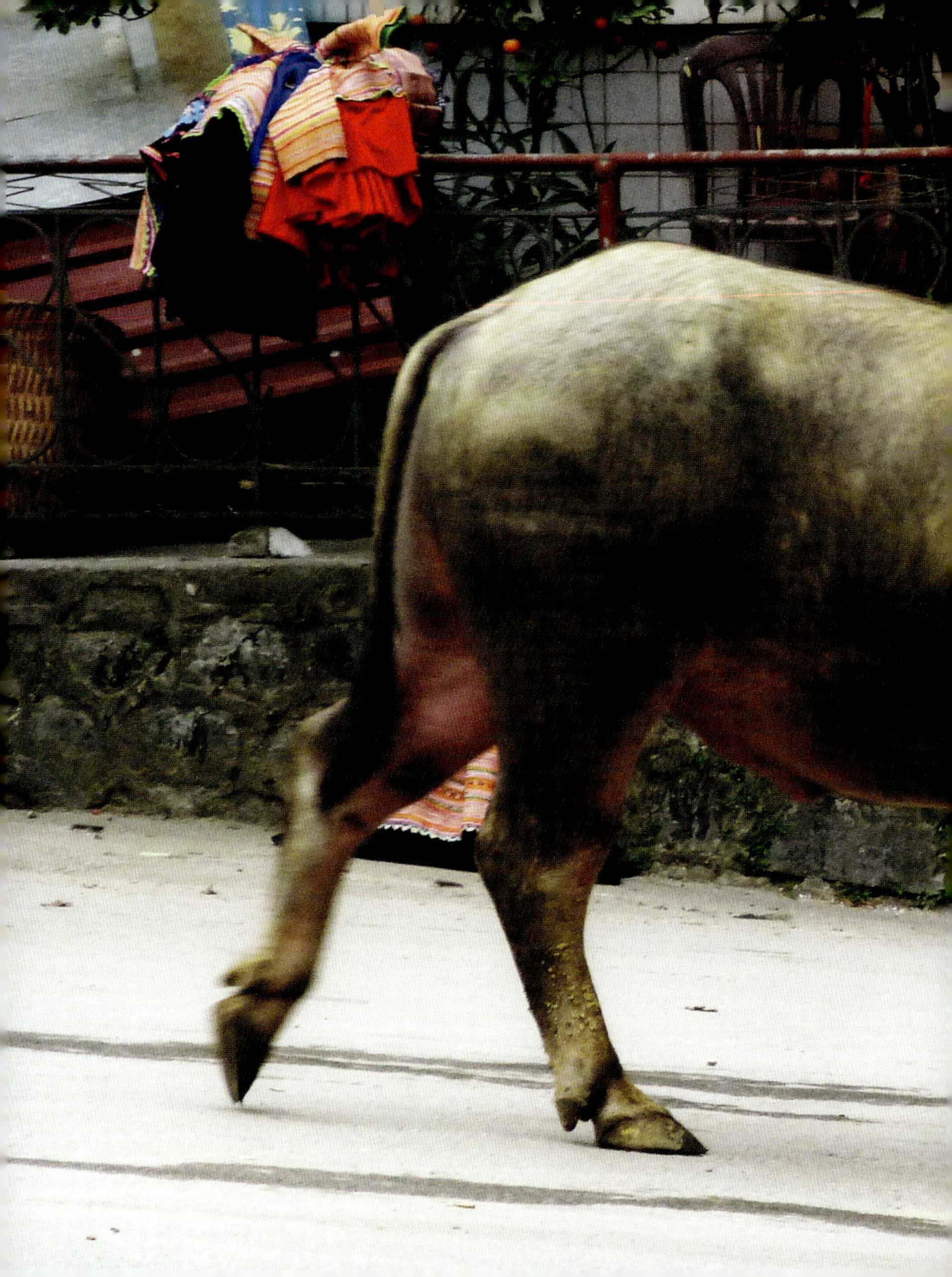

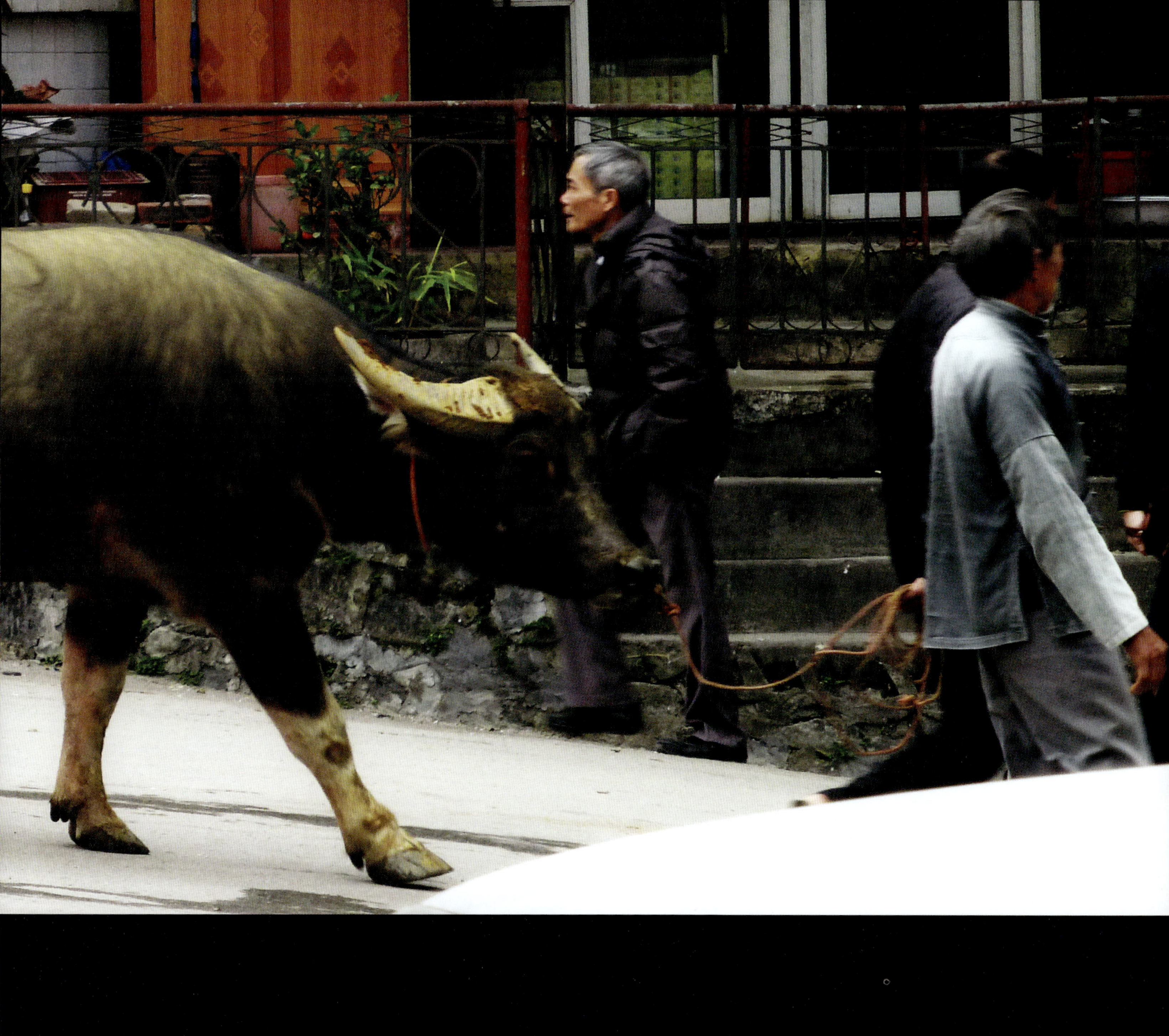

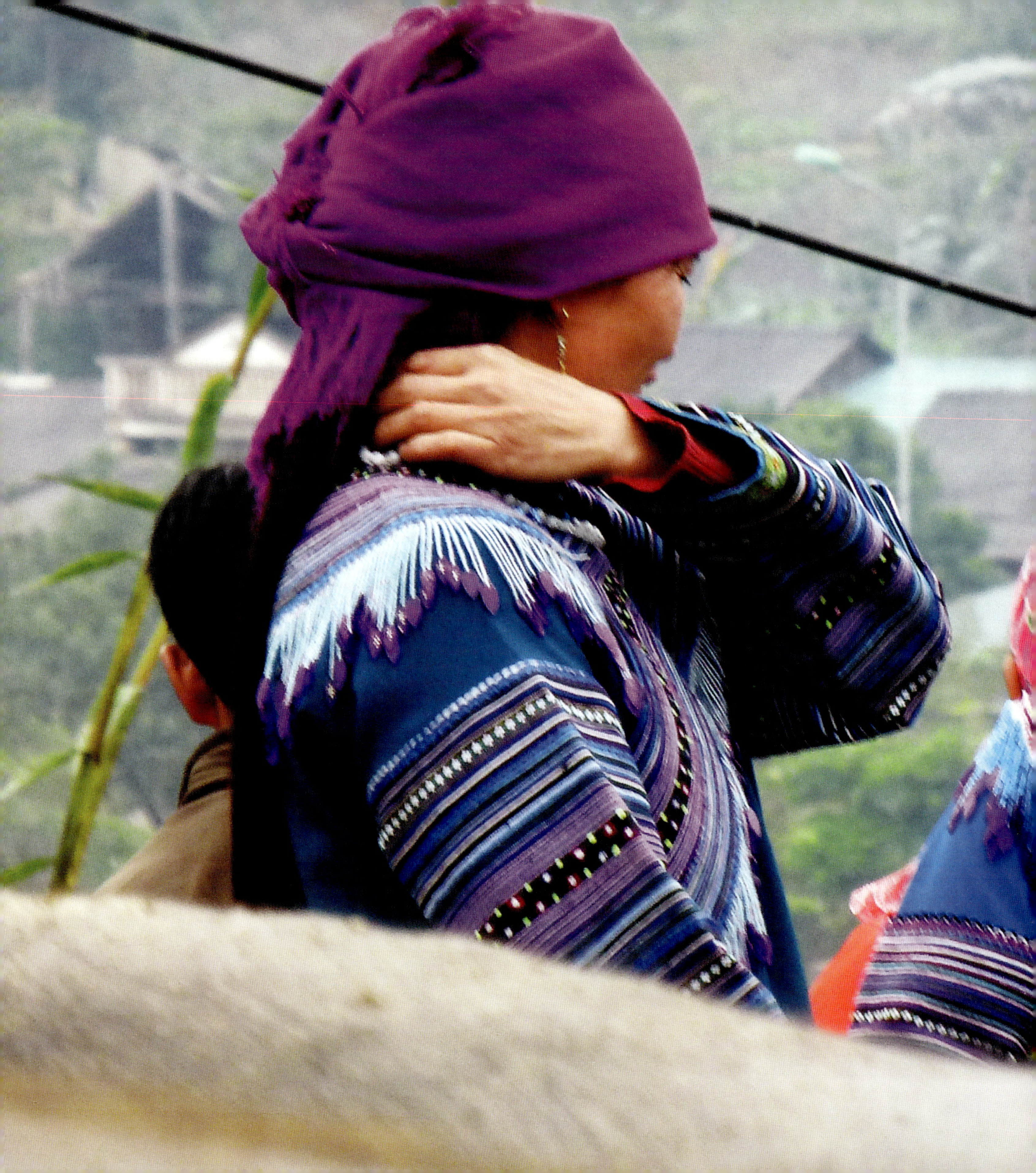

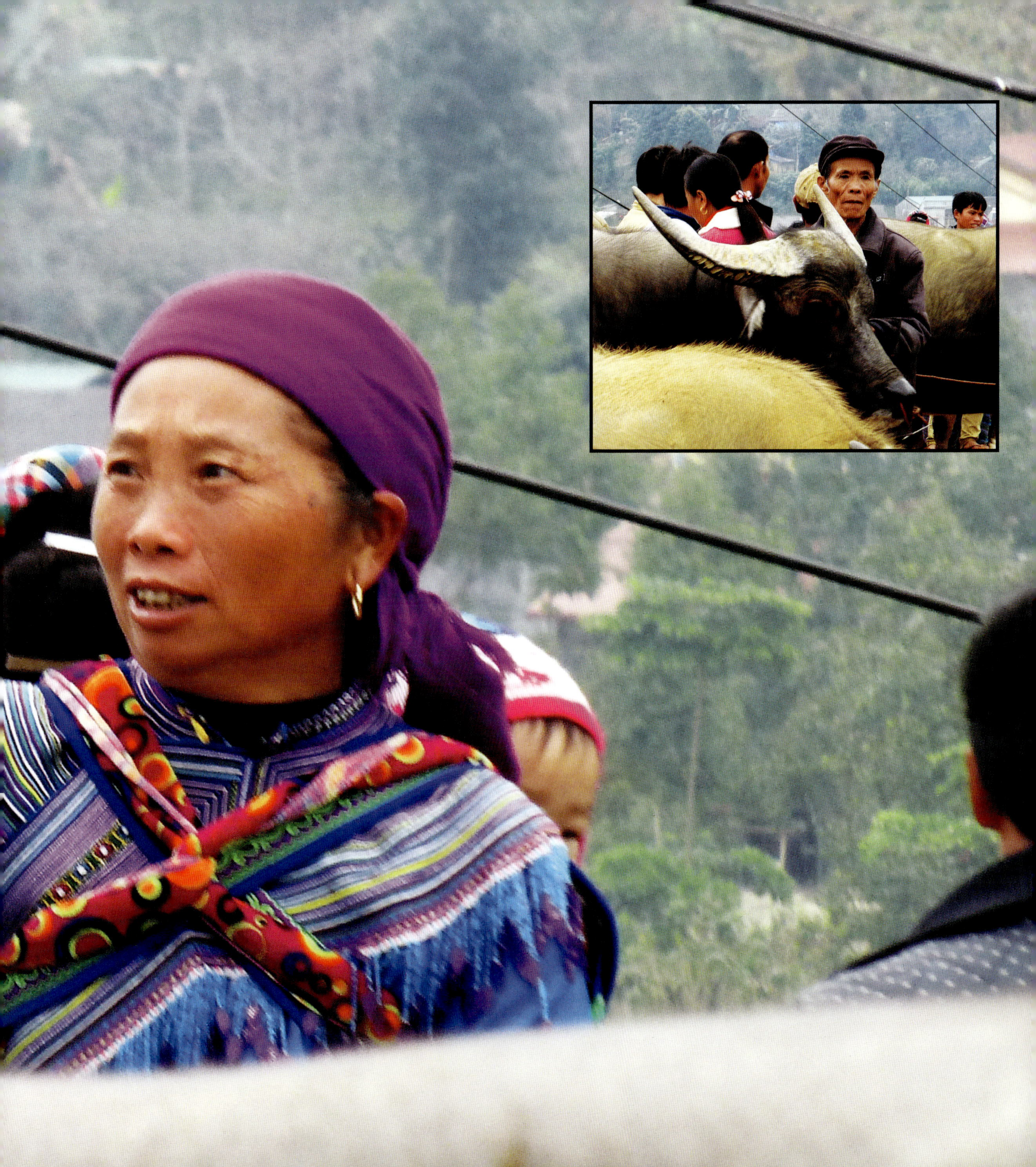

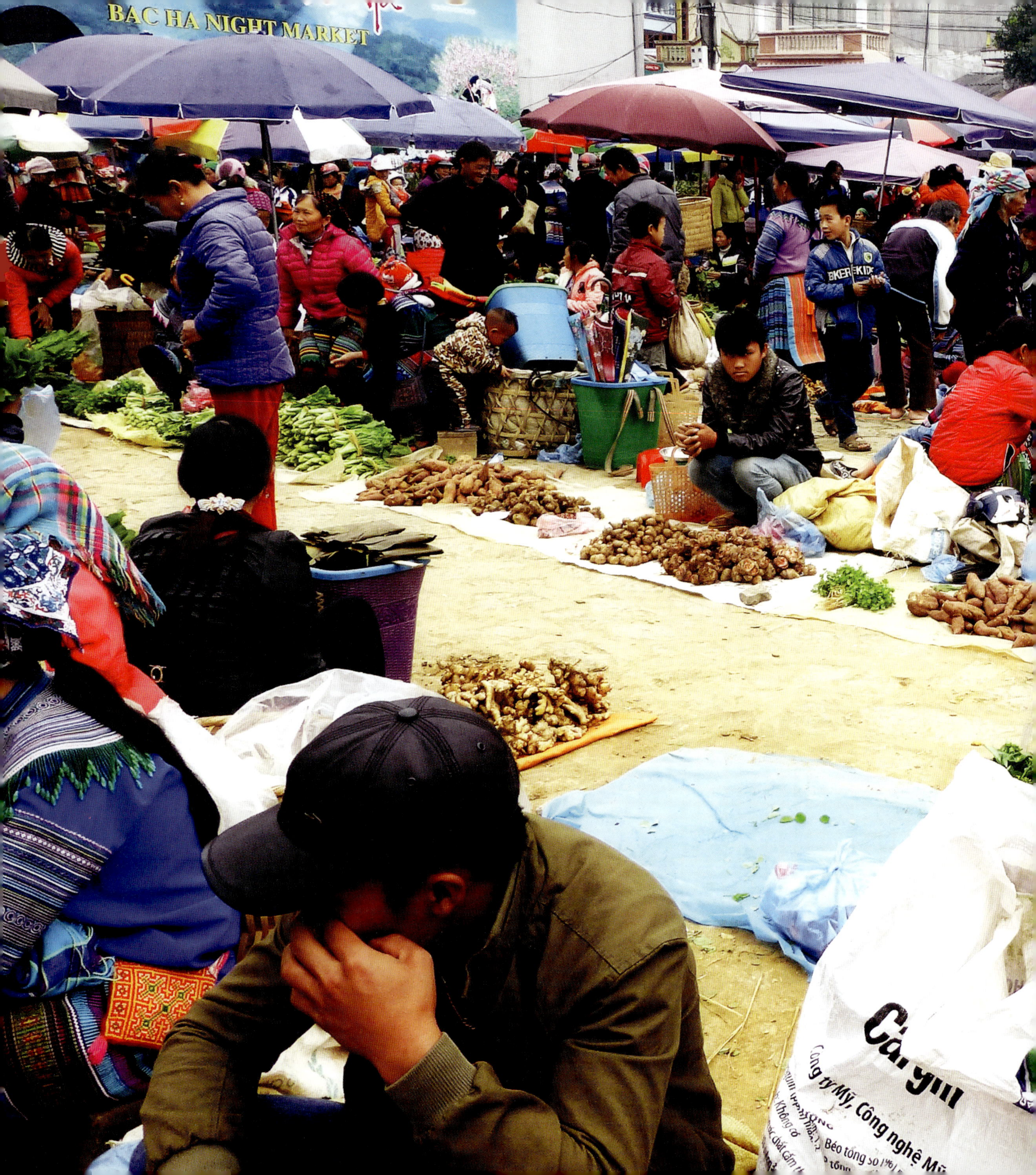
BAC HA NIGHT MARKET
Công ty Mỹ, Công nghệ Mỹ

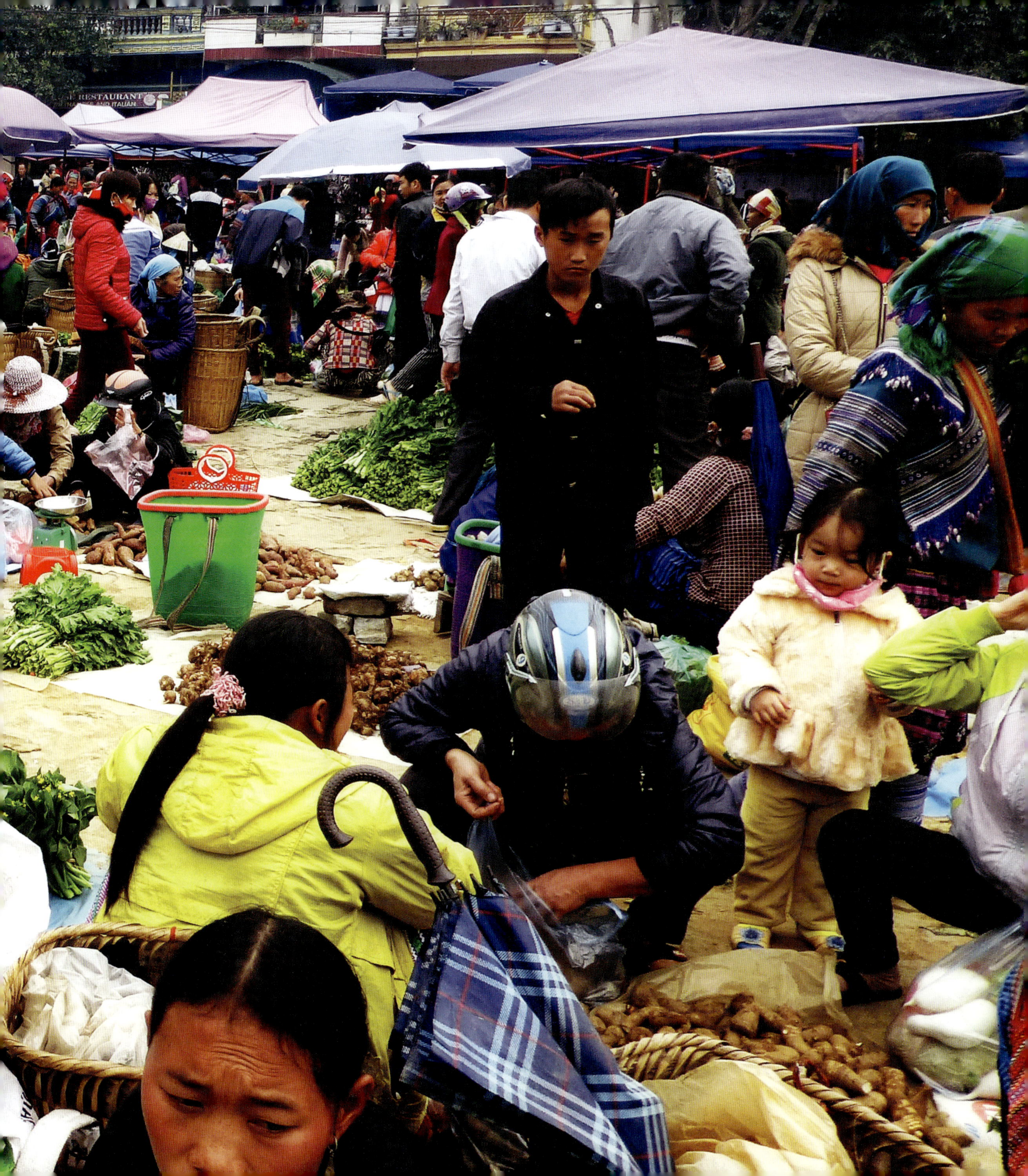
RESTAURANT

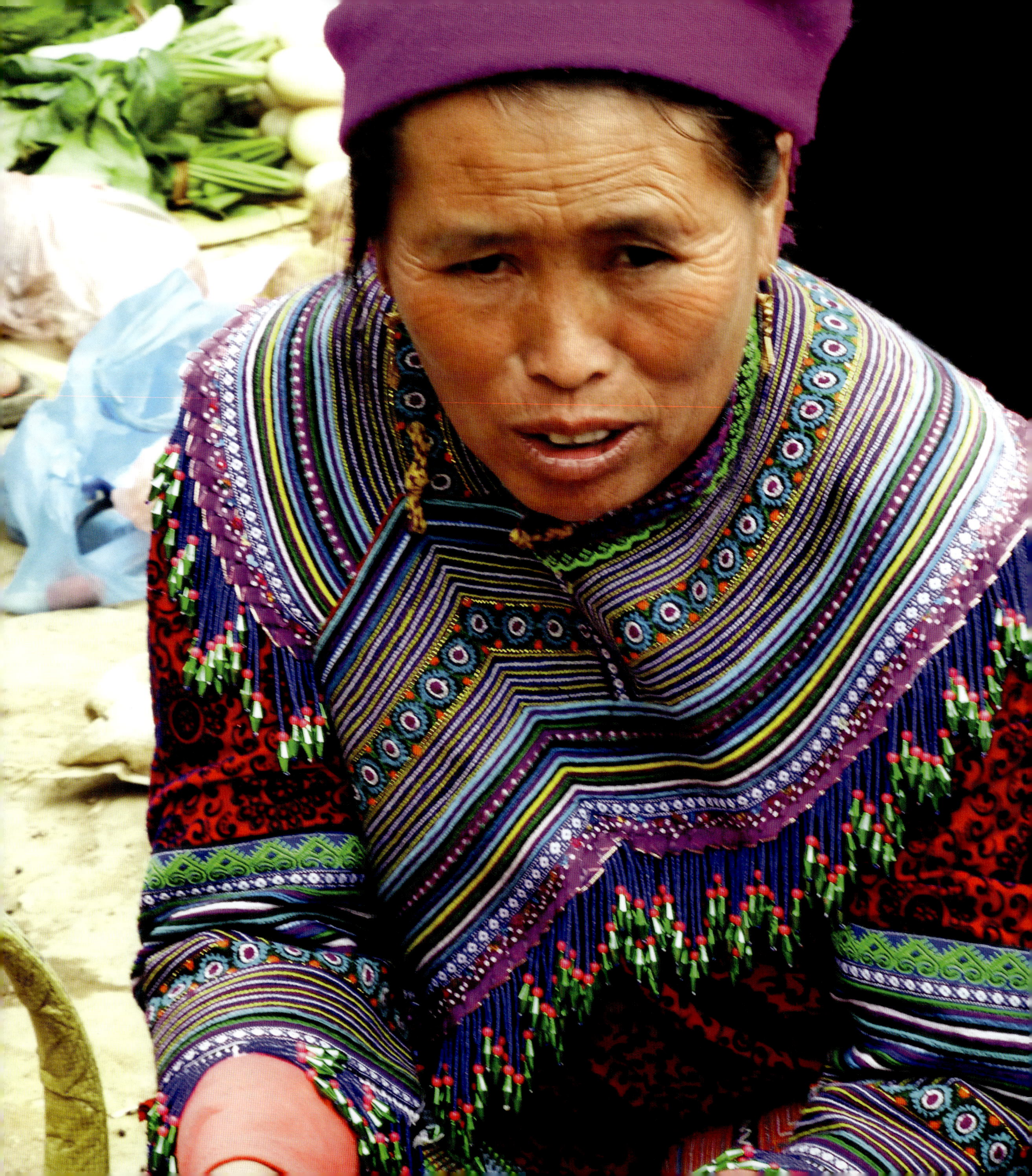

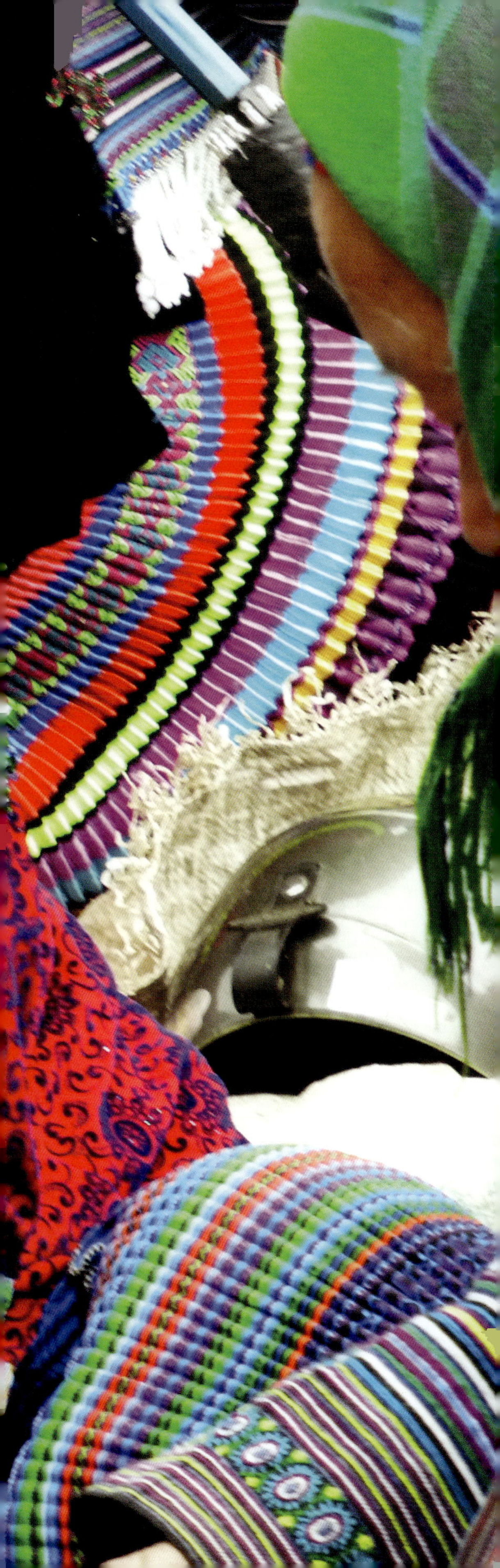

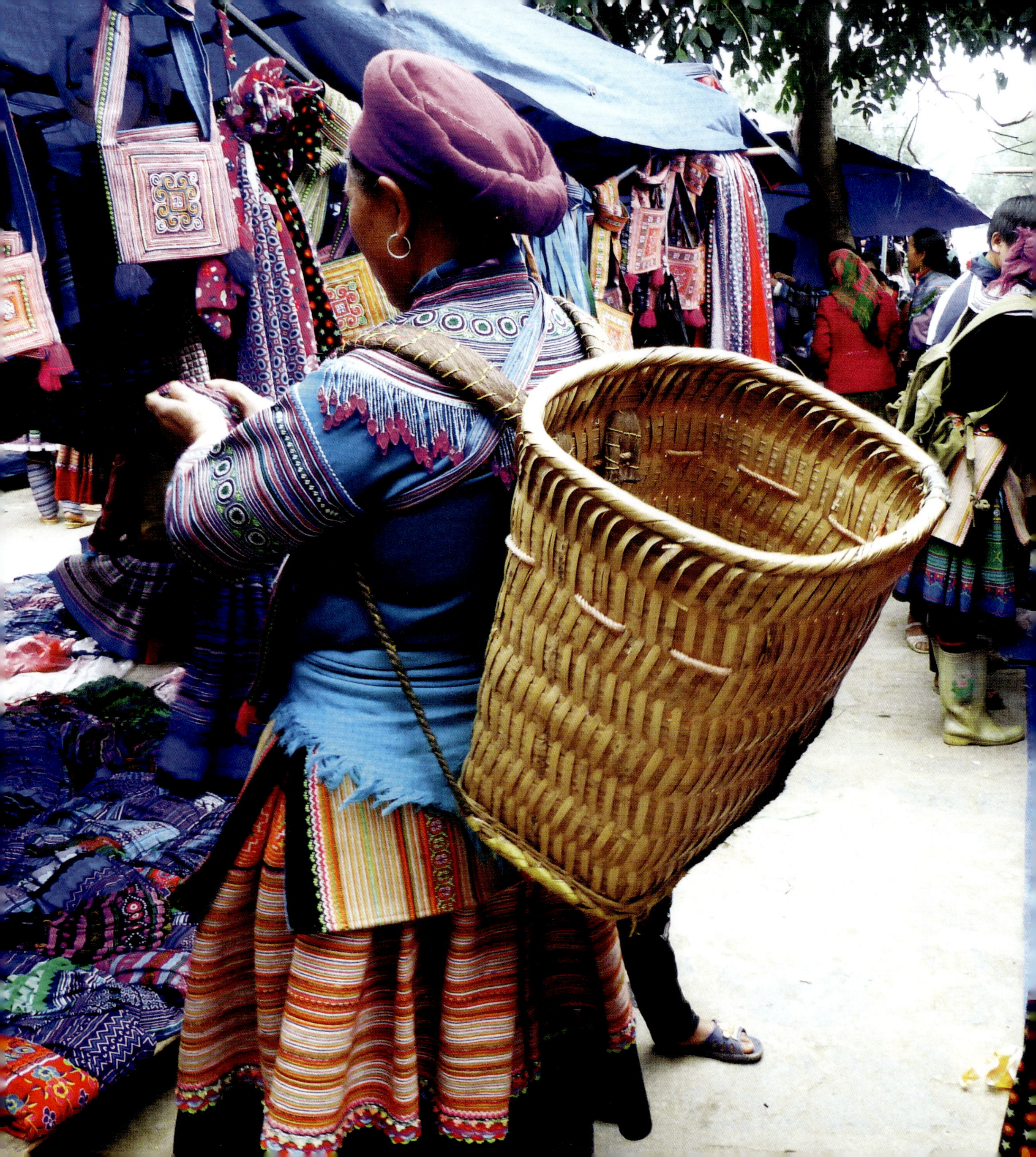

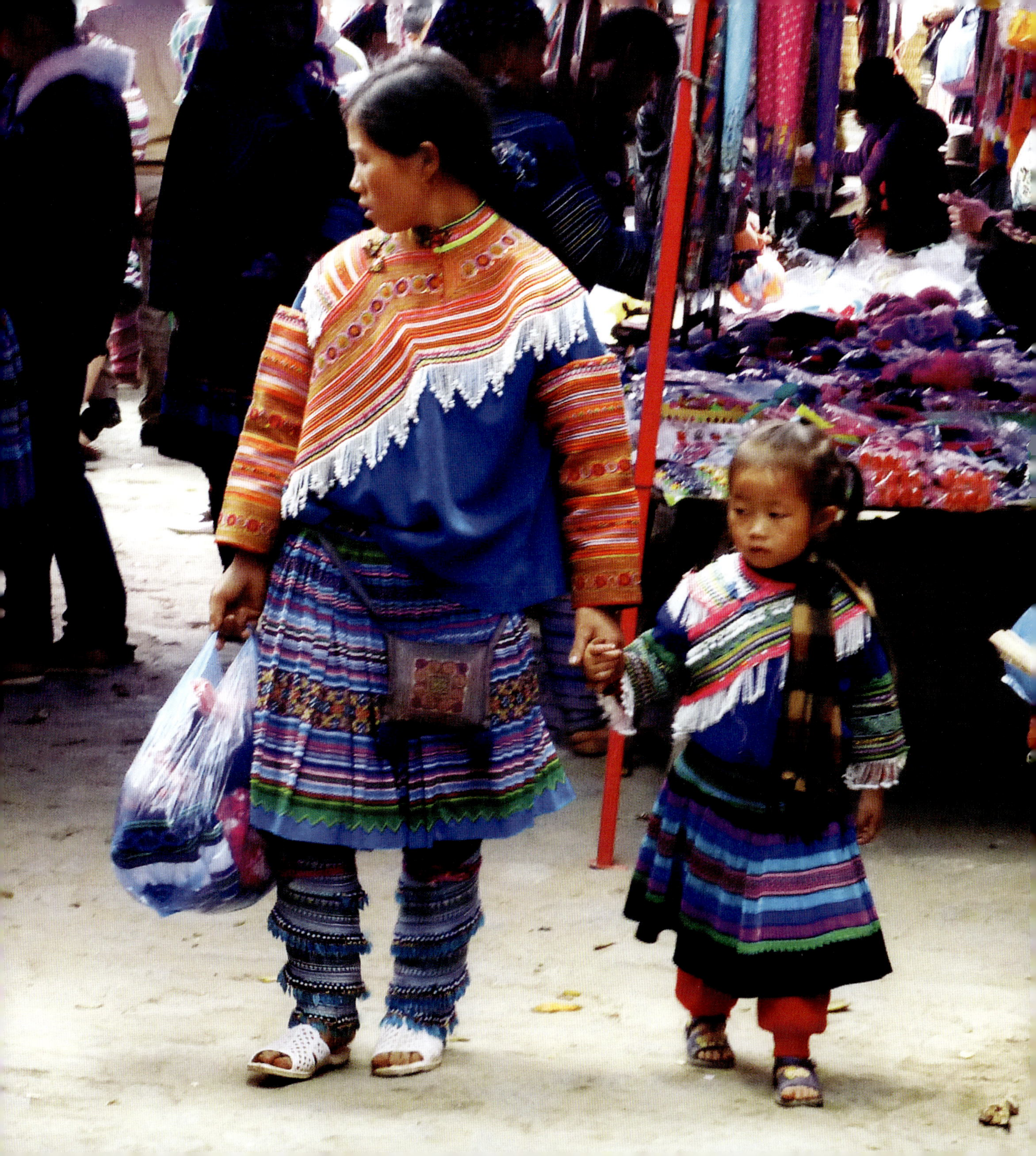

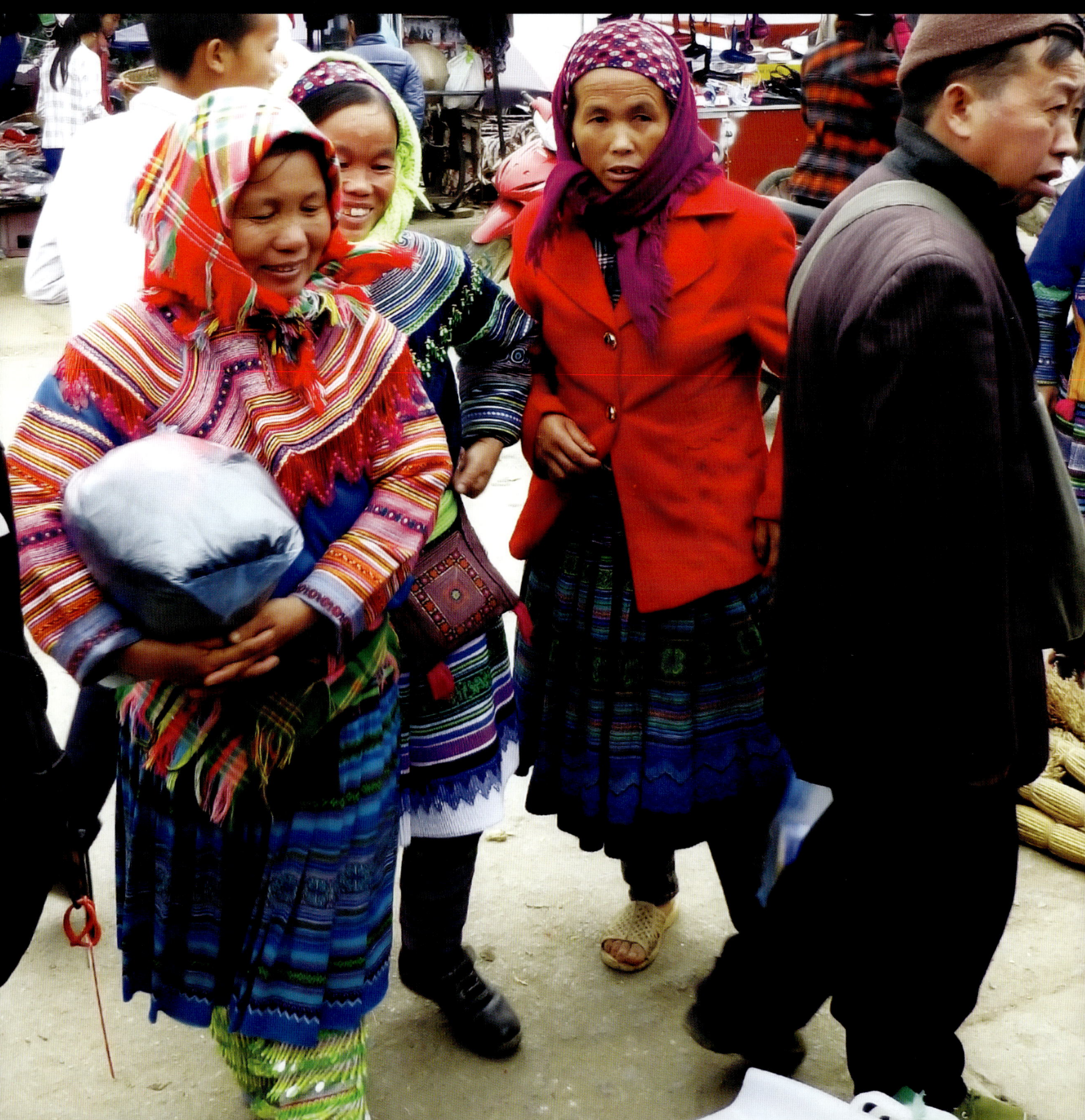

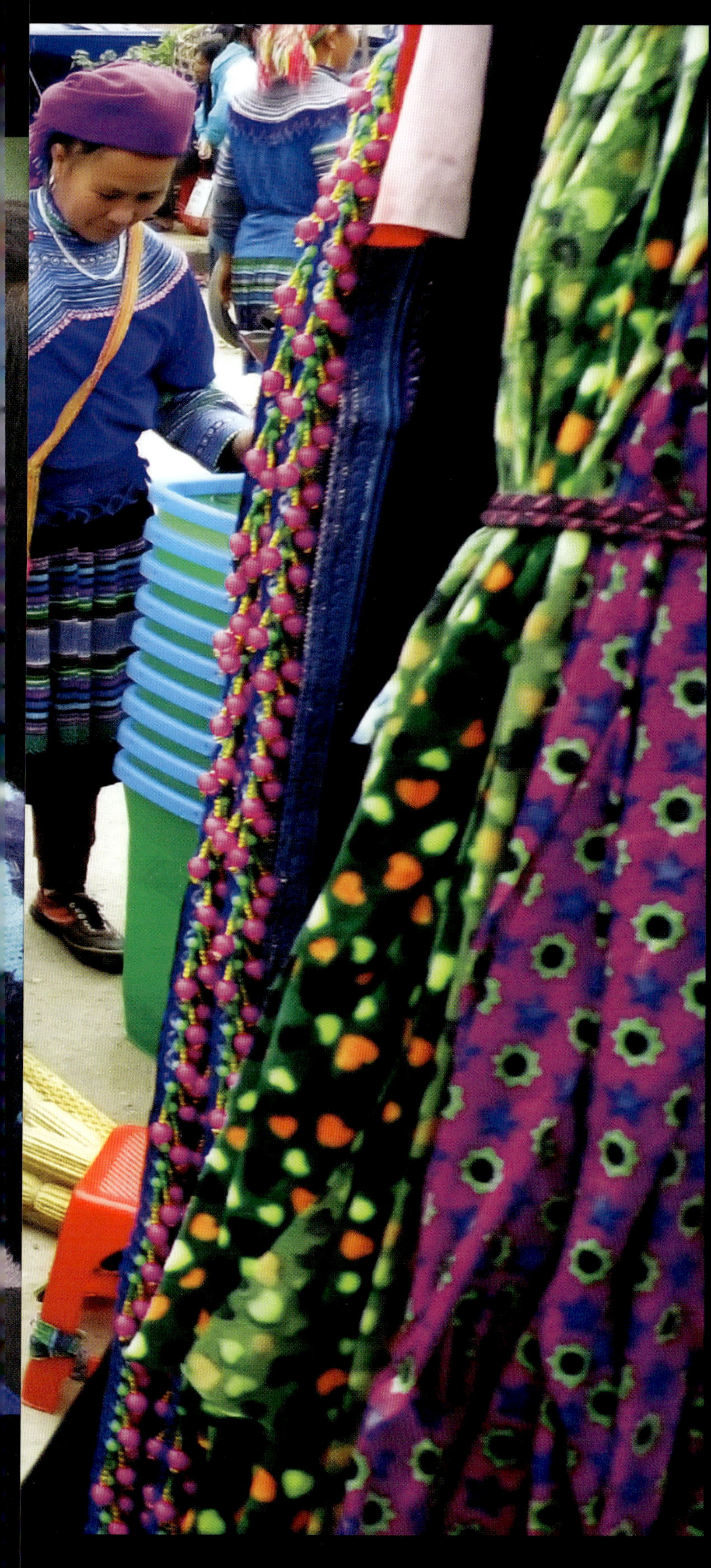

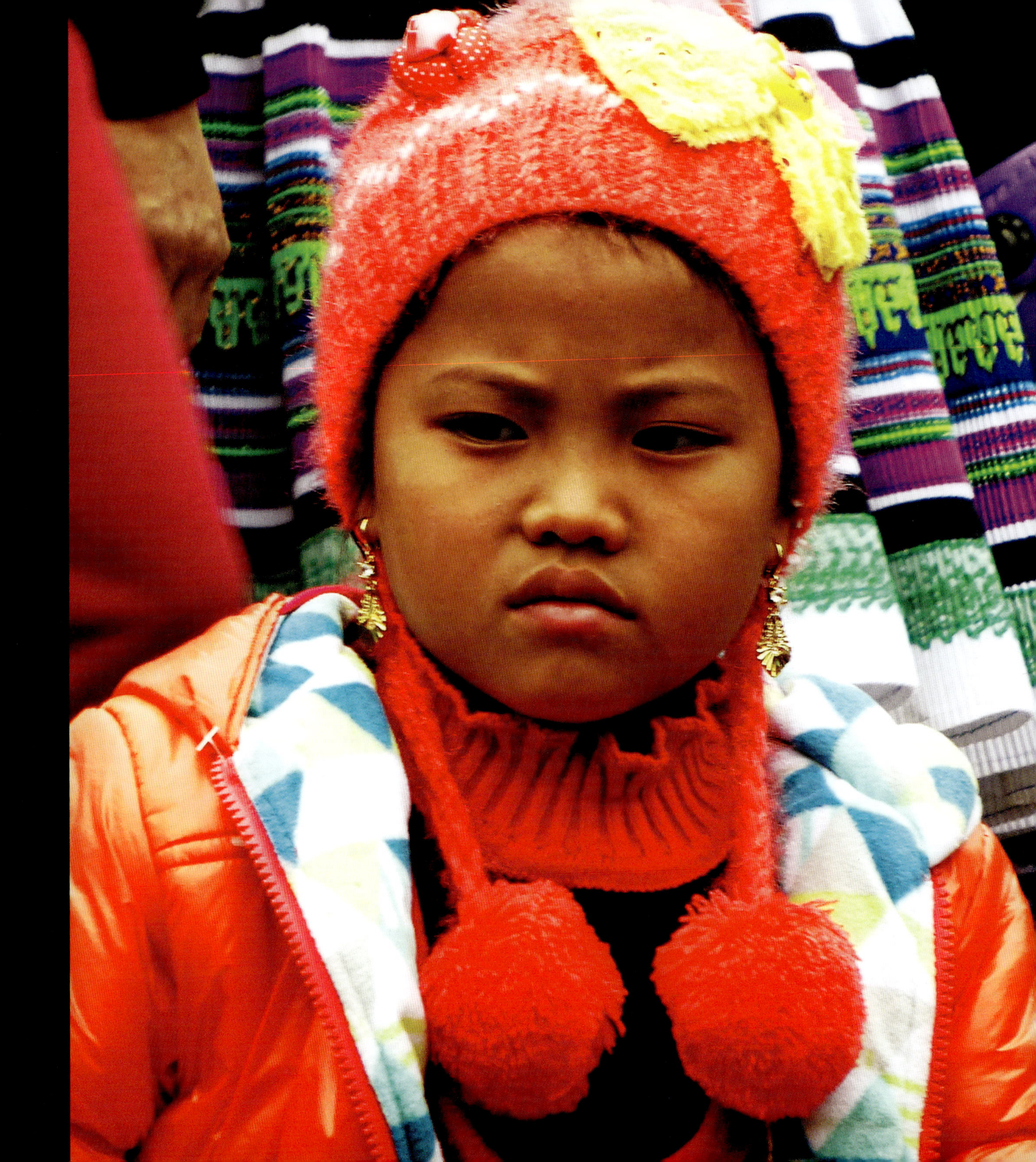

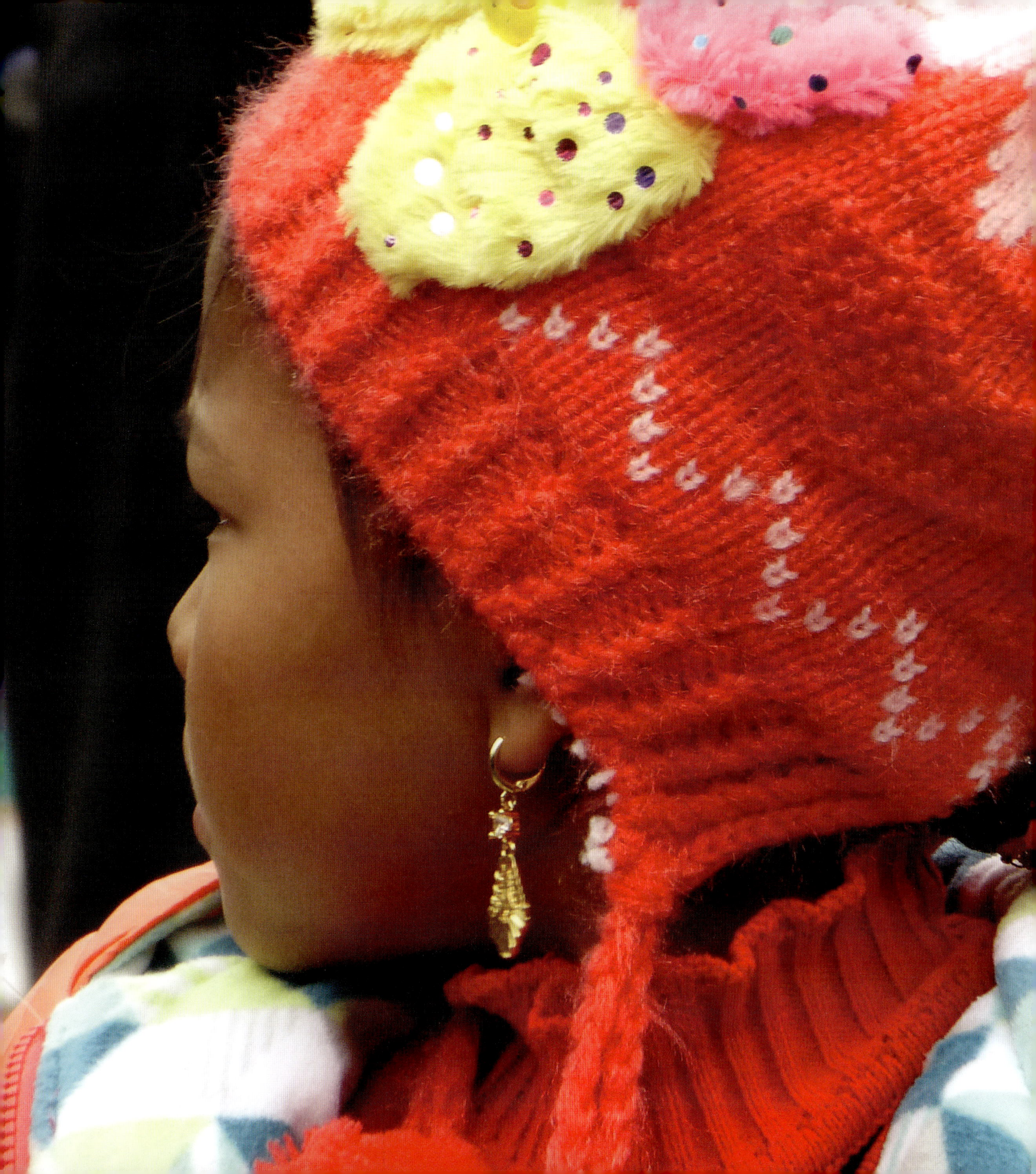

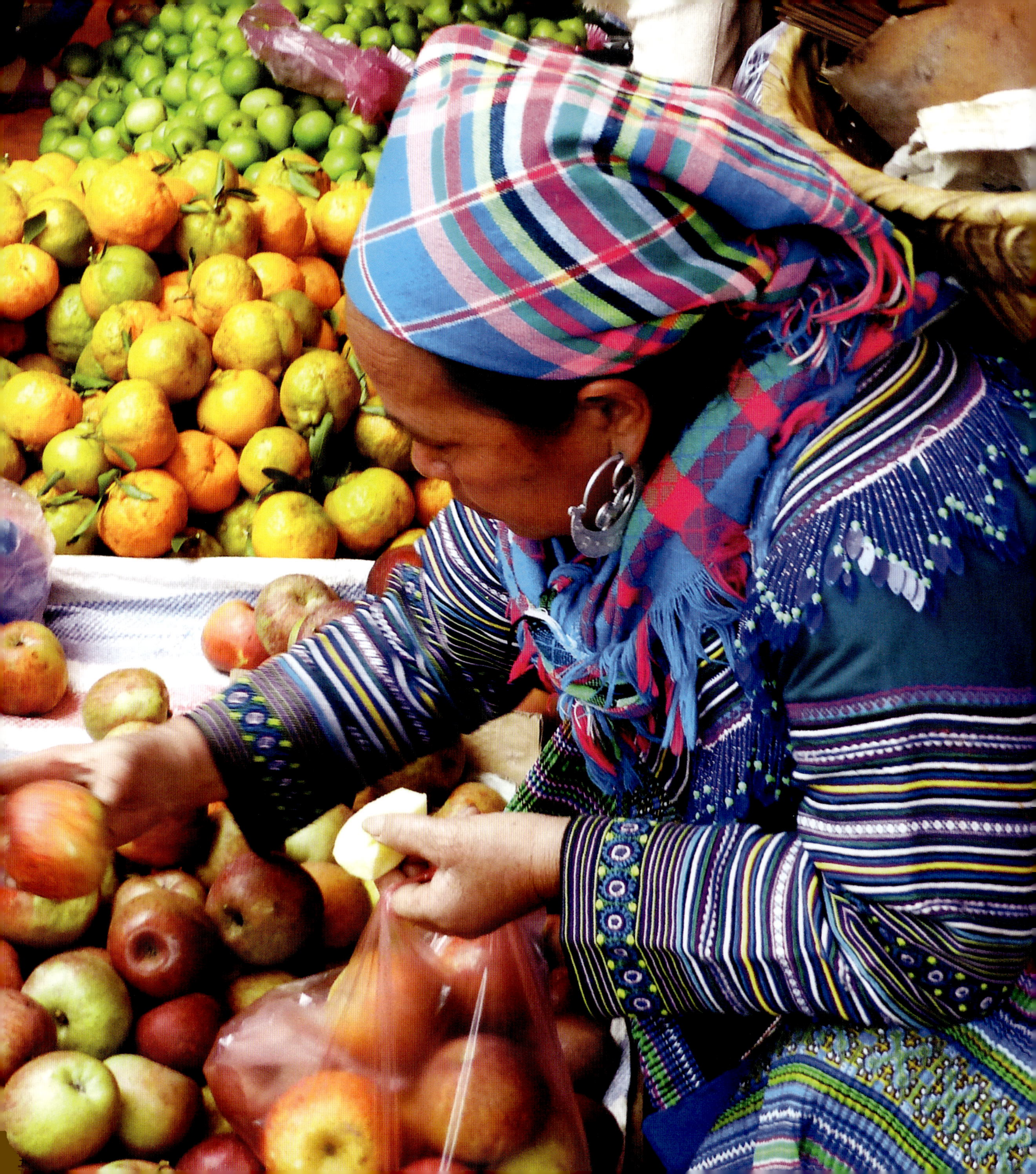

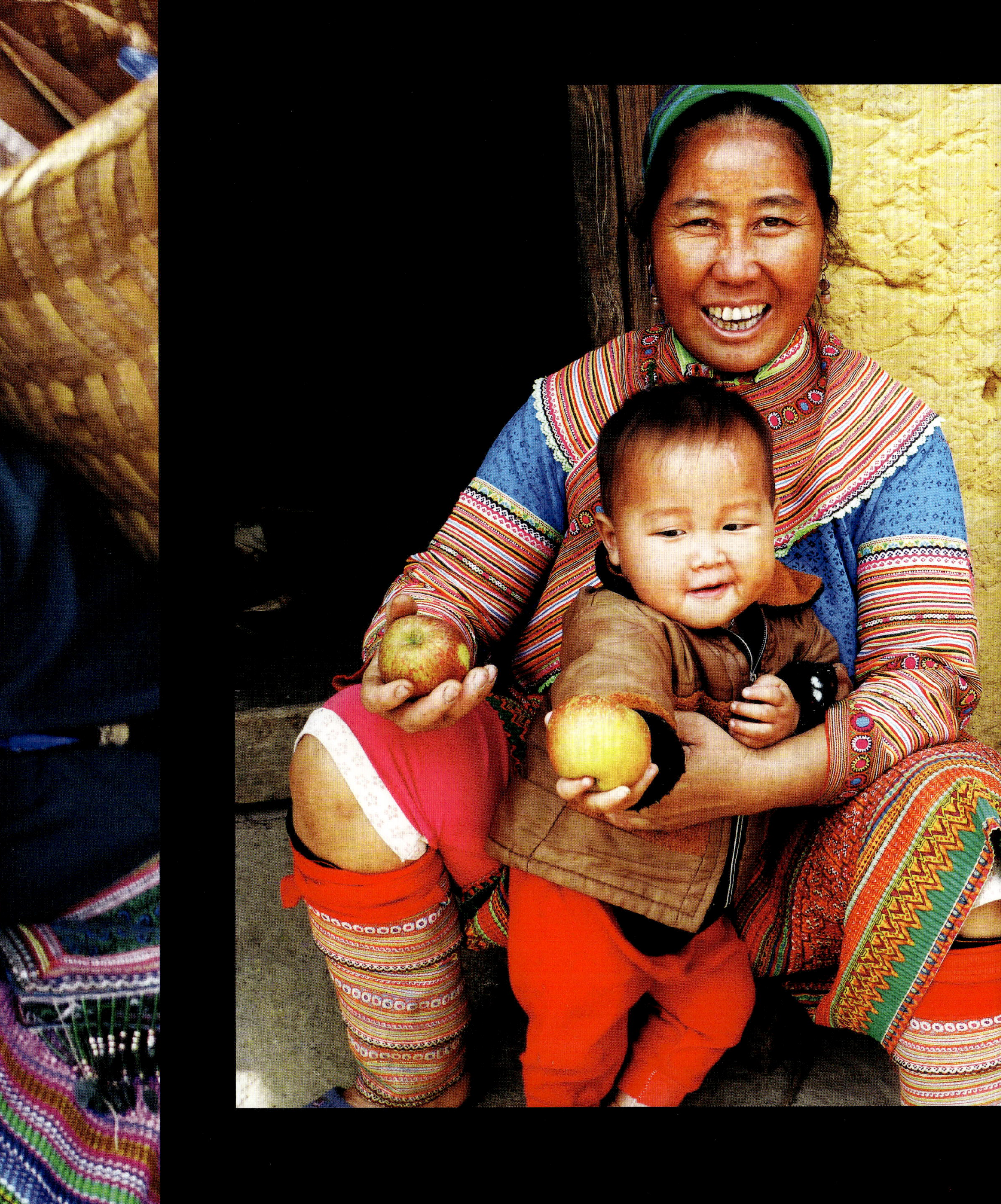

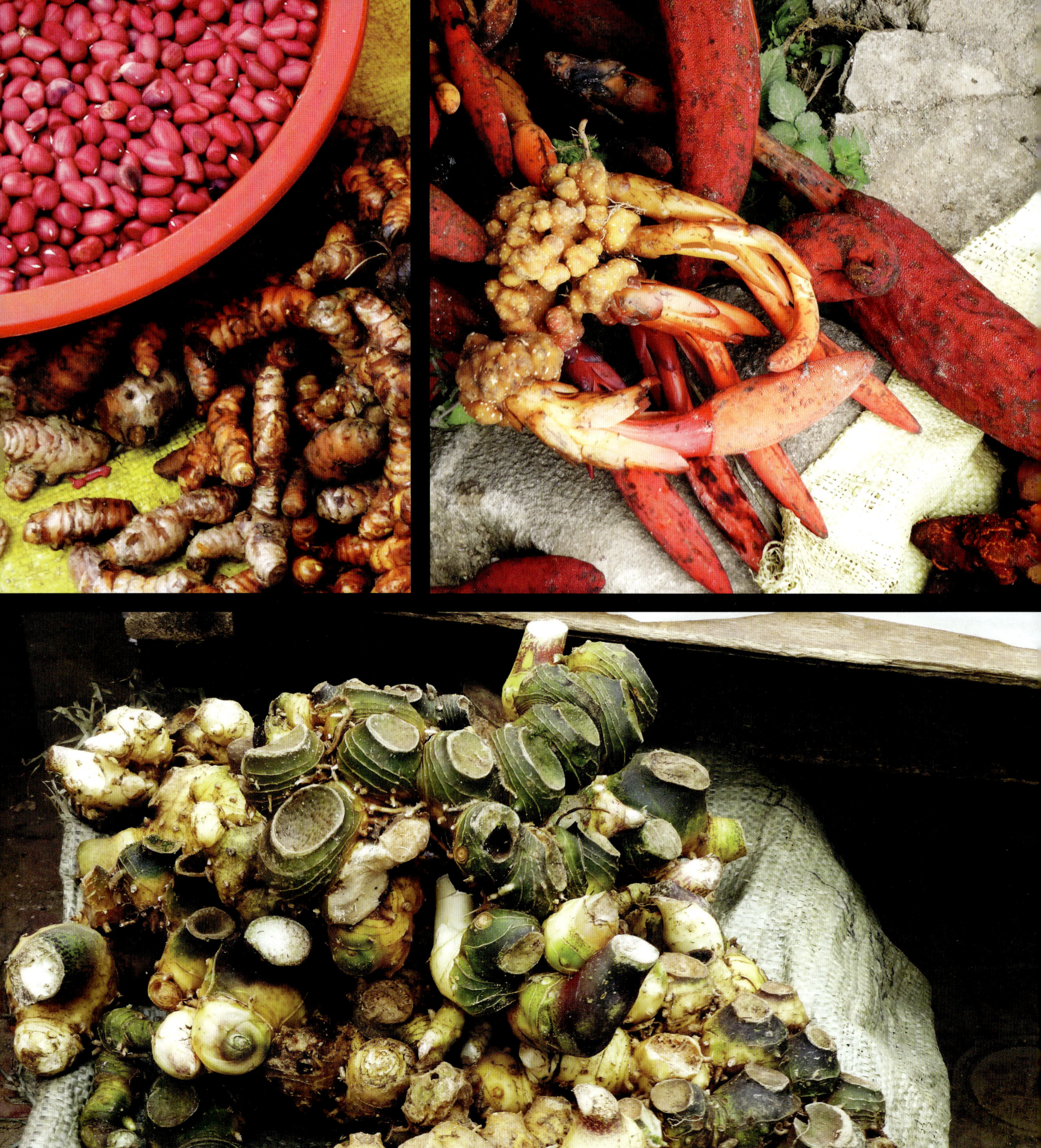

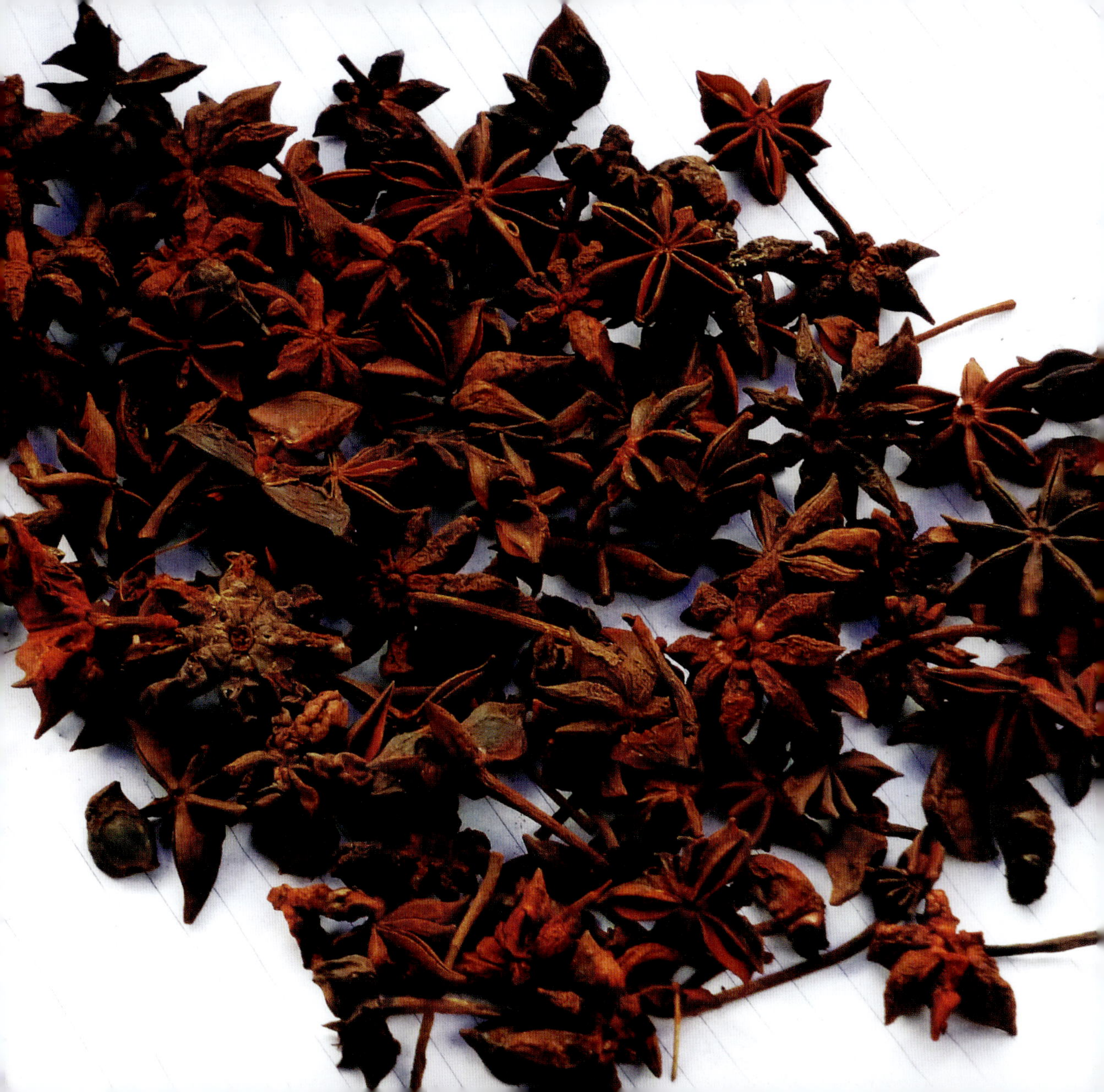

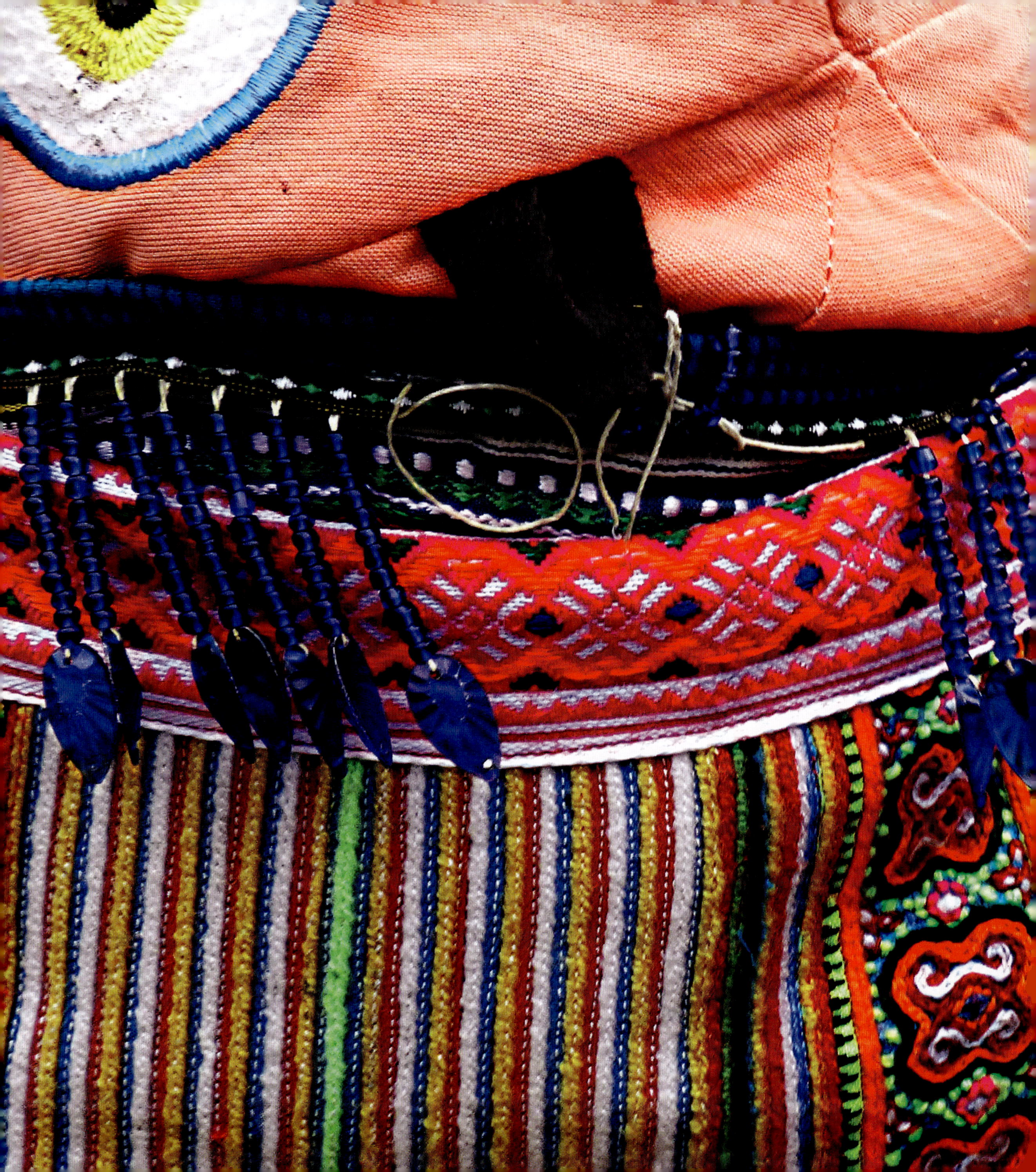

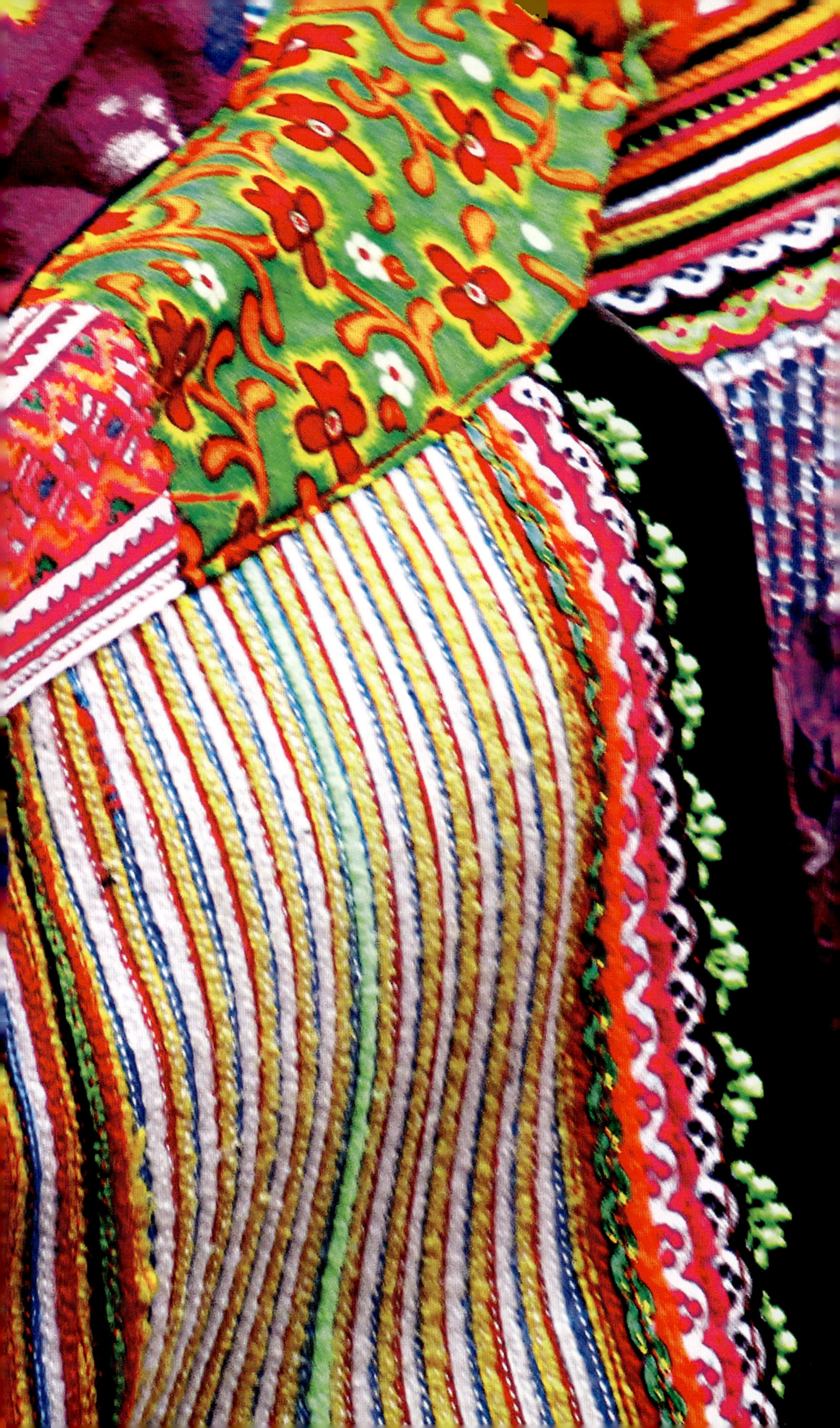

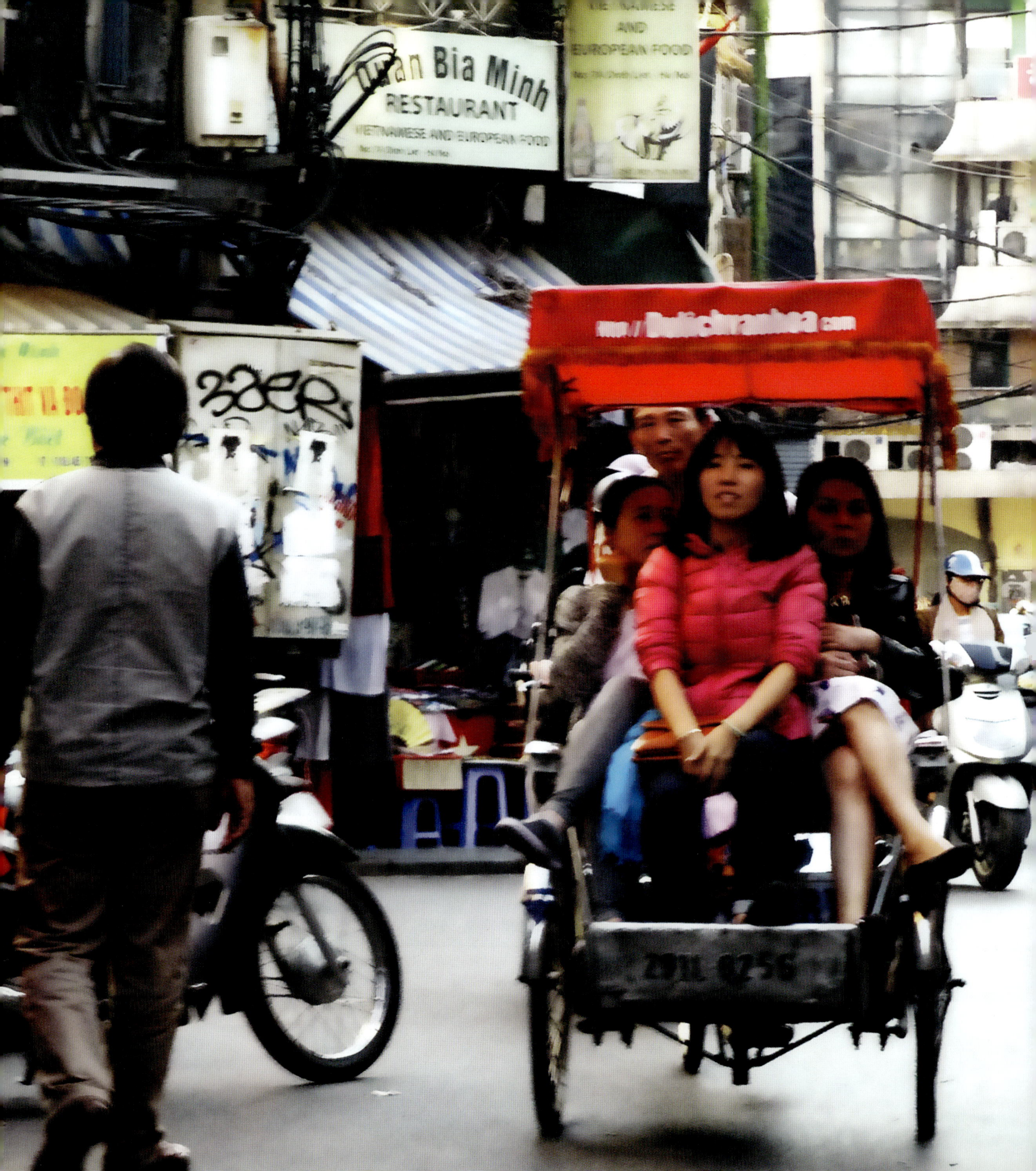

Bia Minh
RESTAURANT
VIETNAMESE AND EUROPEAN FOOD
AND
EUROPEAN FOOD

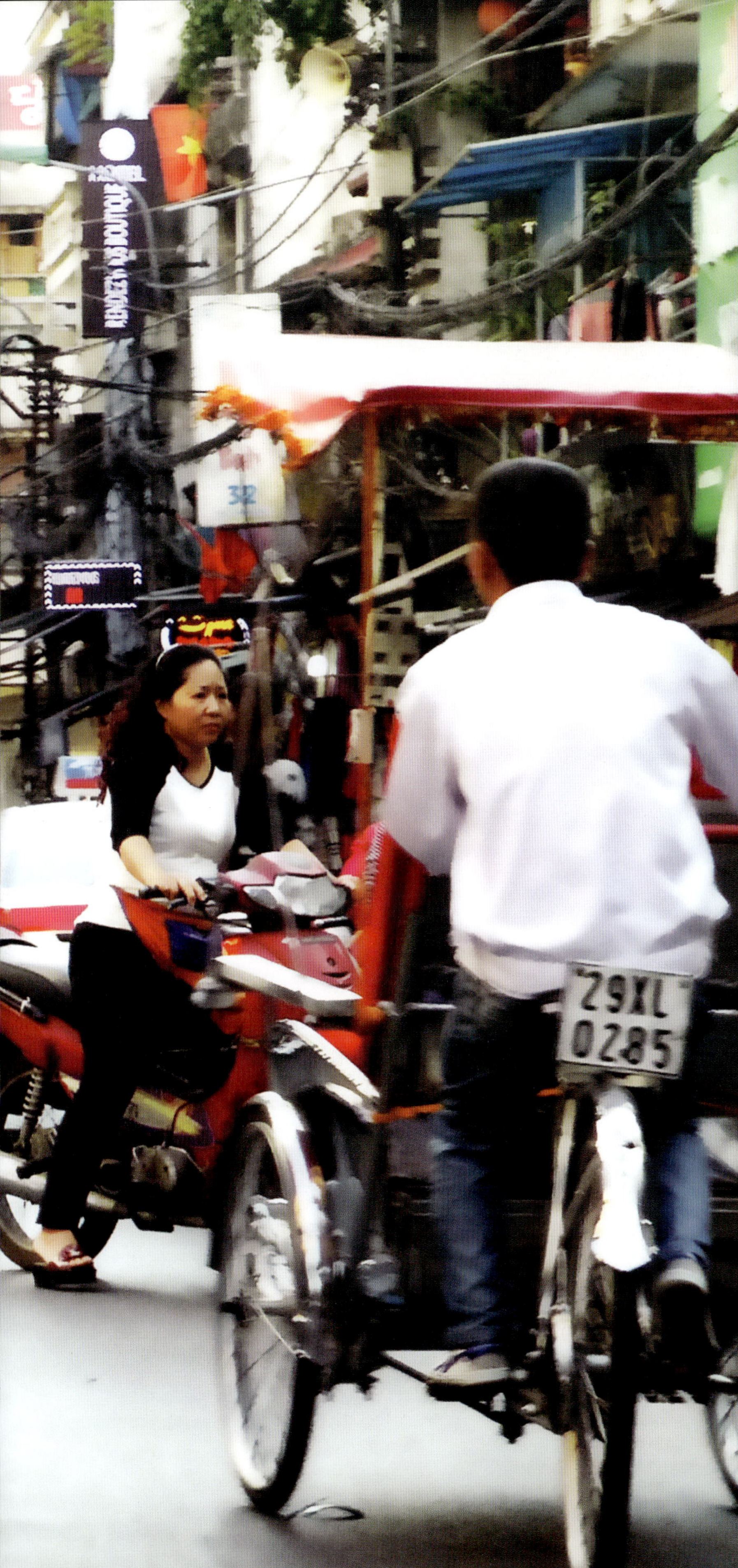

Urban life is only 200 miles (320 km) to the southeast – the capital city of Hanoi.

Thrust into 21st-century commercialism and expansion, Hanoi is a bustling mixture of cultural influences – a fast-paced city with a thousand-year history. Tall buildings peppering the skyline spring forth from colonial streets filled with plastic-stool sidewalk eateries and roving street vendors – migrant women from the countryside. The second largest city in Vietnam with increasing urban sprawl and the seat of political power and planning, Hanoi has become a lifeline, albeit a stressful one, for some poor rural families. Women trek long distances daily, leaving before dawn and returning only in time to catch a few hours' sleep, to sell their wares. Hanoi is a composite of extremes.

Population (2016): 3.79 million

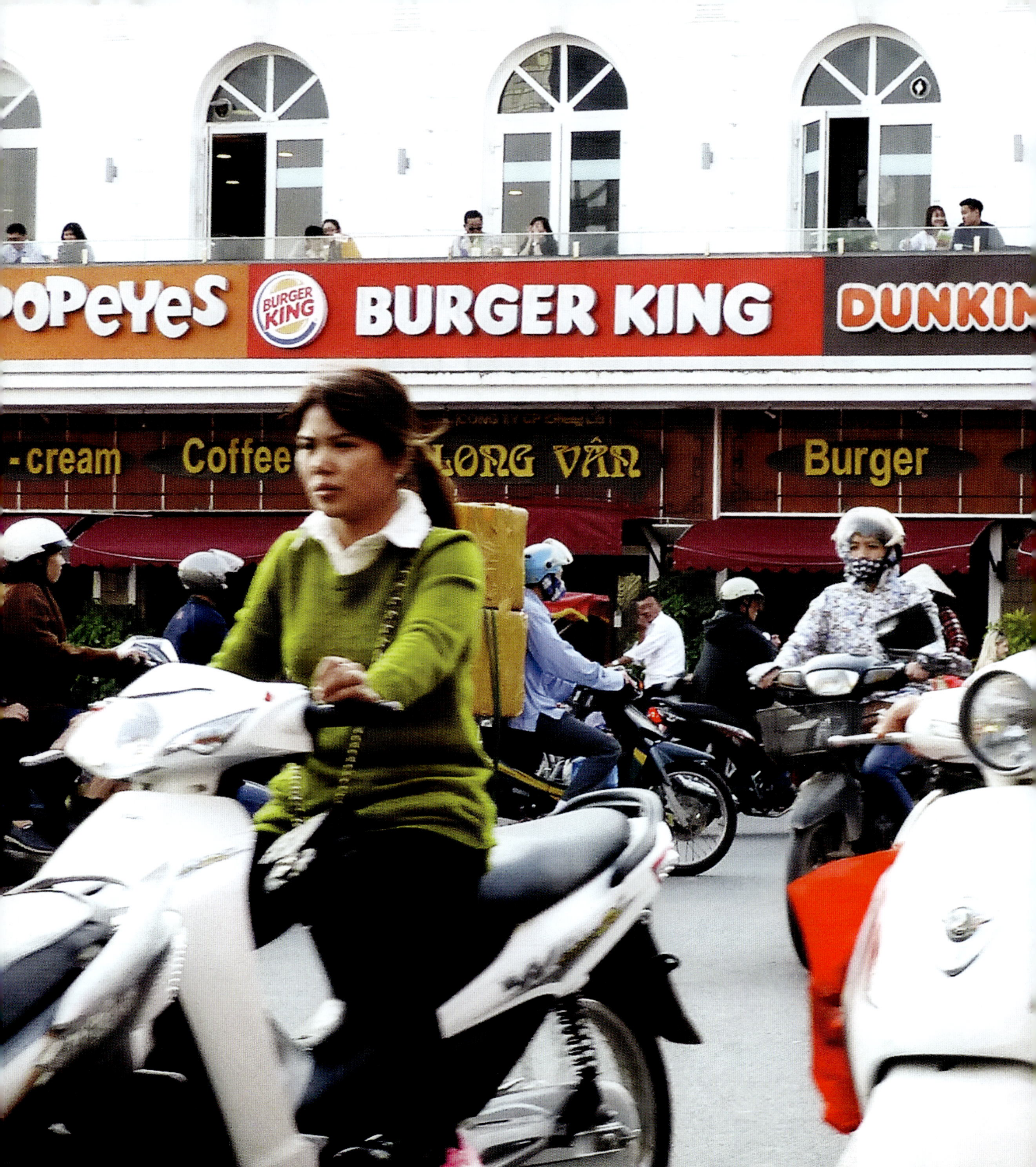
BURGER KING
BURGER KING
Coffee
LONG VÂN
Burger

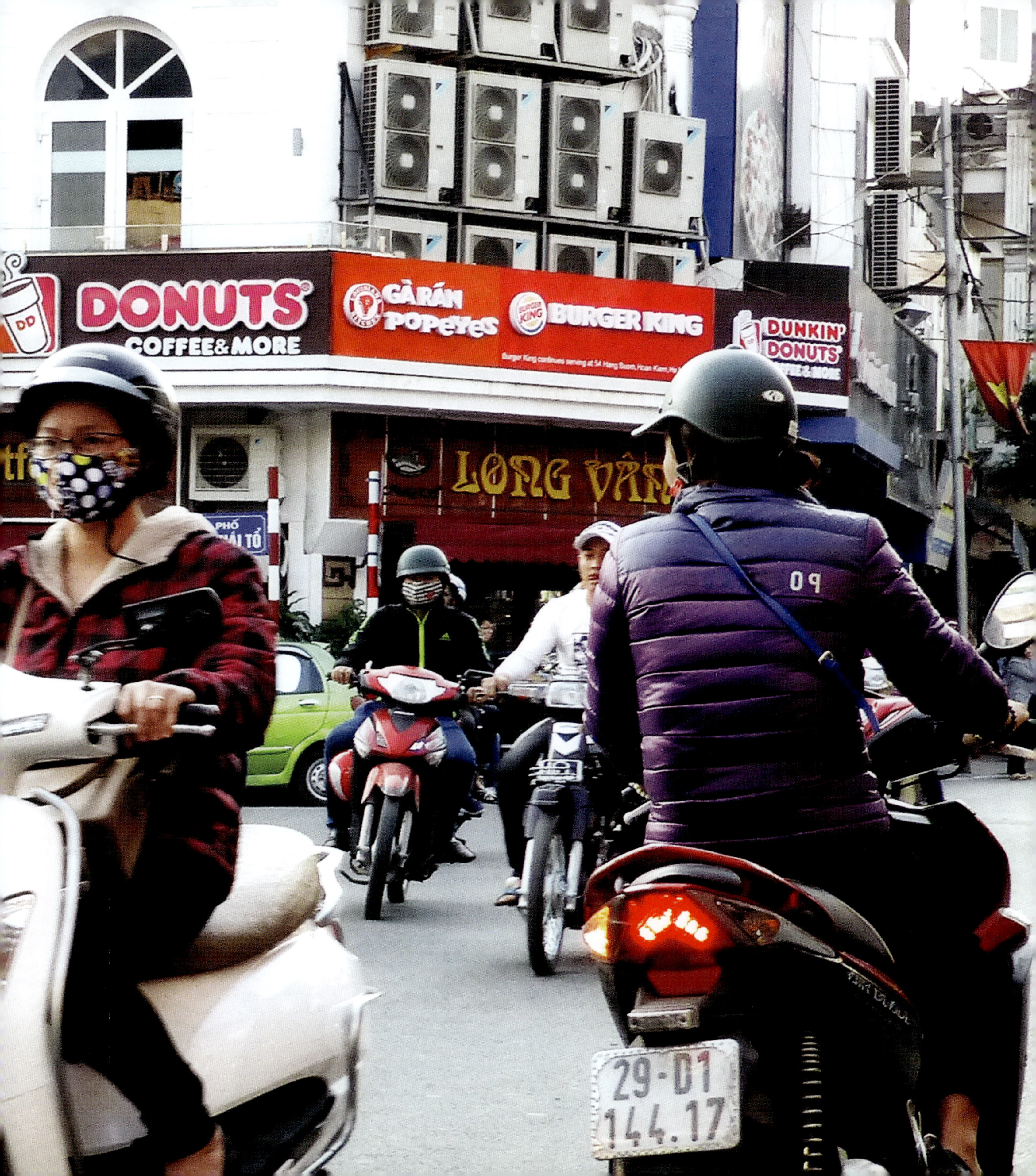
DONUTS
COFFEE&MORE
GÀ RÁN
POPEYES
BURGER KING
DUNKIN'
DONUTS
LONG VÂN
29-01
144.17

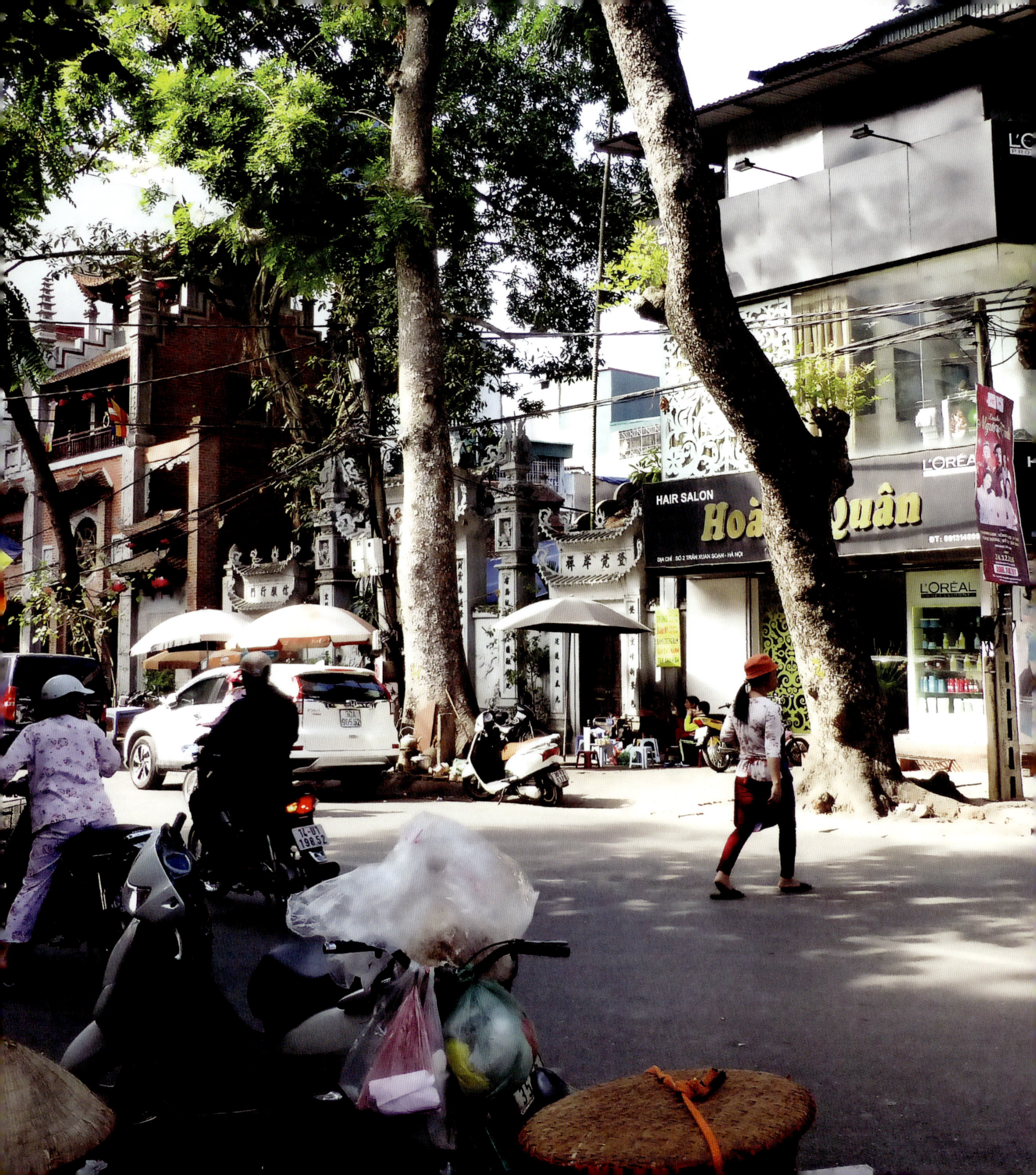
HAIR SALON
Quân
L'ORÉAL

Hoàng

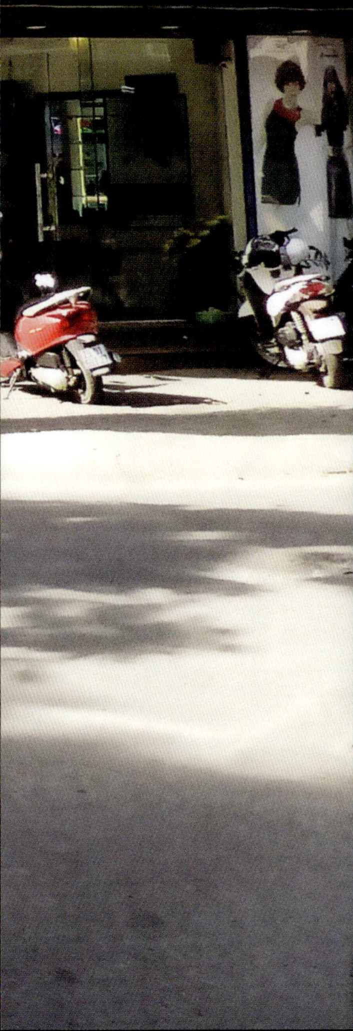

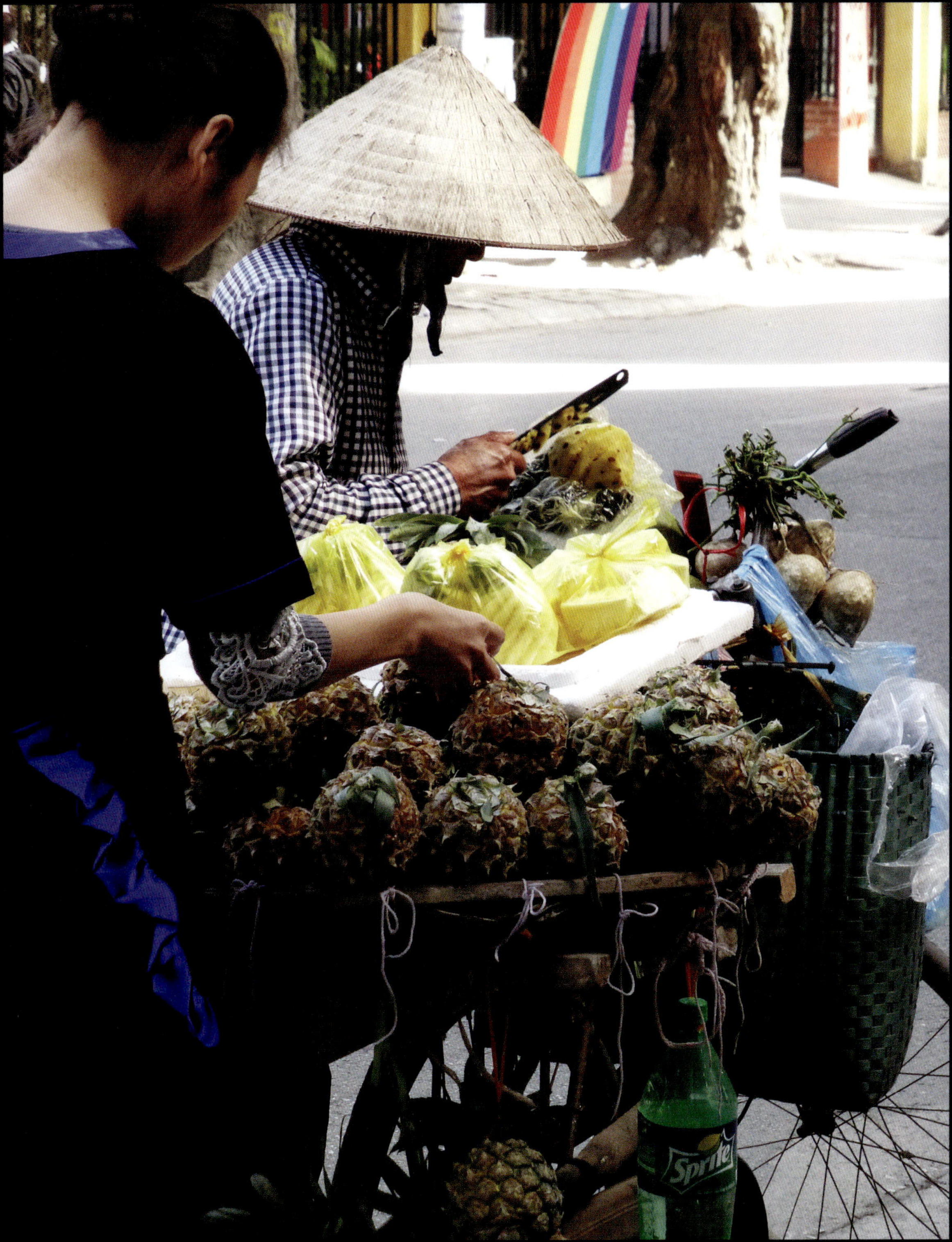

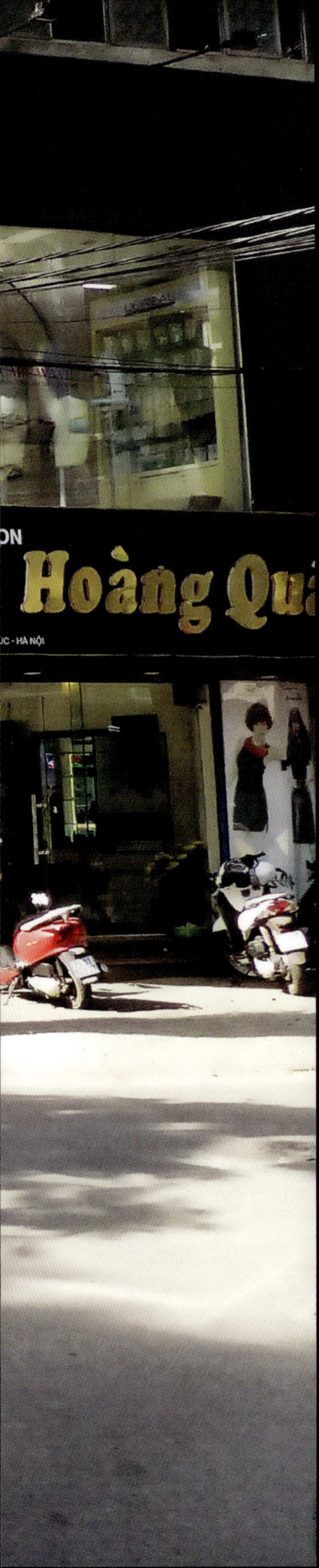

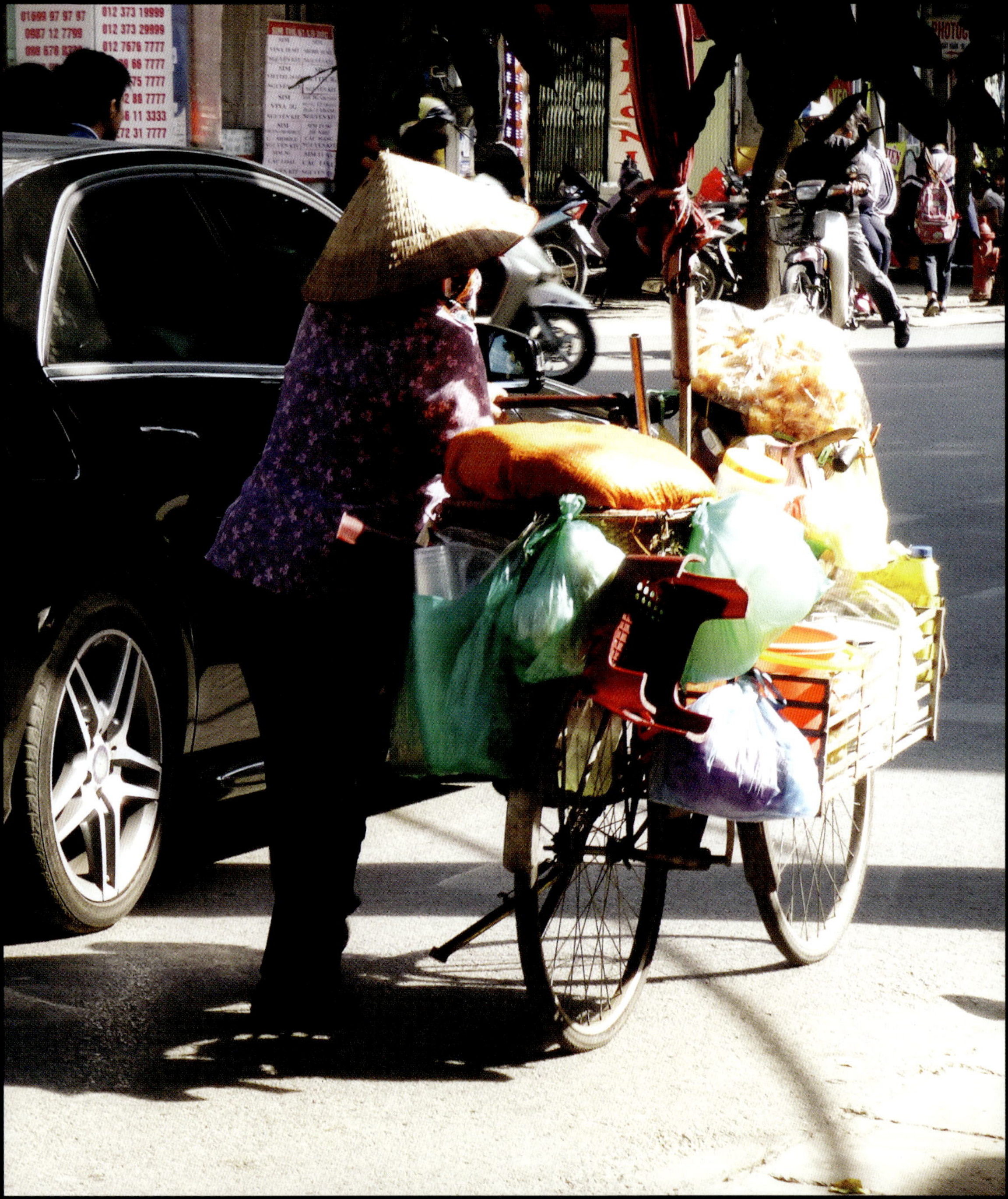

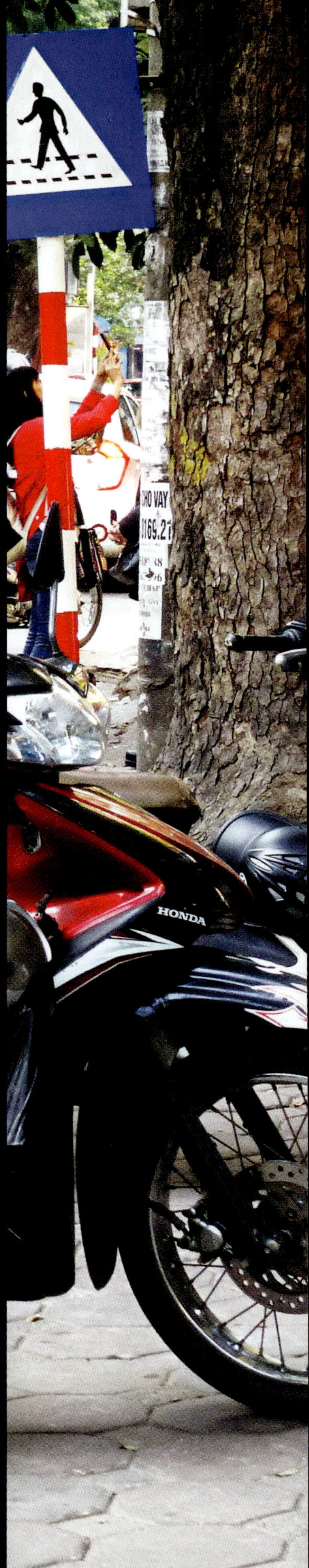
CHO VAY
HONDA

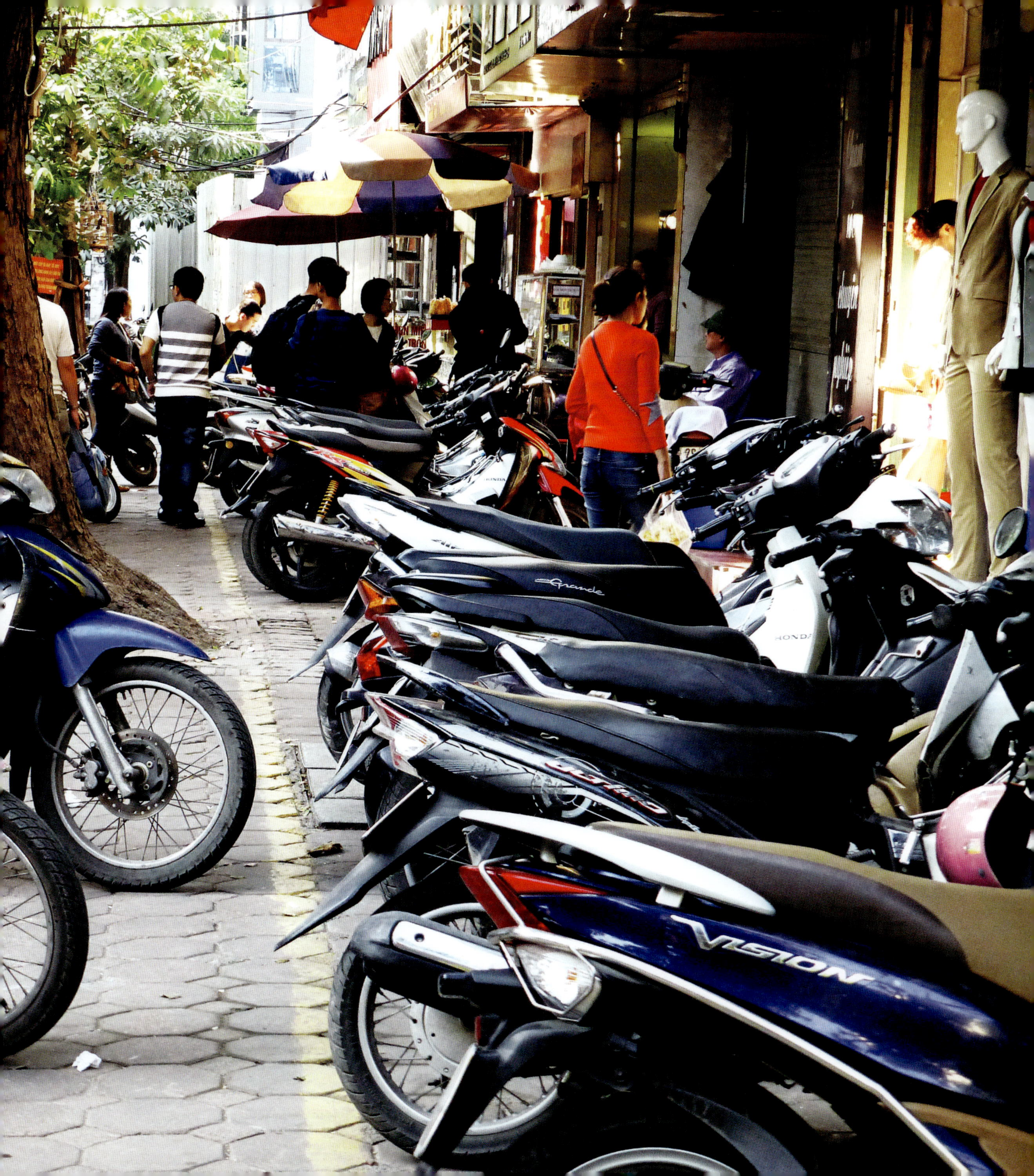
Grande
VISION

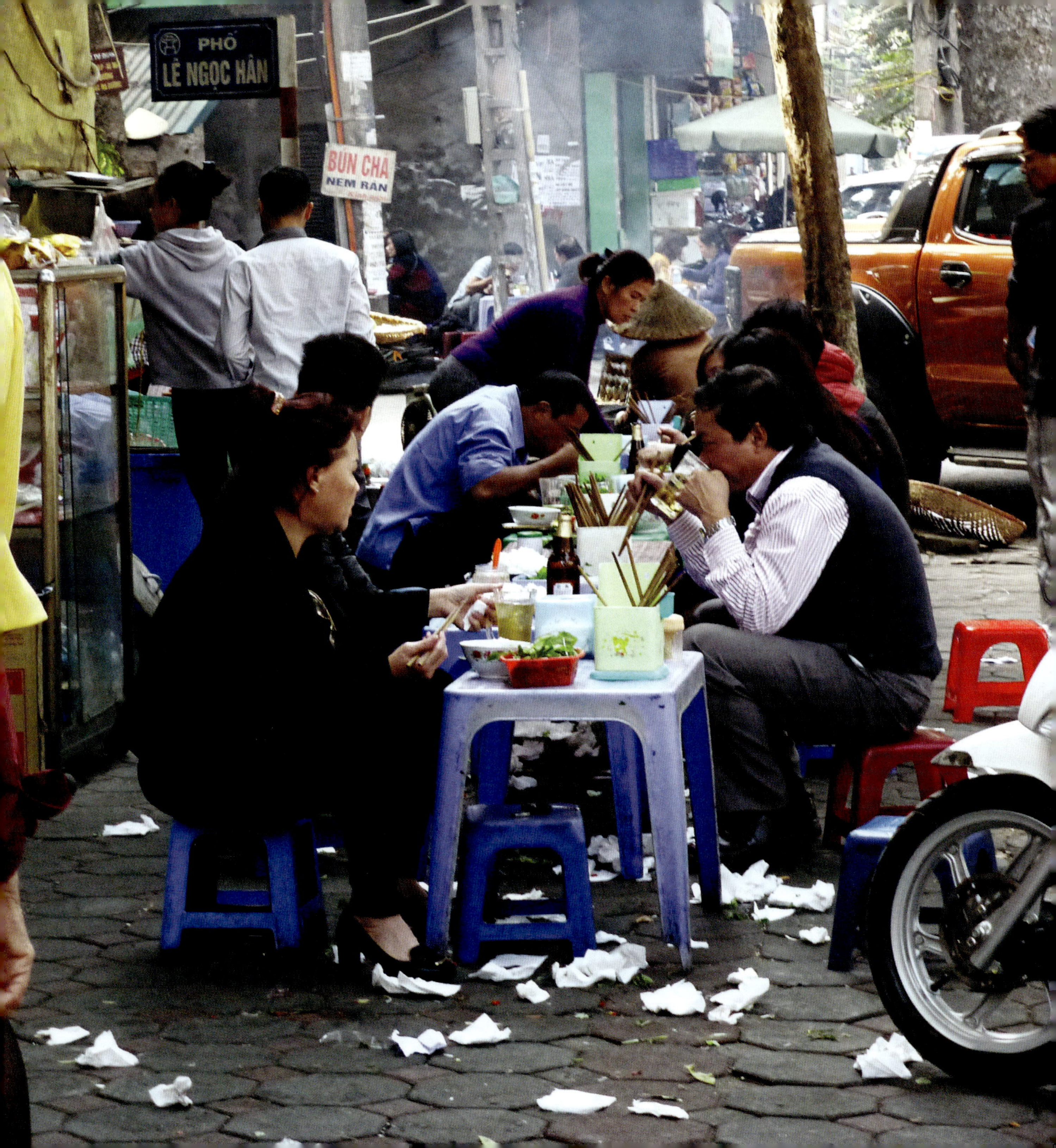
PHỐ
LÊ NGỌC HÂN
BÚN CHẢ
NEM RÁN

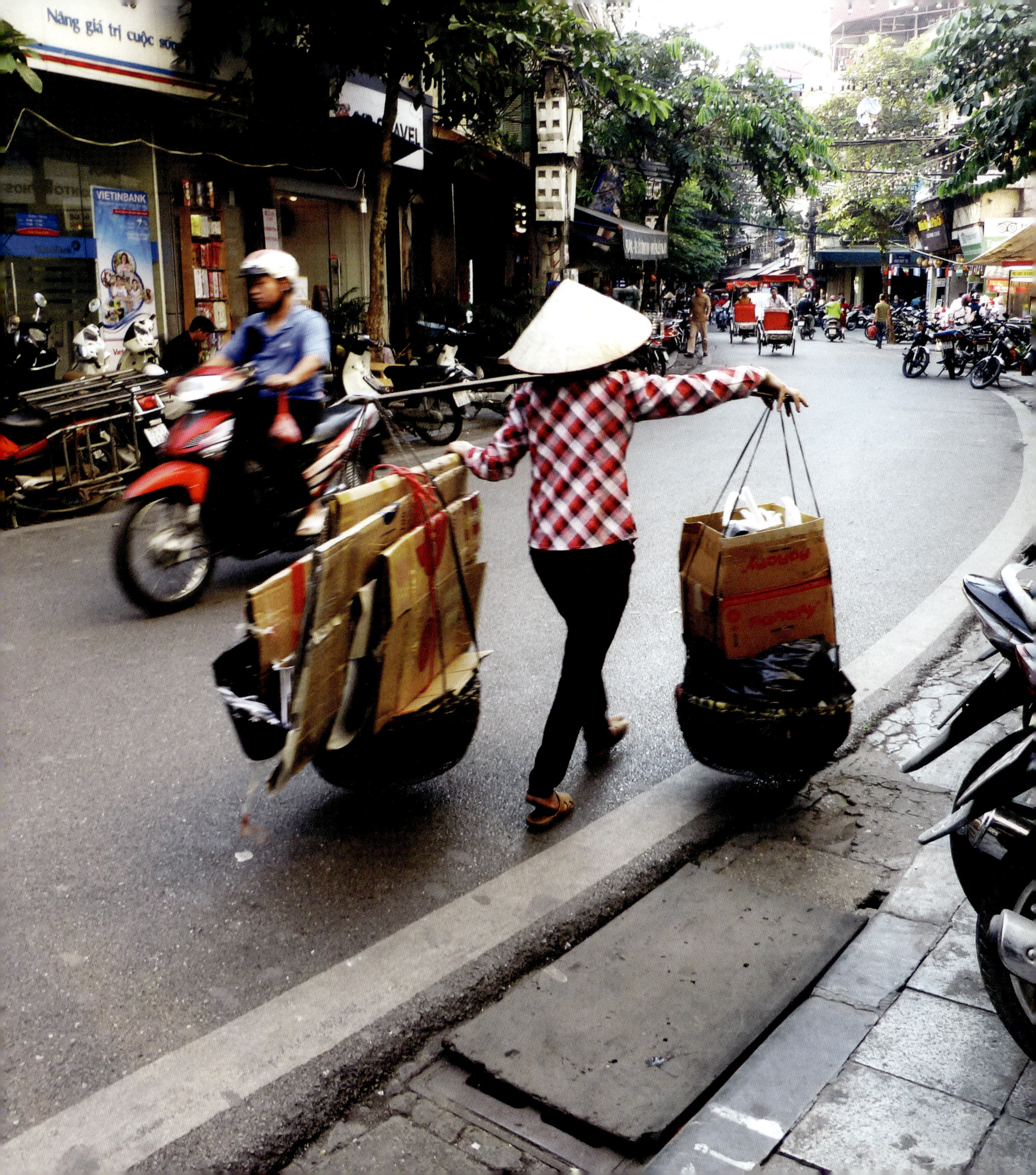
Nâng giá trị cuộc
VIETINBANK

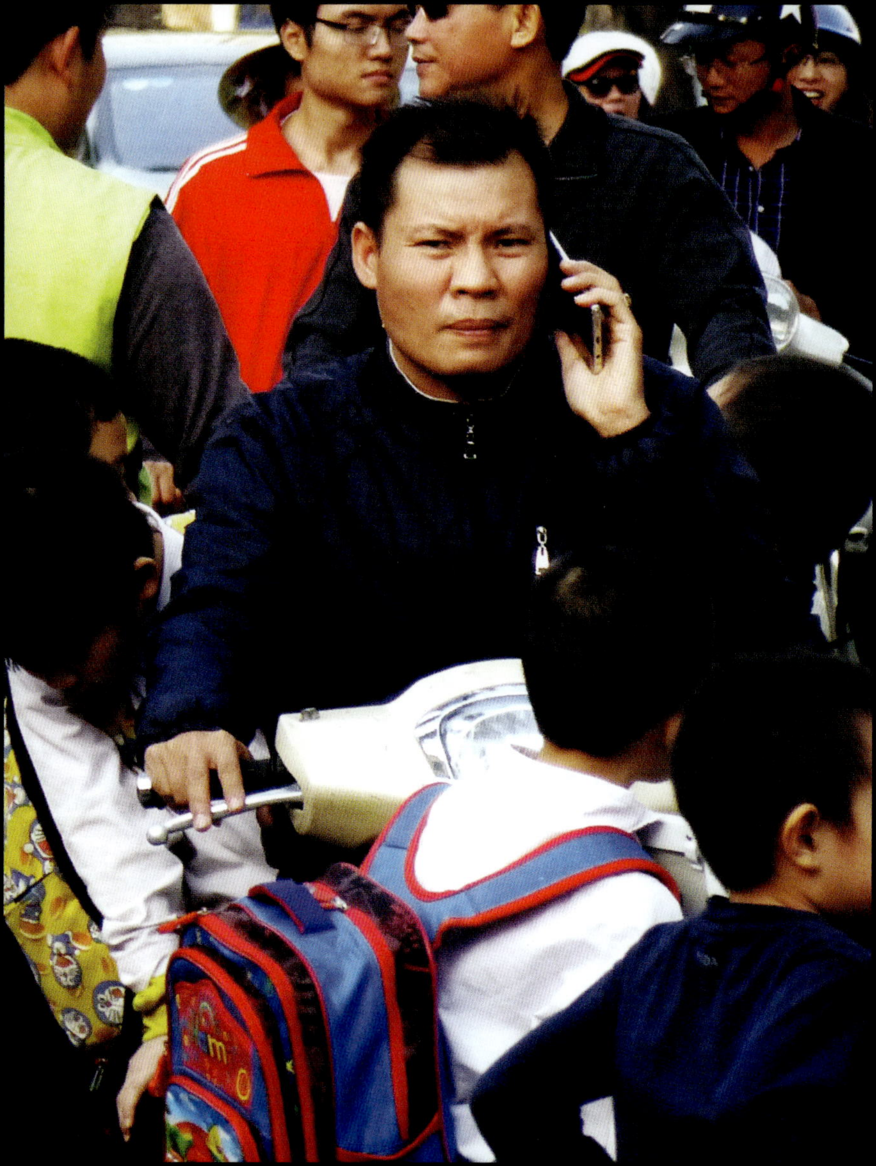

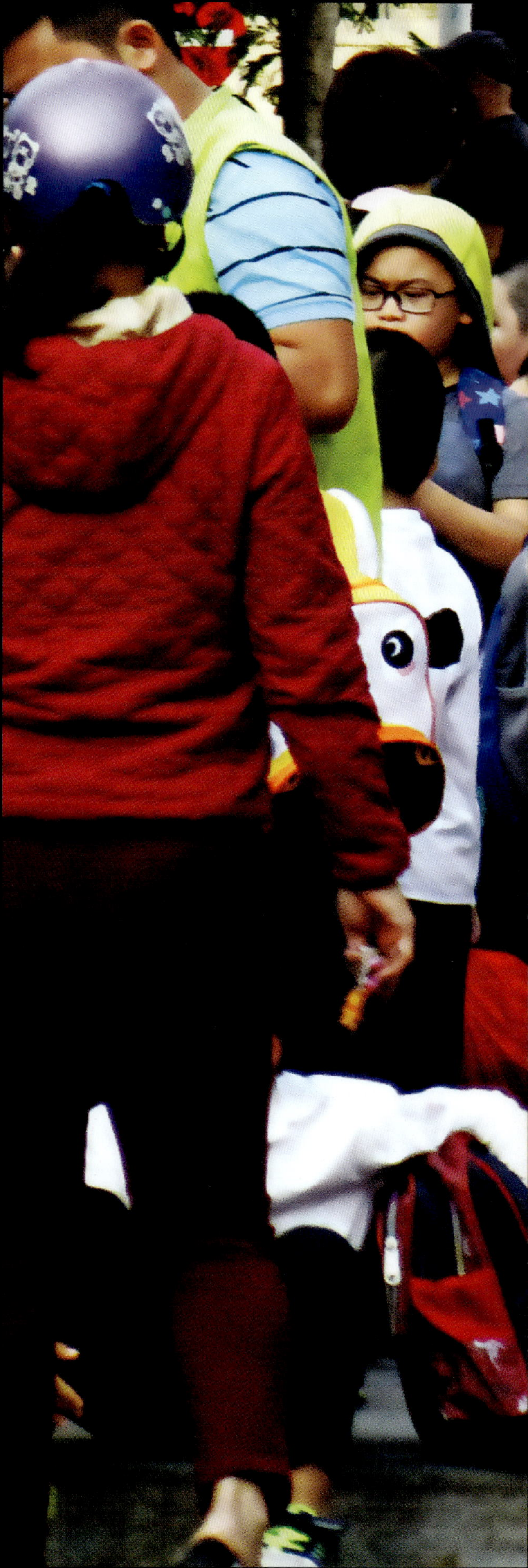

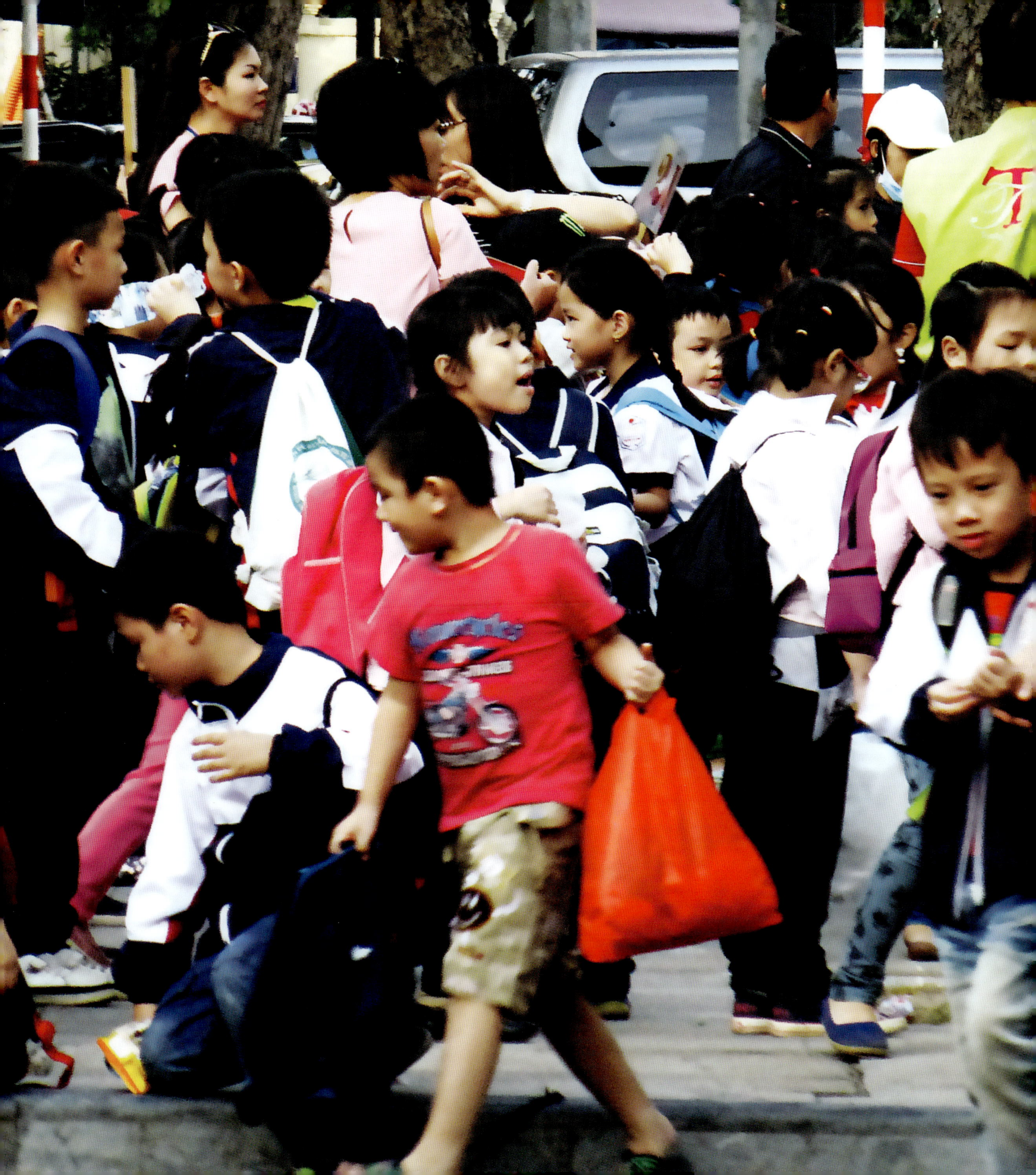

TWO

In the mountains of northern Laos

200 miles due west of Hanoi (390km) lie the mountainous northwestern highlands of Laos. Ethnic minority groups in this area and its adjacent central highlands constitute approximately seventy percent of this sector's population. Tropical and sub-tropical monsoon climates render this region lush with abundant vegetation.

The government of Laos recognizes forty-nine ethnic groups, forty-eight of which are minorities. Although the majority of all Laotians are Buddhists, and the highland minorities are primarily animists, animism is common throughout the population.

The hamlets and villages portray poverty in varying degrees – visages of earth and dust, split and pole bamboo, thatch, wood, shakes and corrugated metal. Architecture and innovation spring from necessity and superstition, created from whatever is available. Subsistence agriculture is the norm.

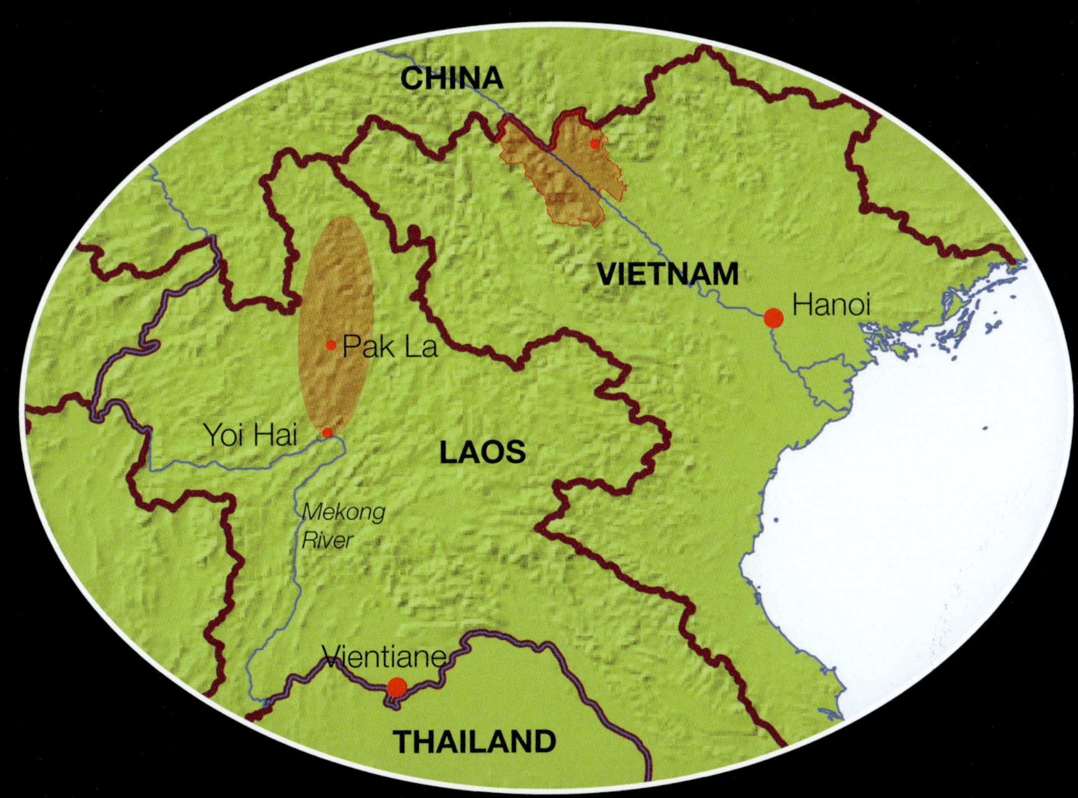

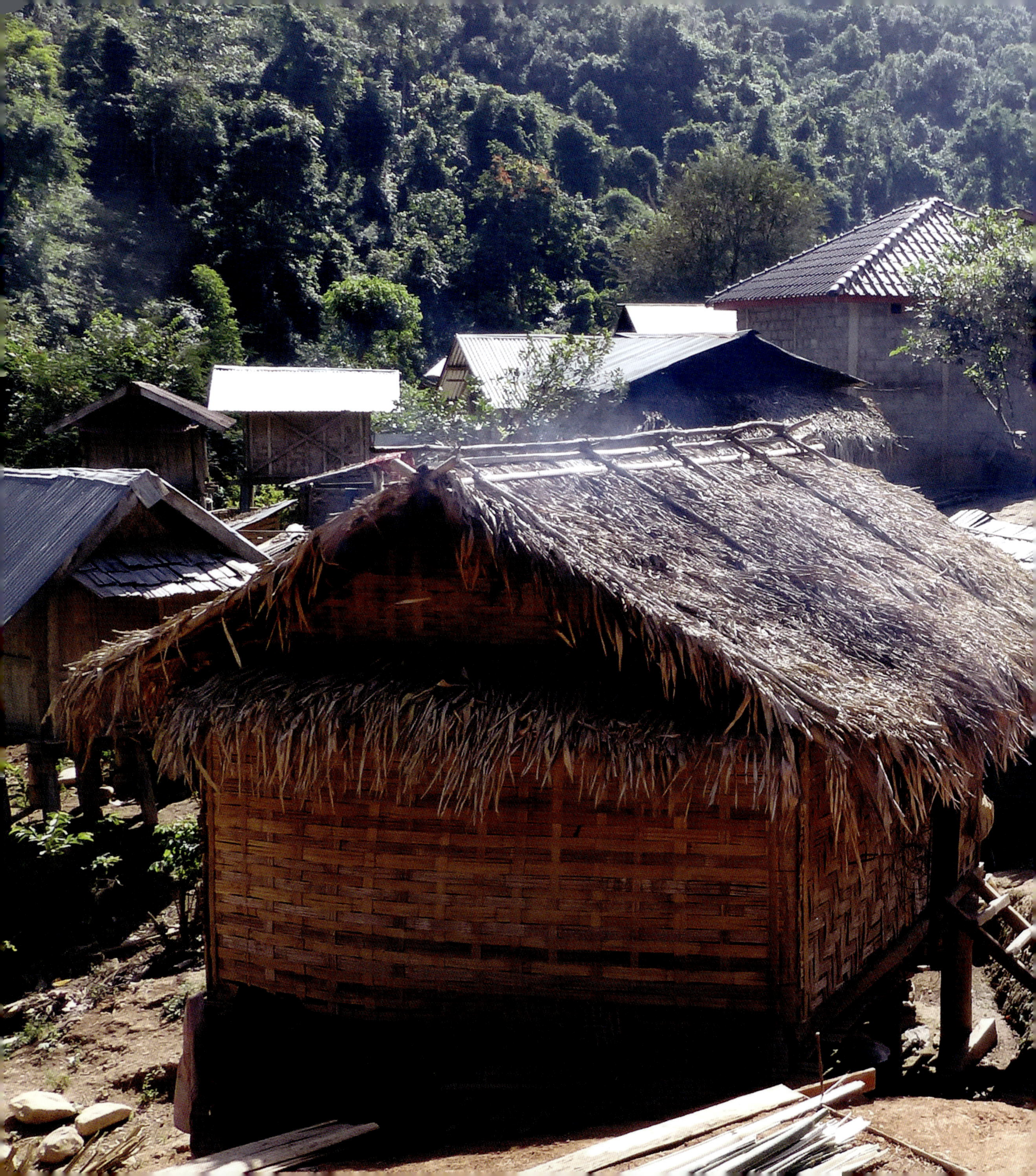

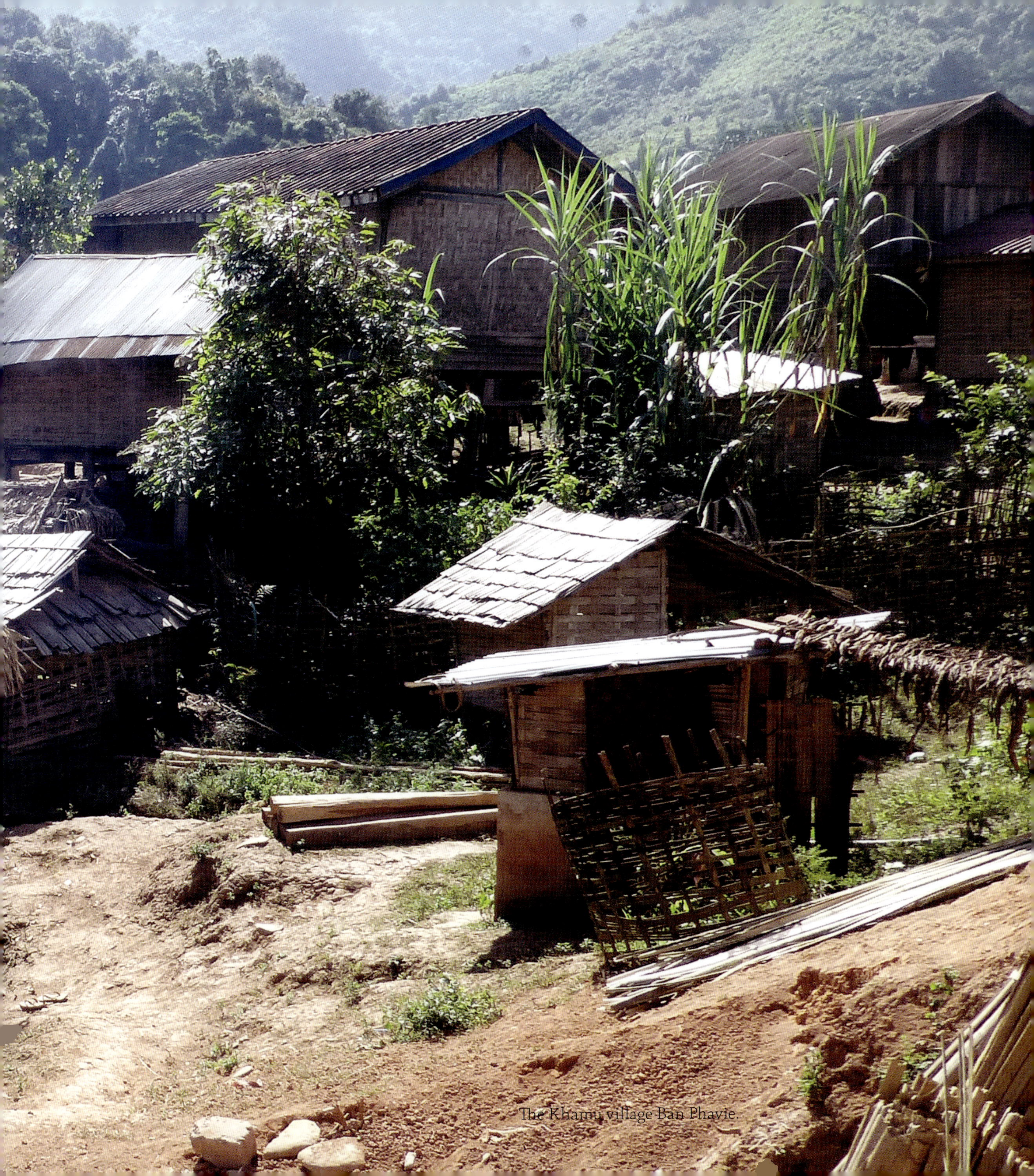

The Khamu village Ban Phavie.

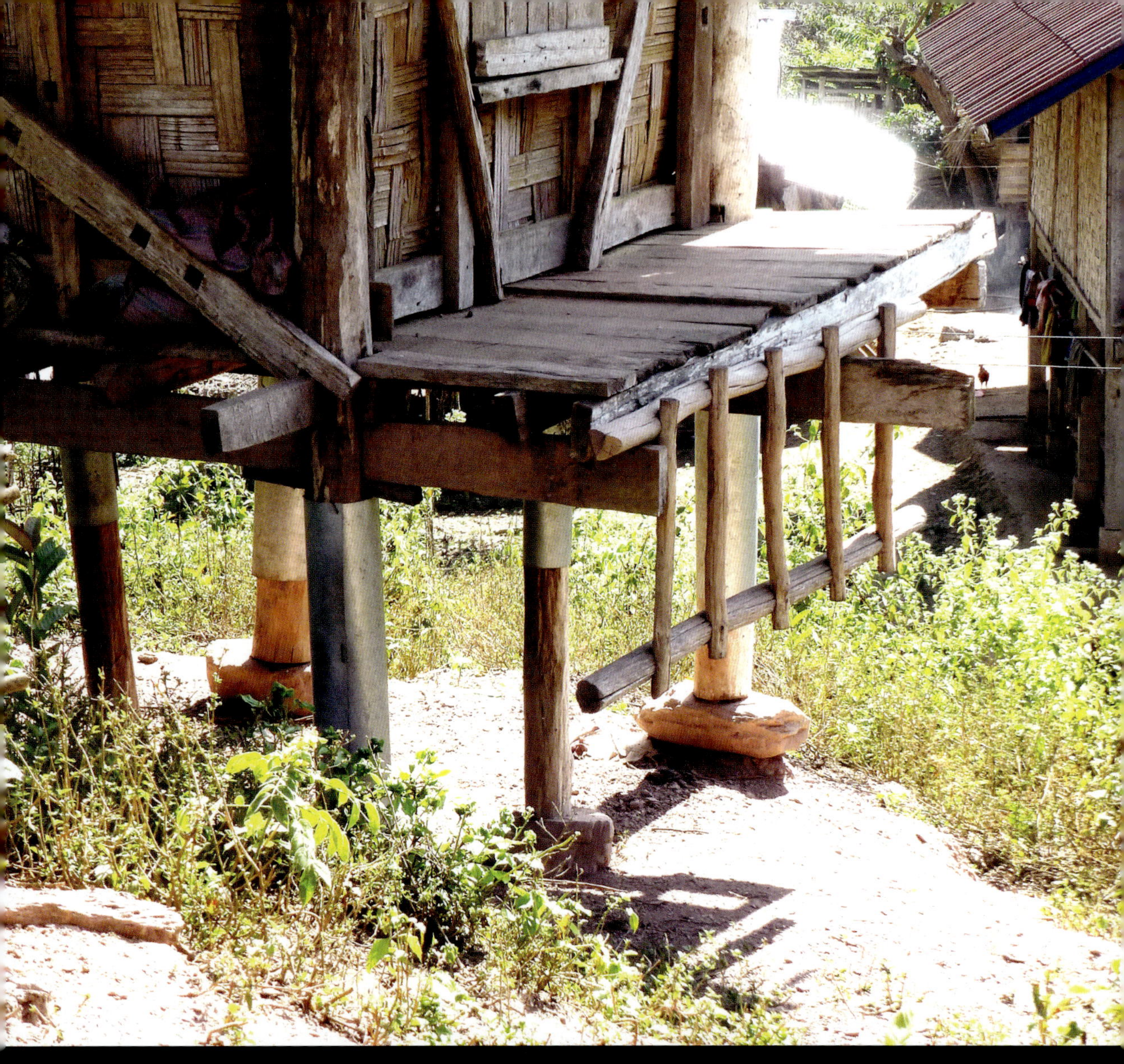

Some villages are built on stilts.

In the highlands, simple innovations are effective. Stone footings discourage snakes, metal sleeves foil rats, and stilt height discourages animals and people. Foraged bamboo and wood – split and sawed – form

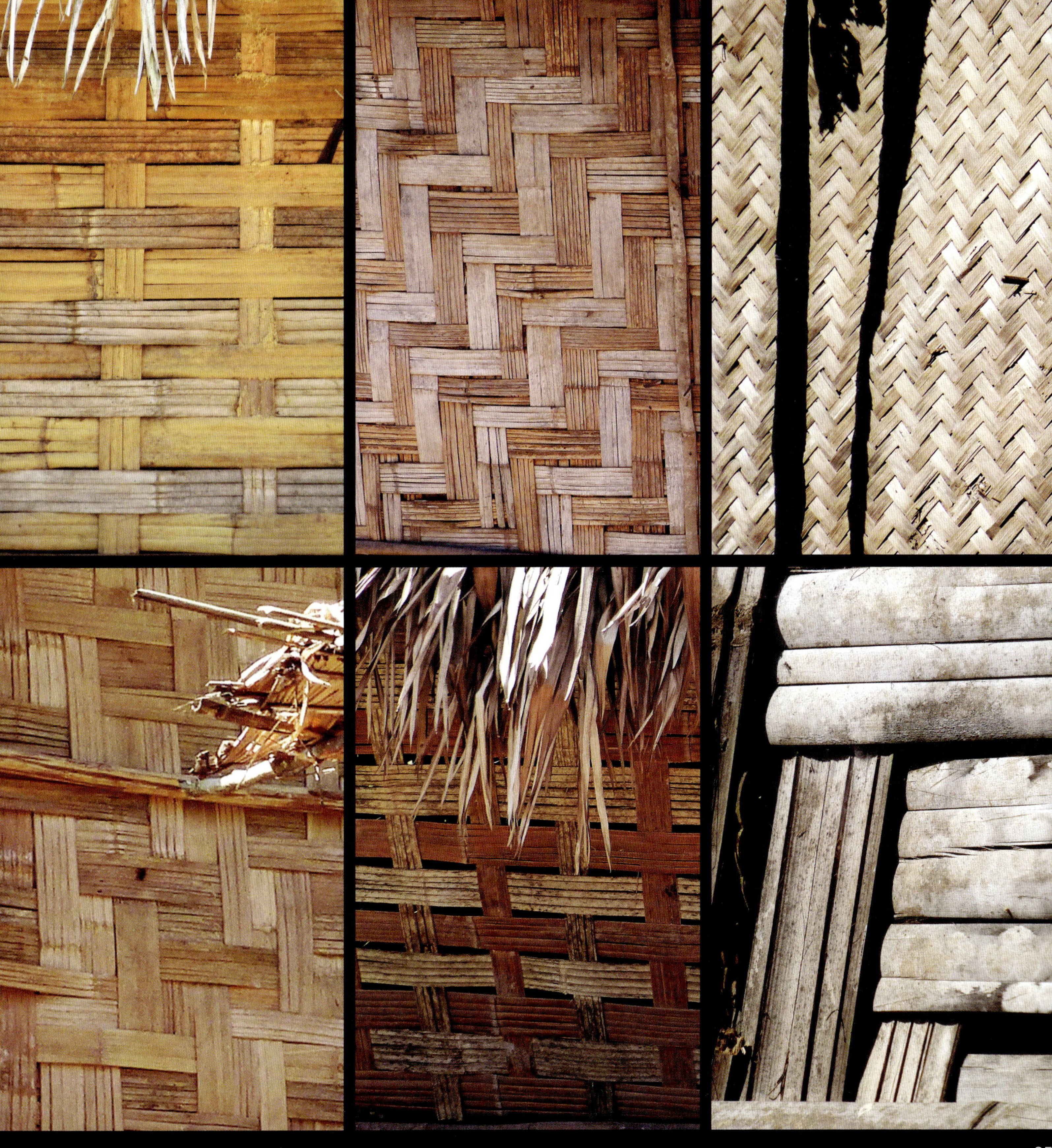

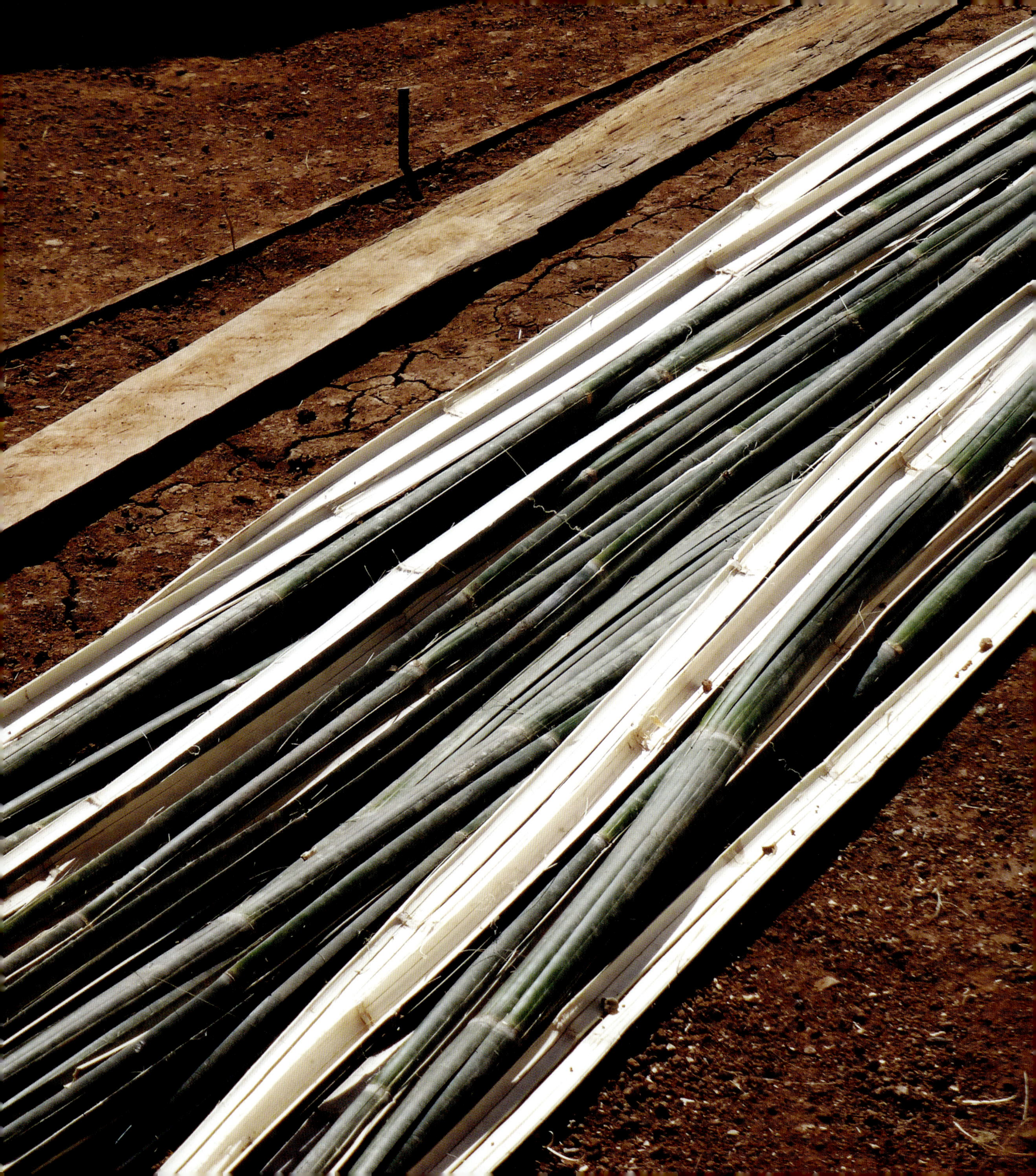

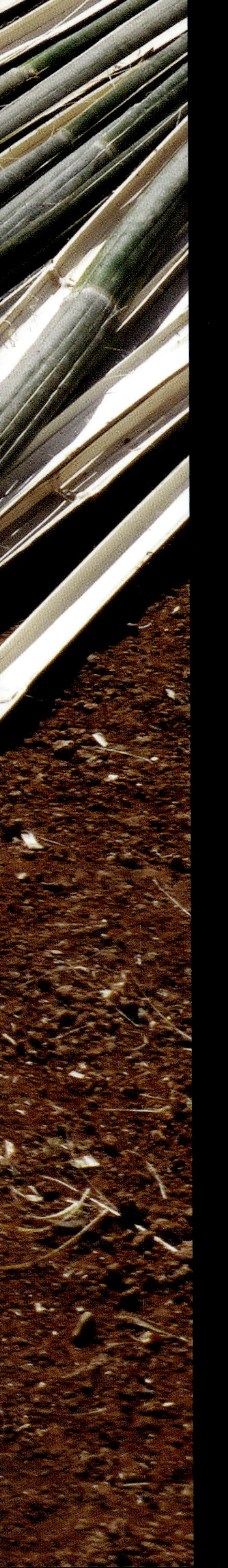

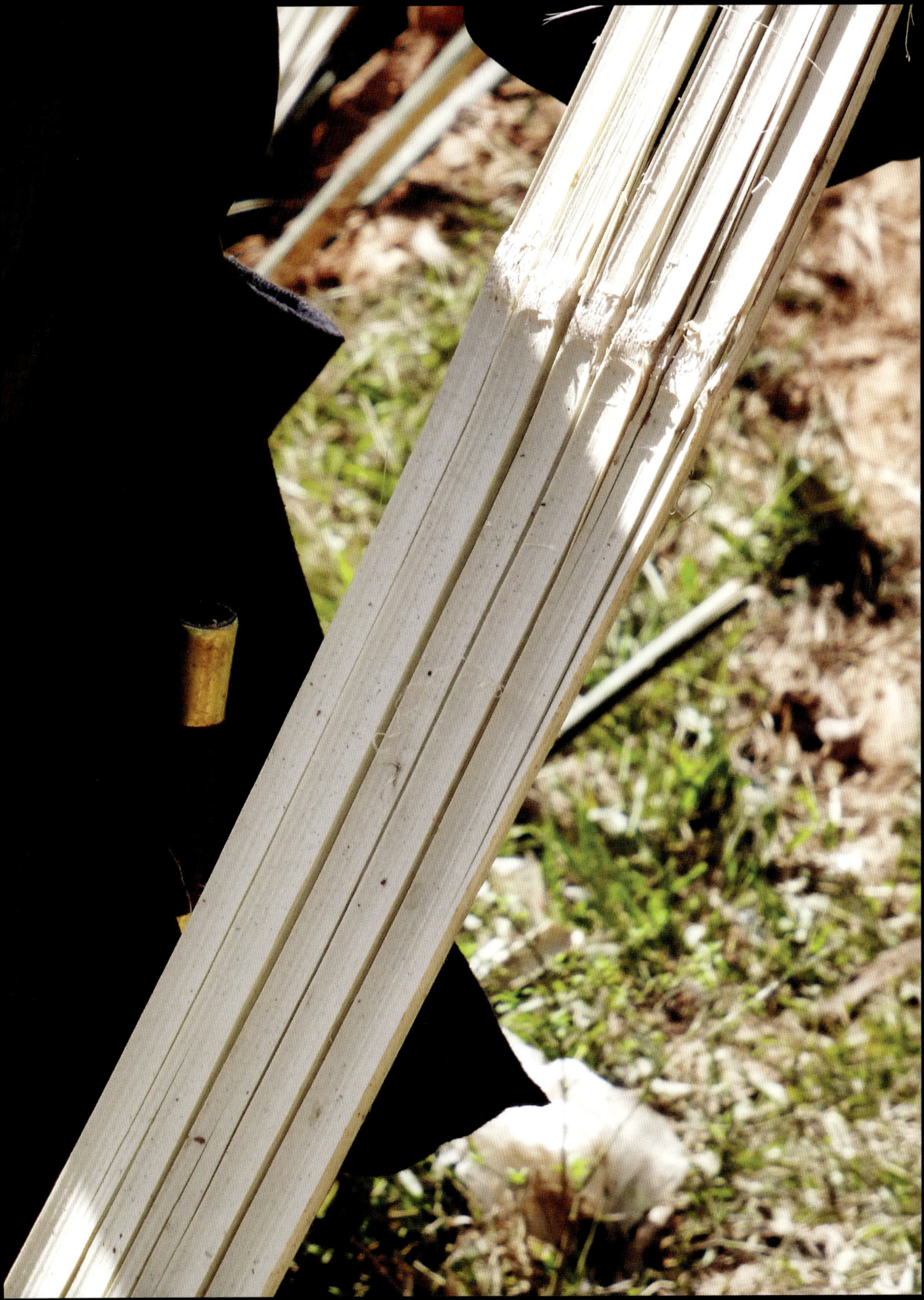

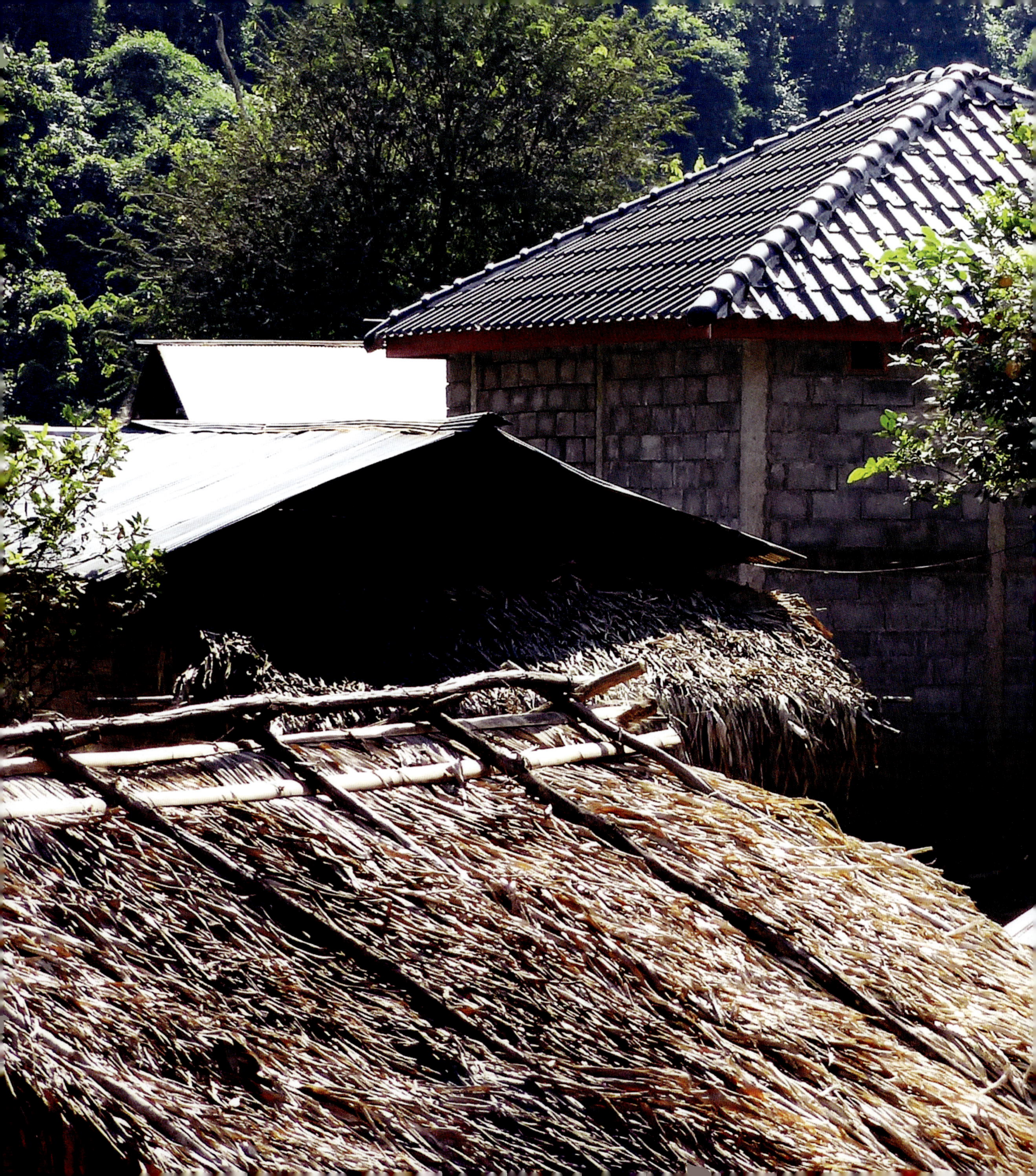

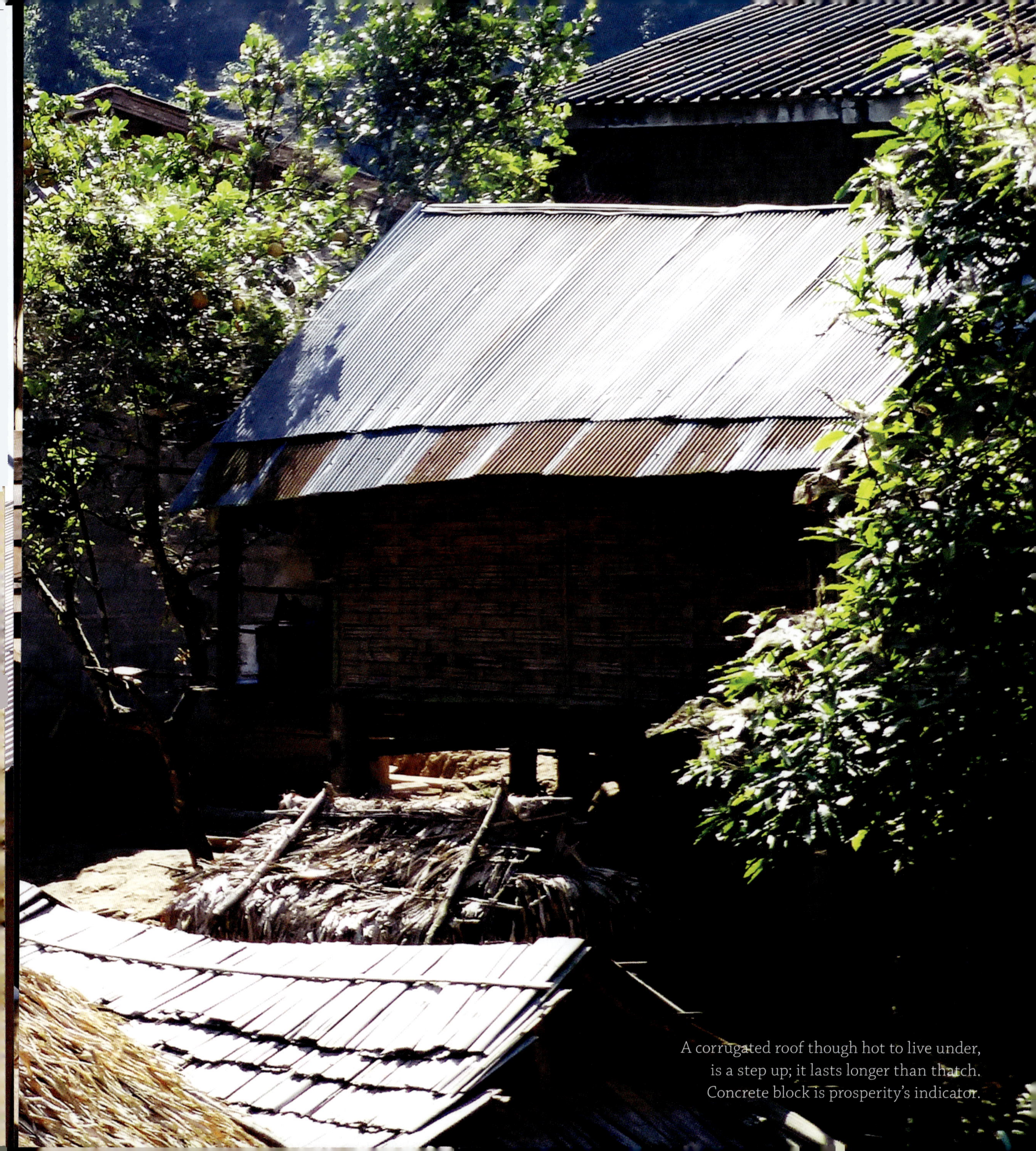

A corrugated roof though hot to live under,
is a step up; it lasts longer than thatch.
Concrete block is prosperity's indicator.

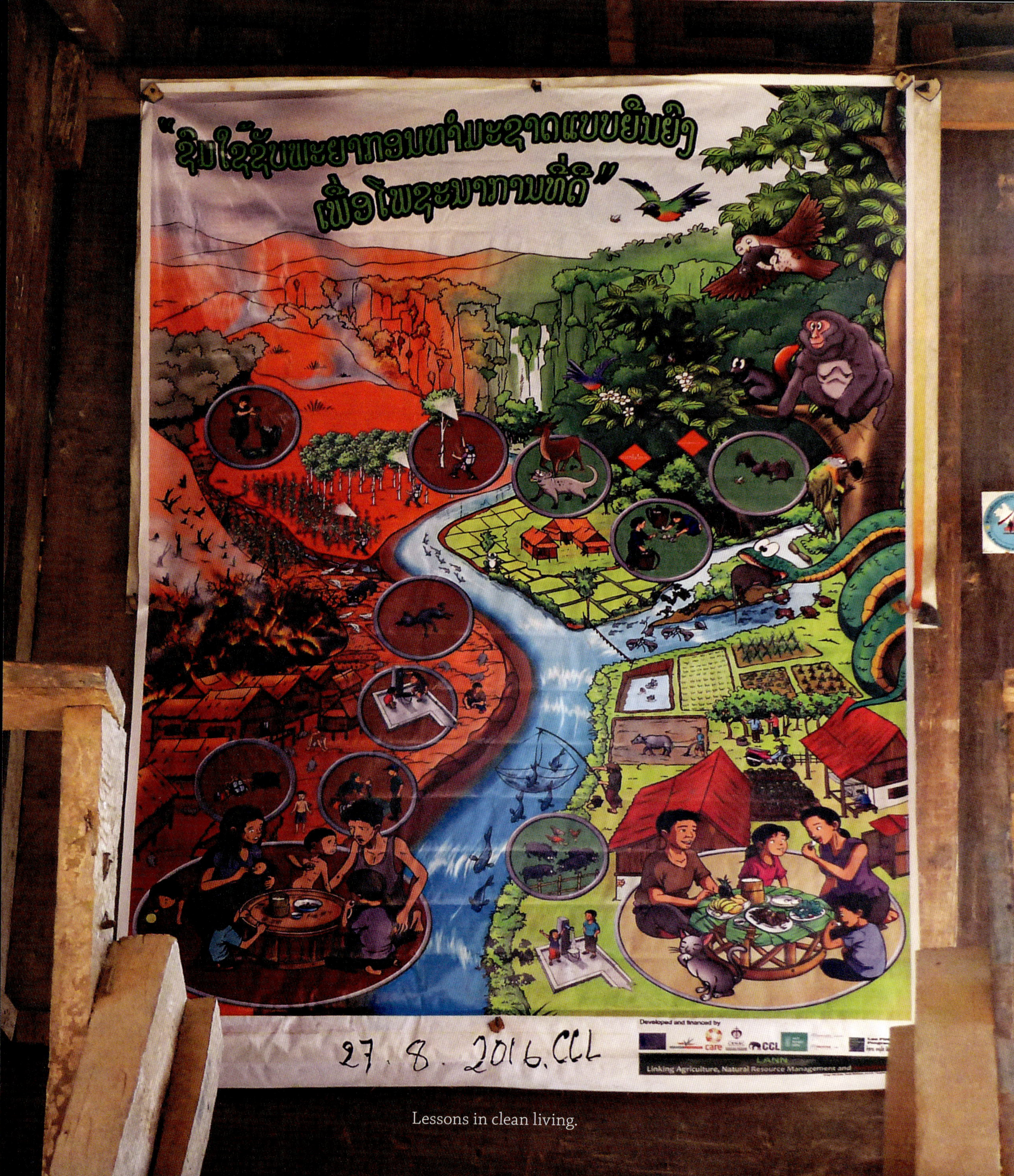

Lessons in clean living.

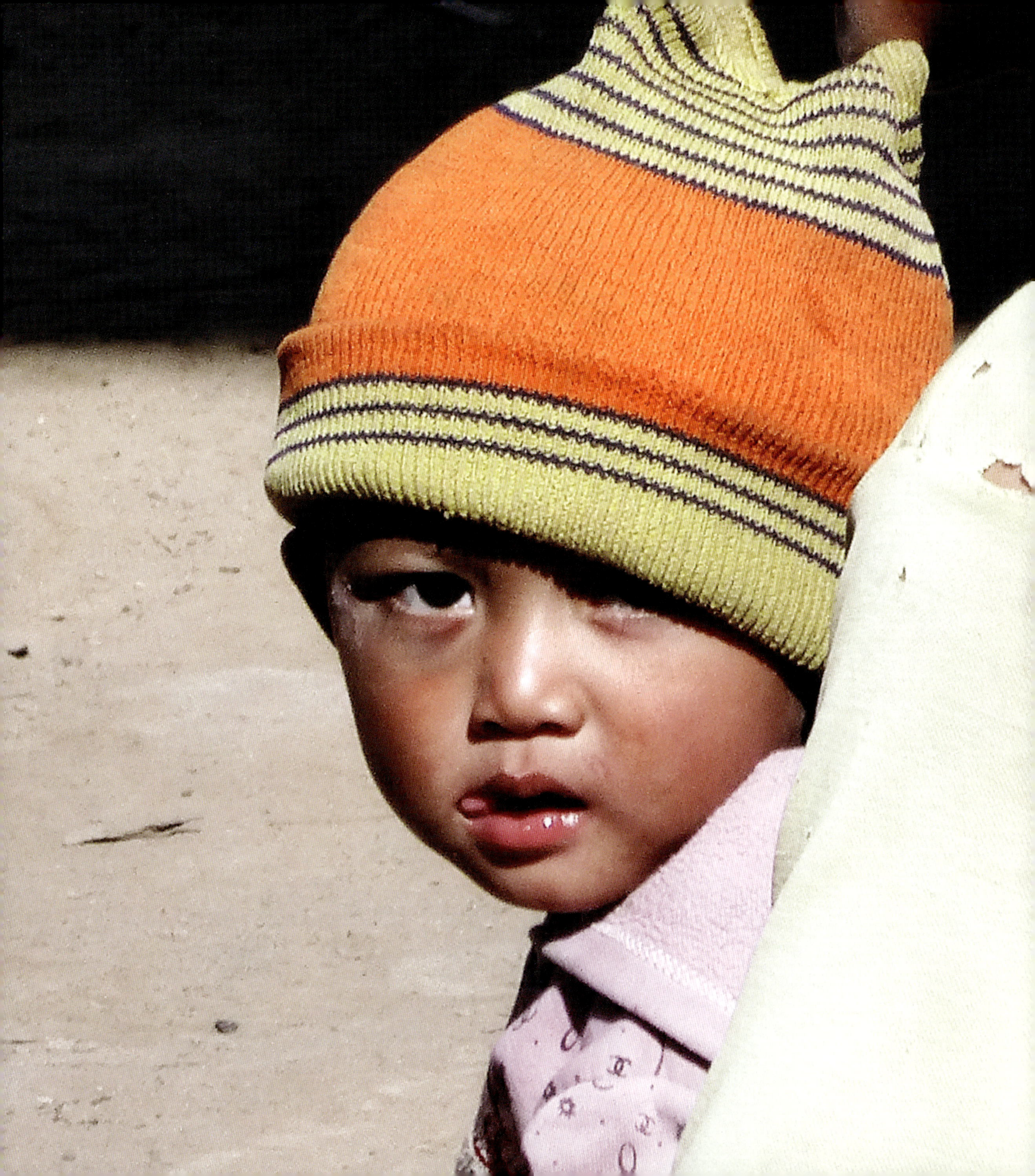

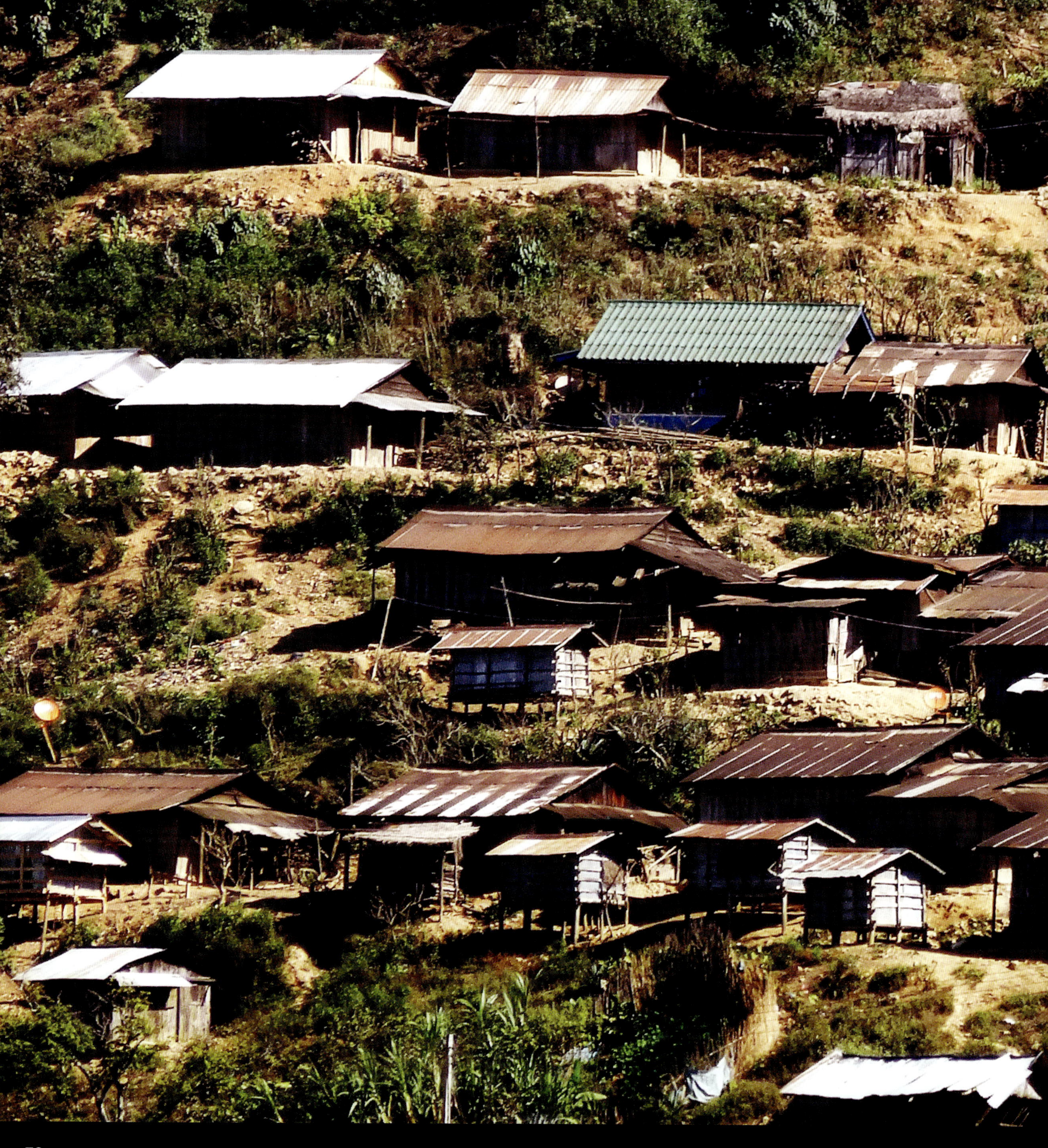

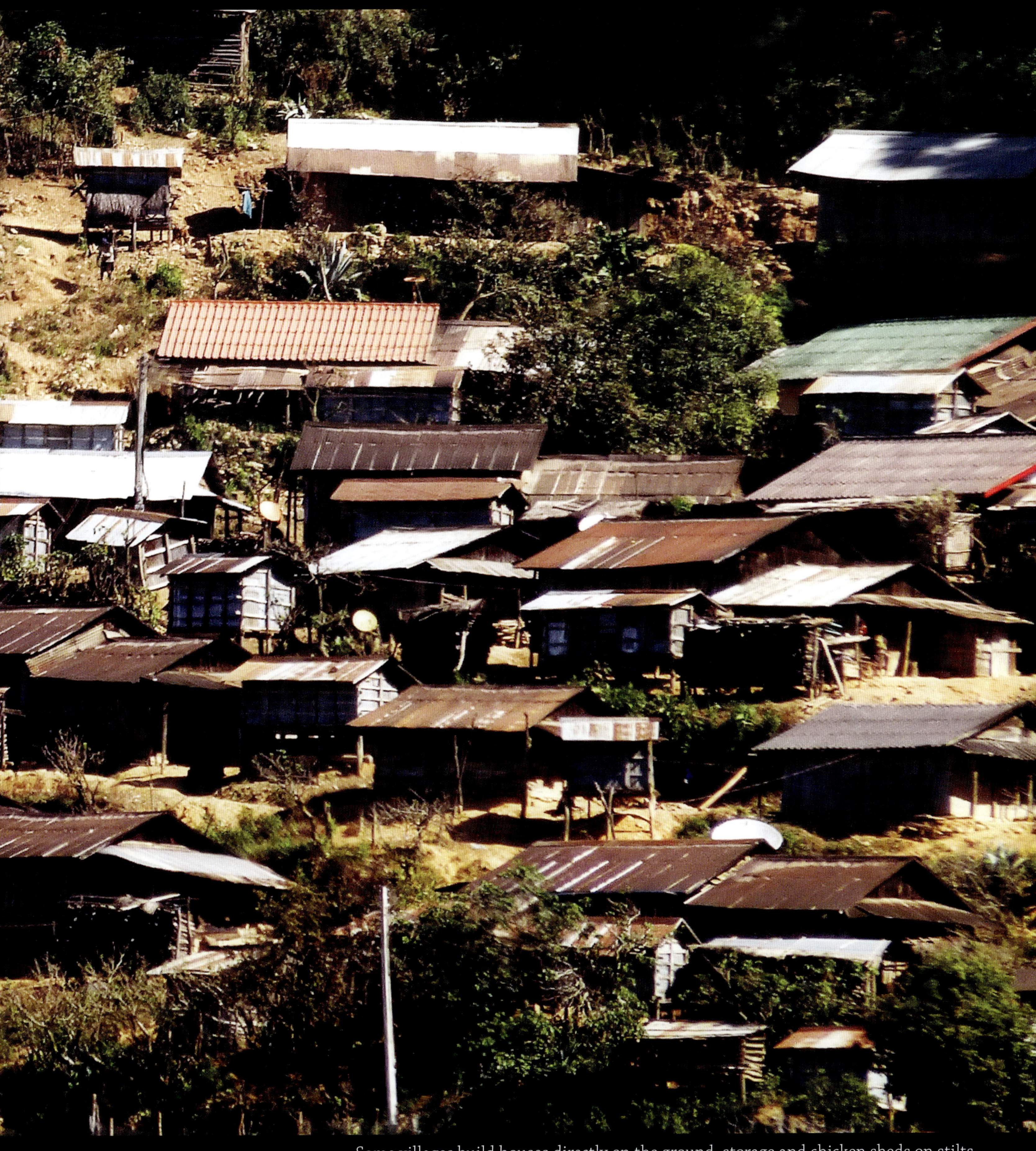

Some villages build houses directly on the ground, storage and chicken sheds on stilts.

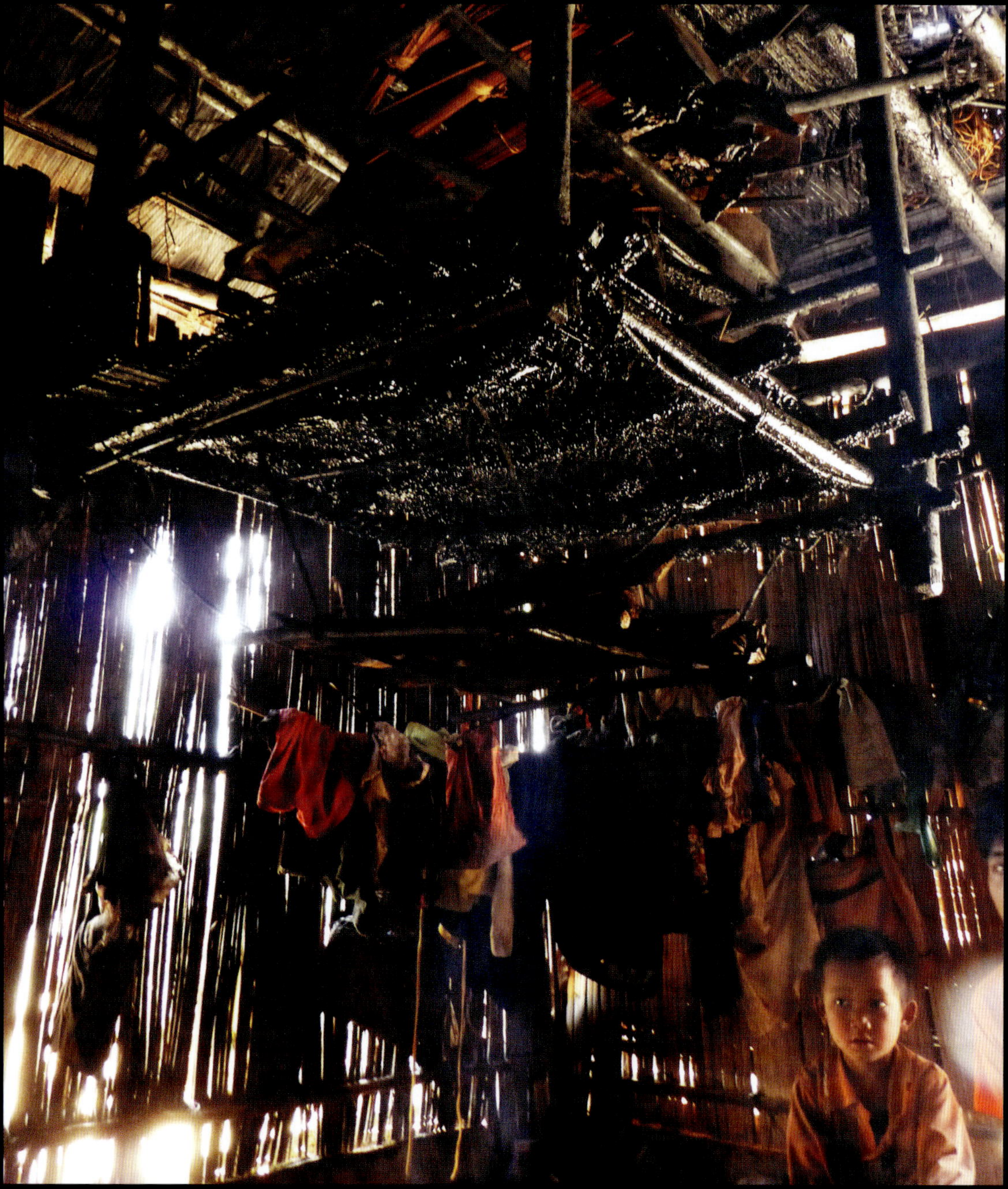

In the Hmong village of Ban Tauser.

Interiors are dark, floors generally earthen, and furniture is minimal. Fires provide cooking and warmth. Smoke and creosote prevail.

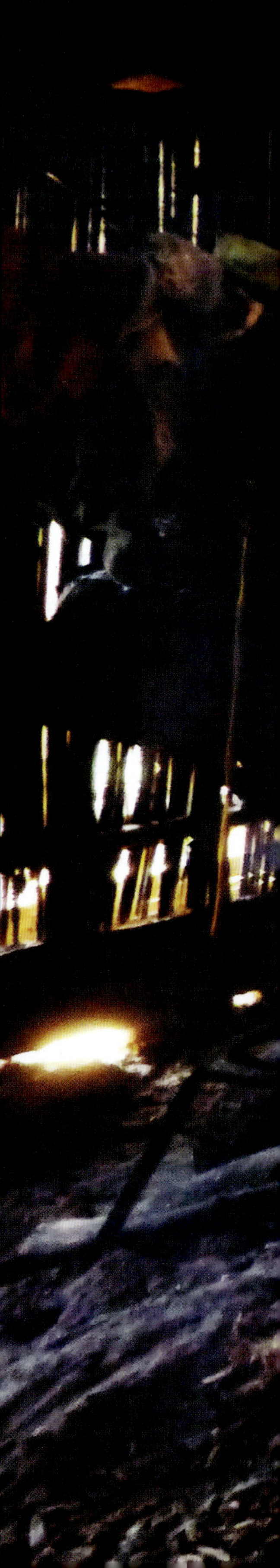

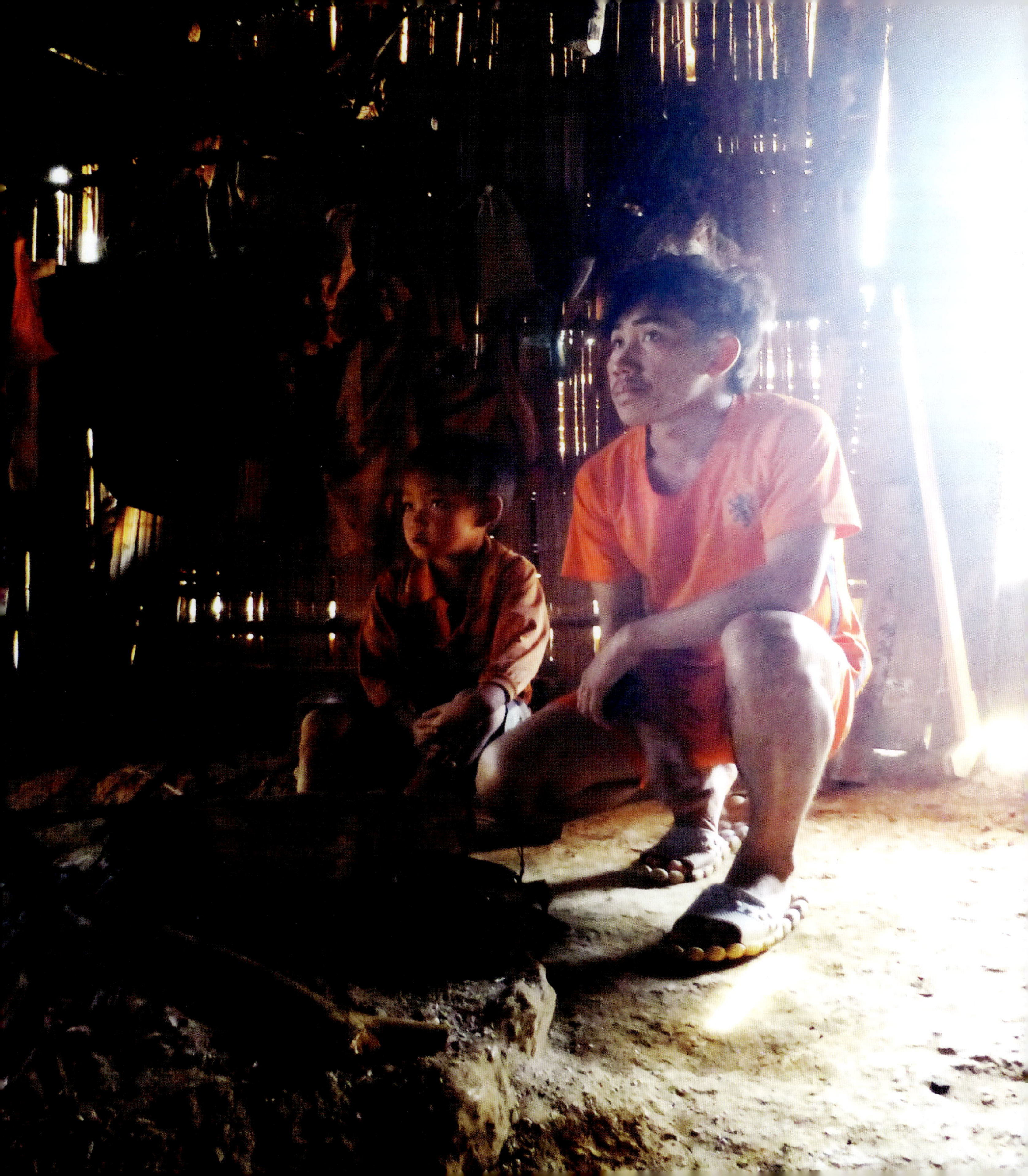

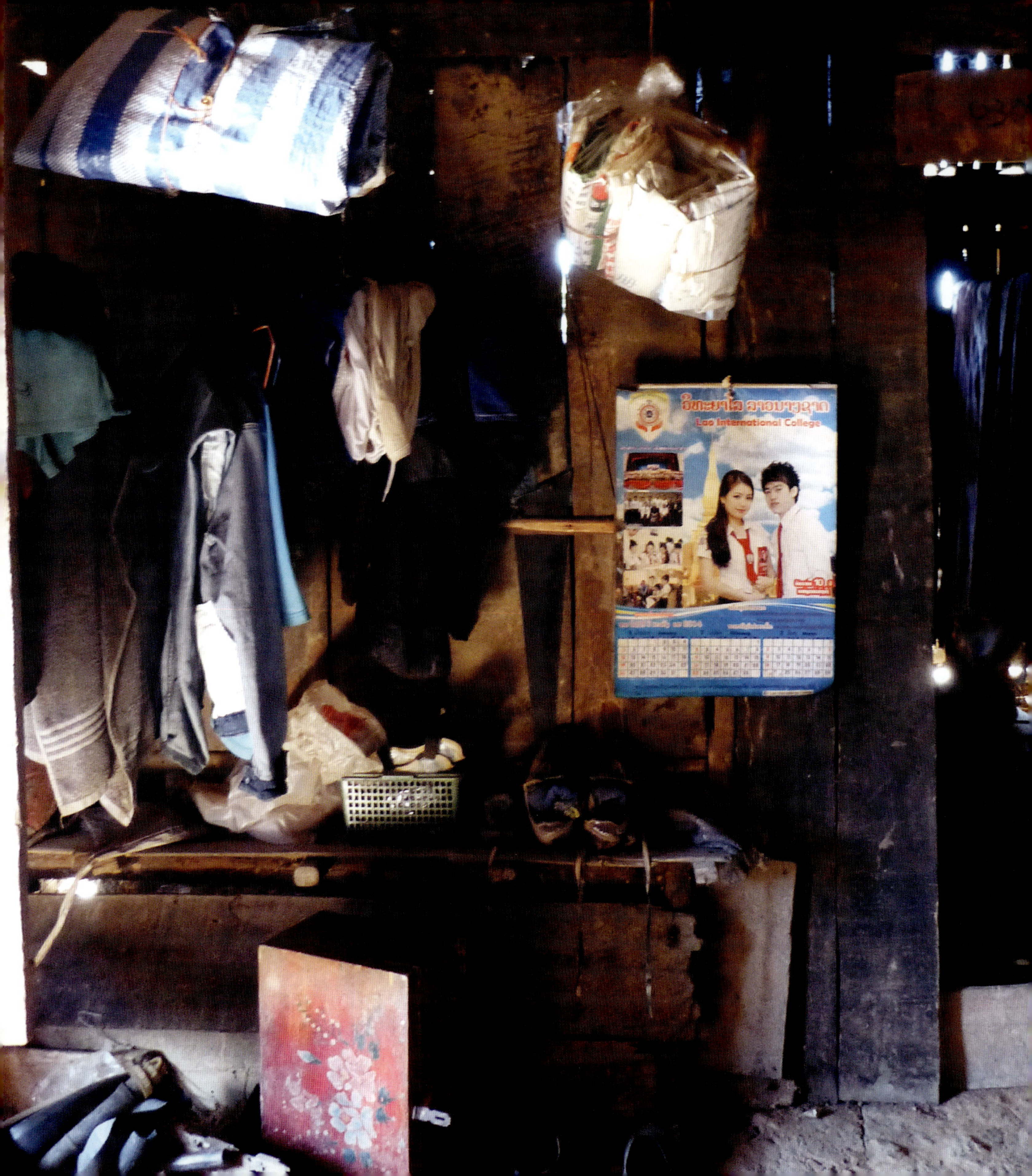
ວິທະຍາໄລ ລາວນາໆຊາດ
Lao International College

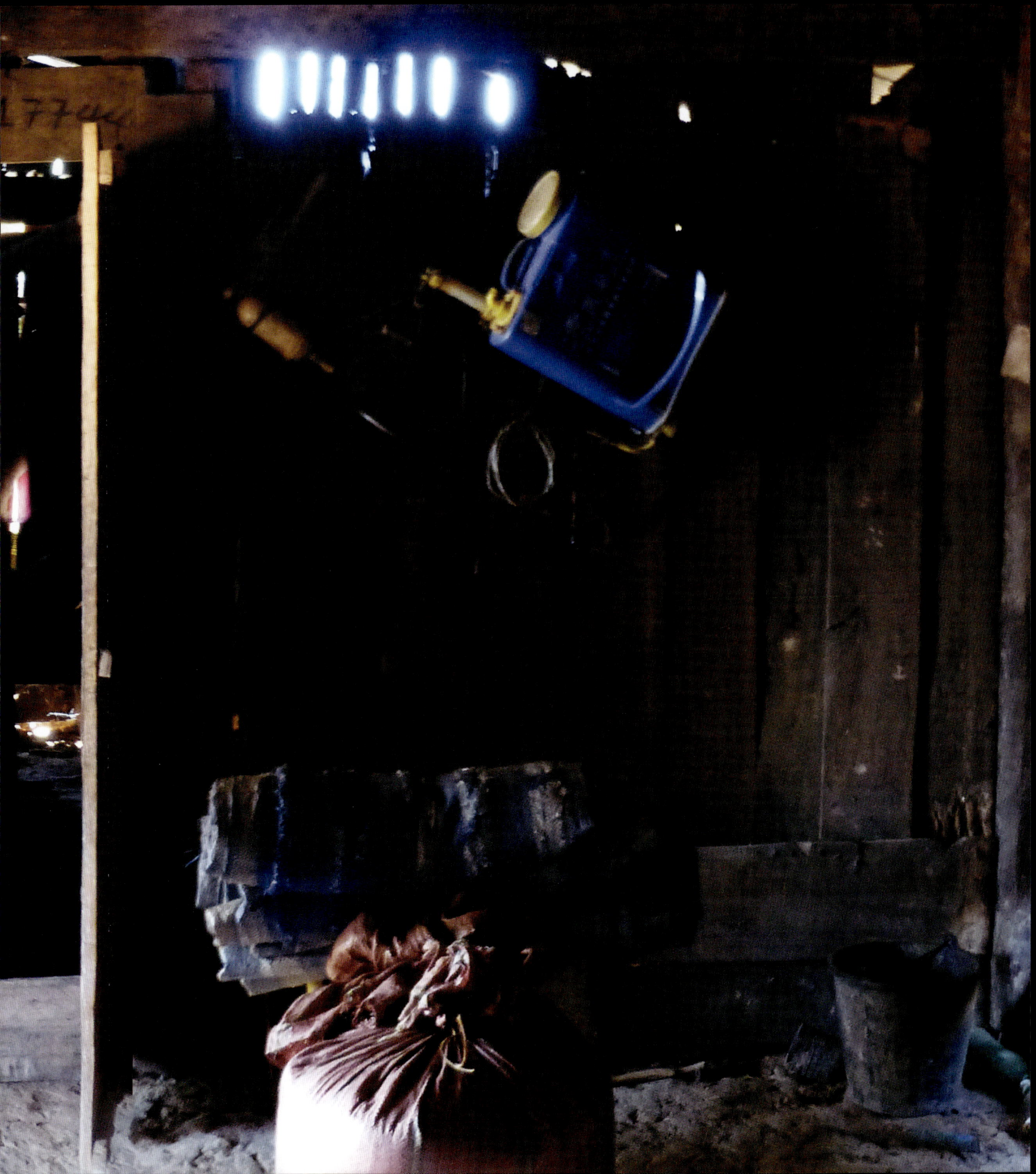

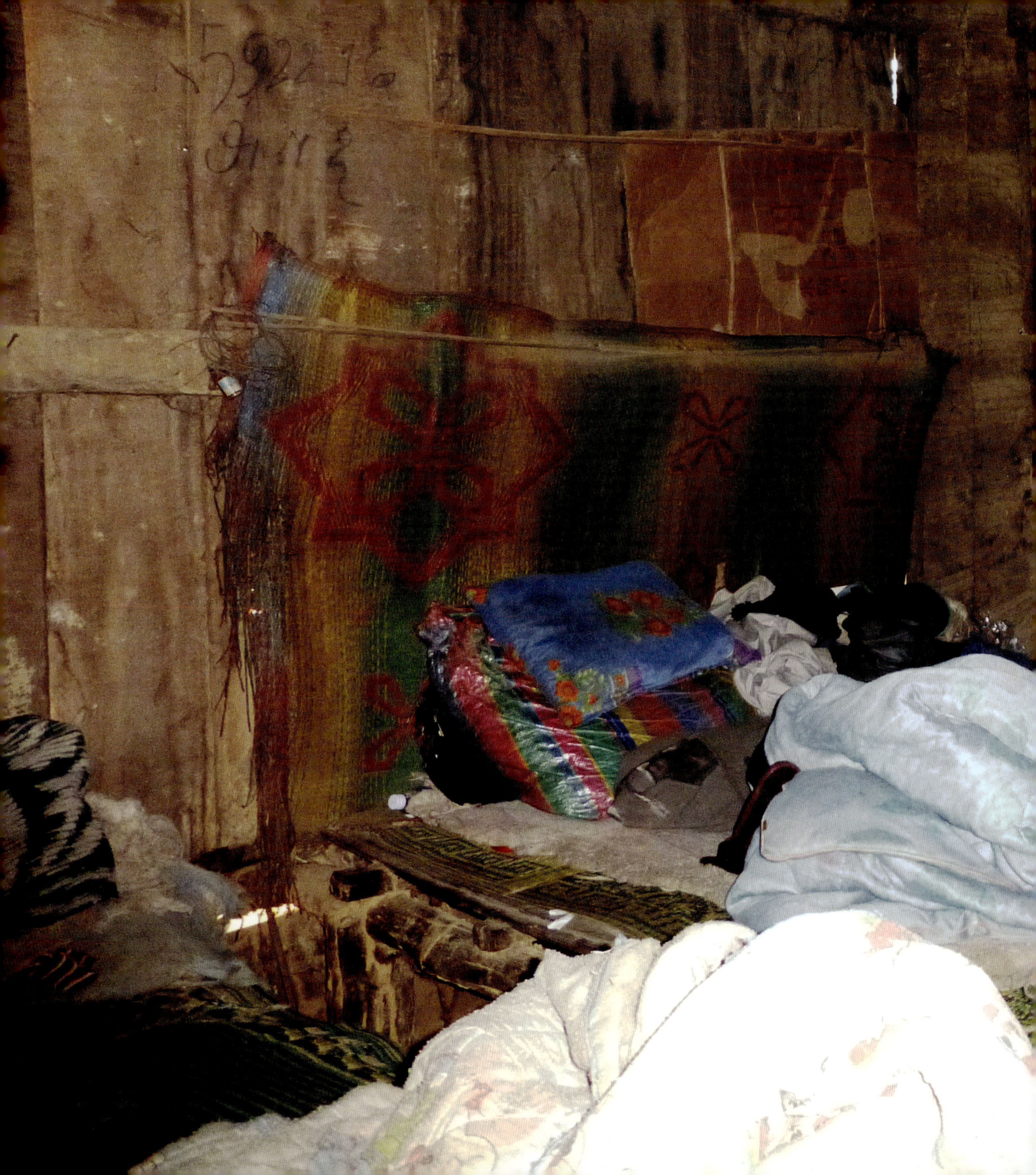

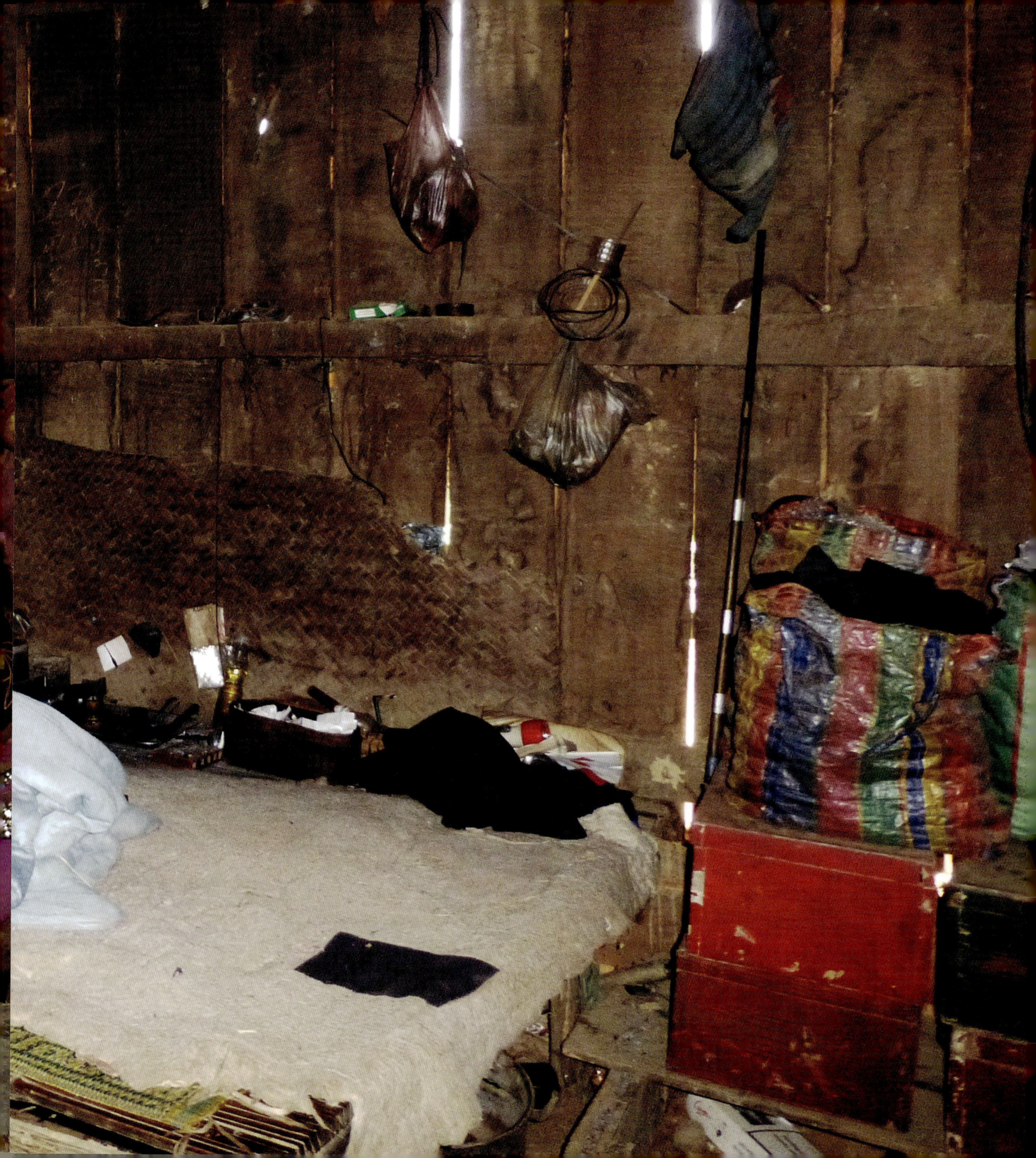

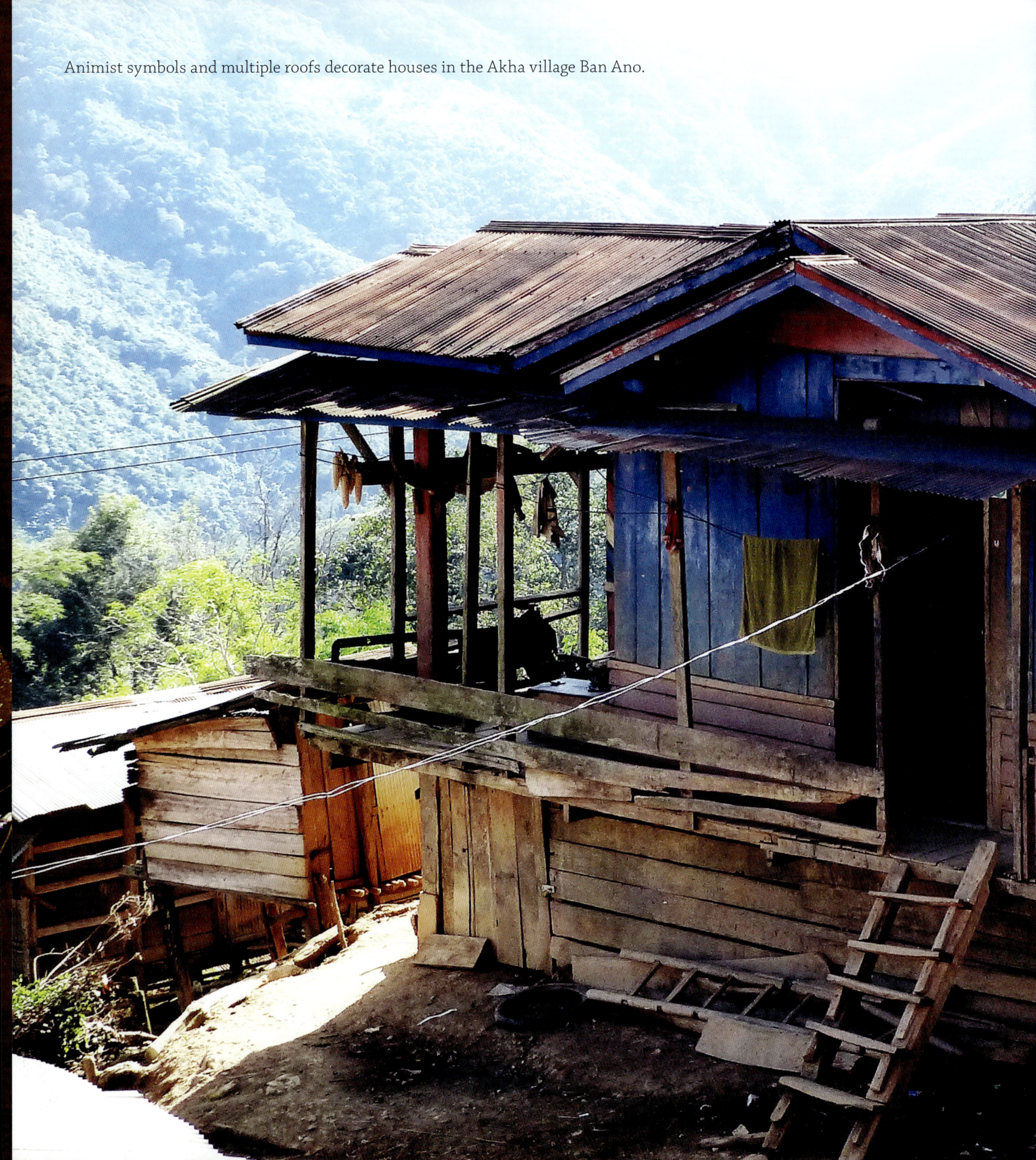

Animist symbols and multiple roofs decorate houses in the Akha village Ban Ano.

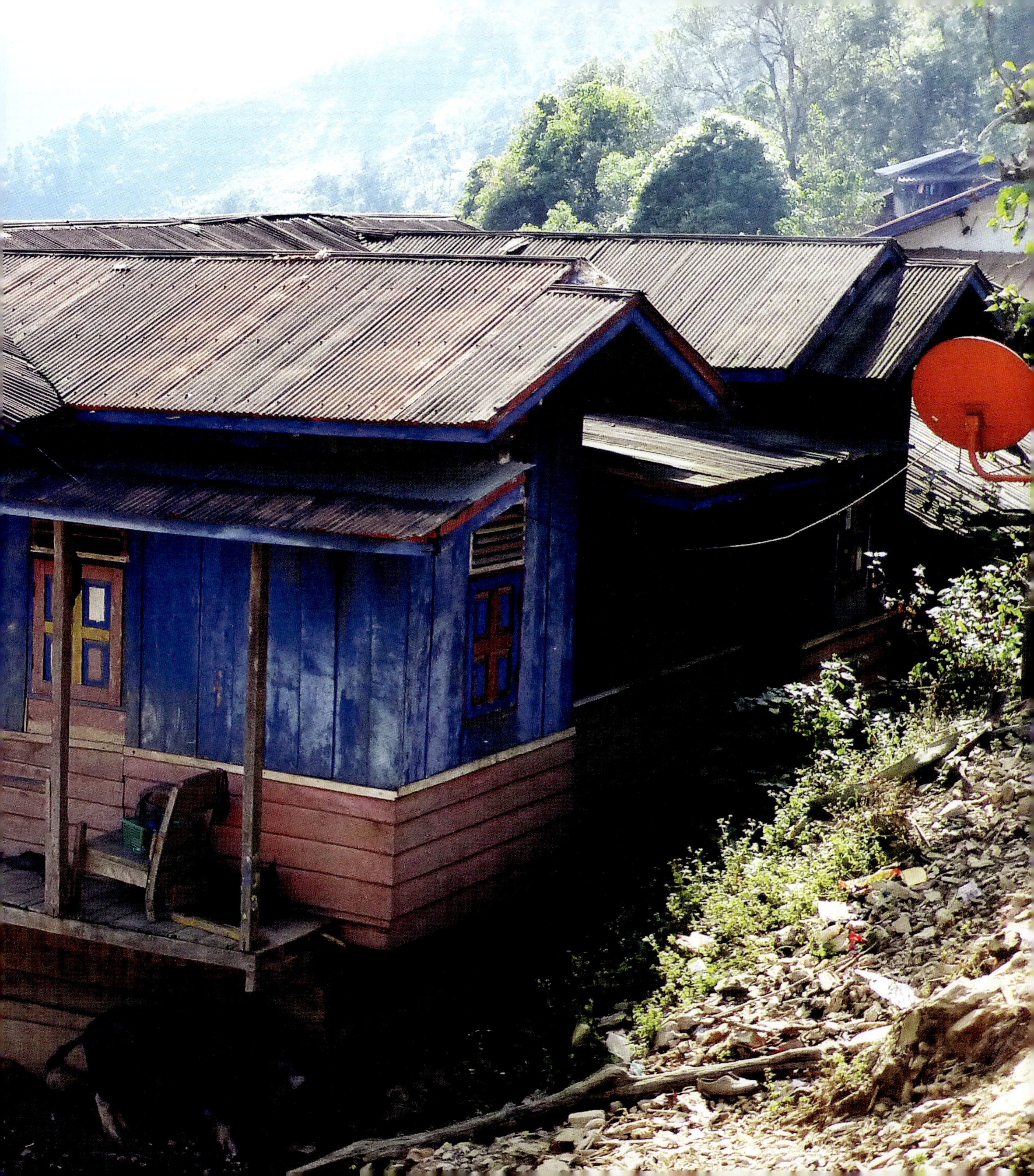

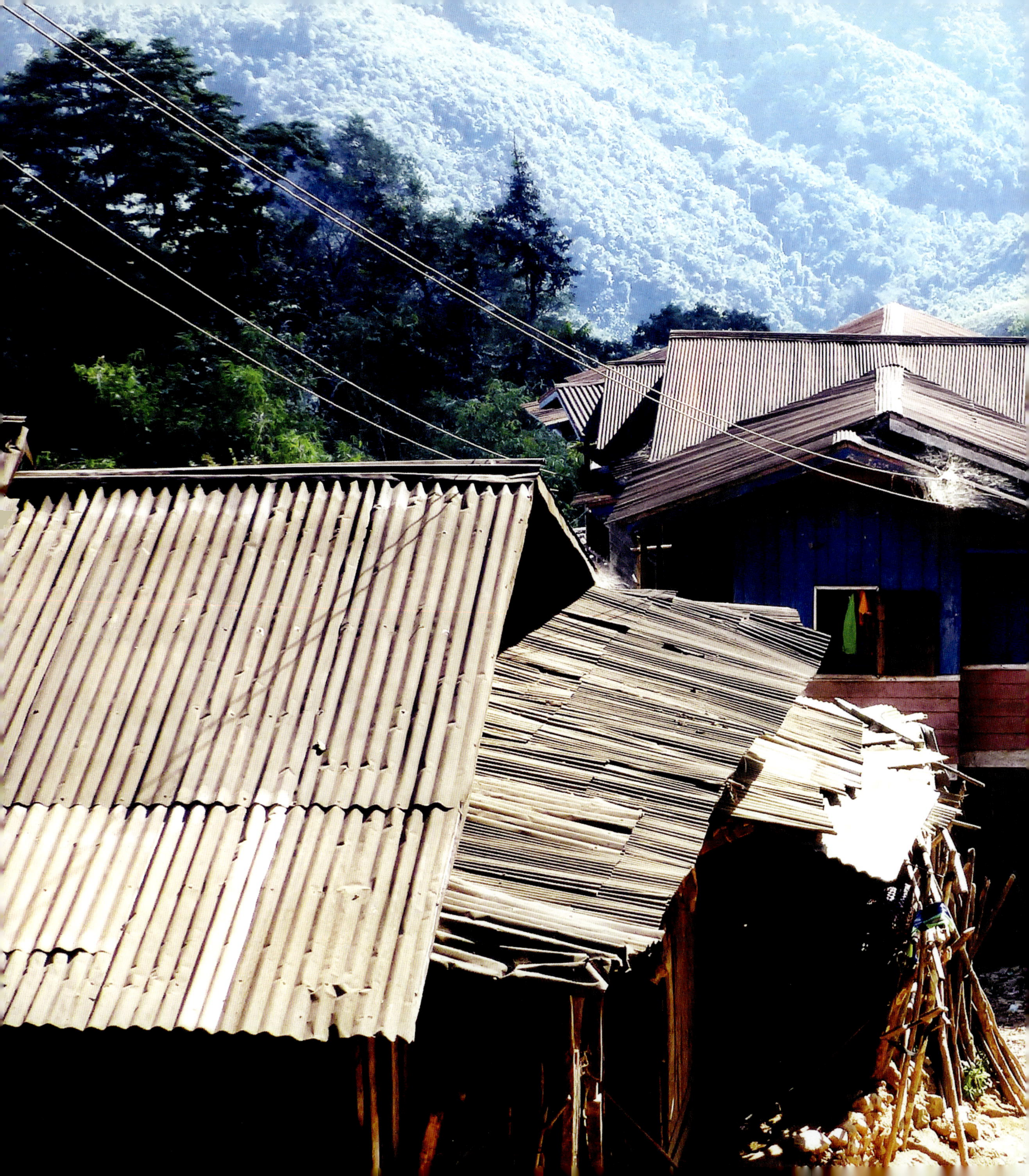

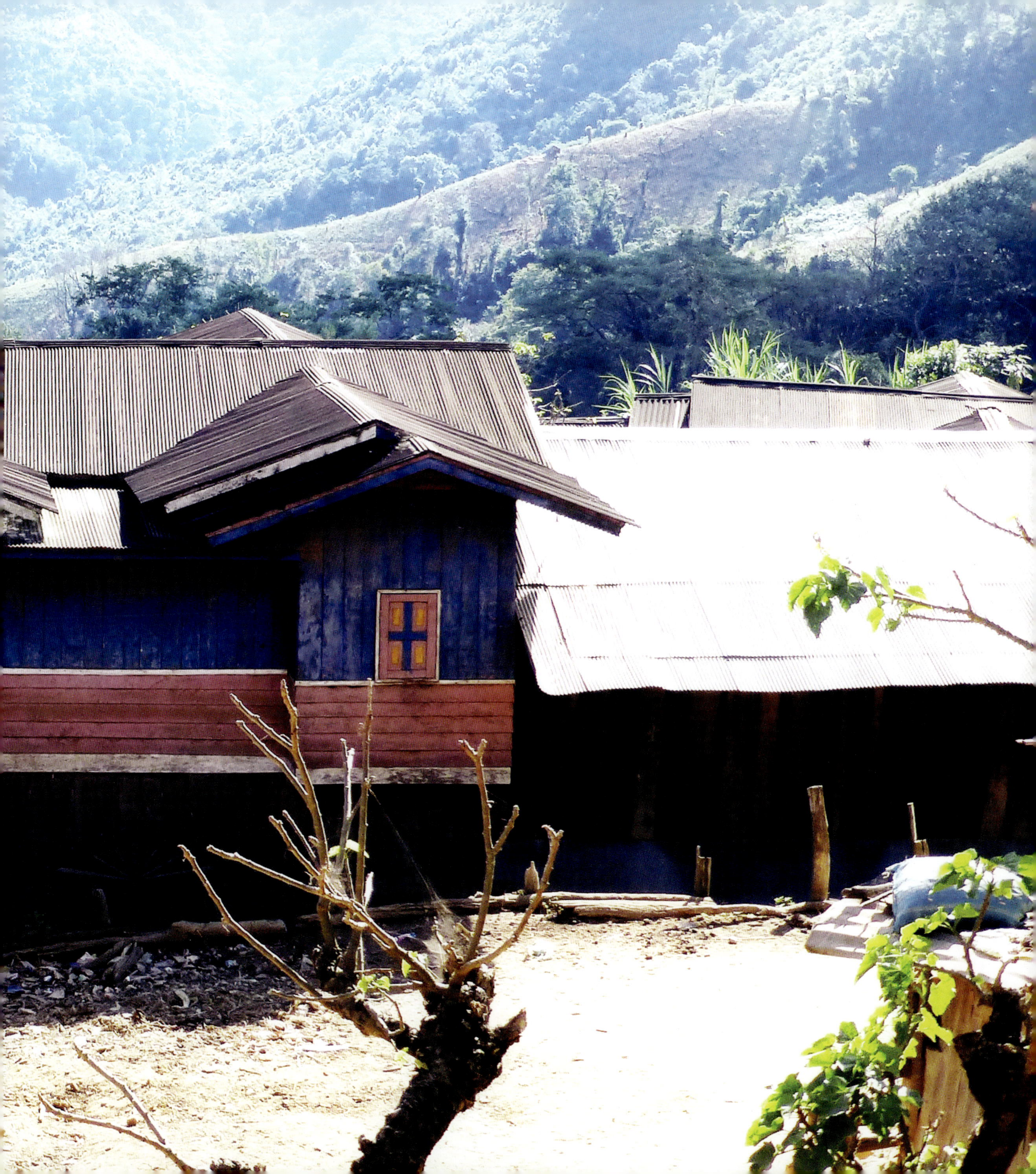

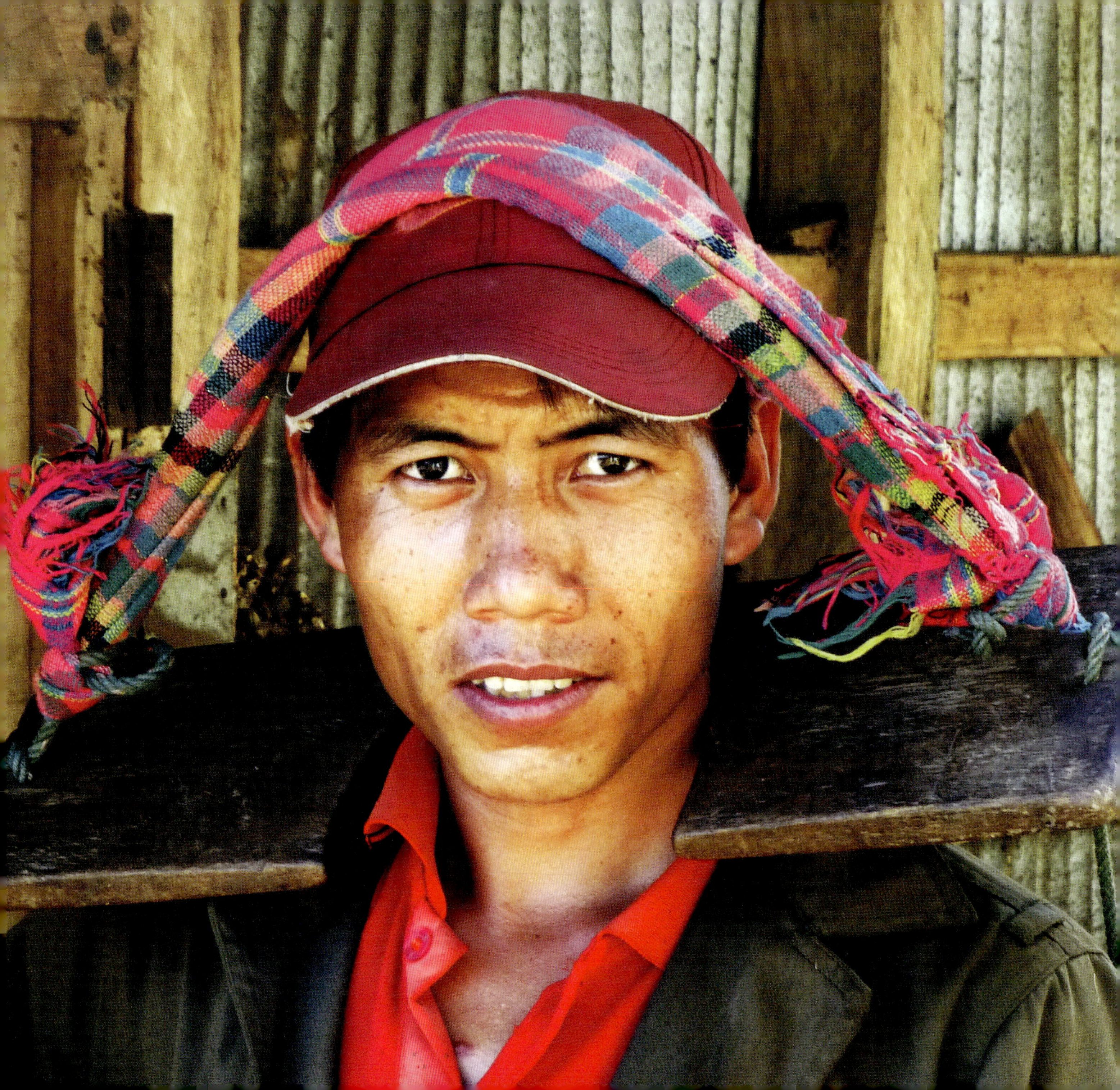

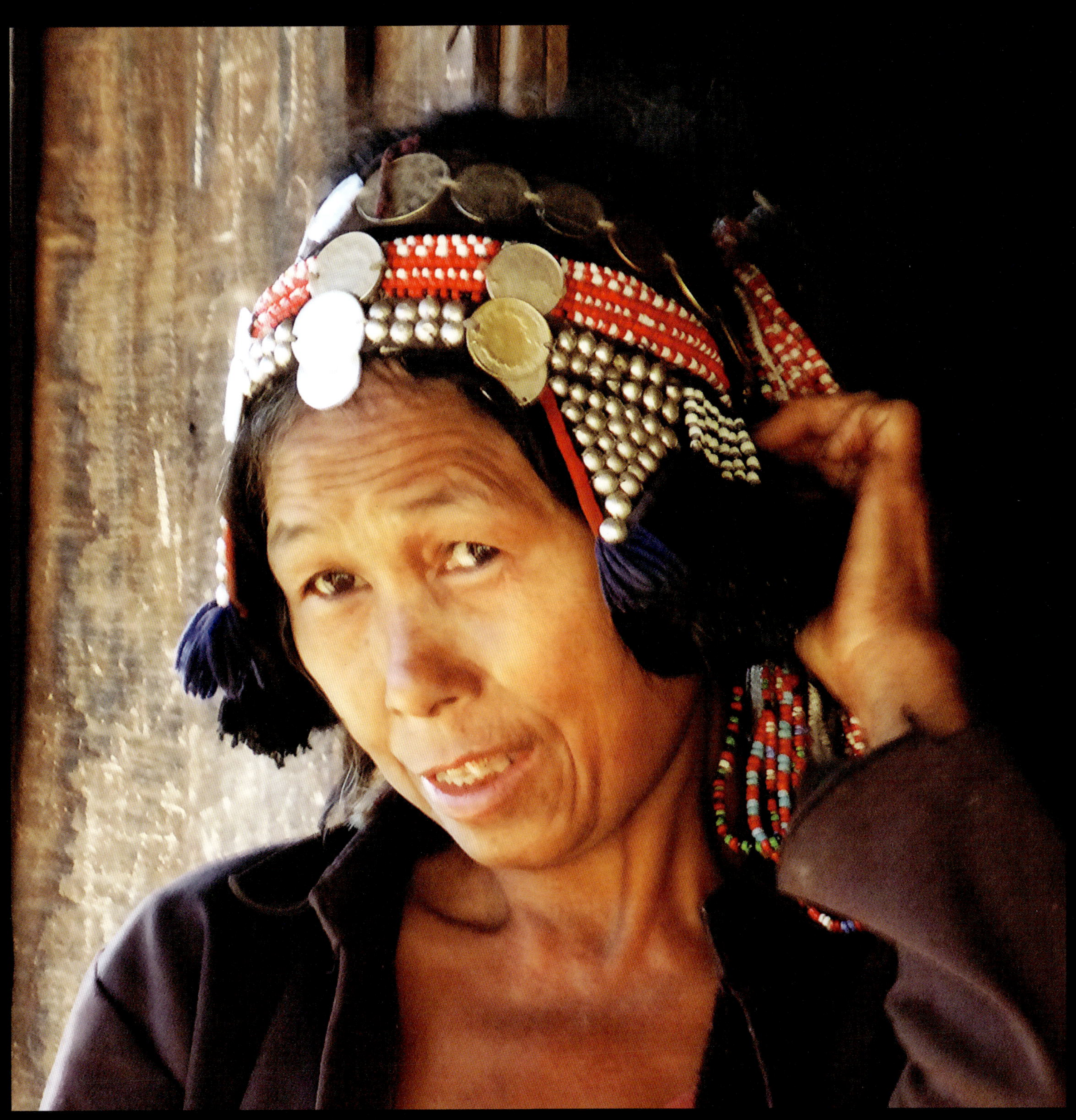

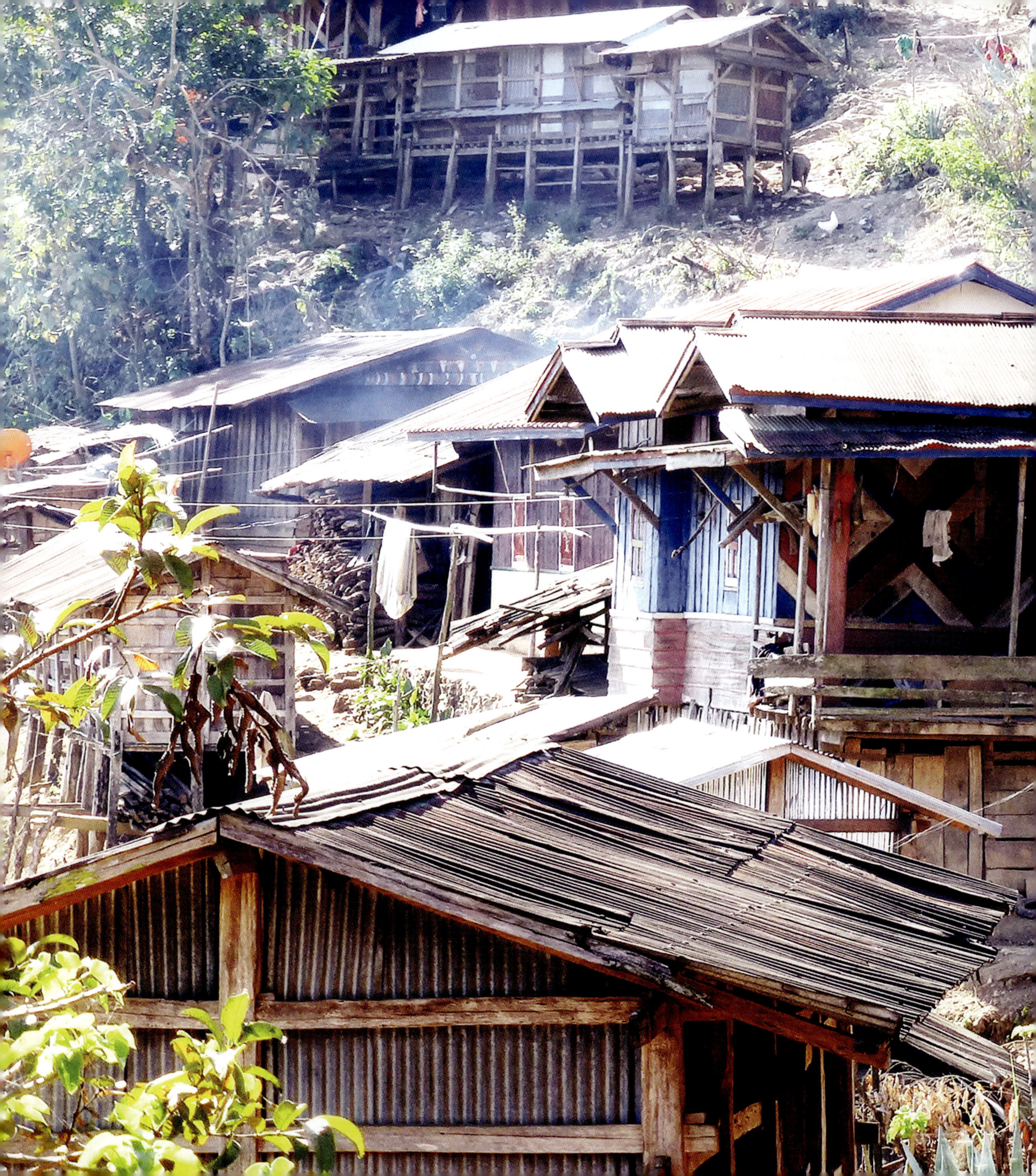

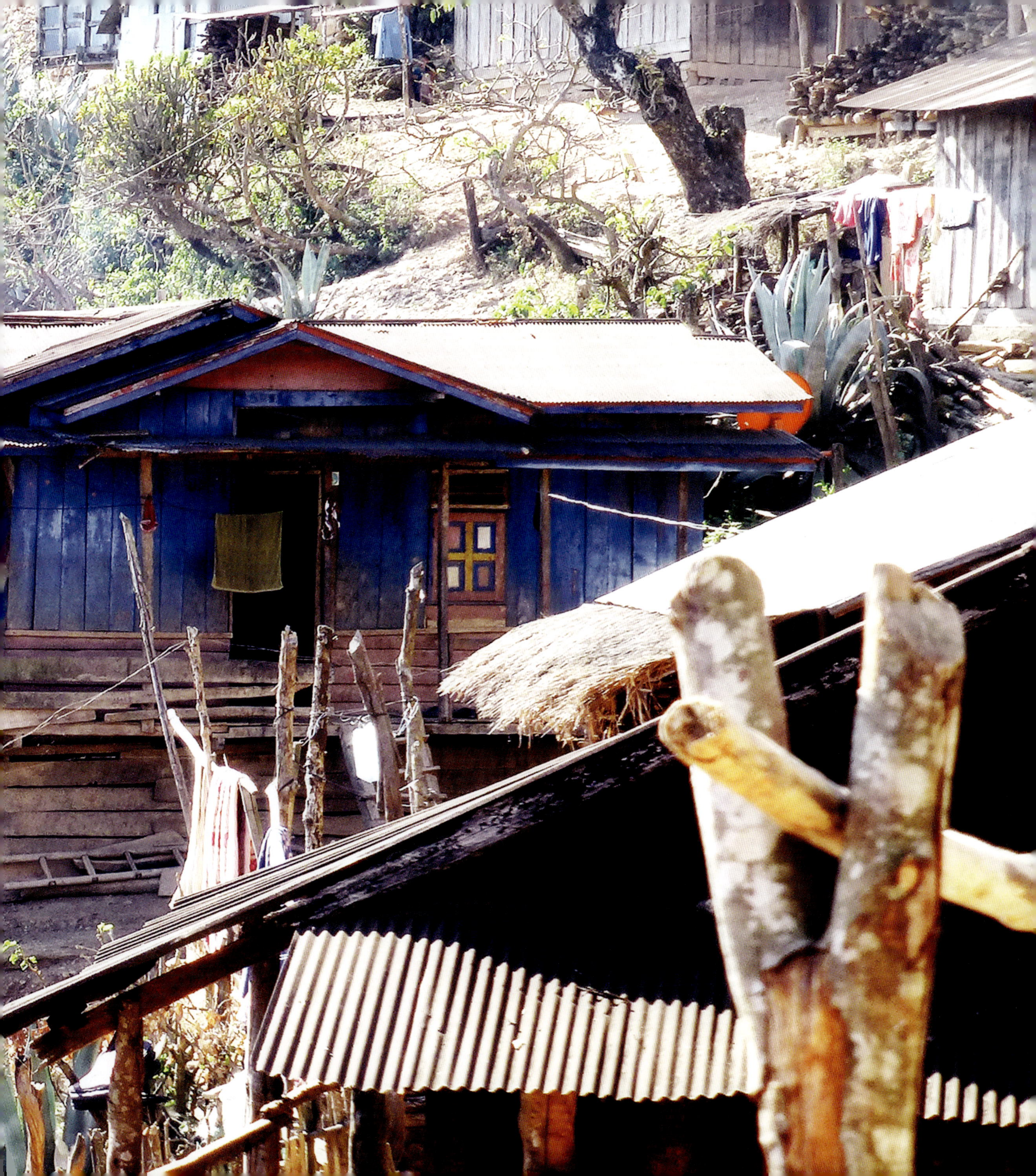

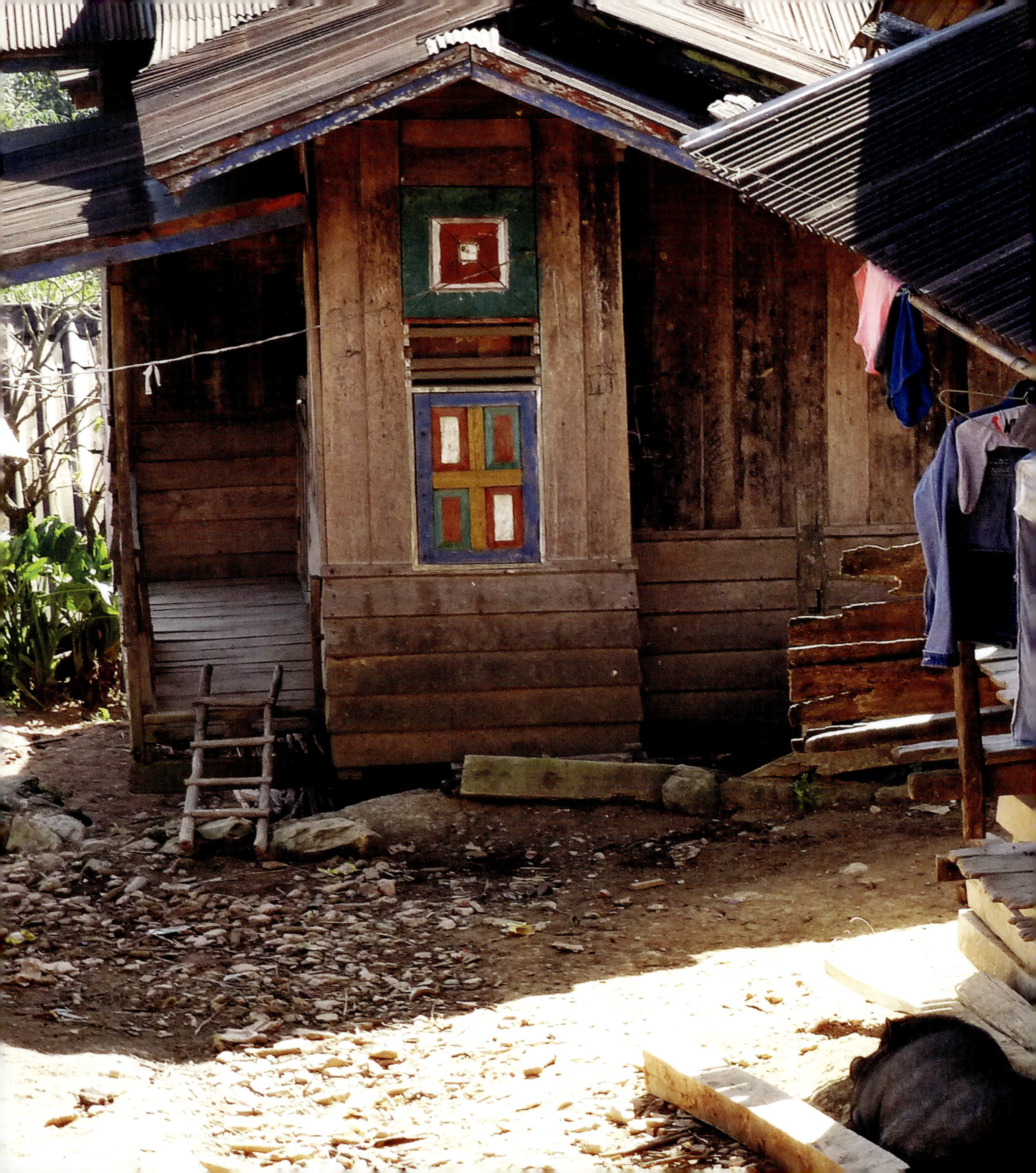

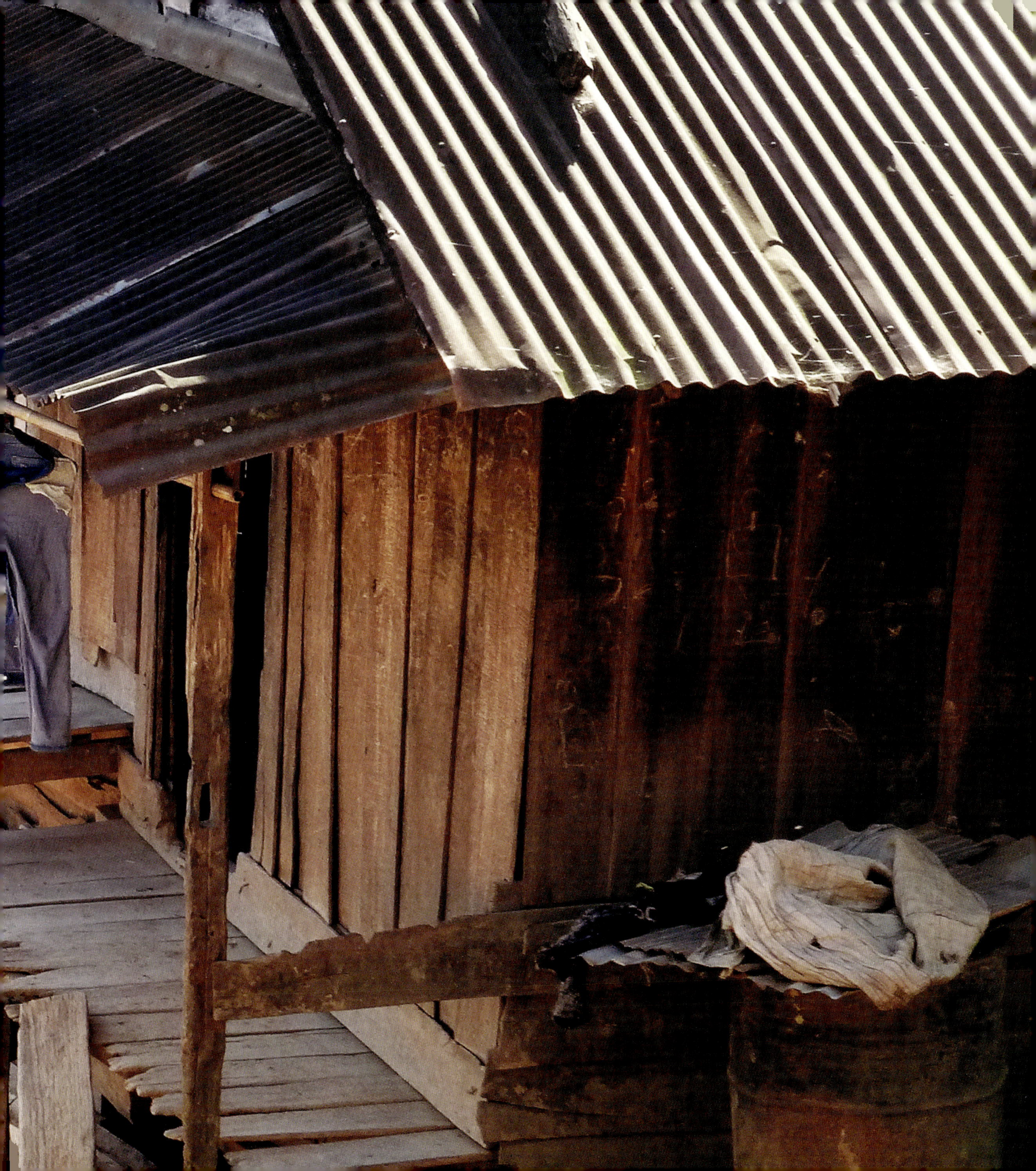

Pigs, chickens and dogs roam listlessly and silently; a food source, supplemented by trapped squirrels, rats and fish. River grass and forest plants, herbs and fruits are foraged and dried. Peppers, corn, squashes, gourds and bananas are farmed, along with water buffalos and cattle.

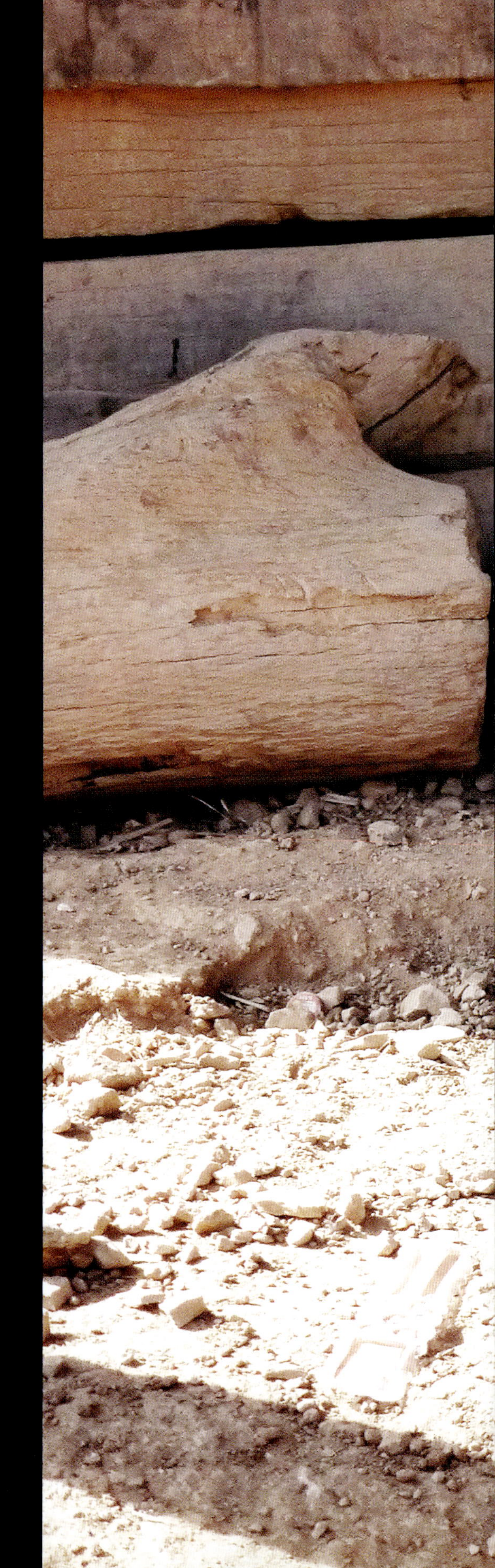

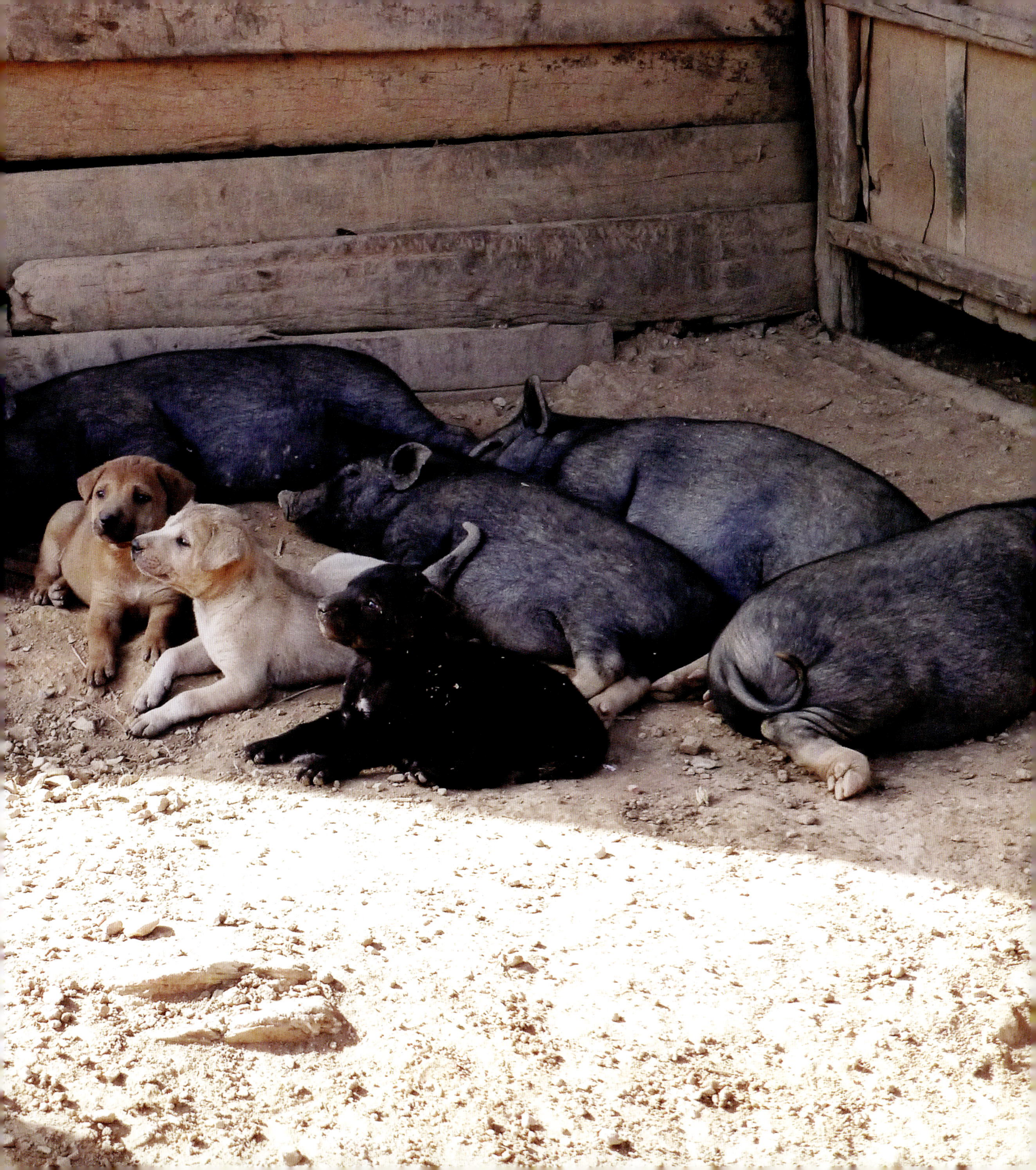

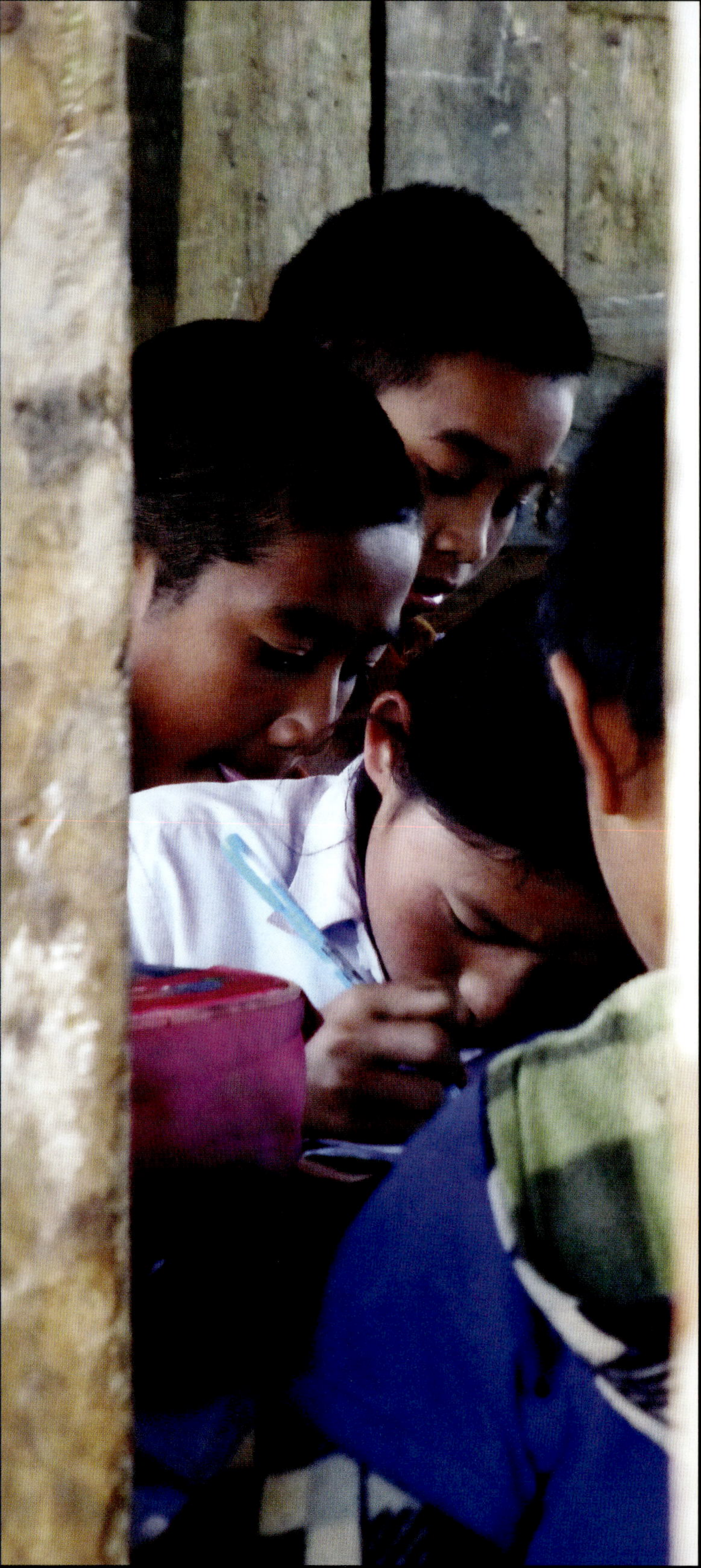

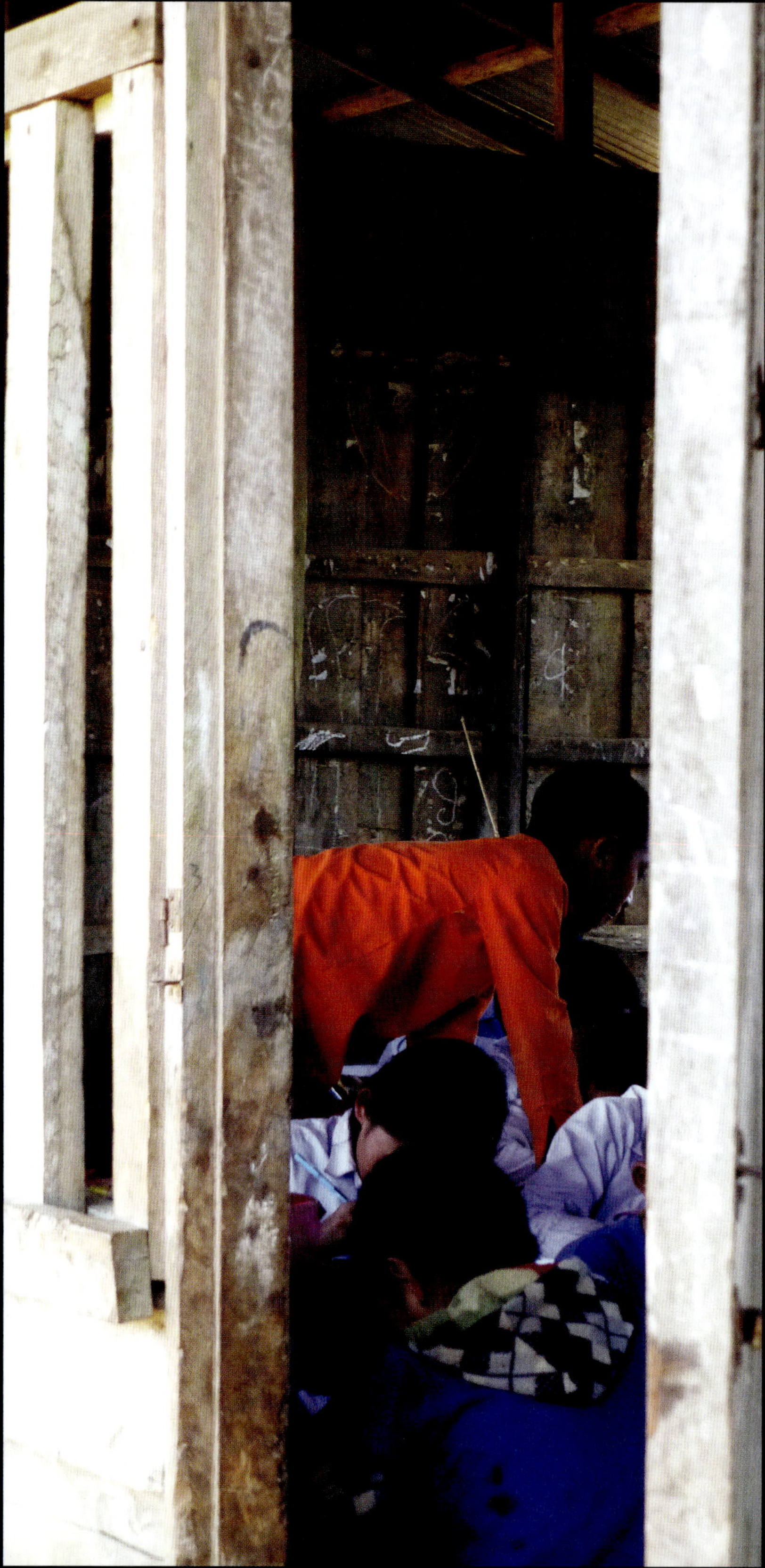

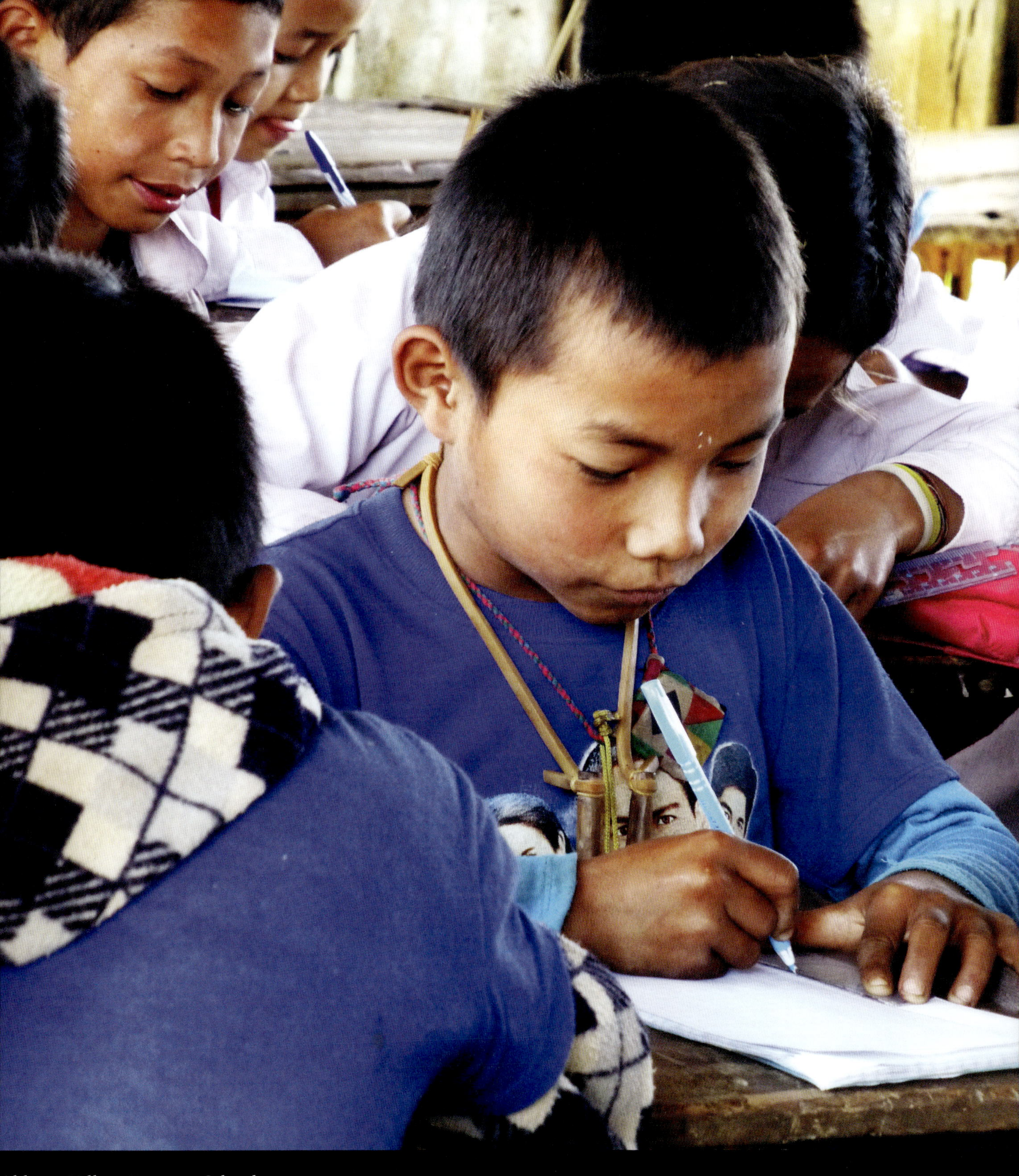

Akhang Village Primary School.

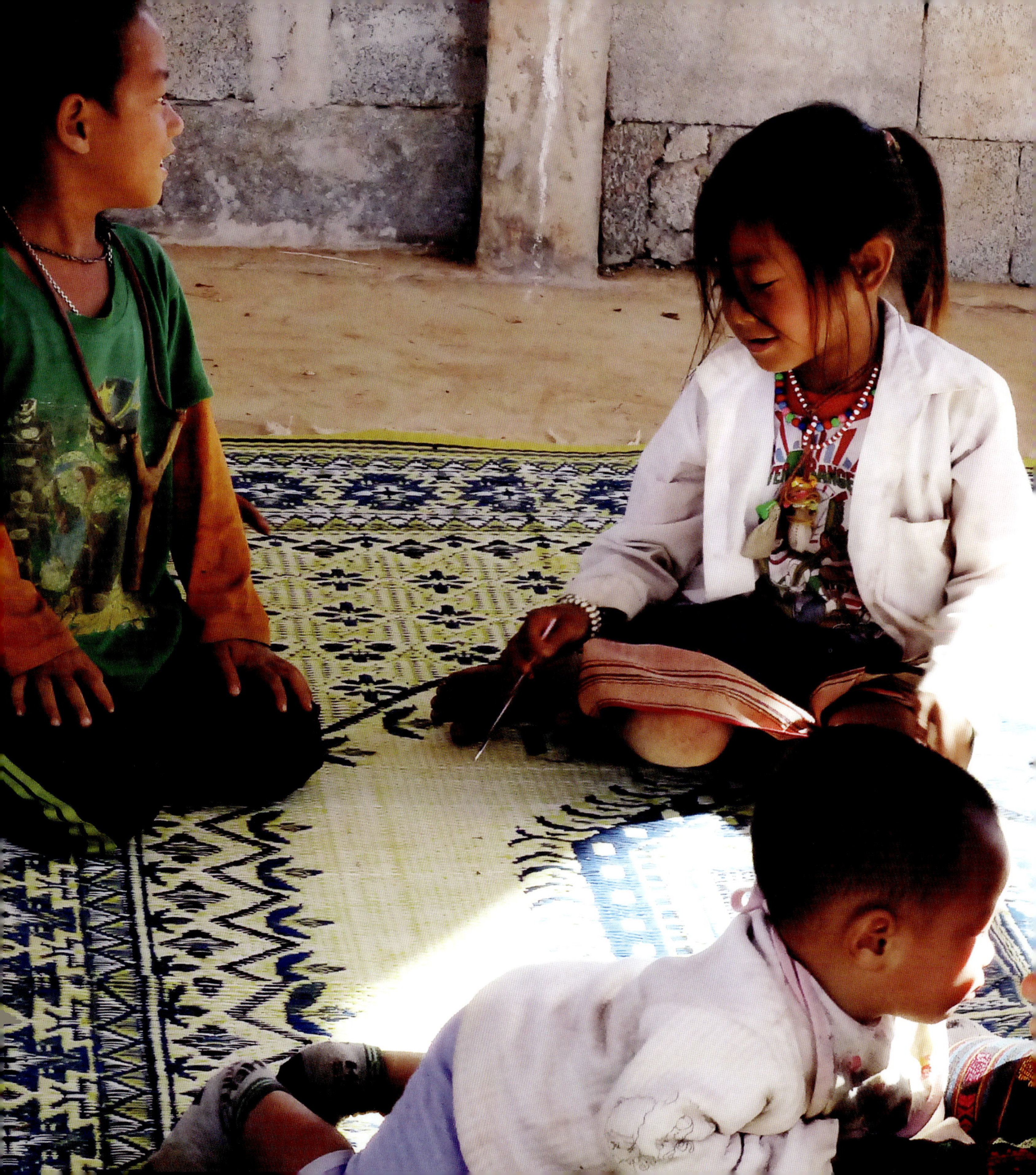

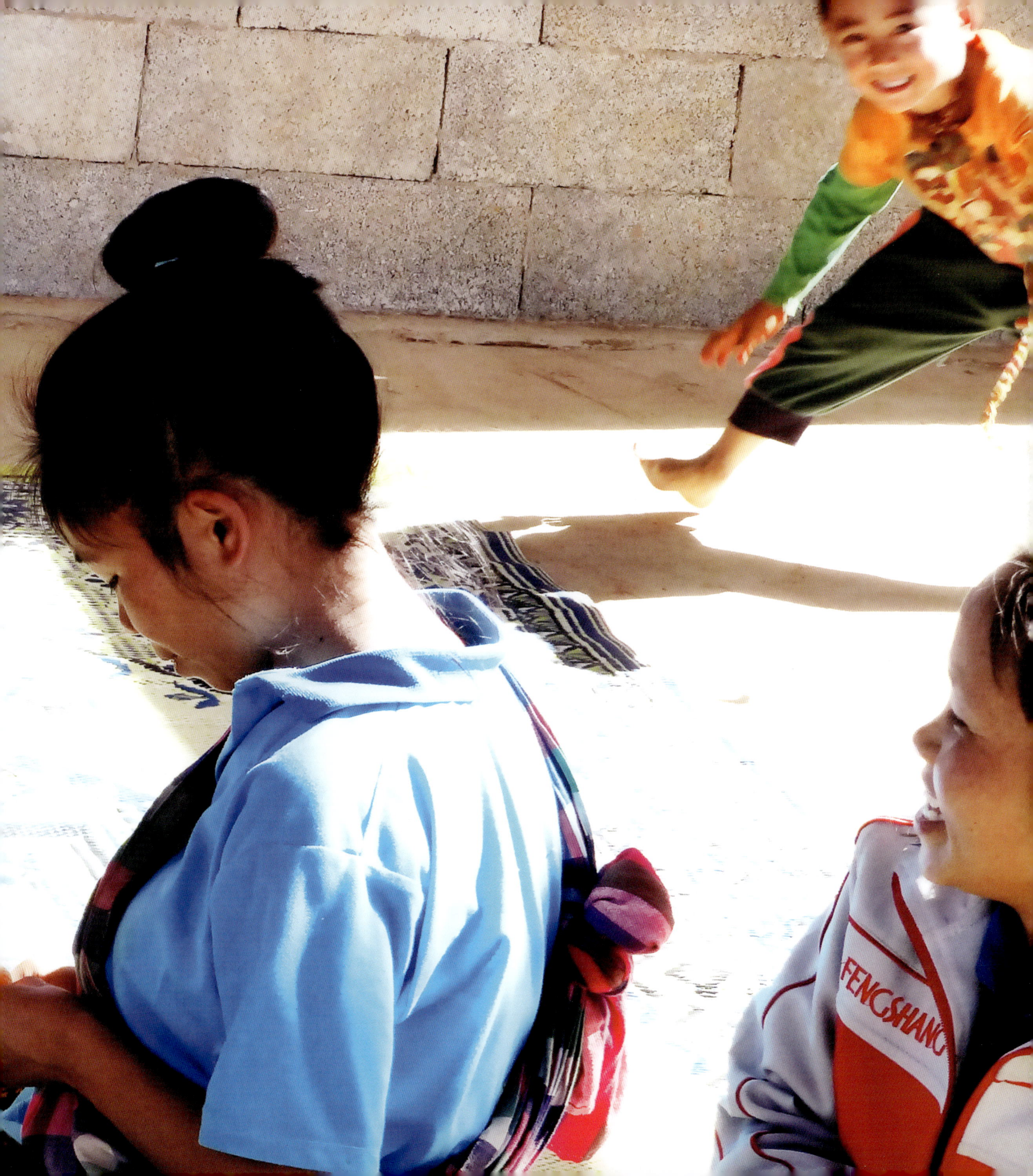
FENGSHANG

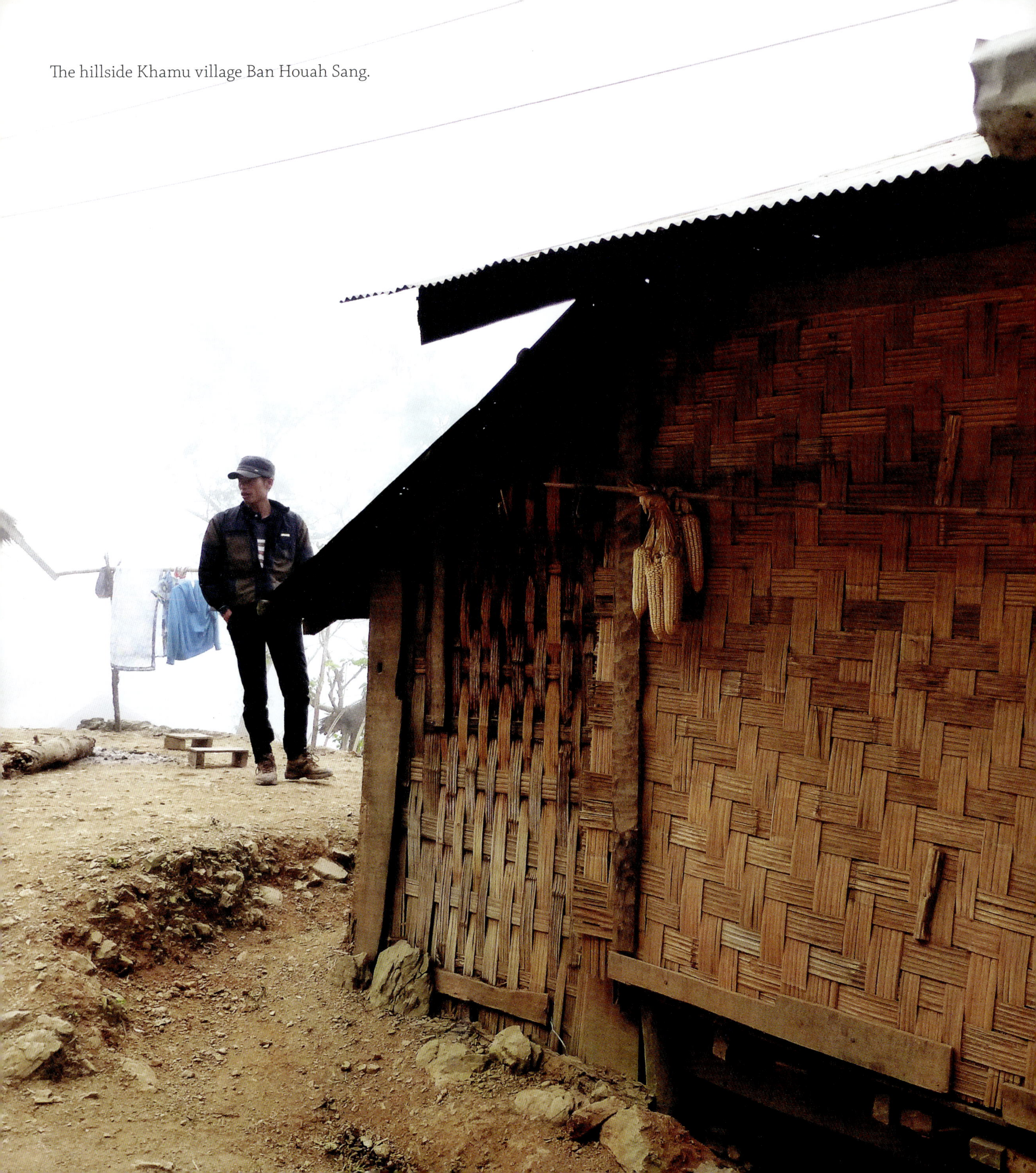

The hillside Khamu village Ban Houah Sang.

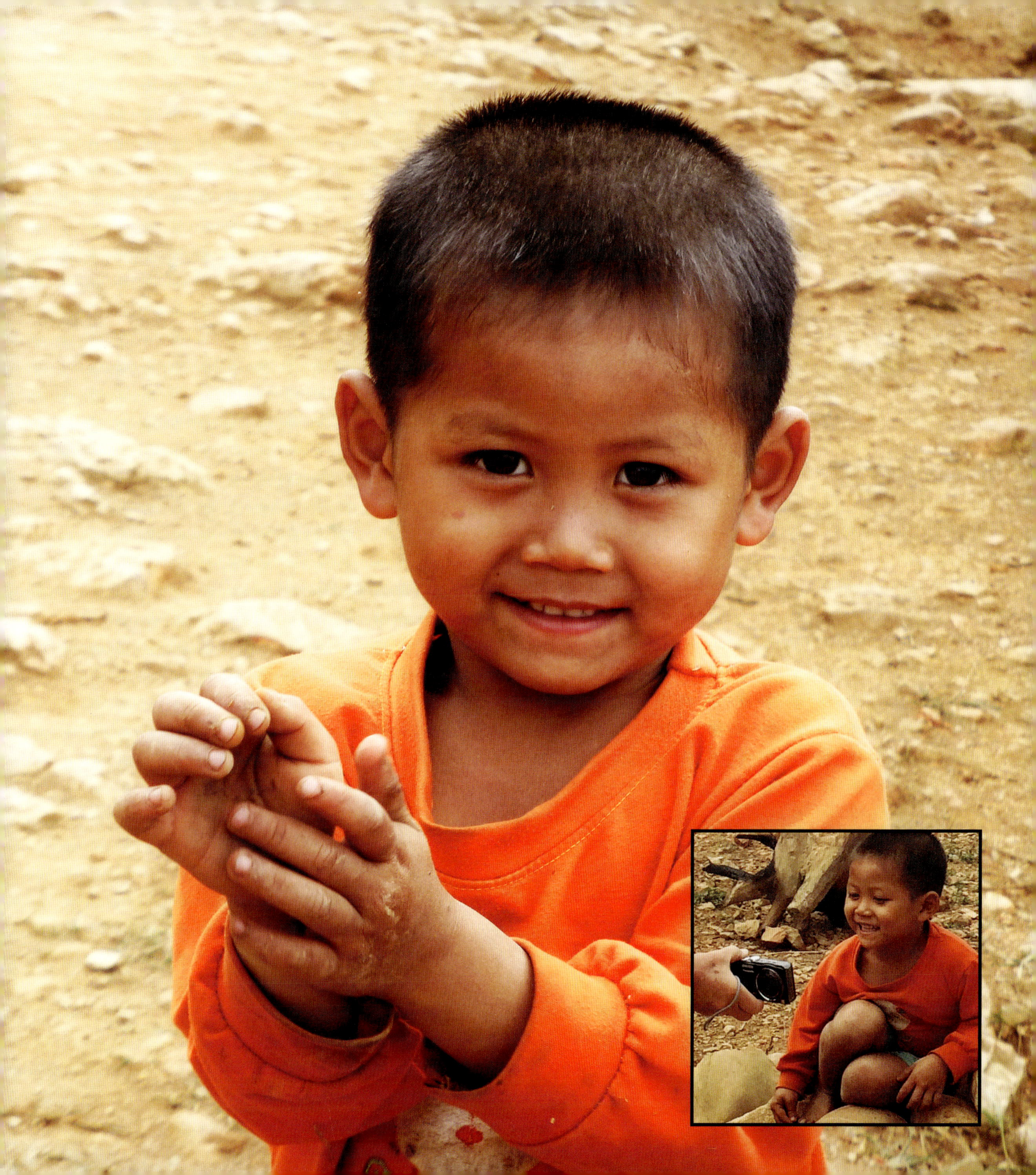

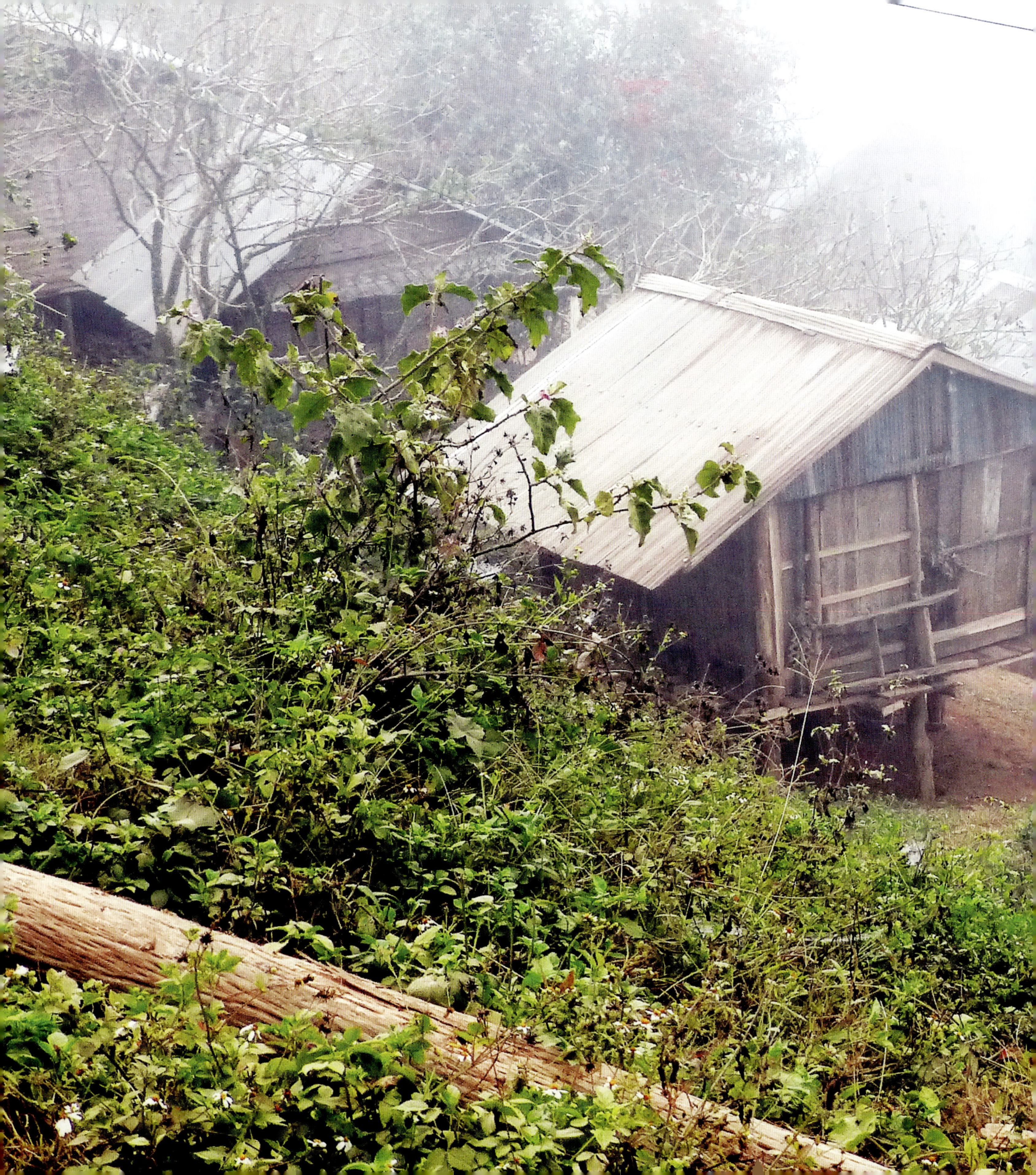

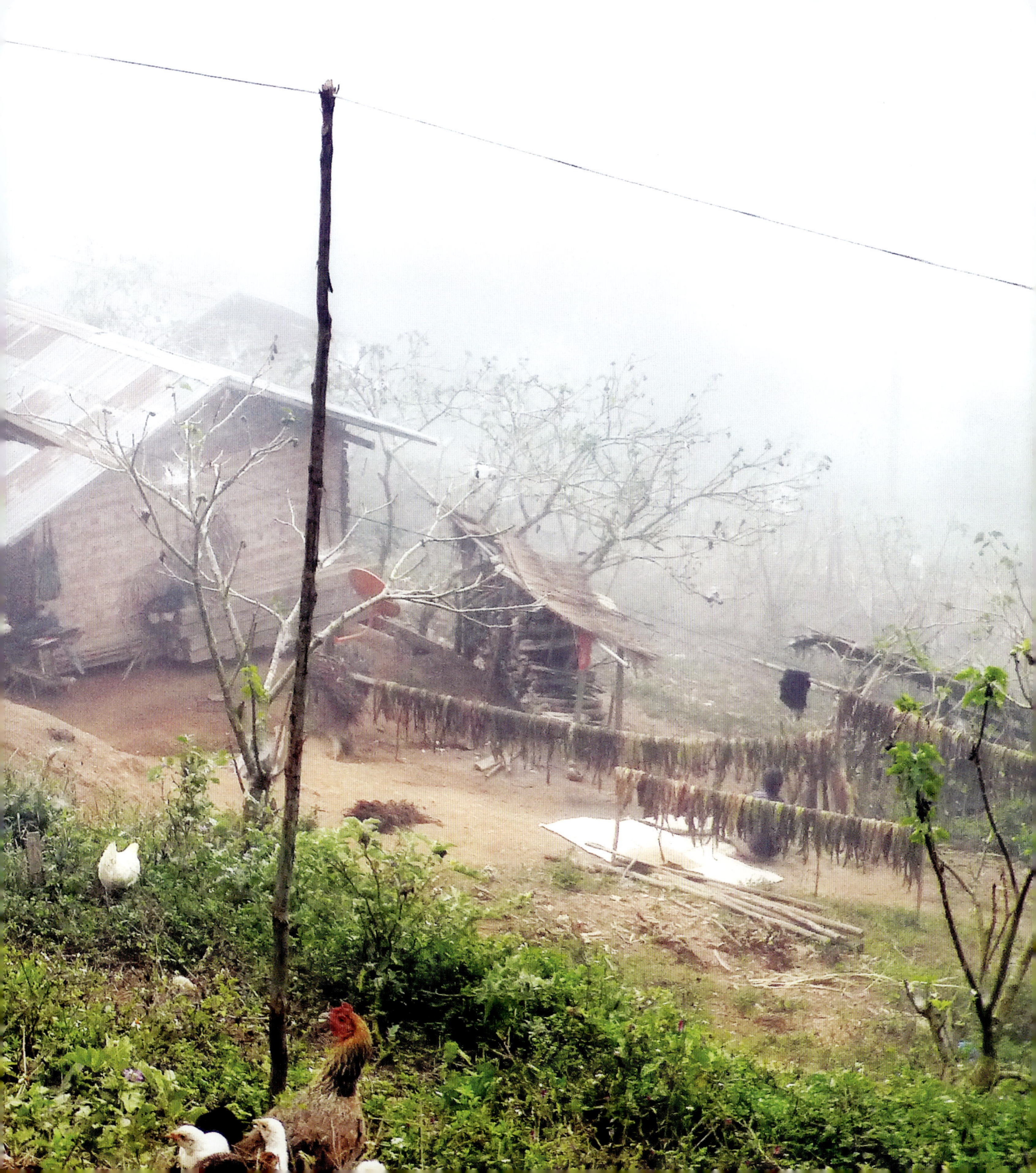

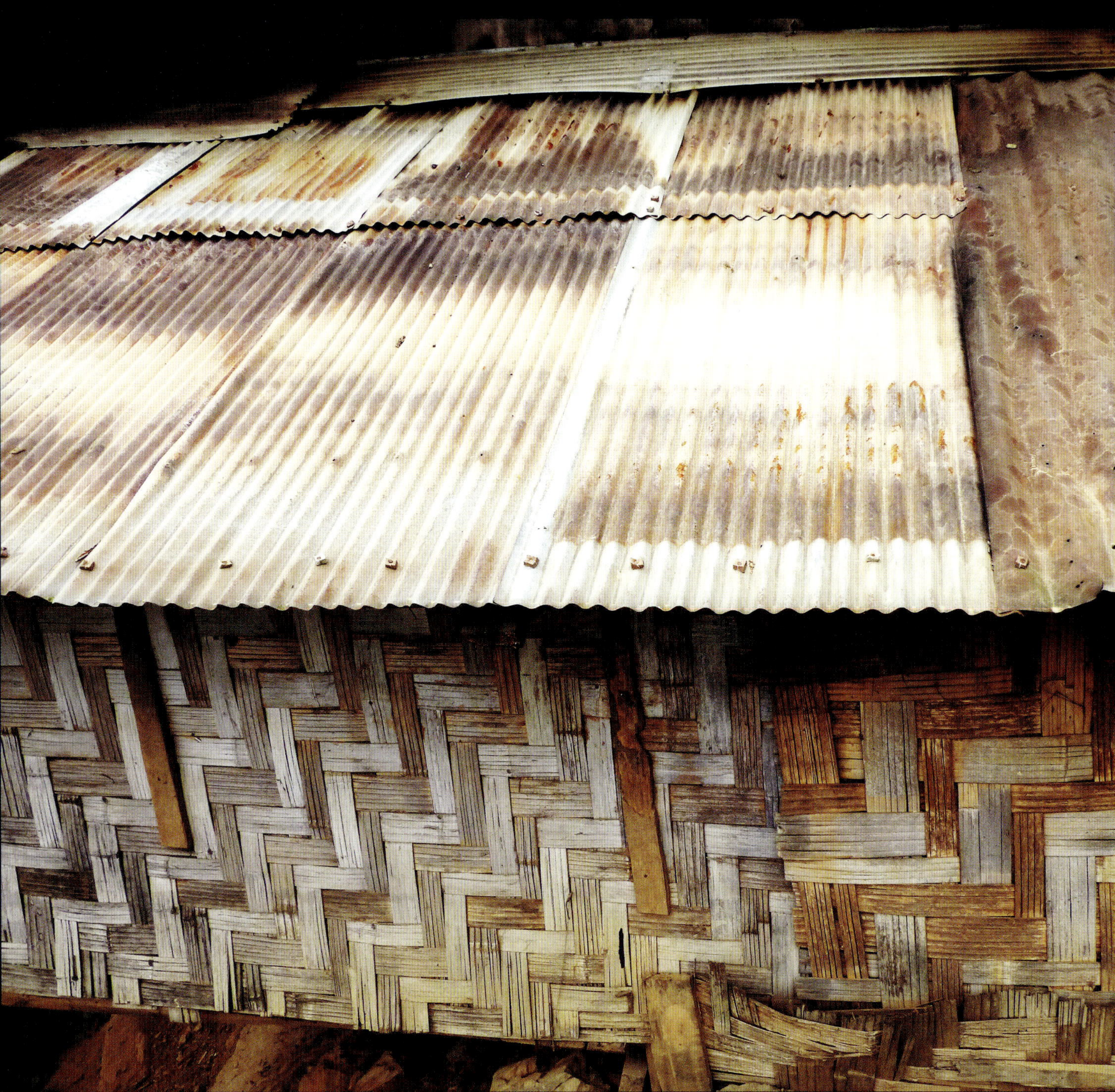

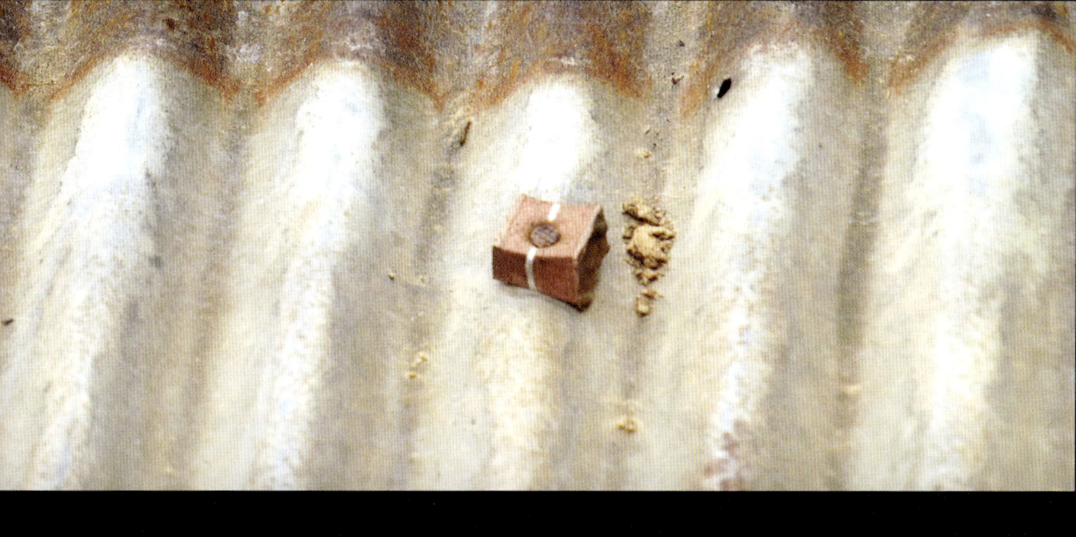

Detail from page 108
Re-use: Roof nail anchor cut from a worn-out flip flop.

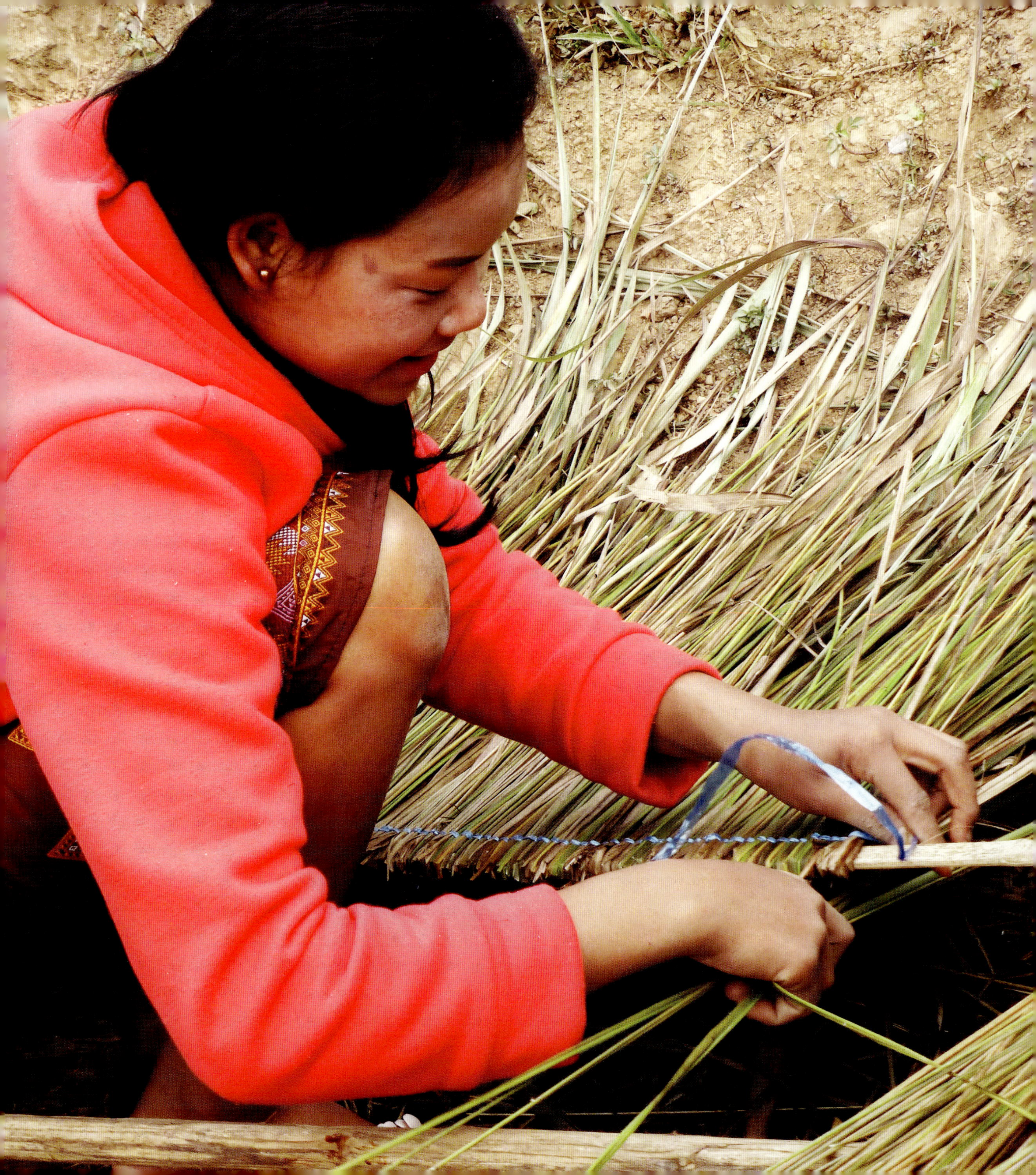

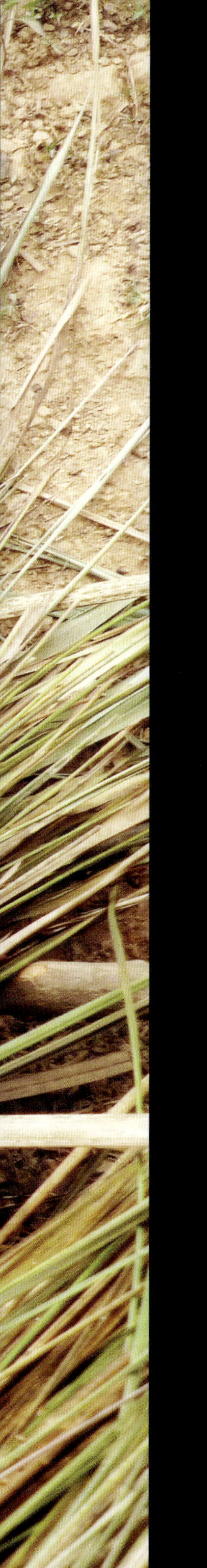

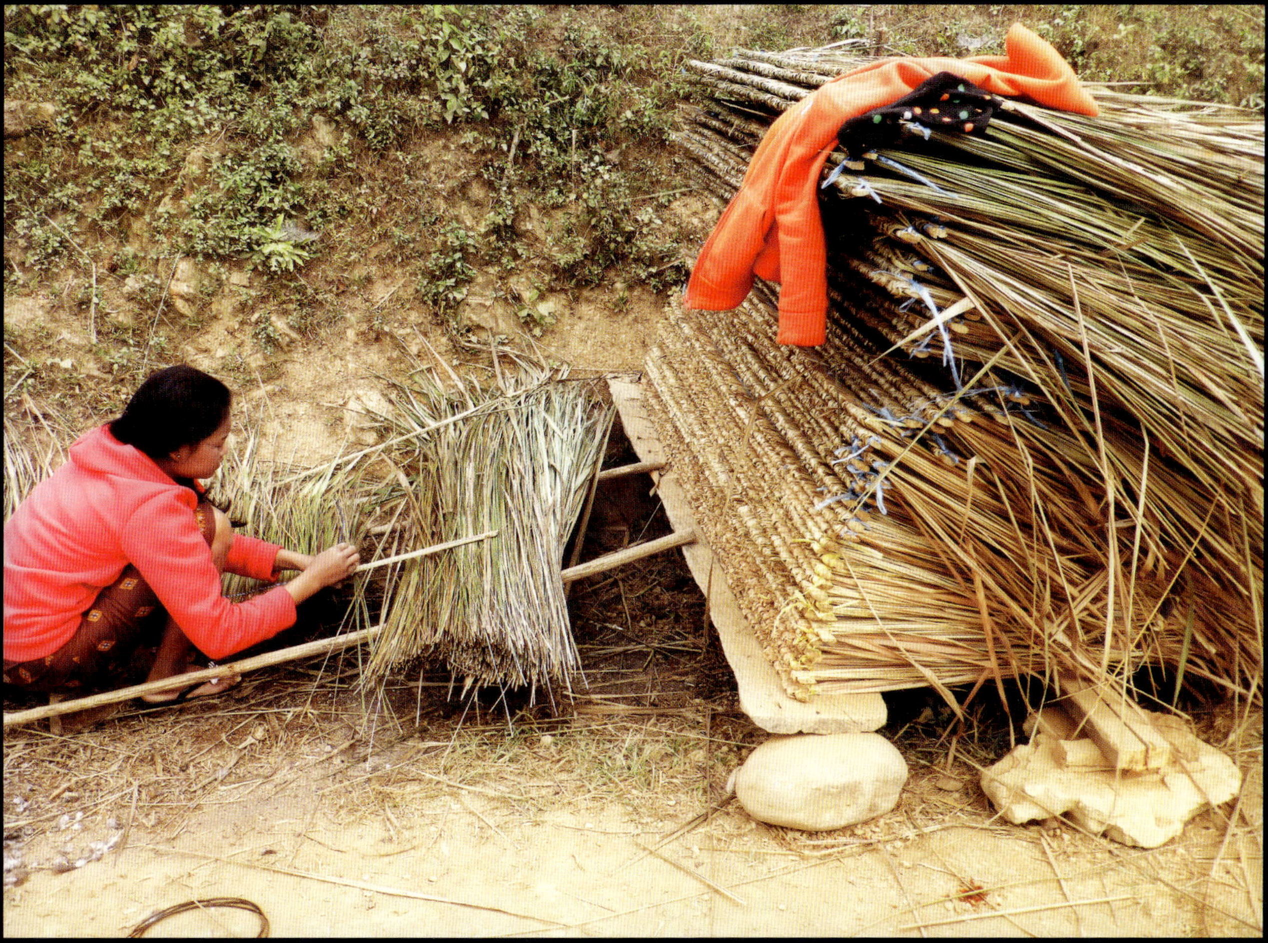

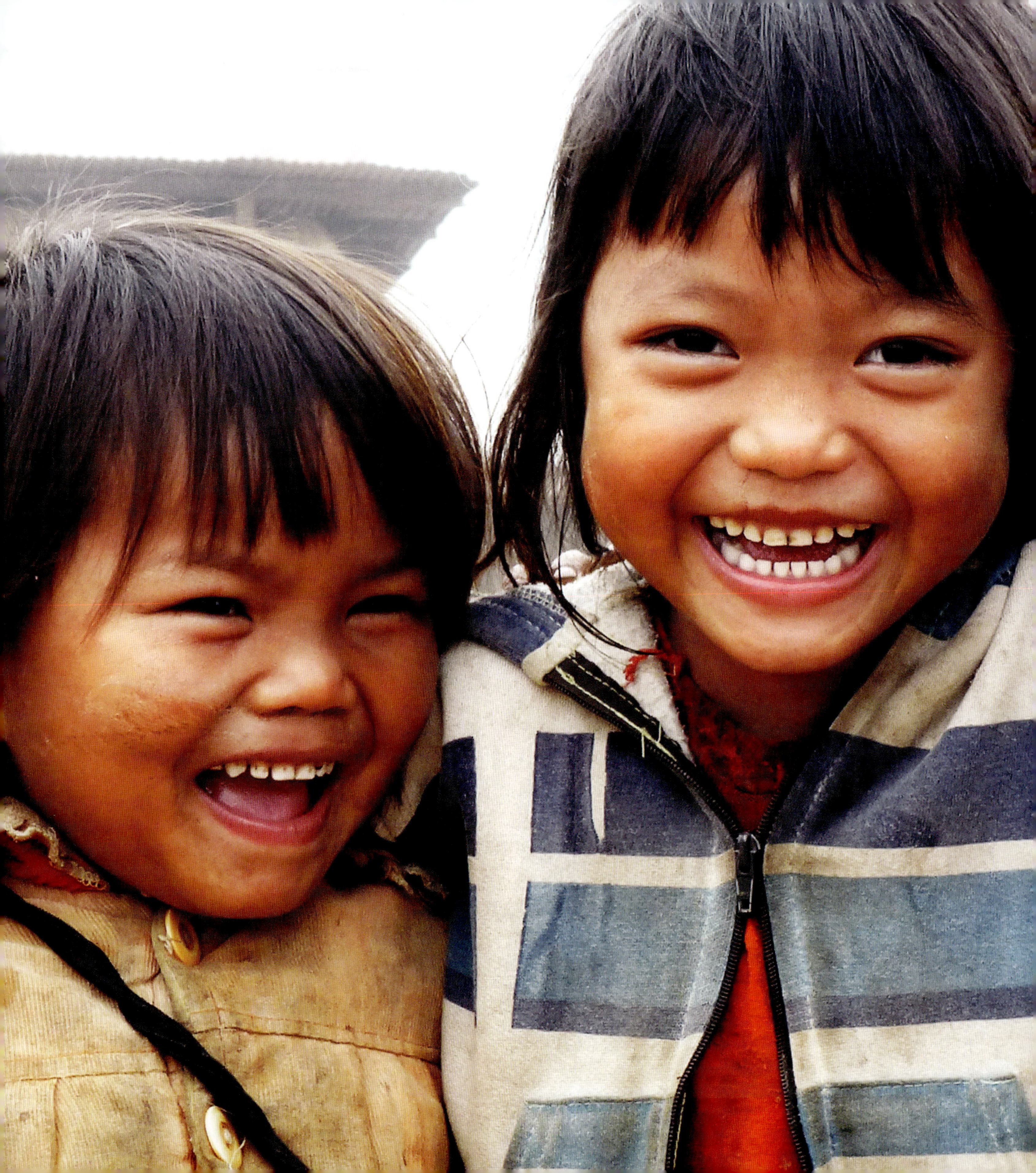

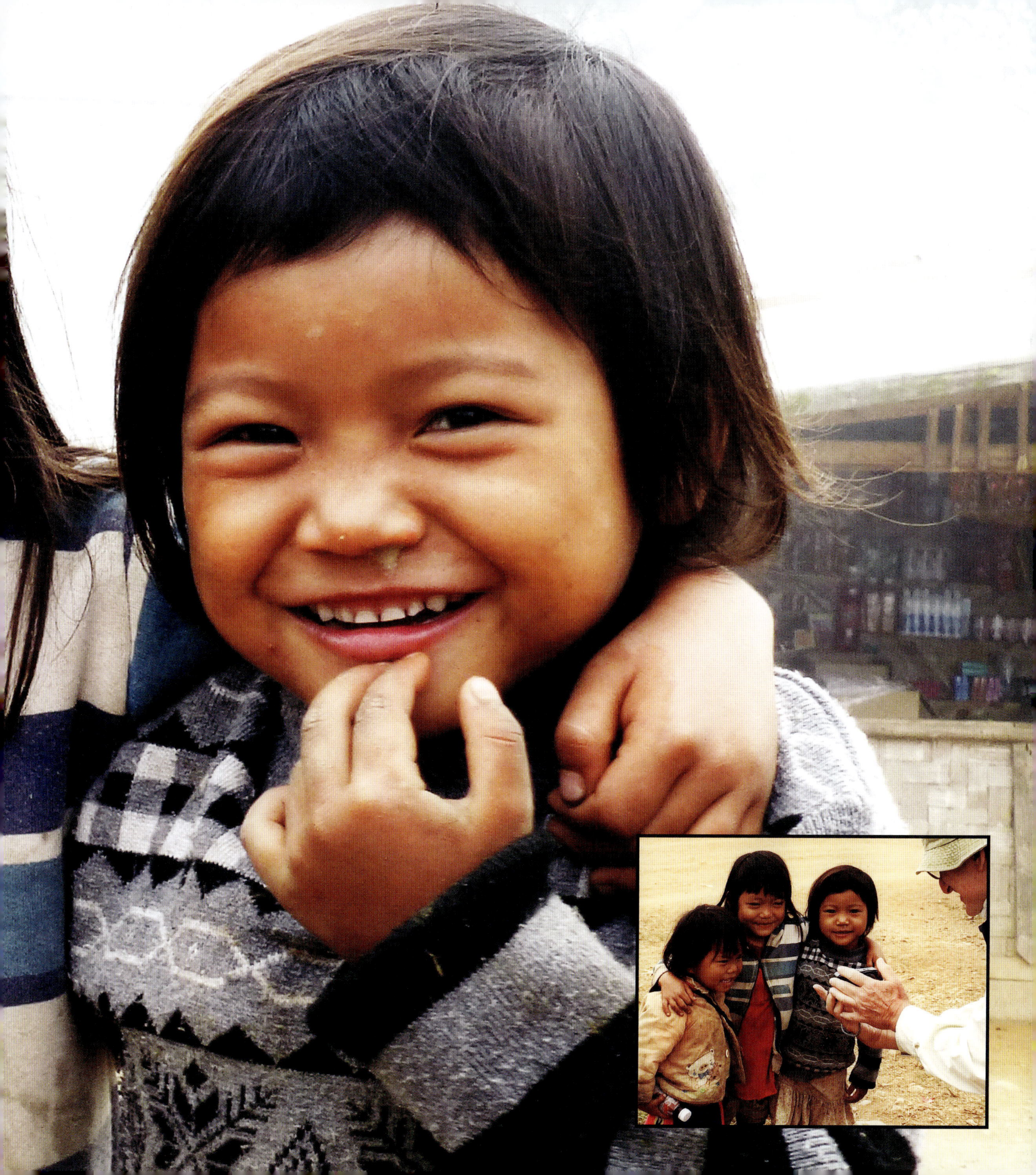

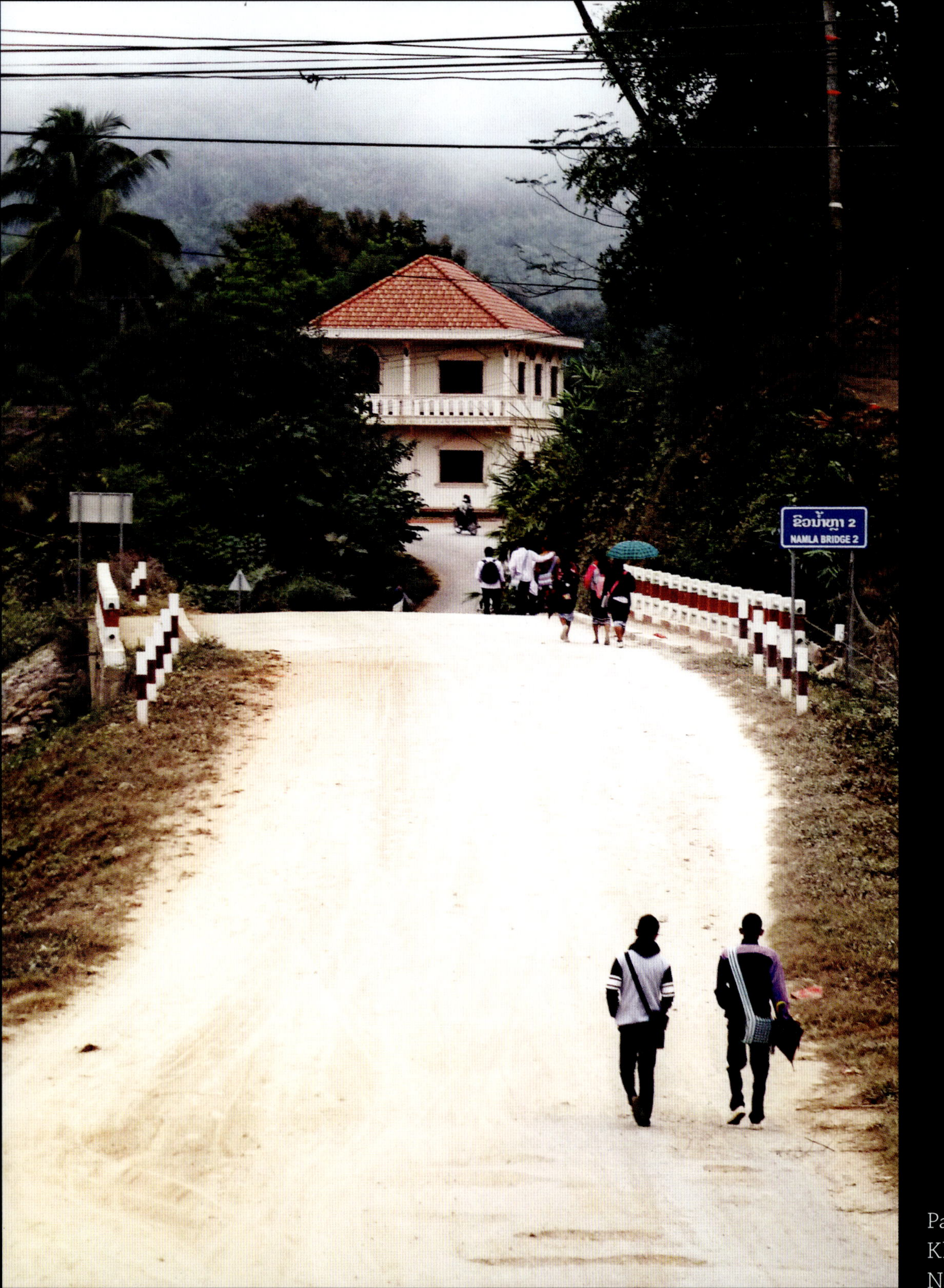

Pak La is a prosperous Khamu village on the Nam Pak River.

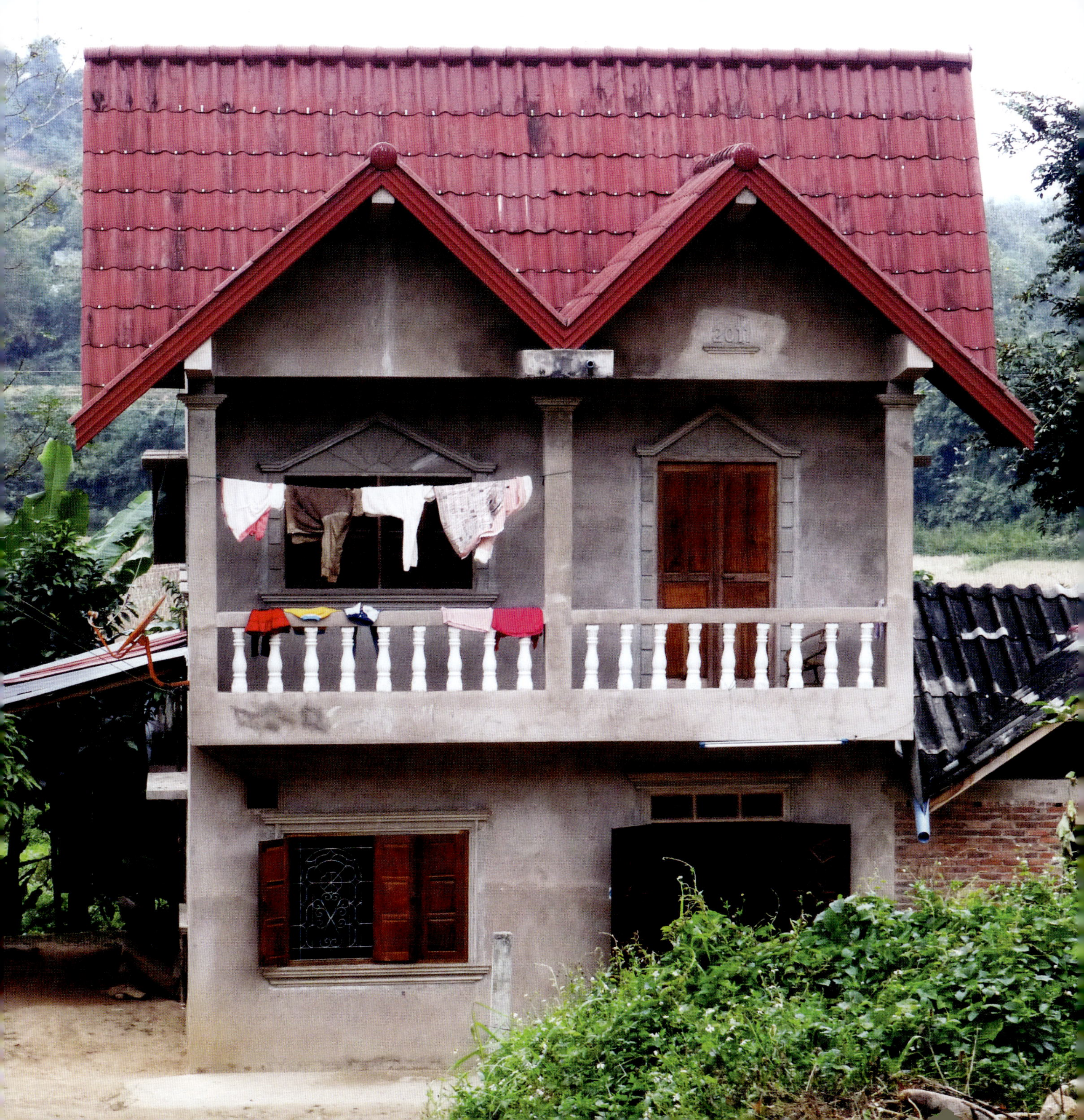
2011

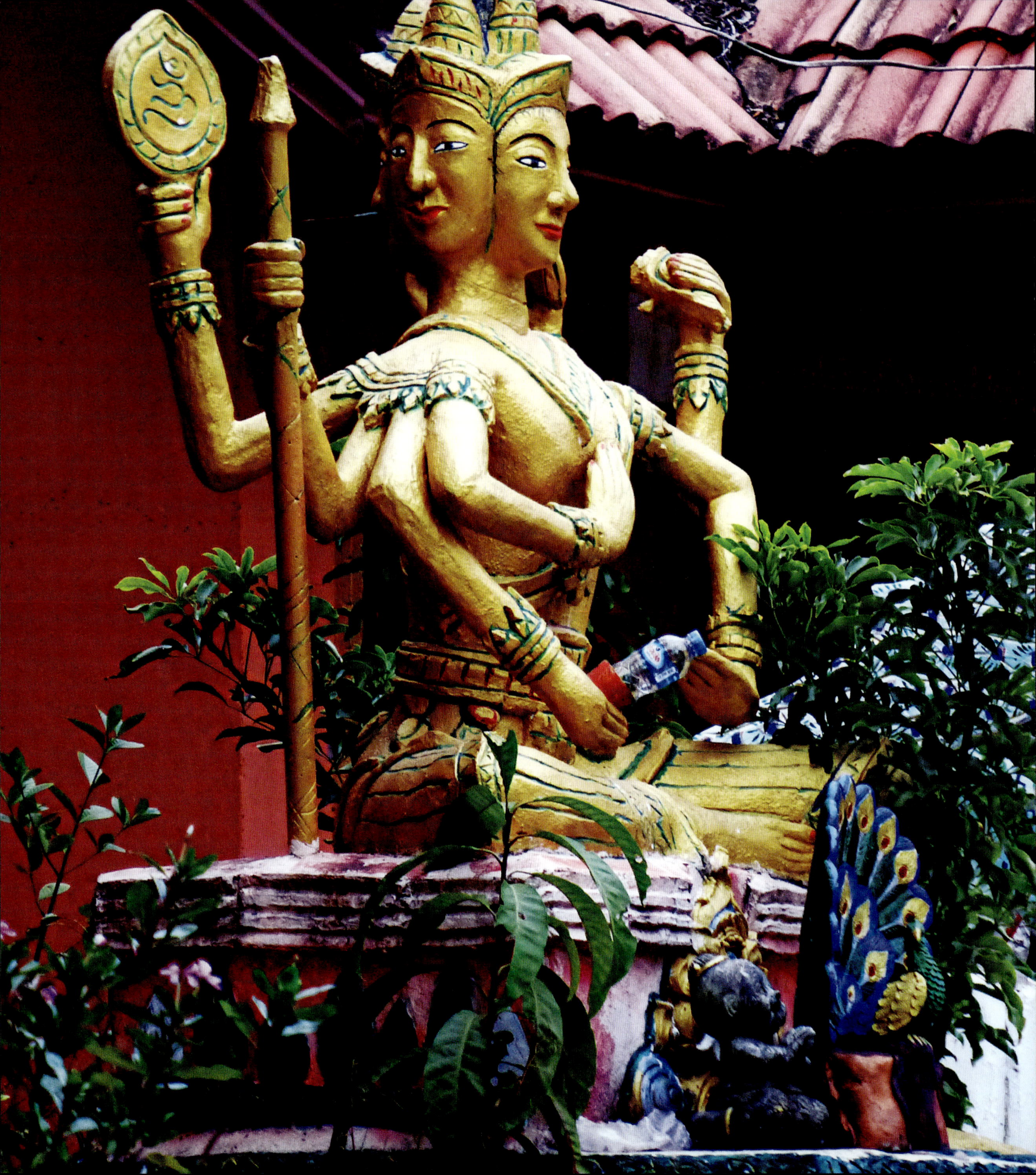

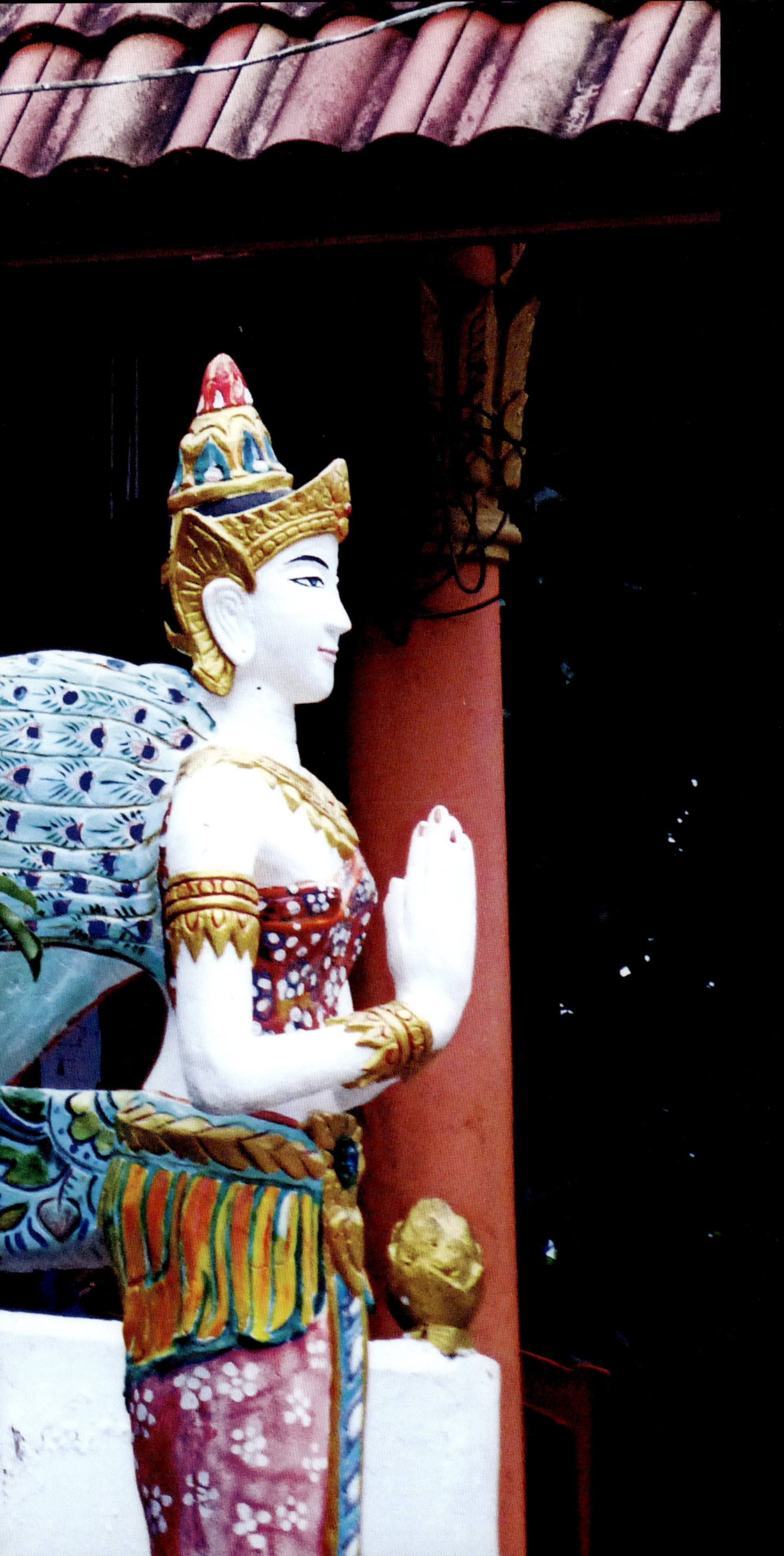

Statuary at Pak La's
Buddhist Temple
Pha Chiao Sing Kham.

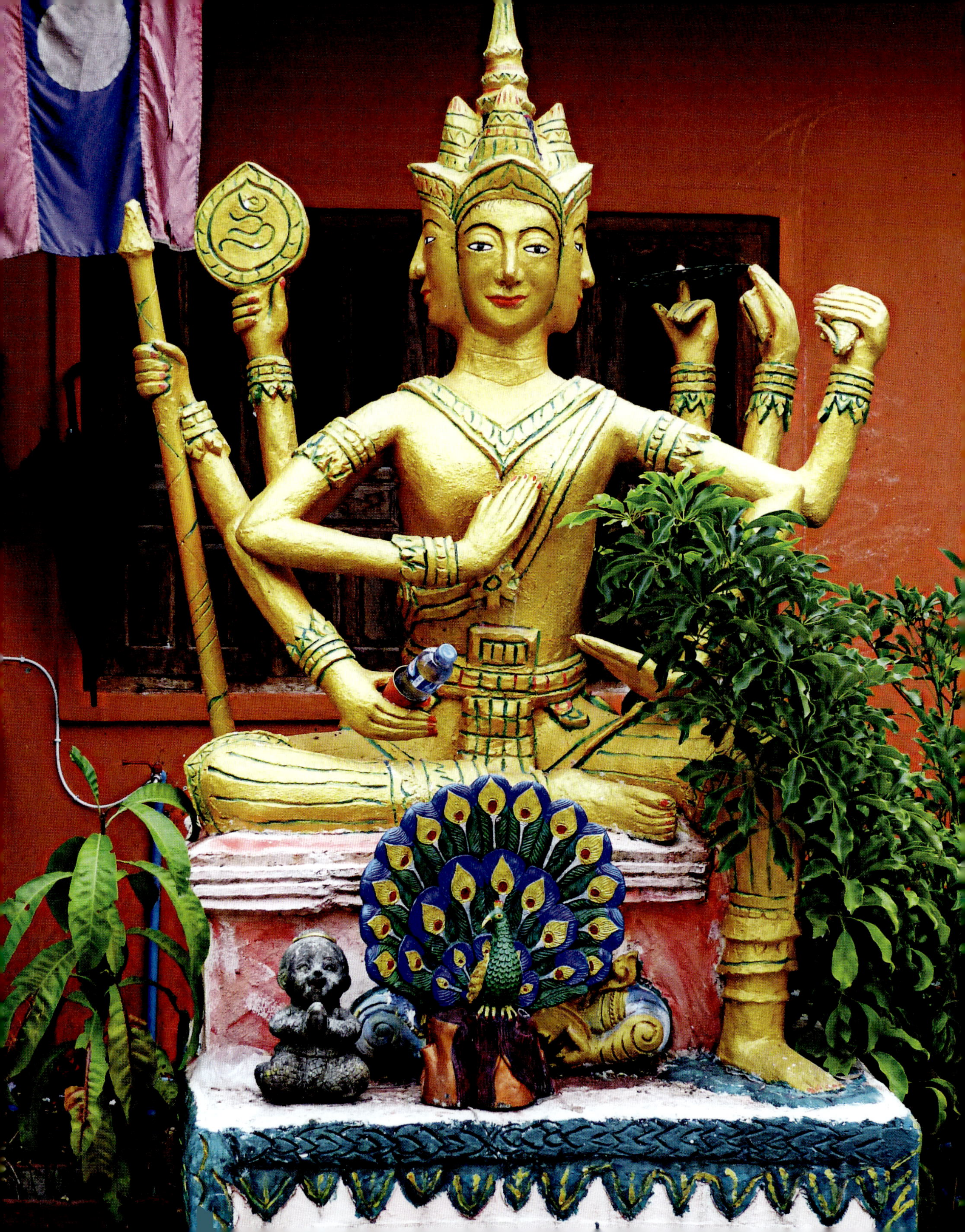

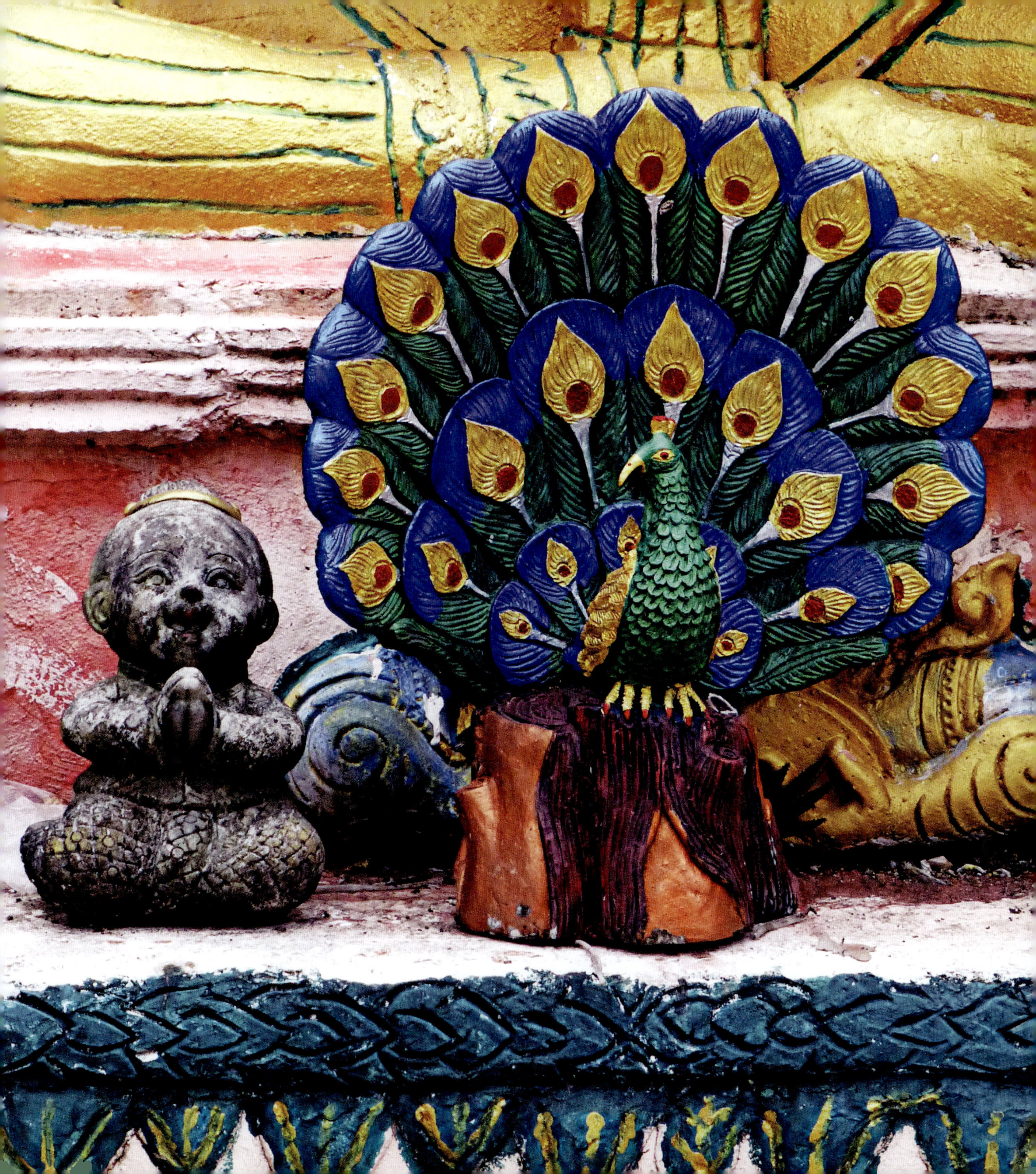

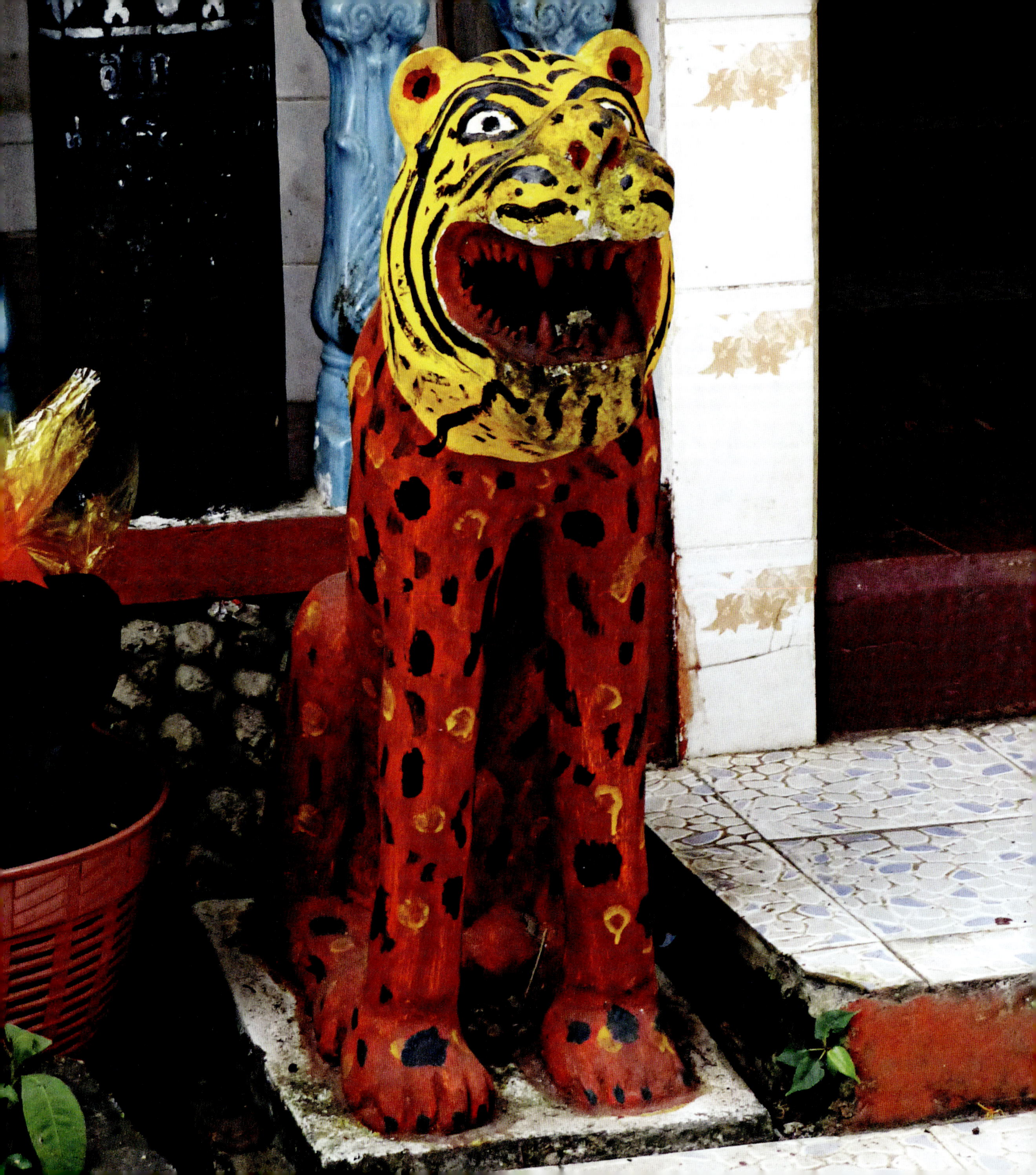

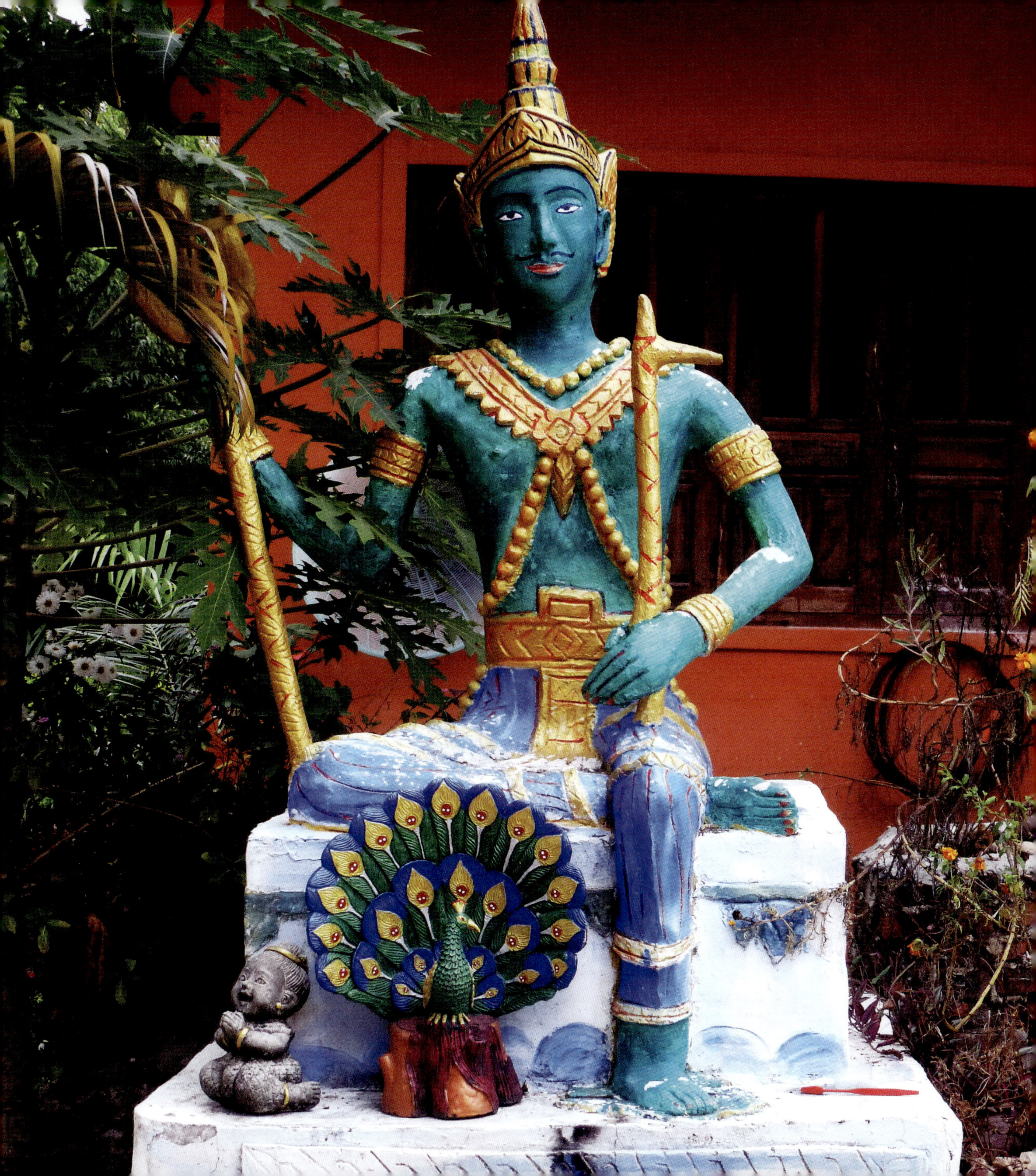

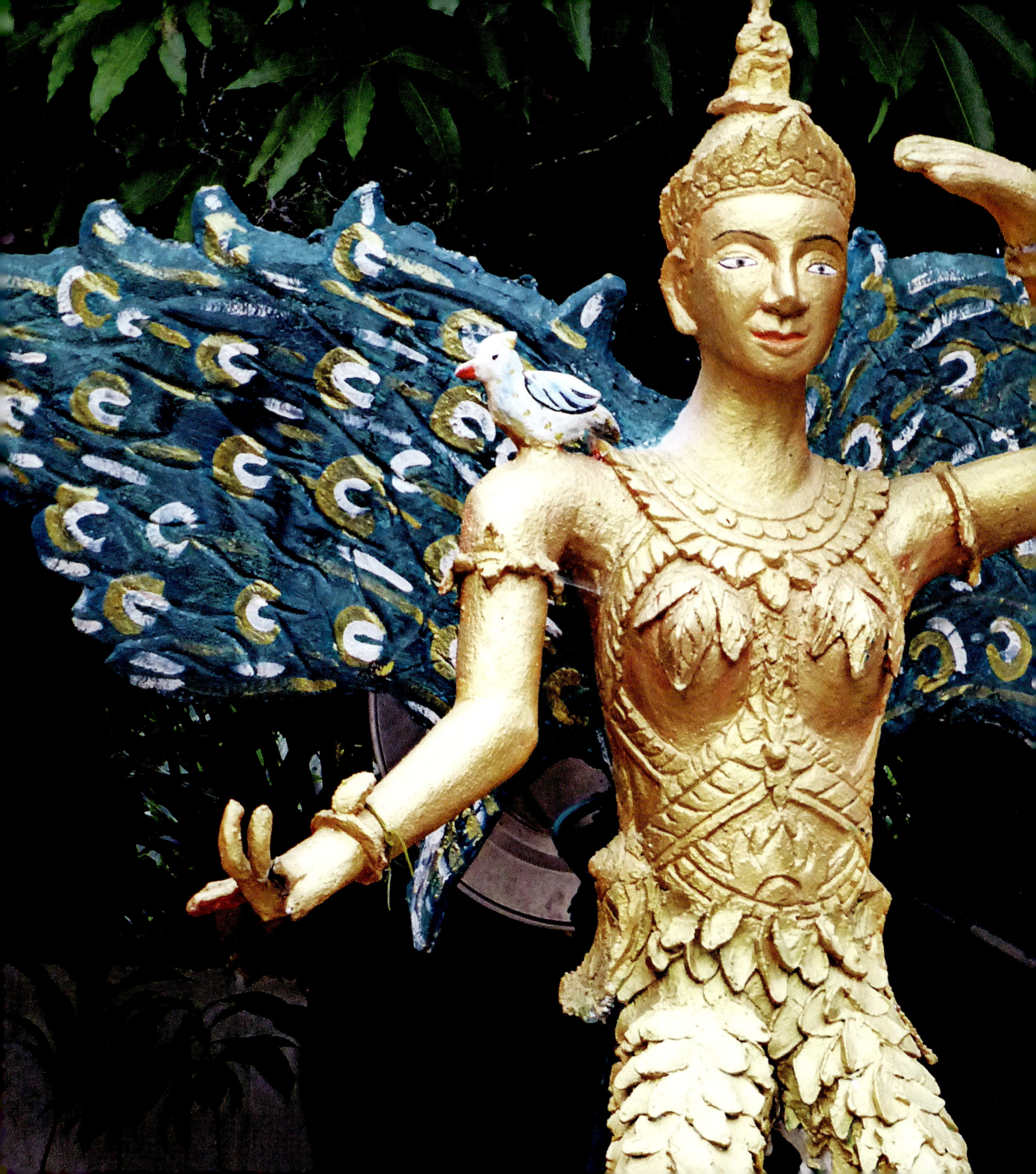

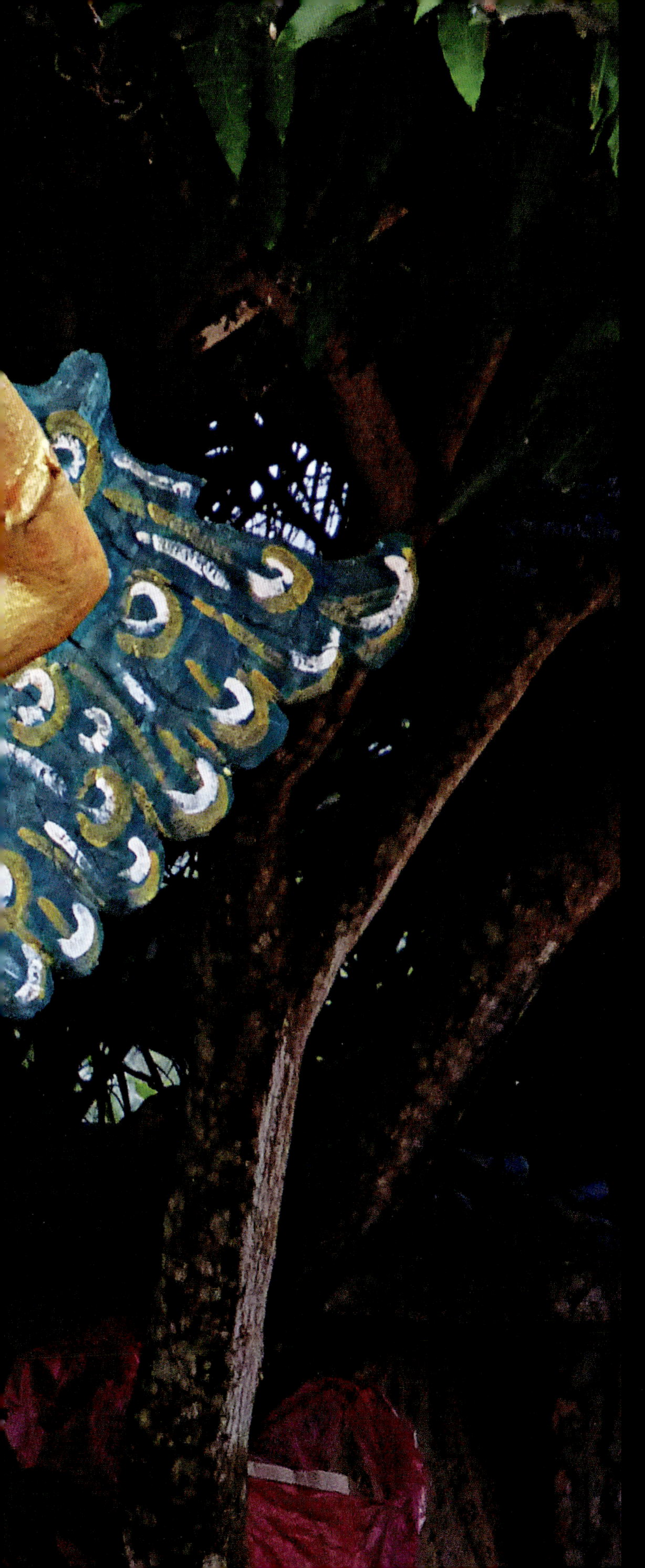

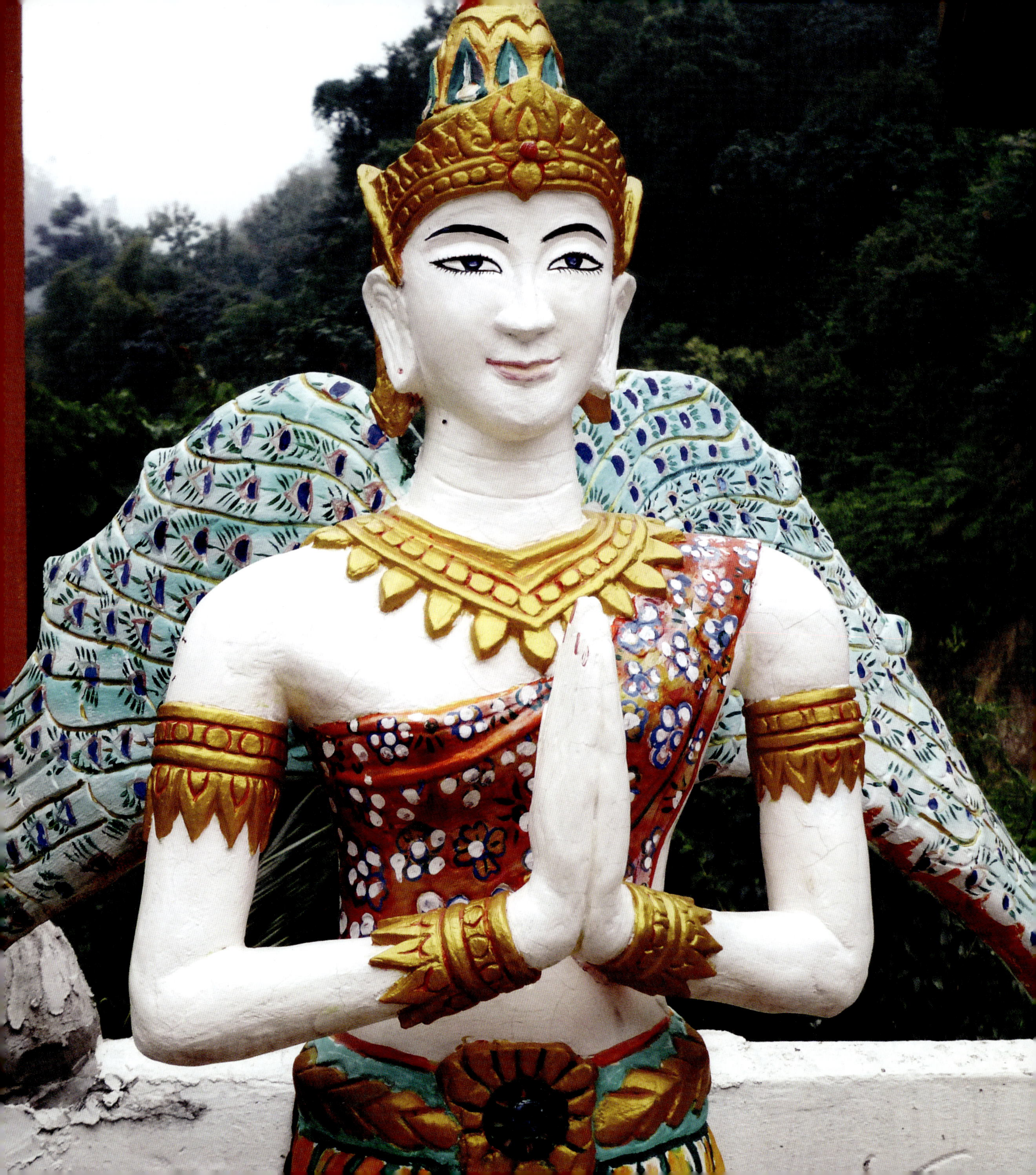

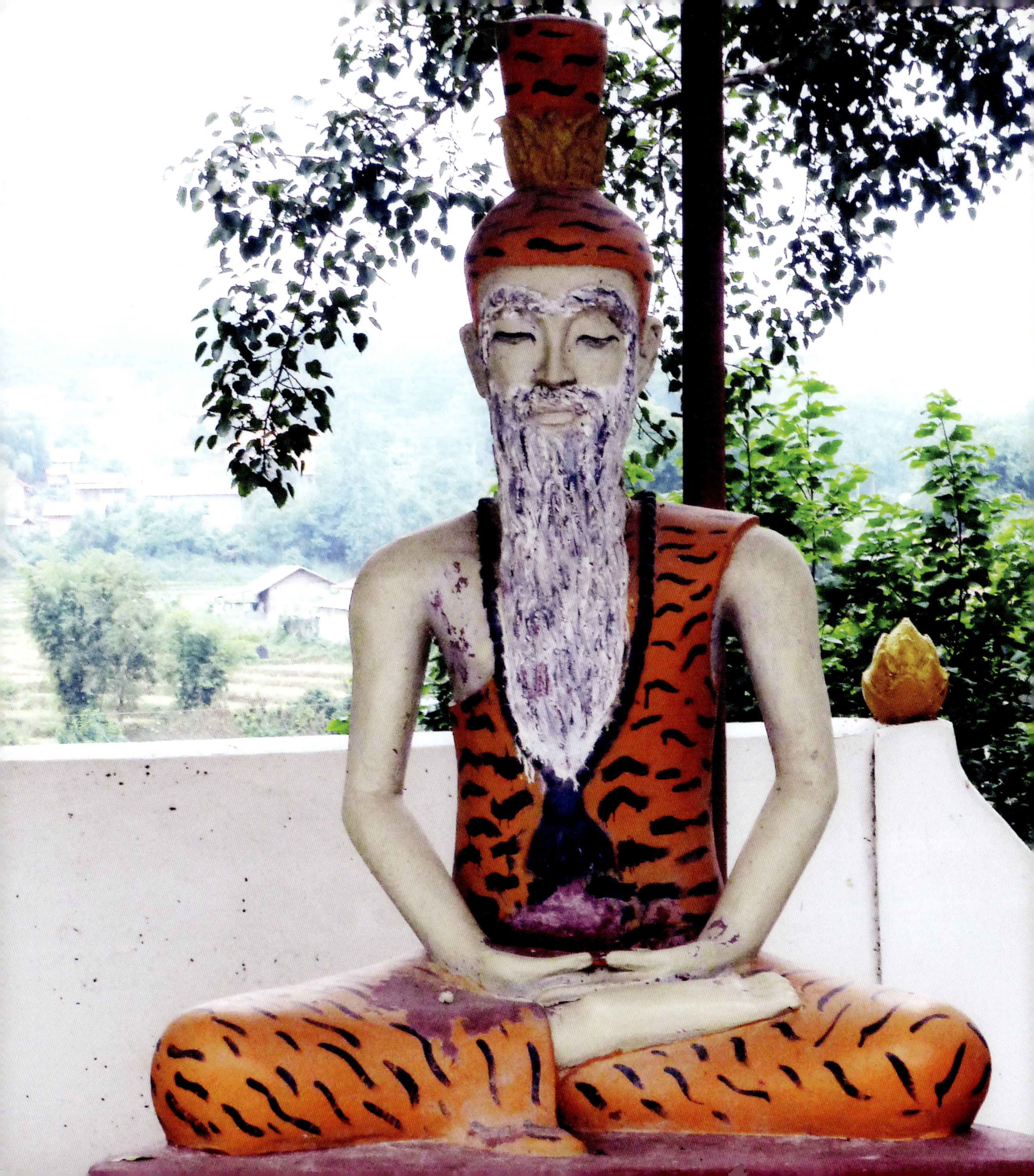

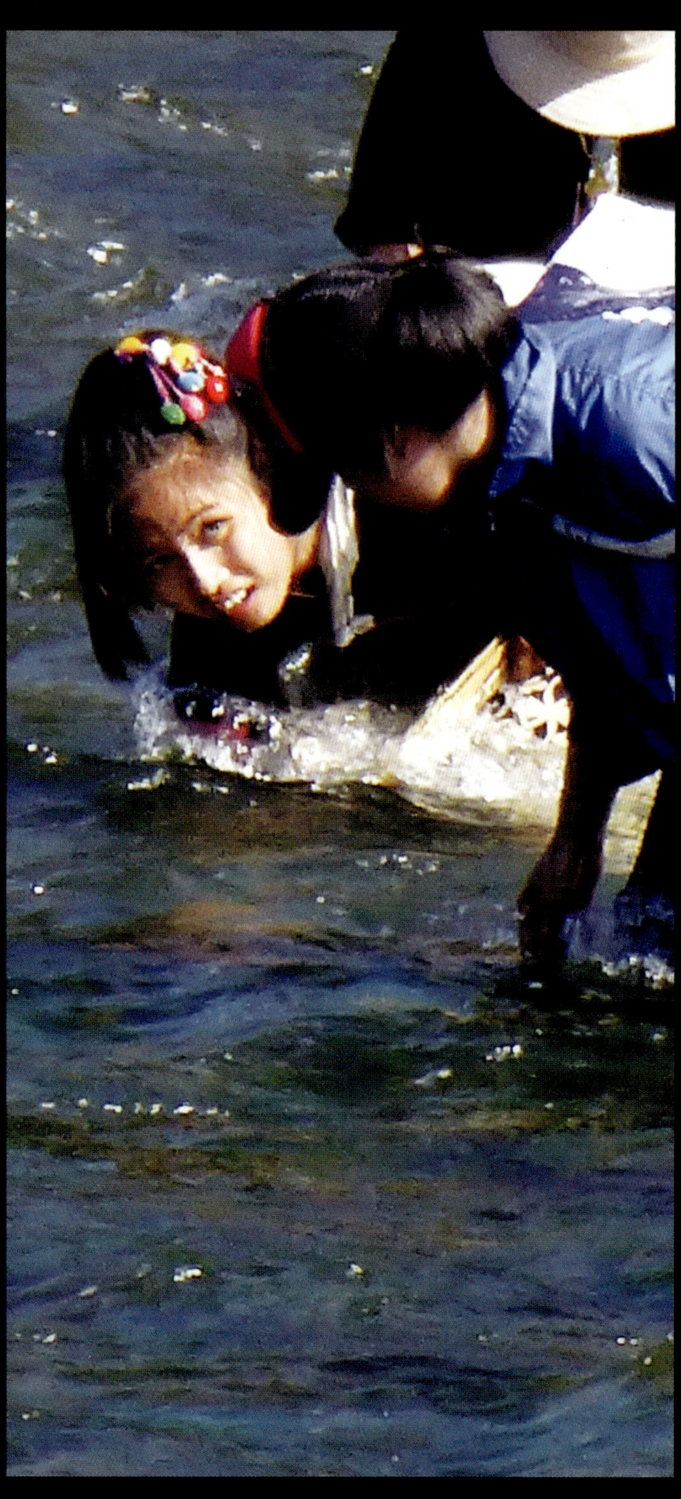

Foraging for river grass.

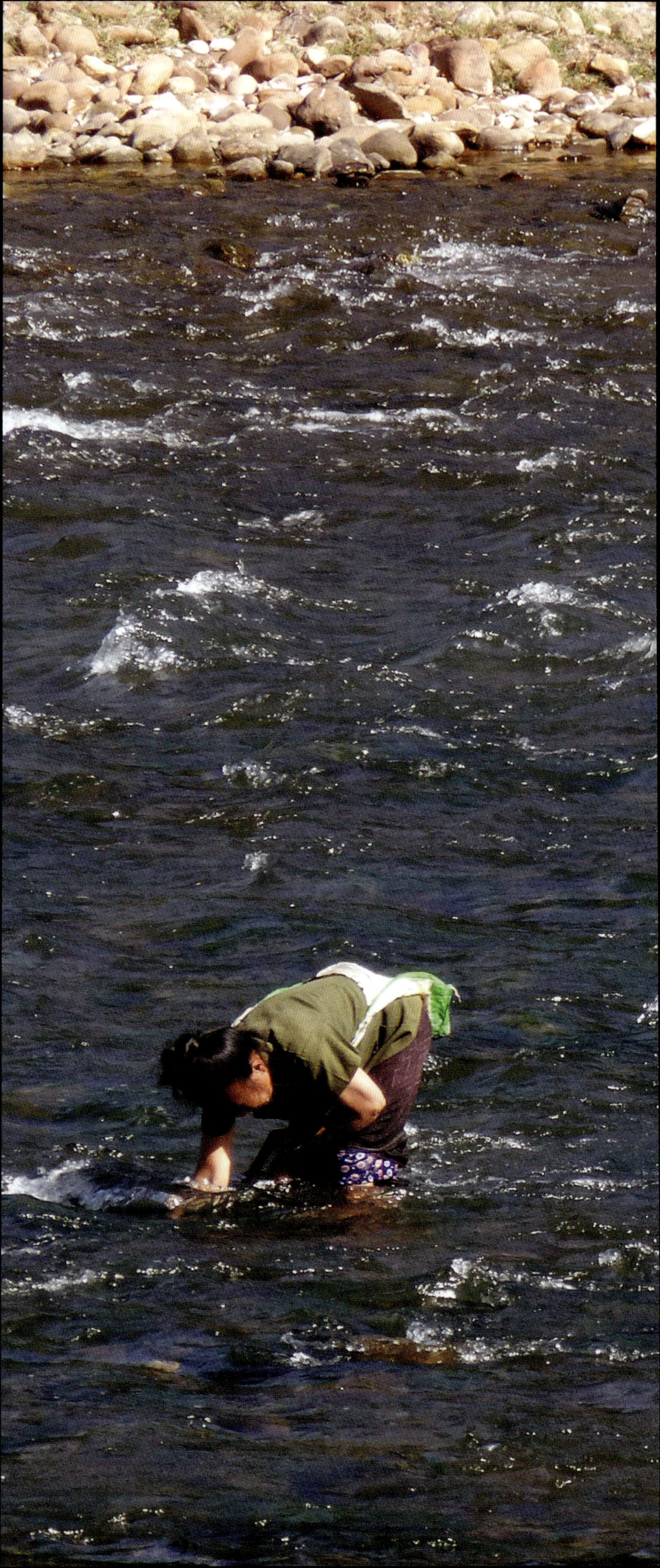

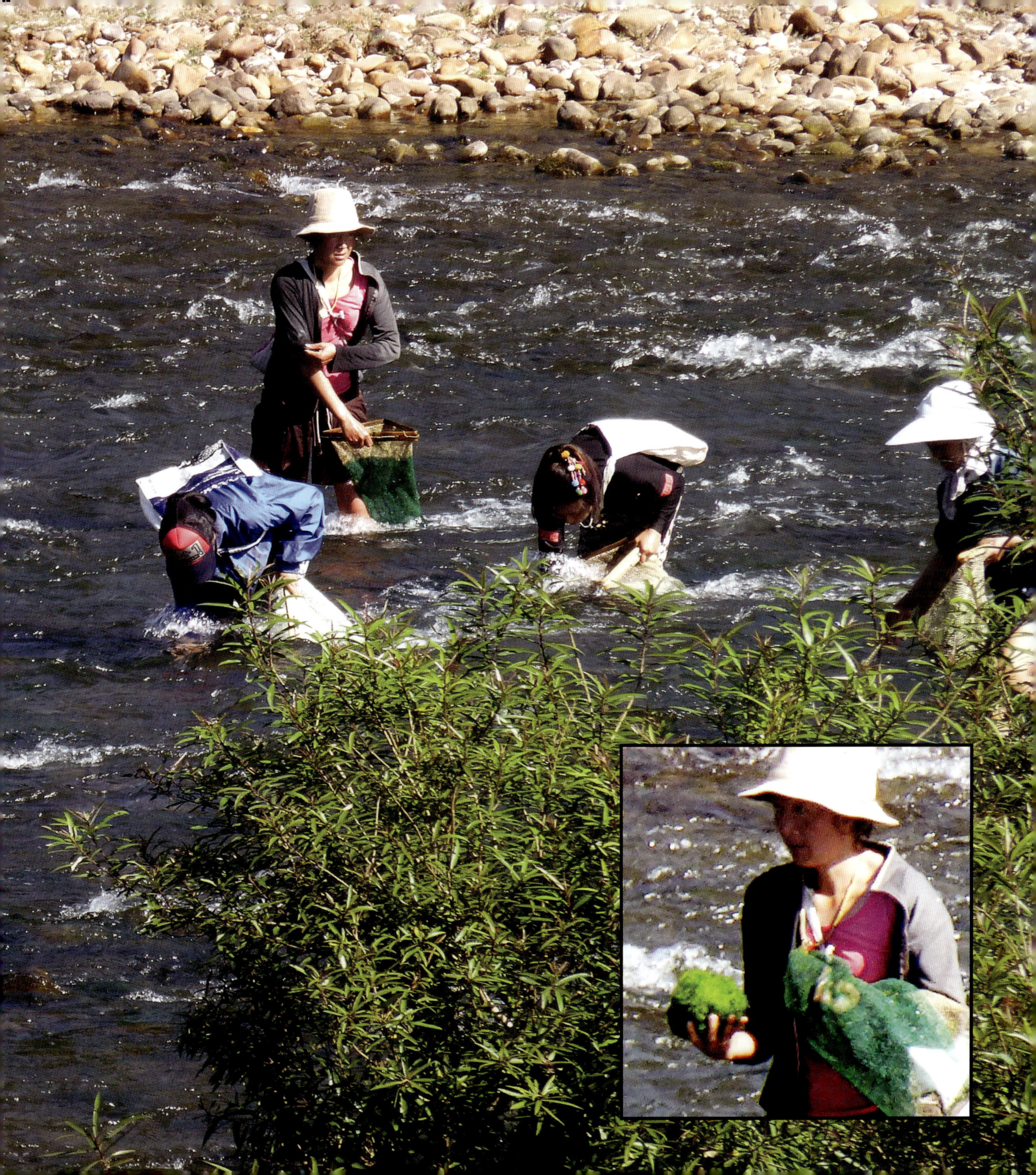

THREE

On the Mekong River in northern Laos

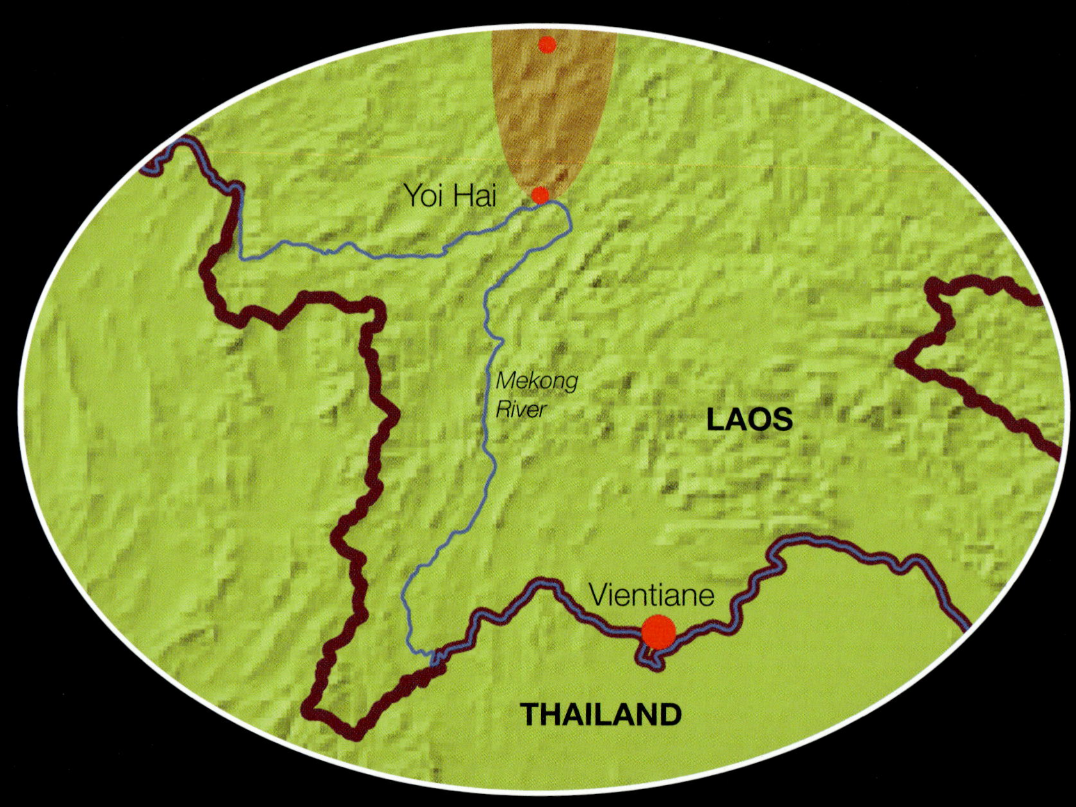

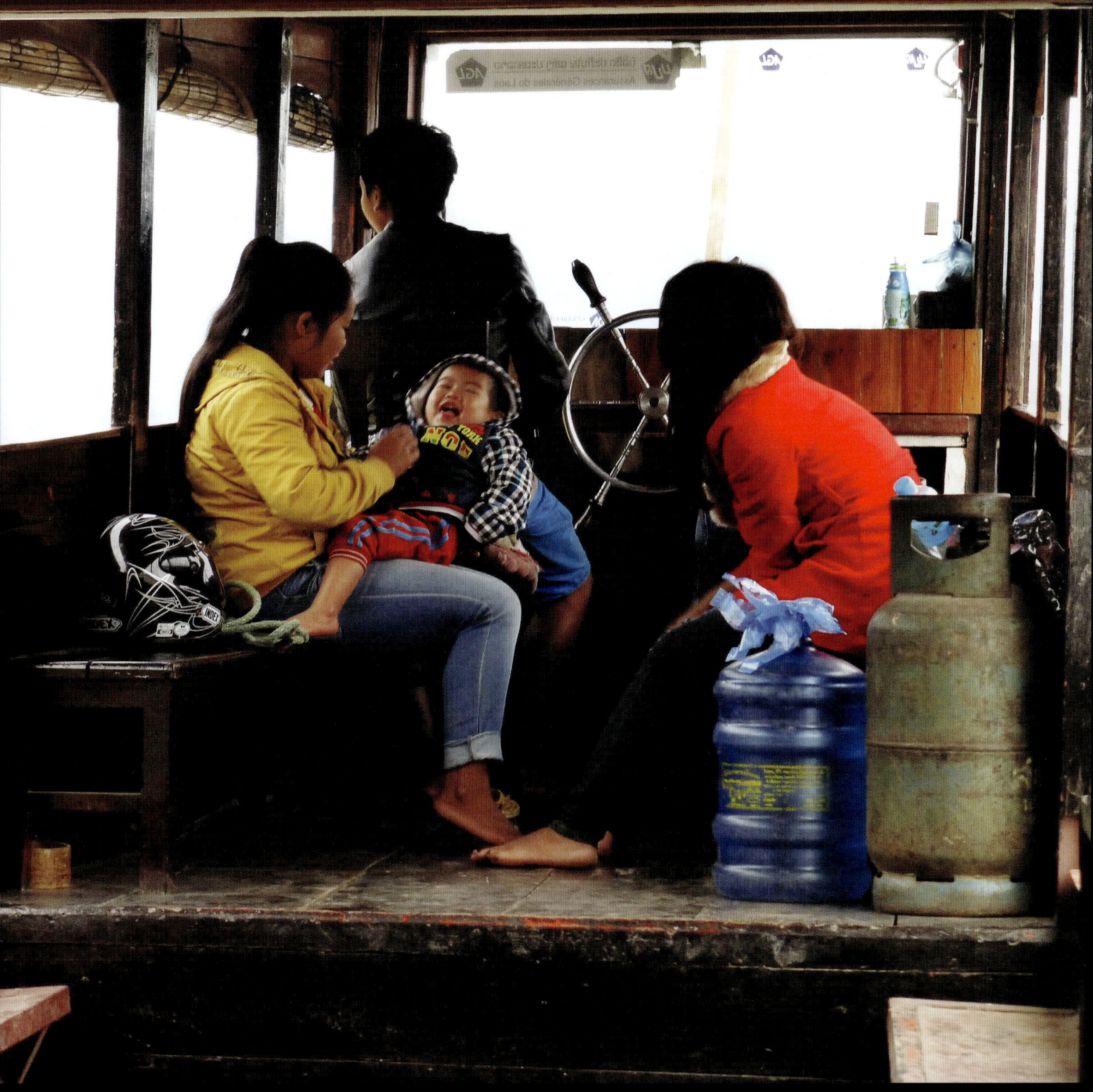
YORK
INDEX

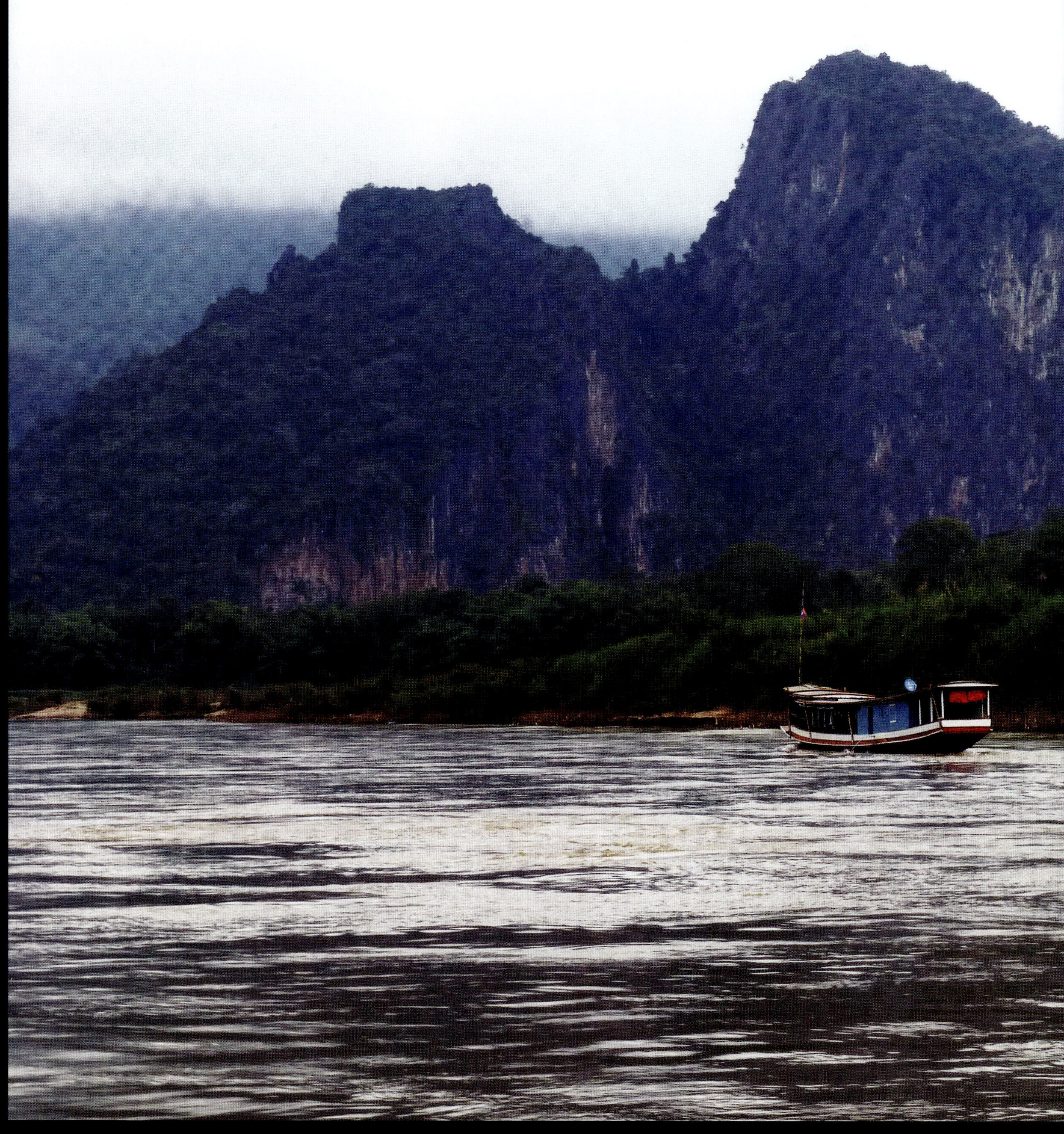

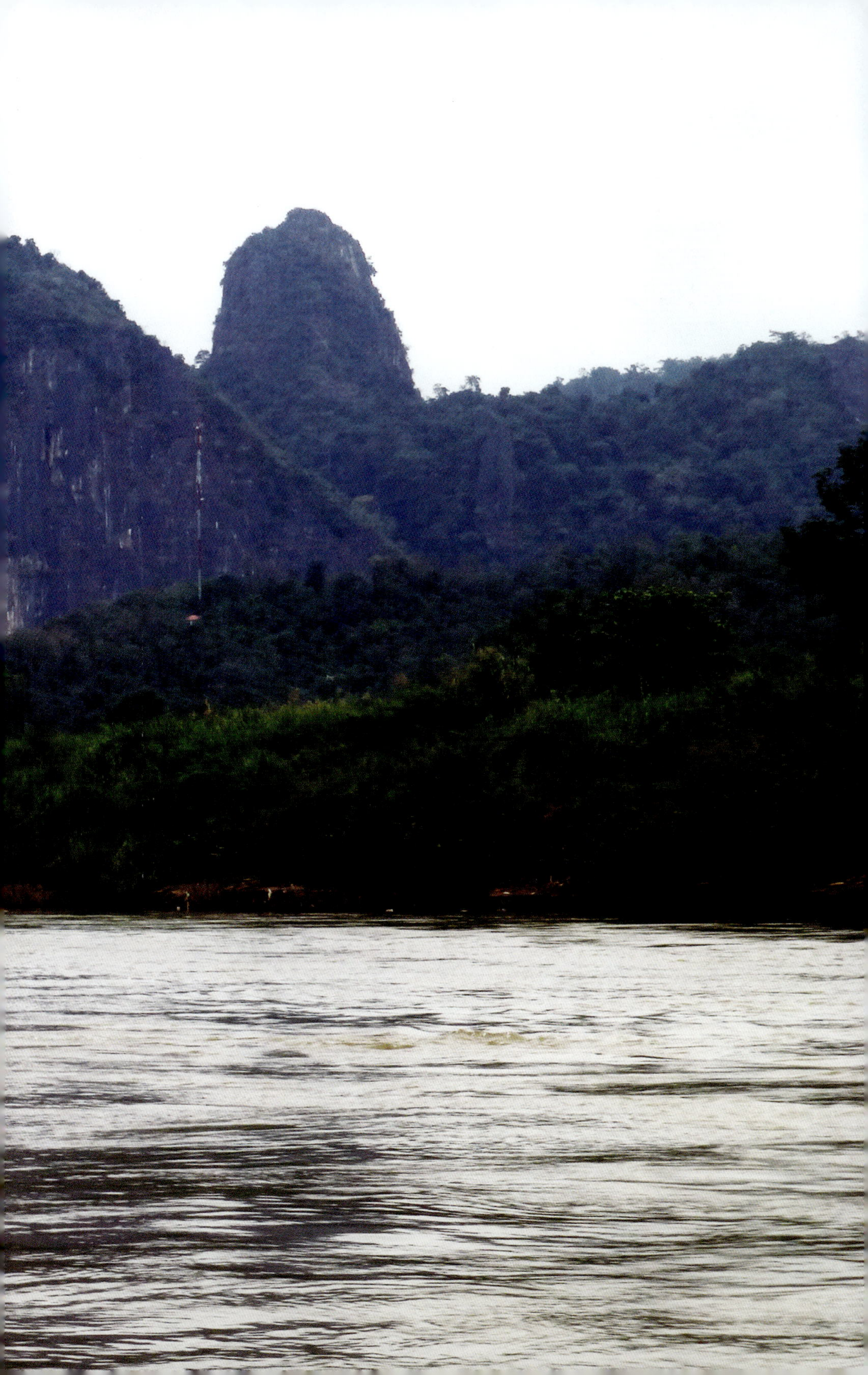

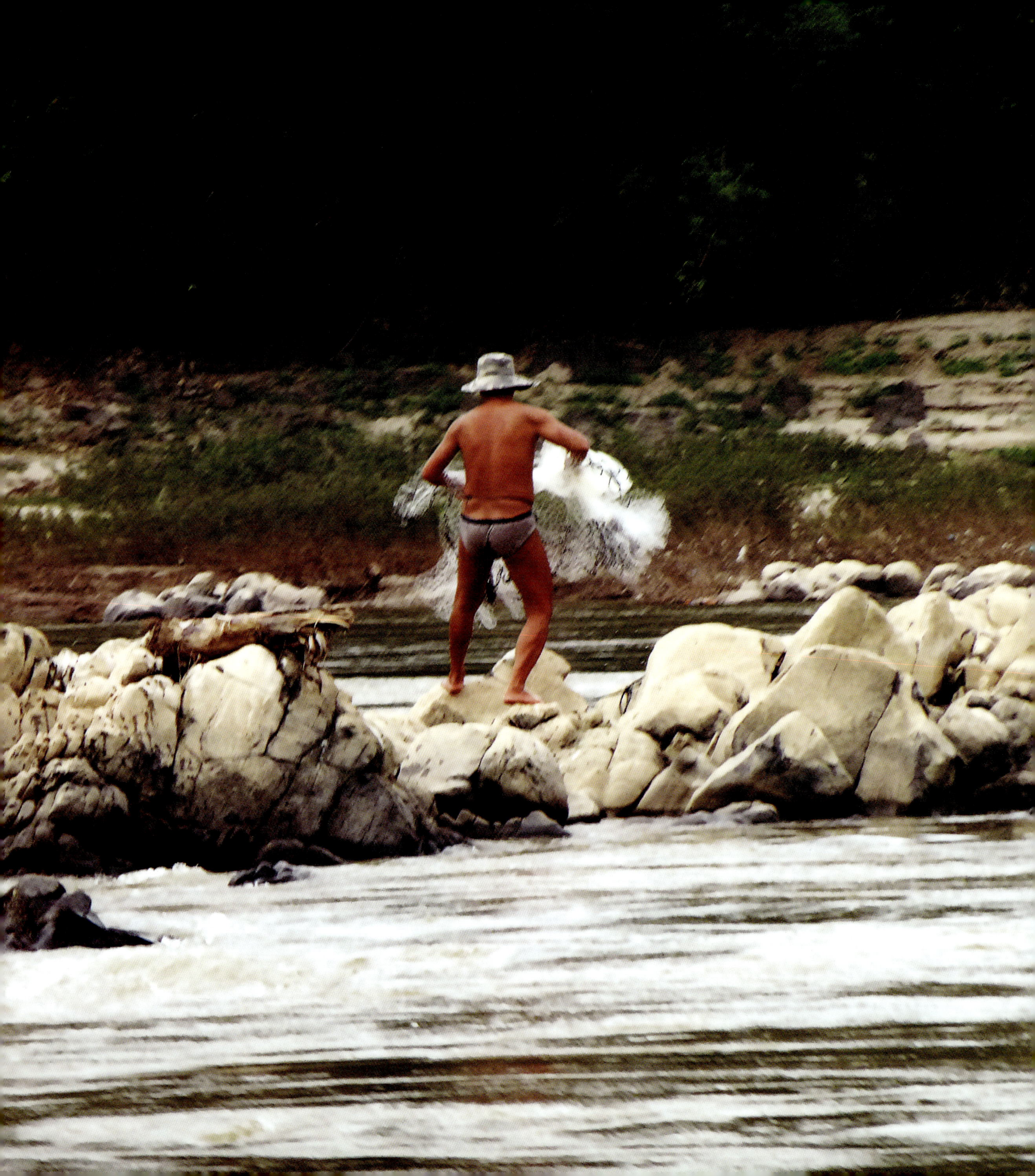

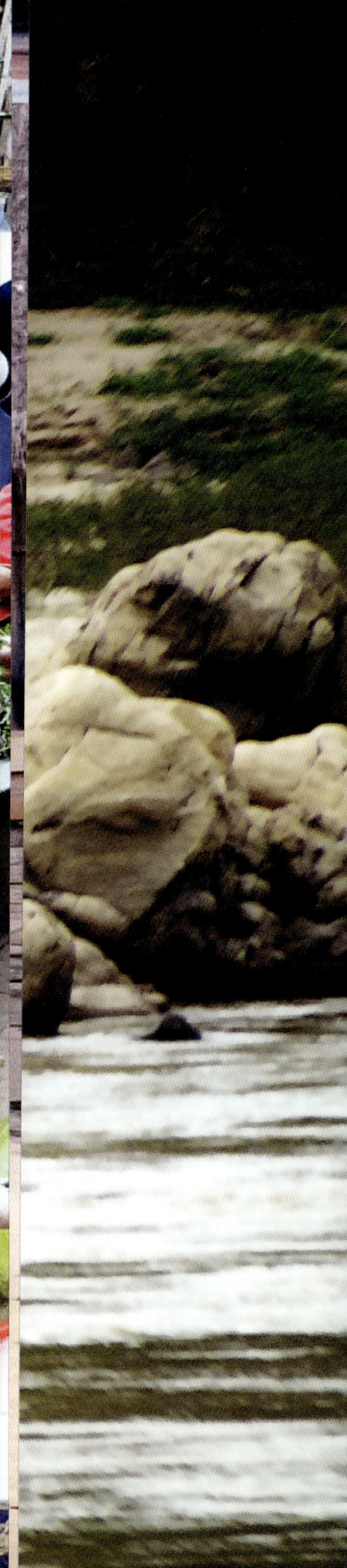

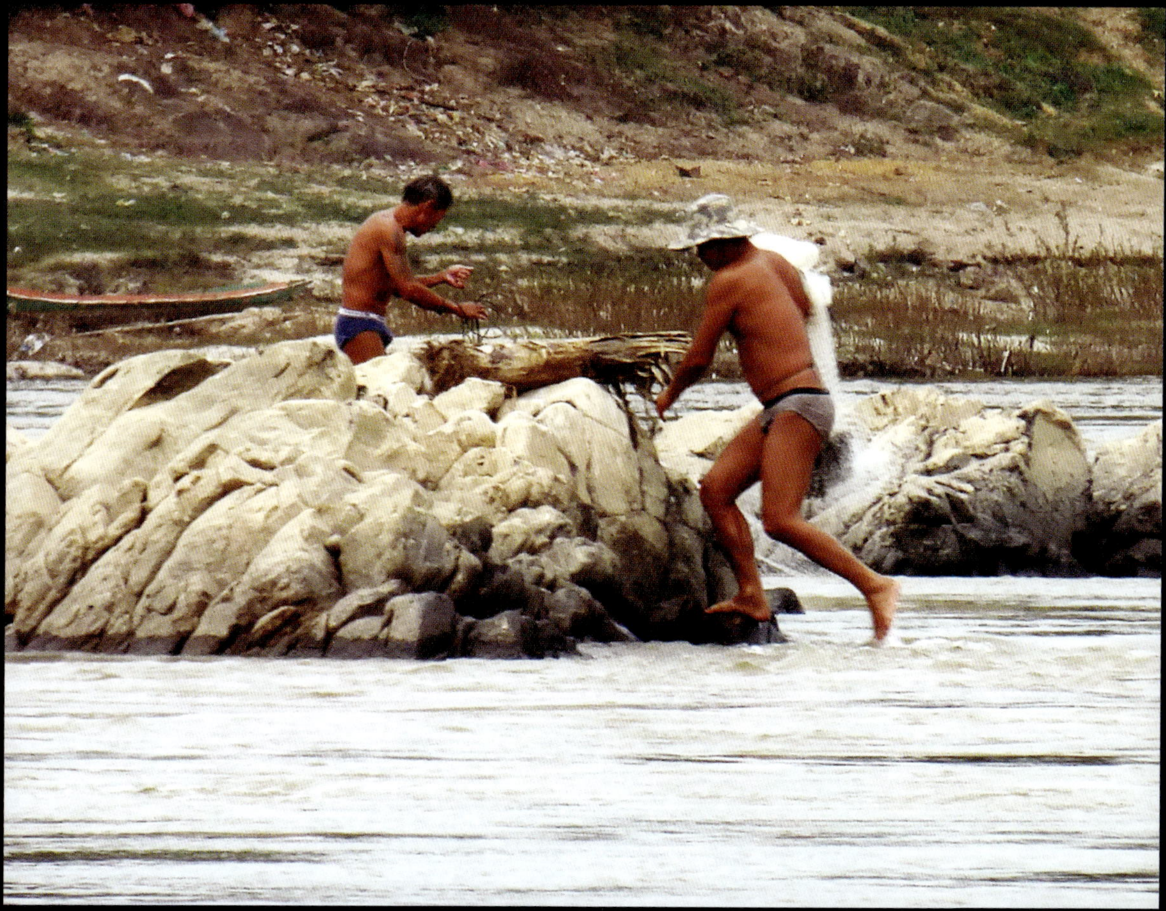

Fishing with nets.

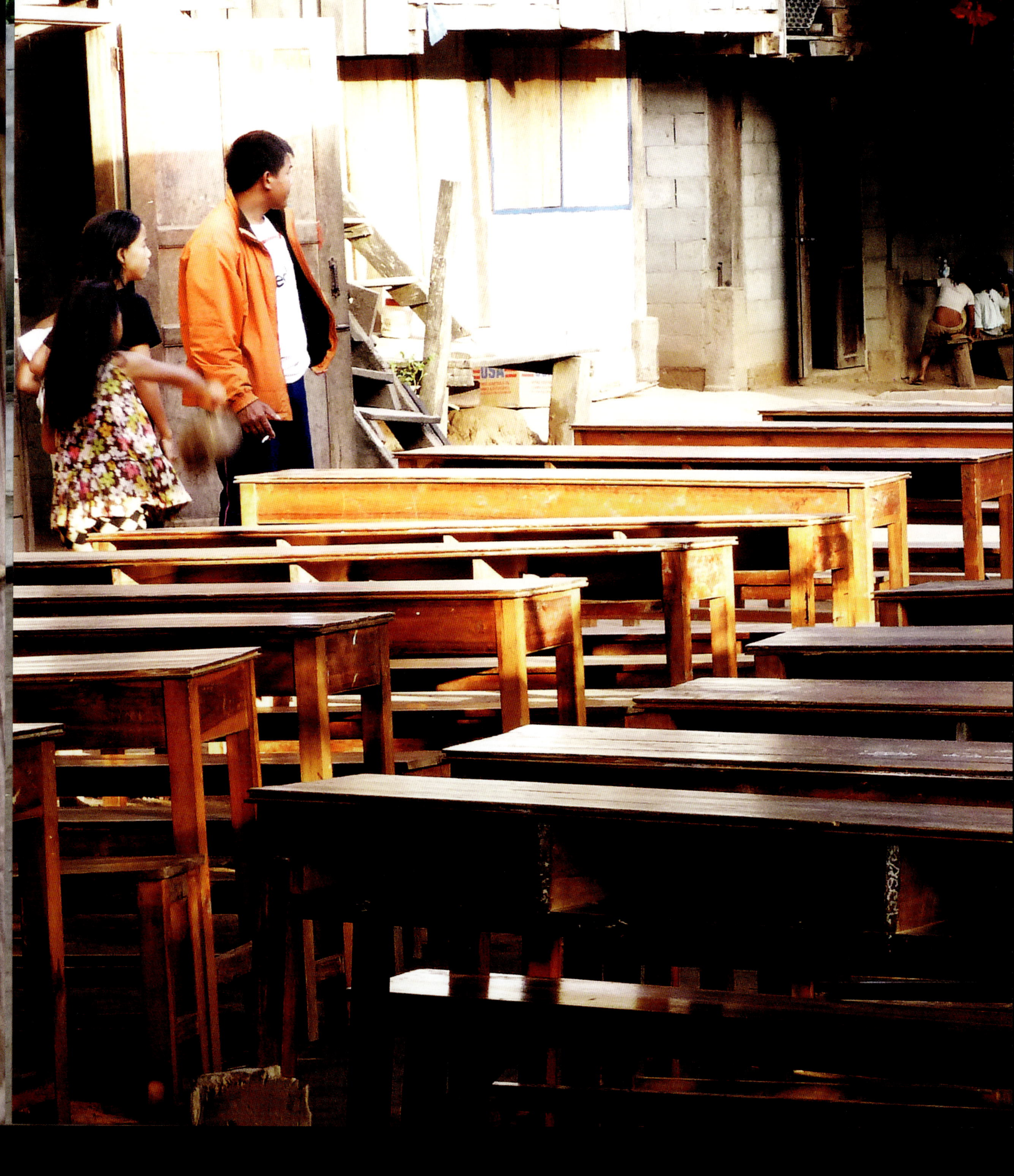
USA

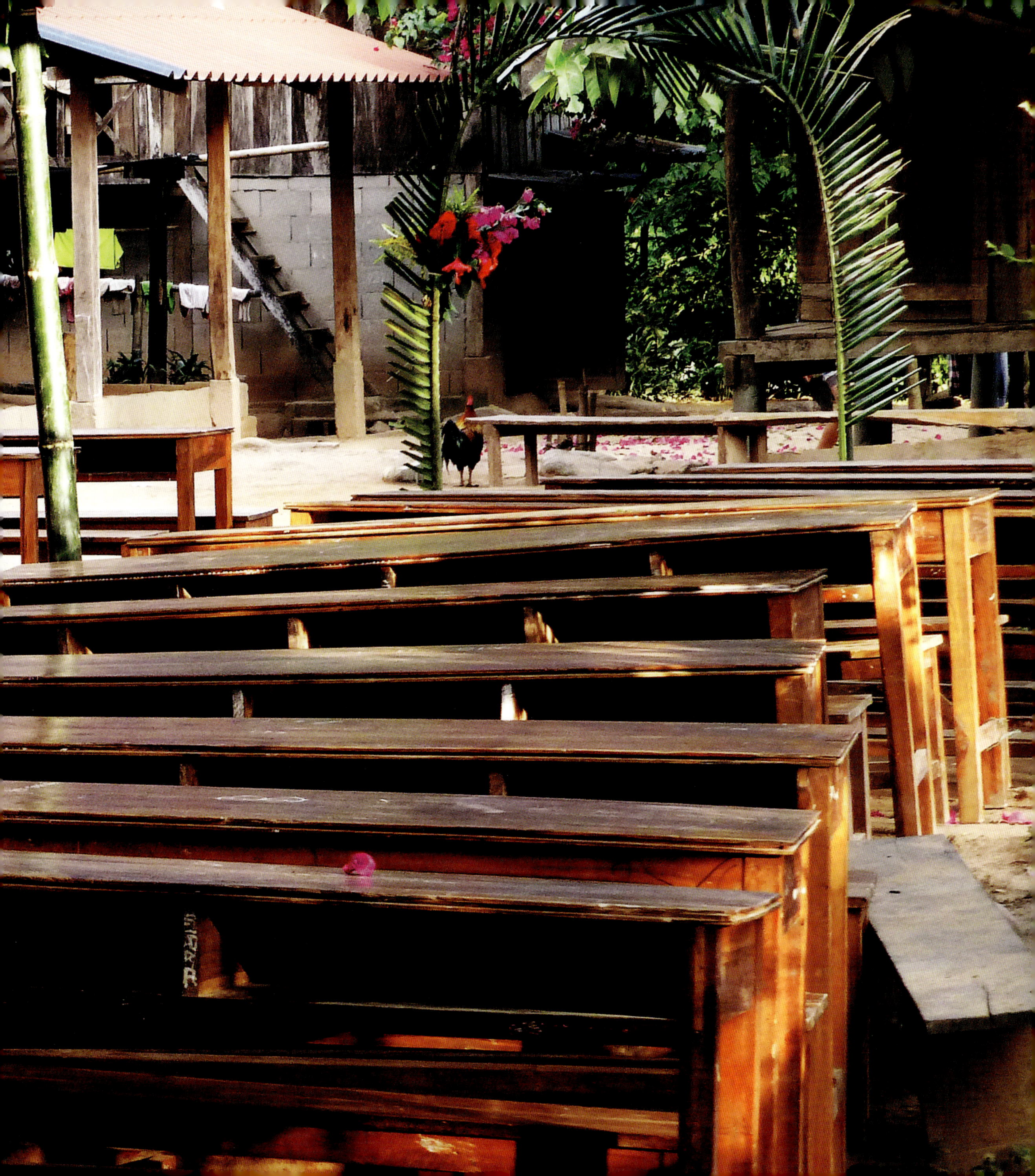

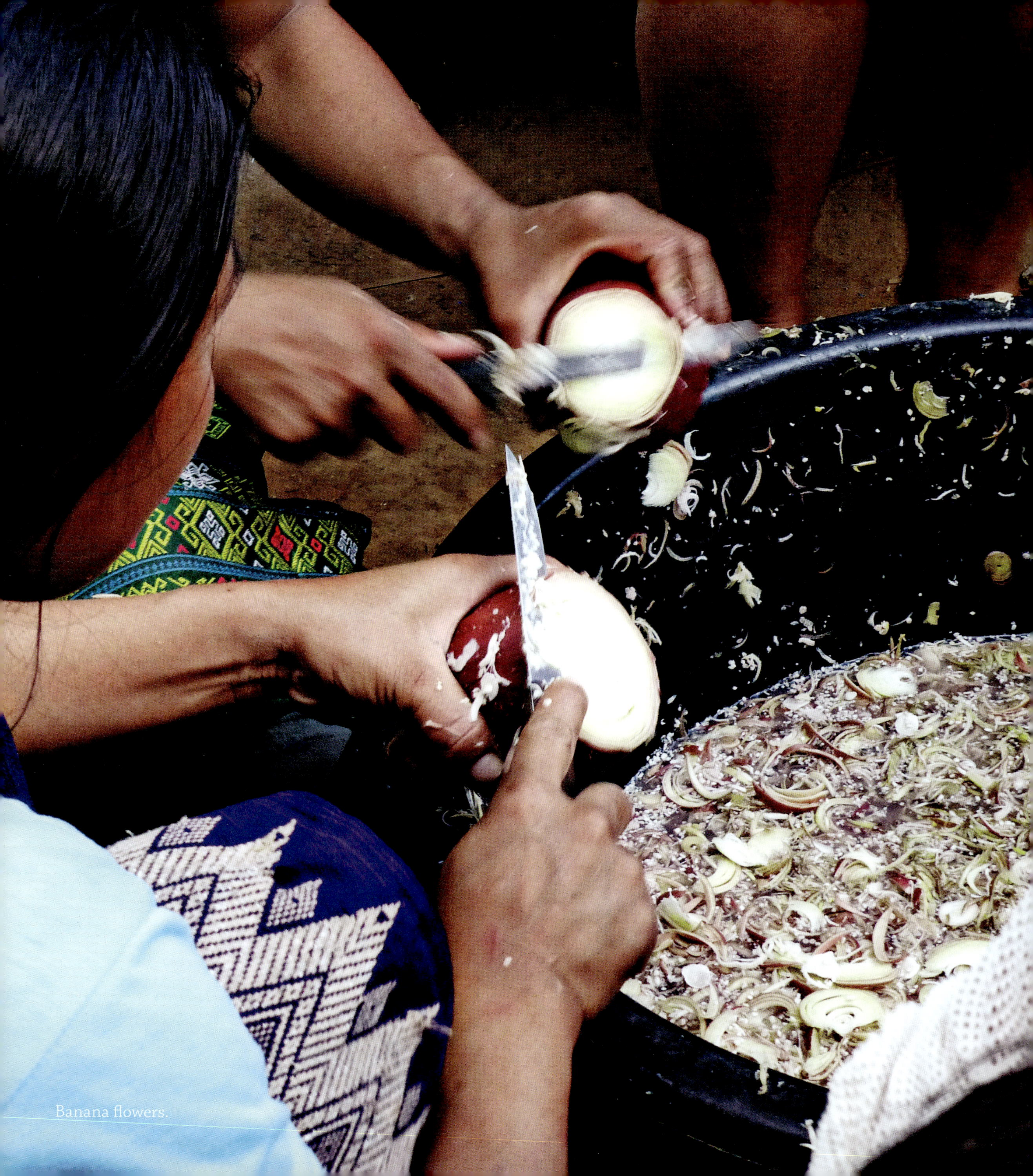

Banana flowers.

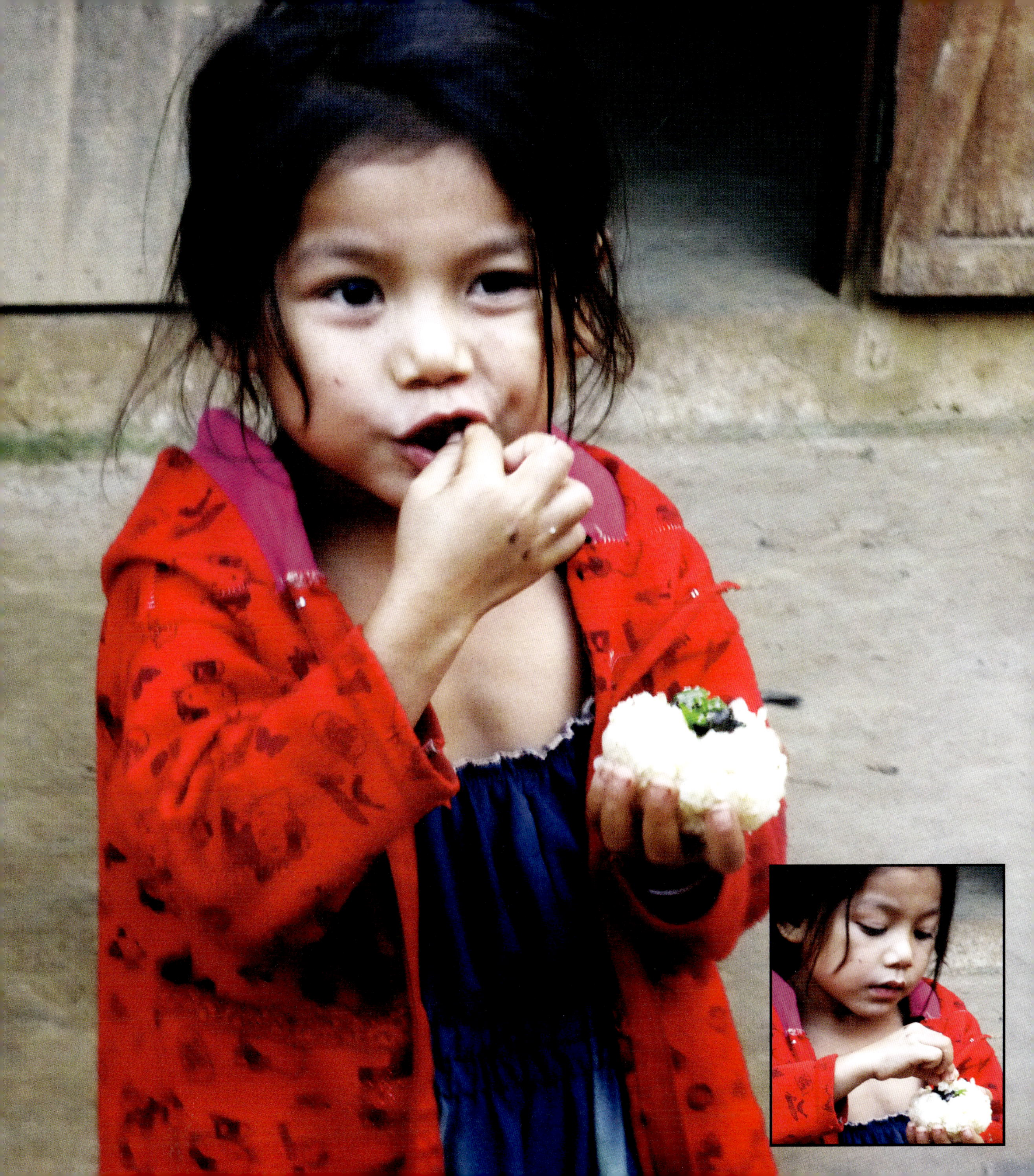

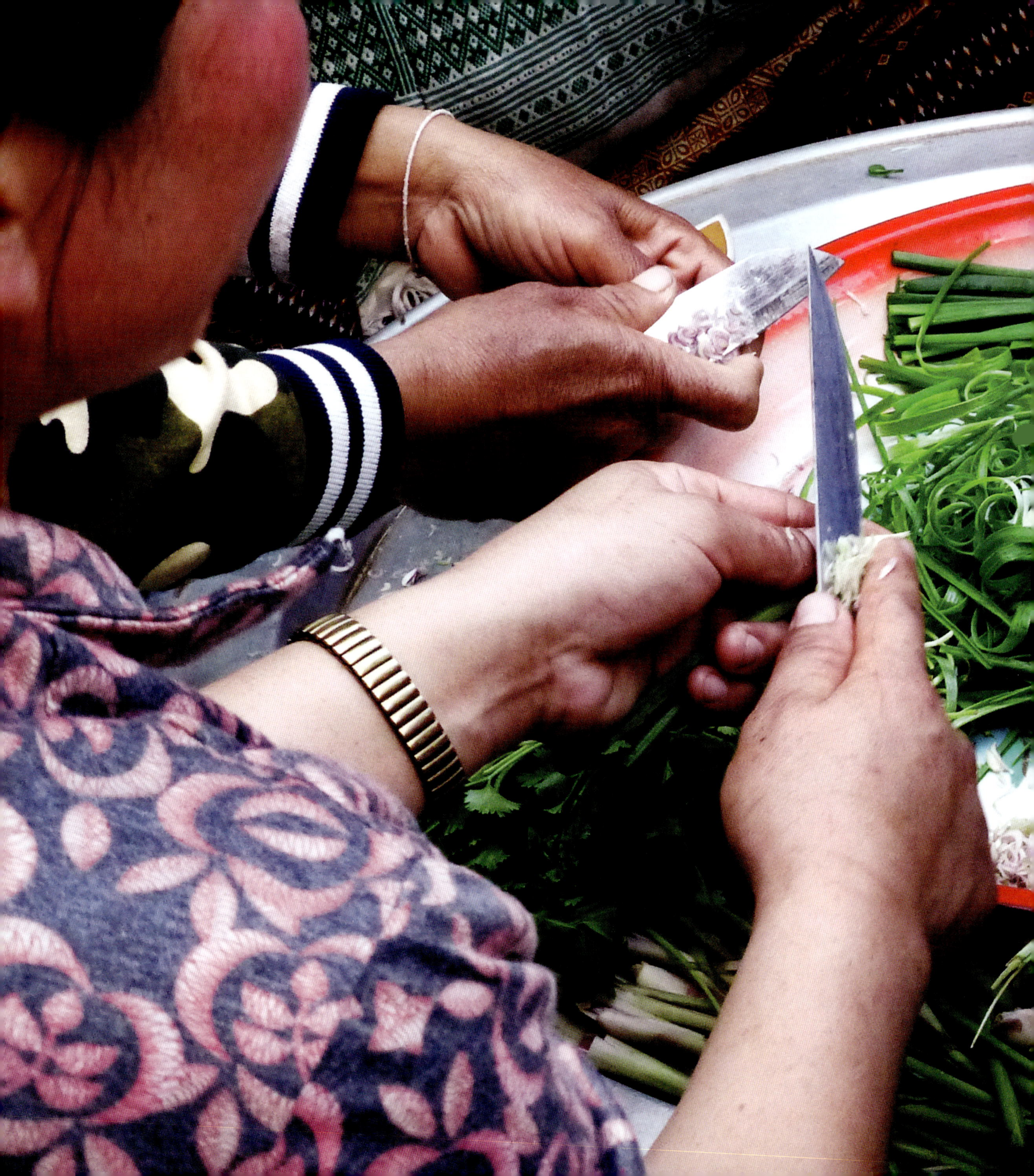

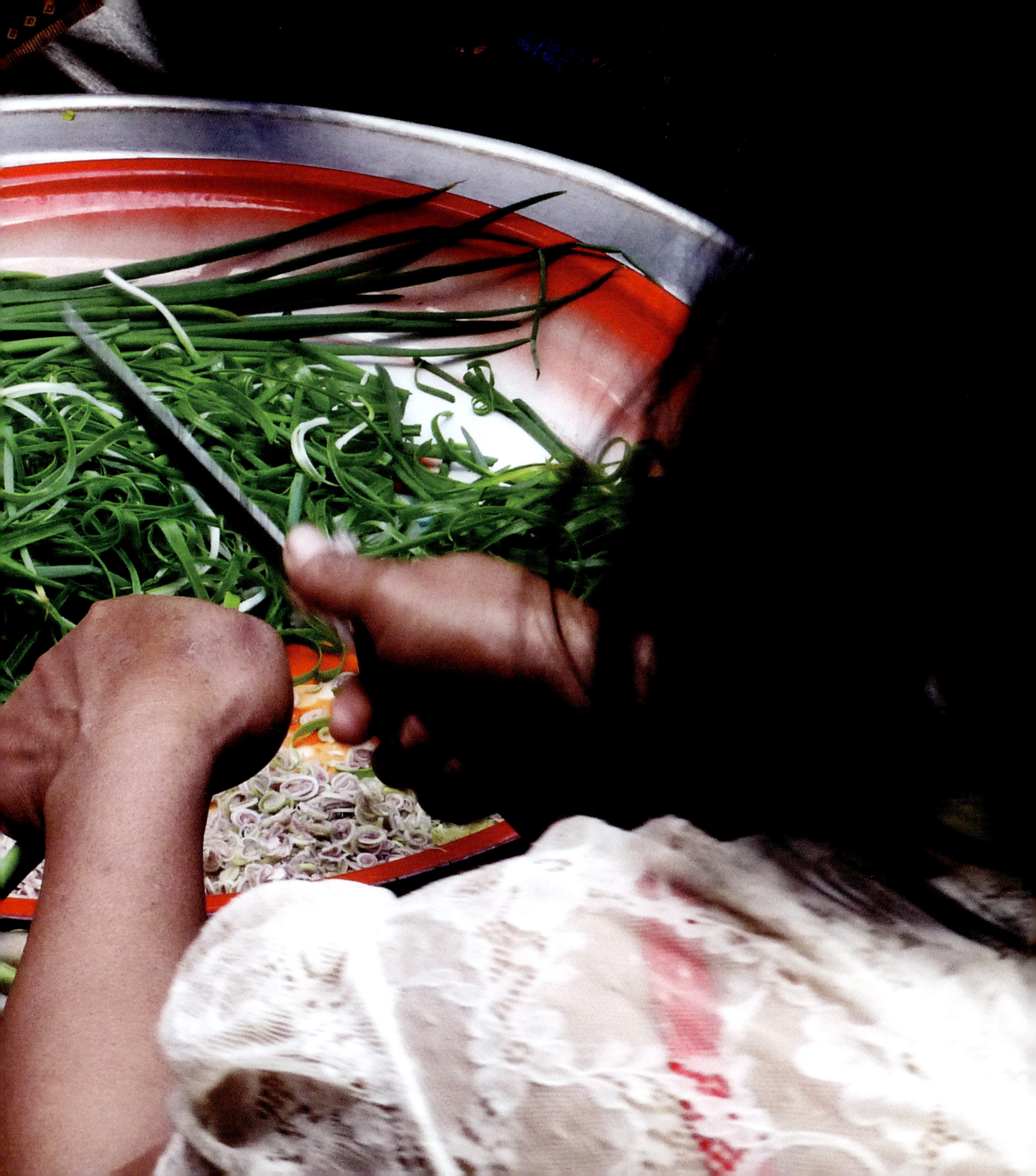

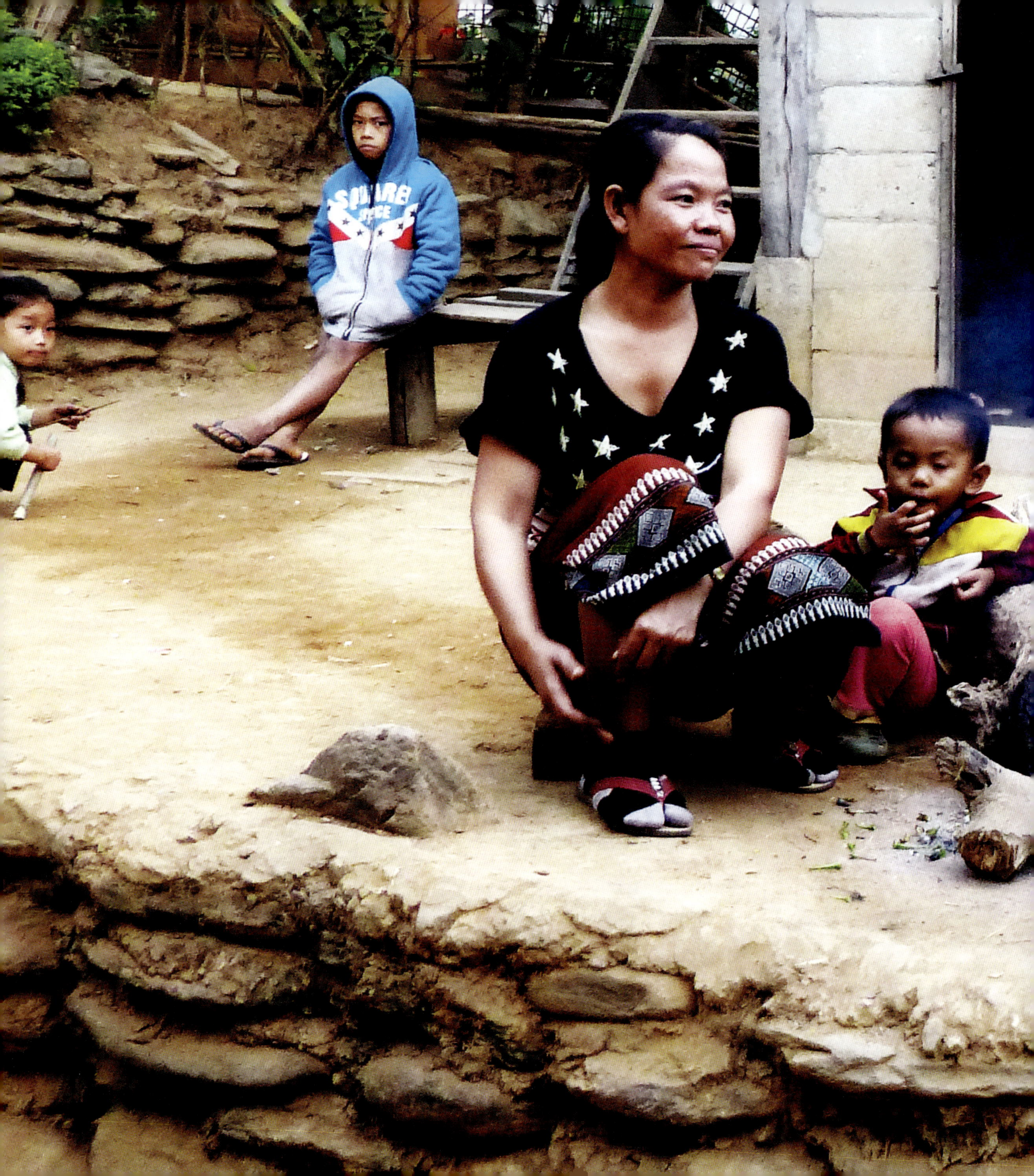

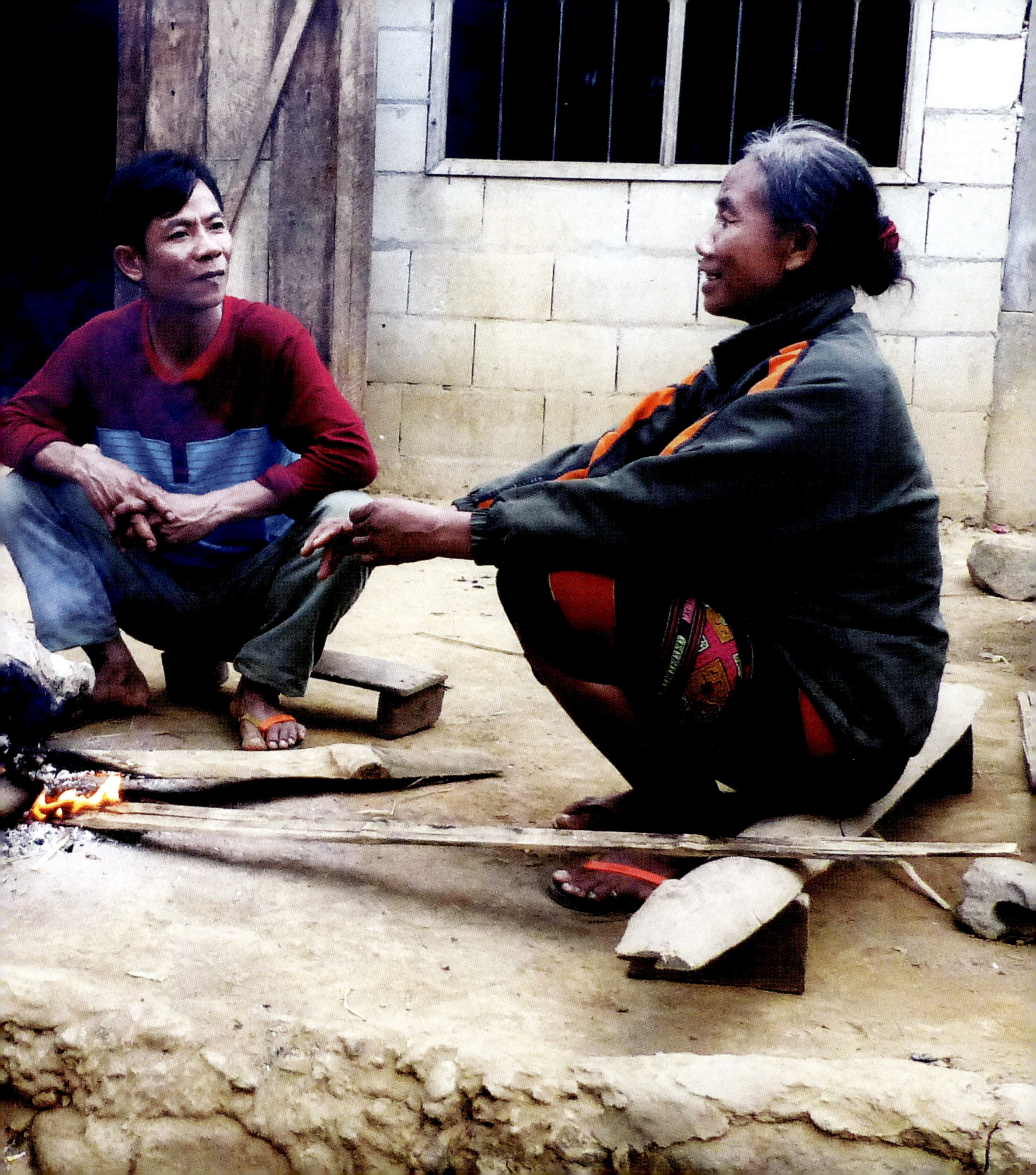

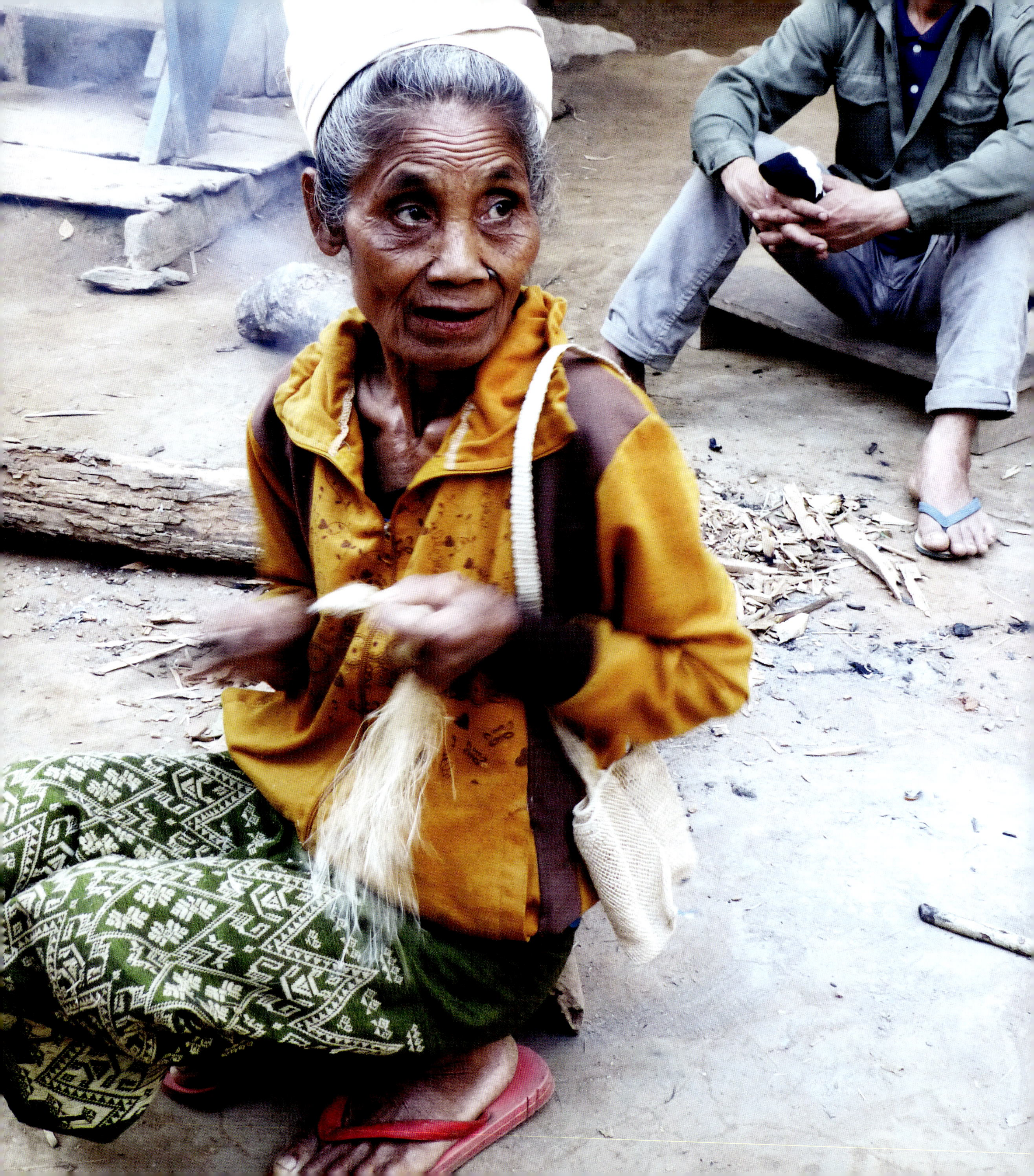

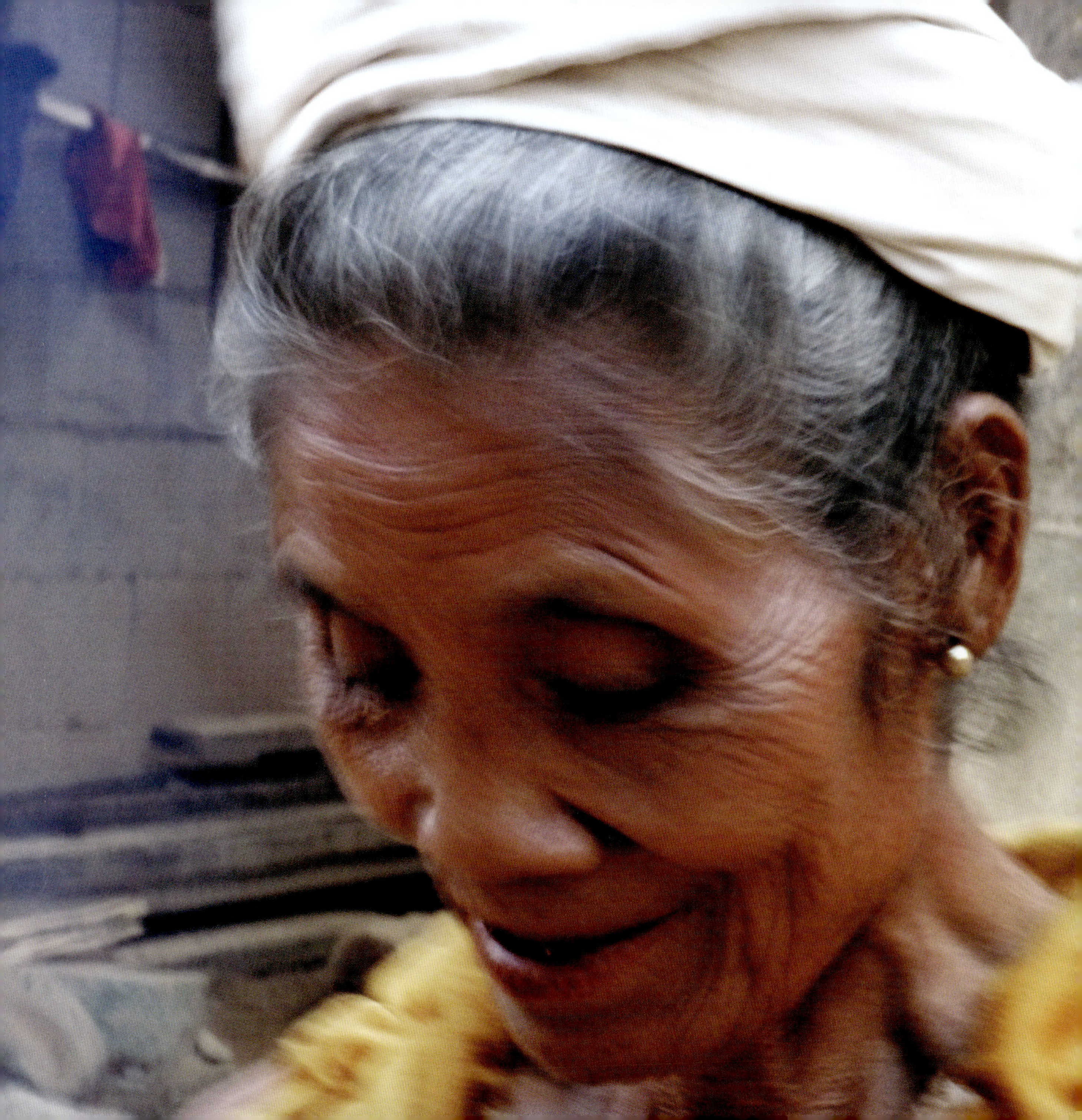

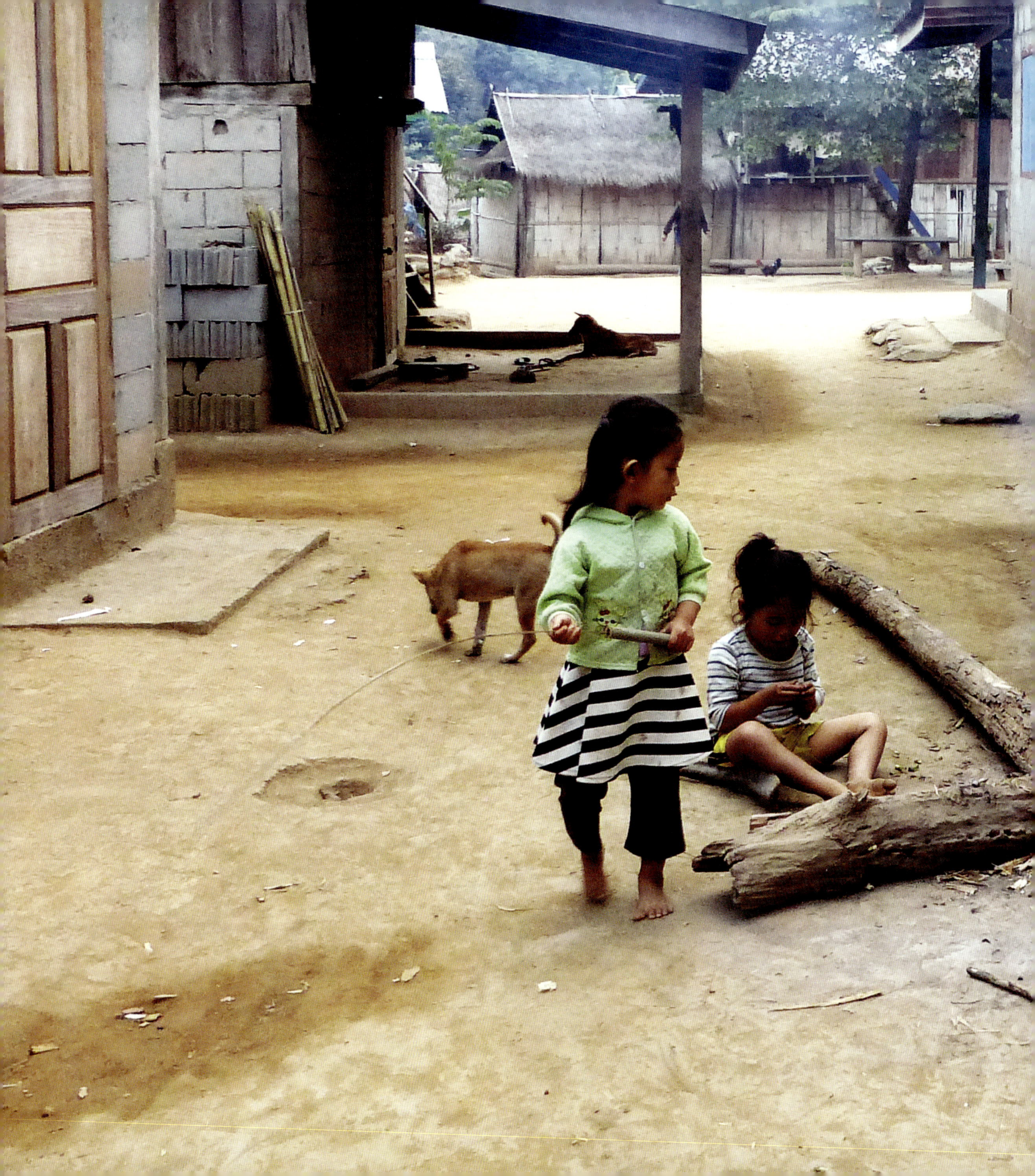

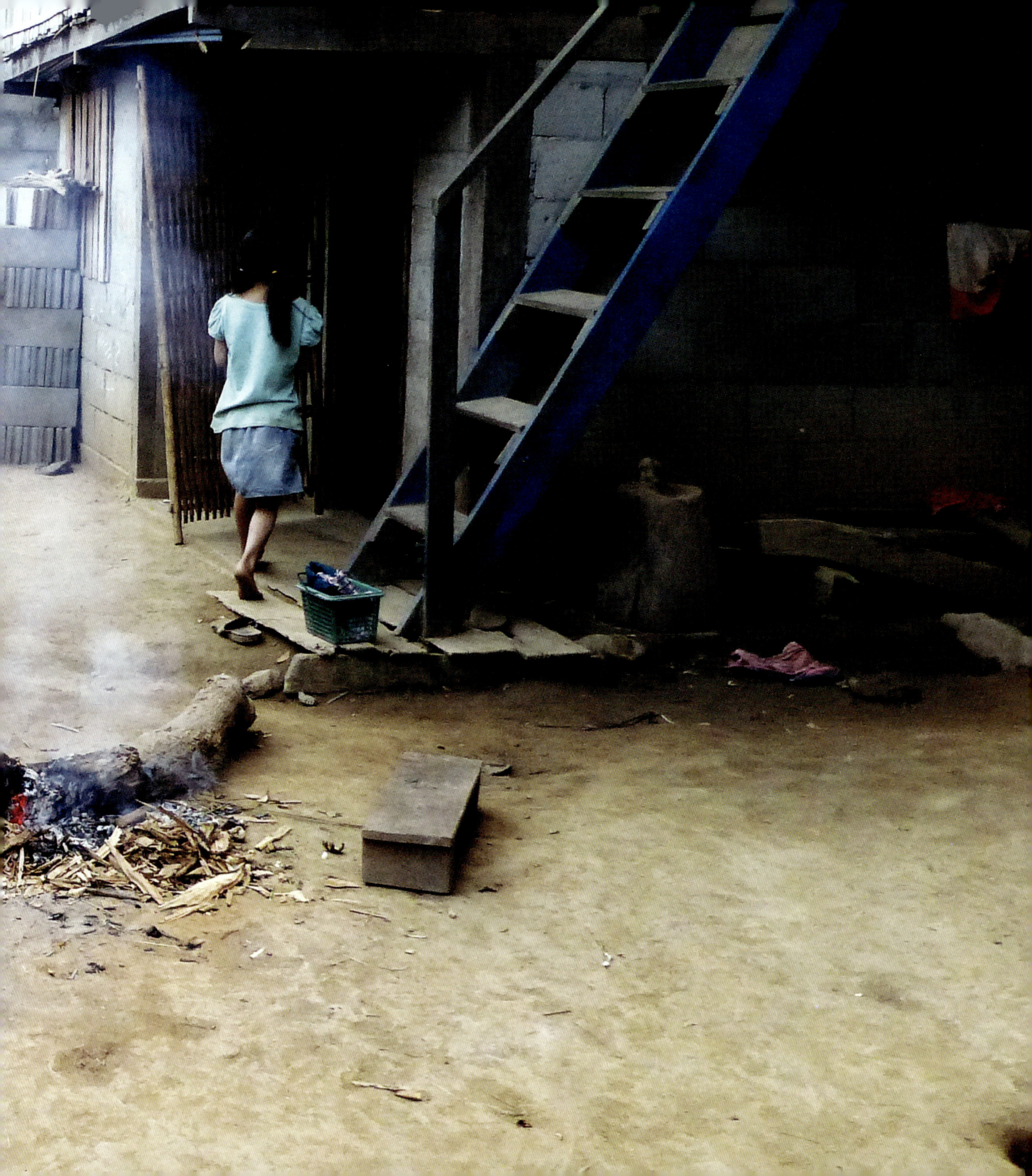

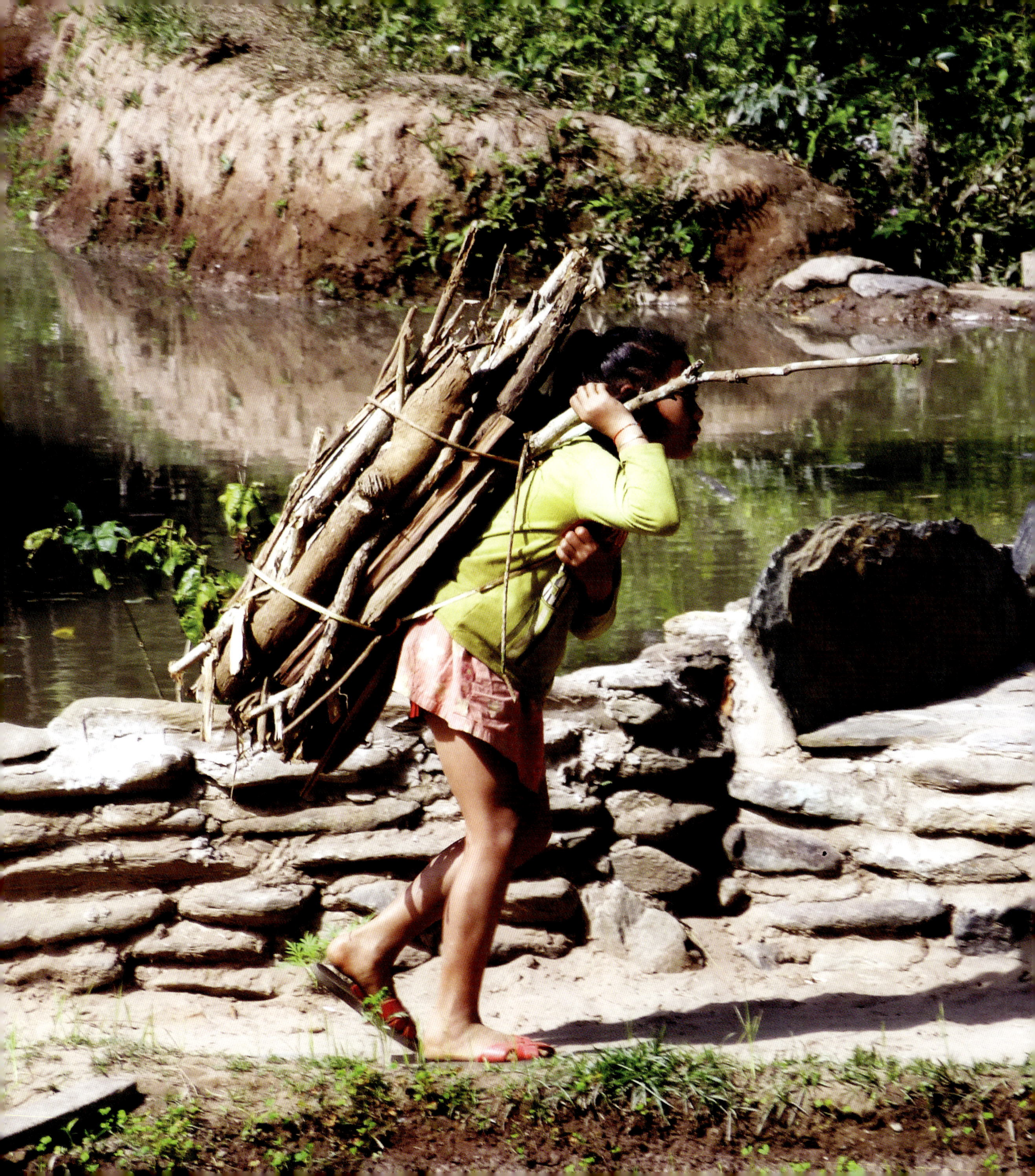

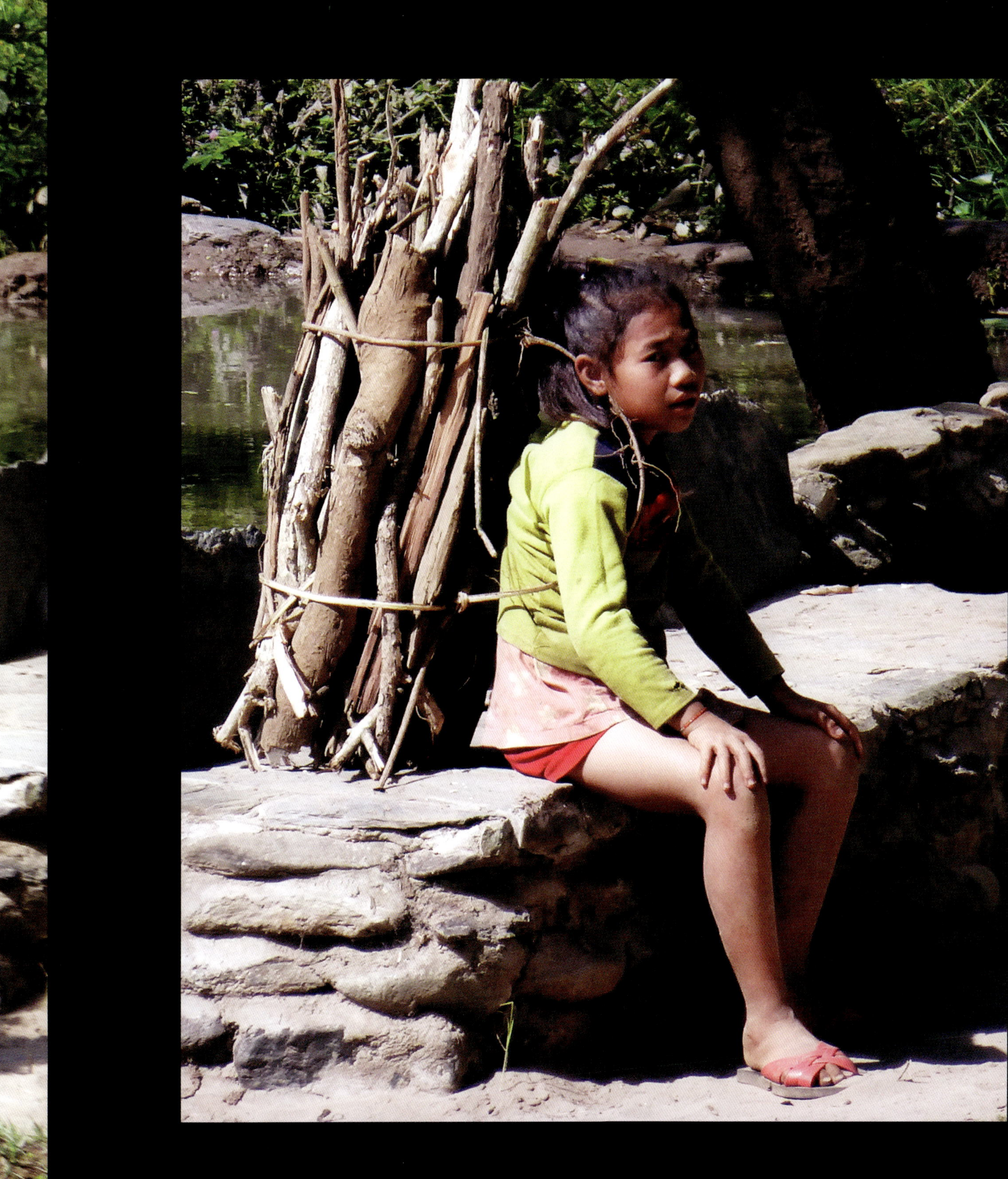

FOUR

On Tonlé Sap Lake Cambodia

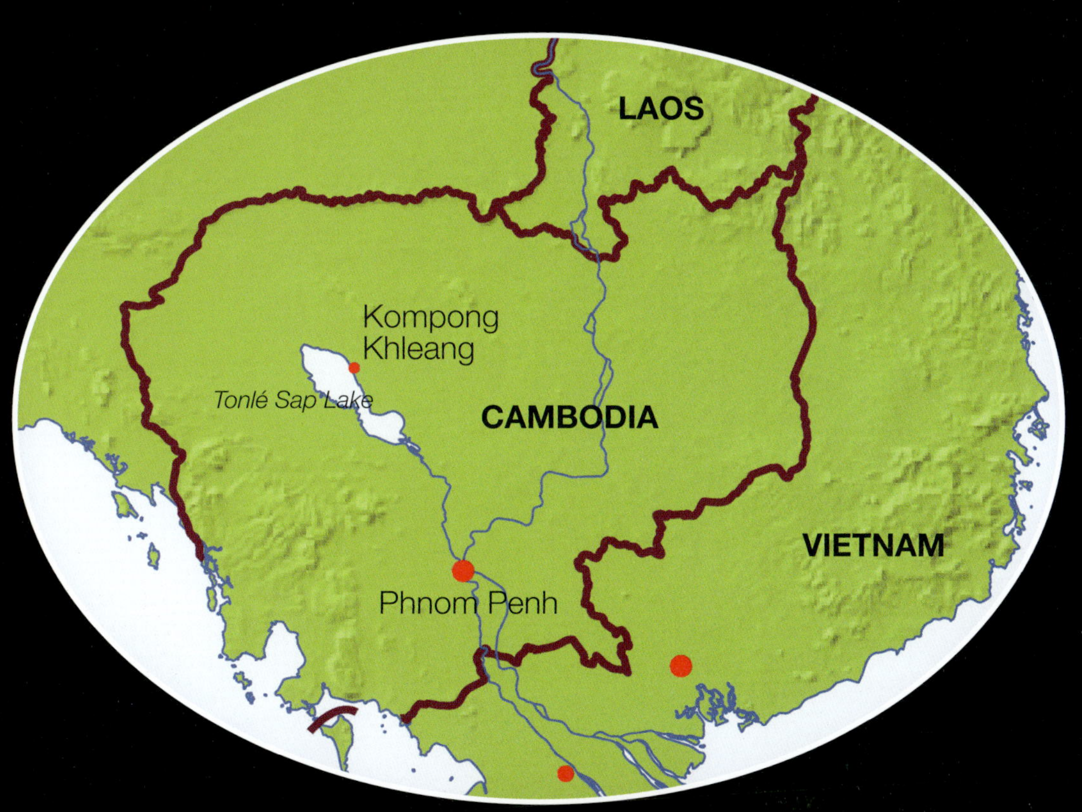

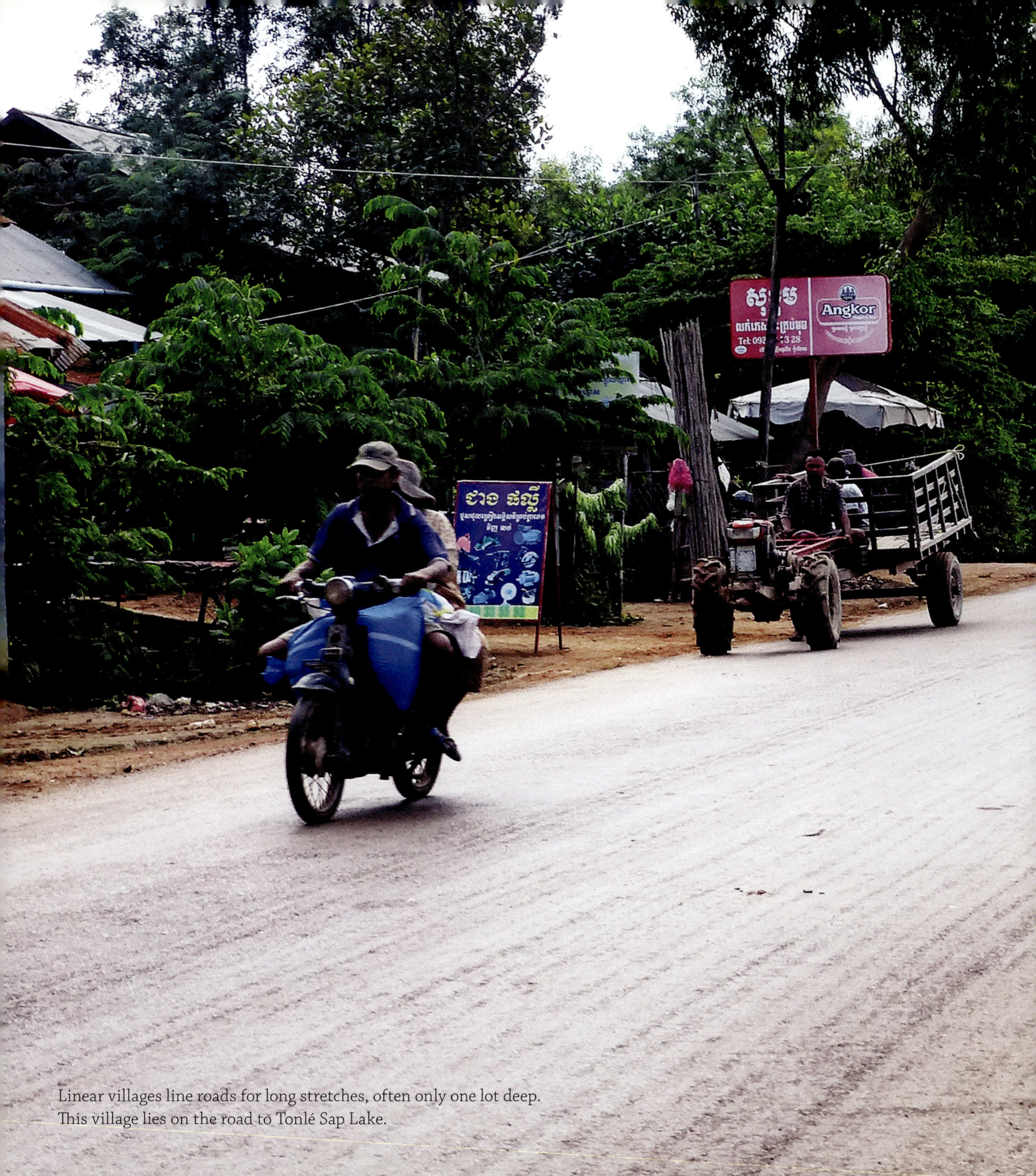

Linear villages line roads for long stretches, often only one lot deep. This village lies on the road to Tonlé Sap Lake.

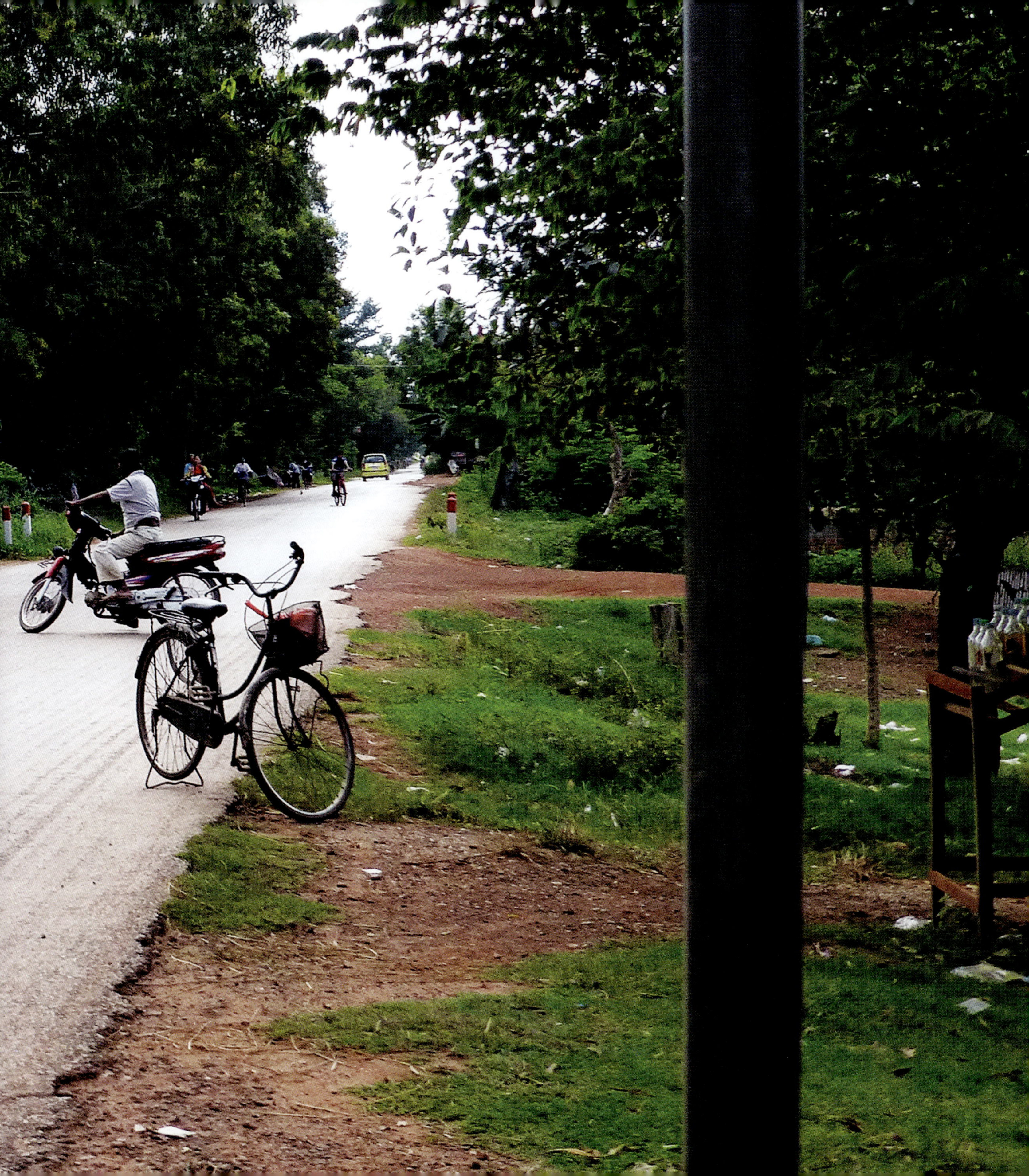

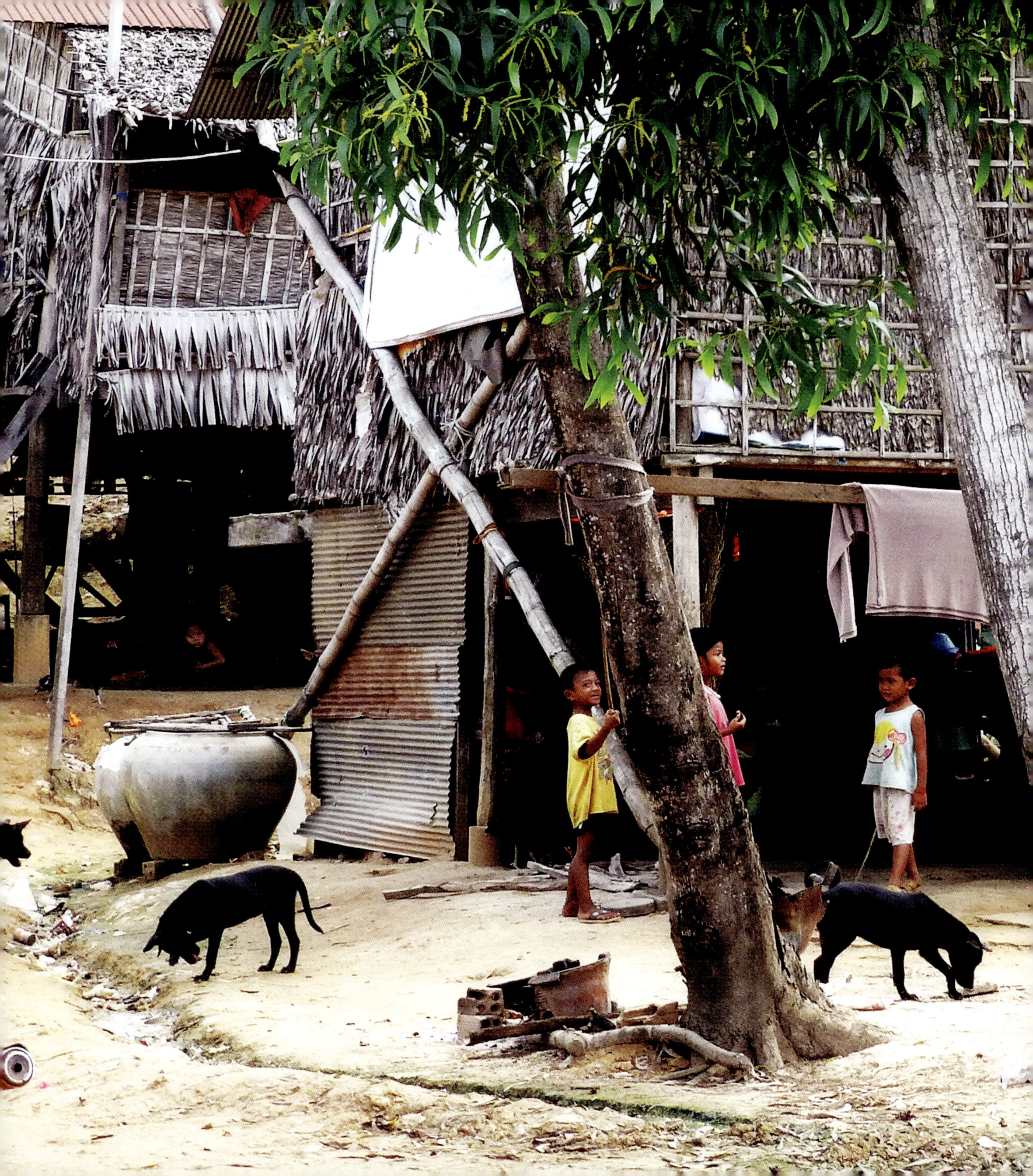

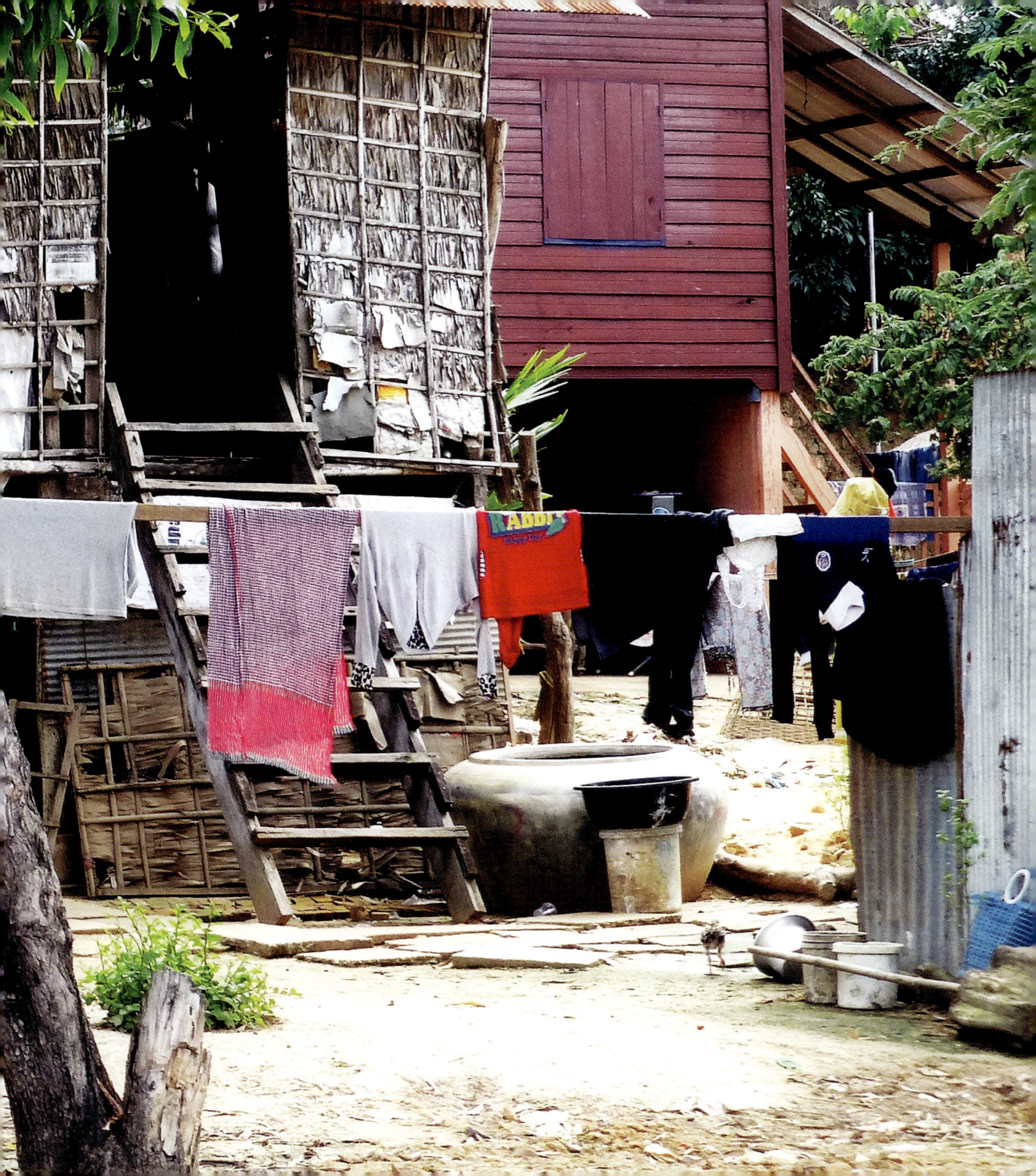

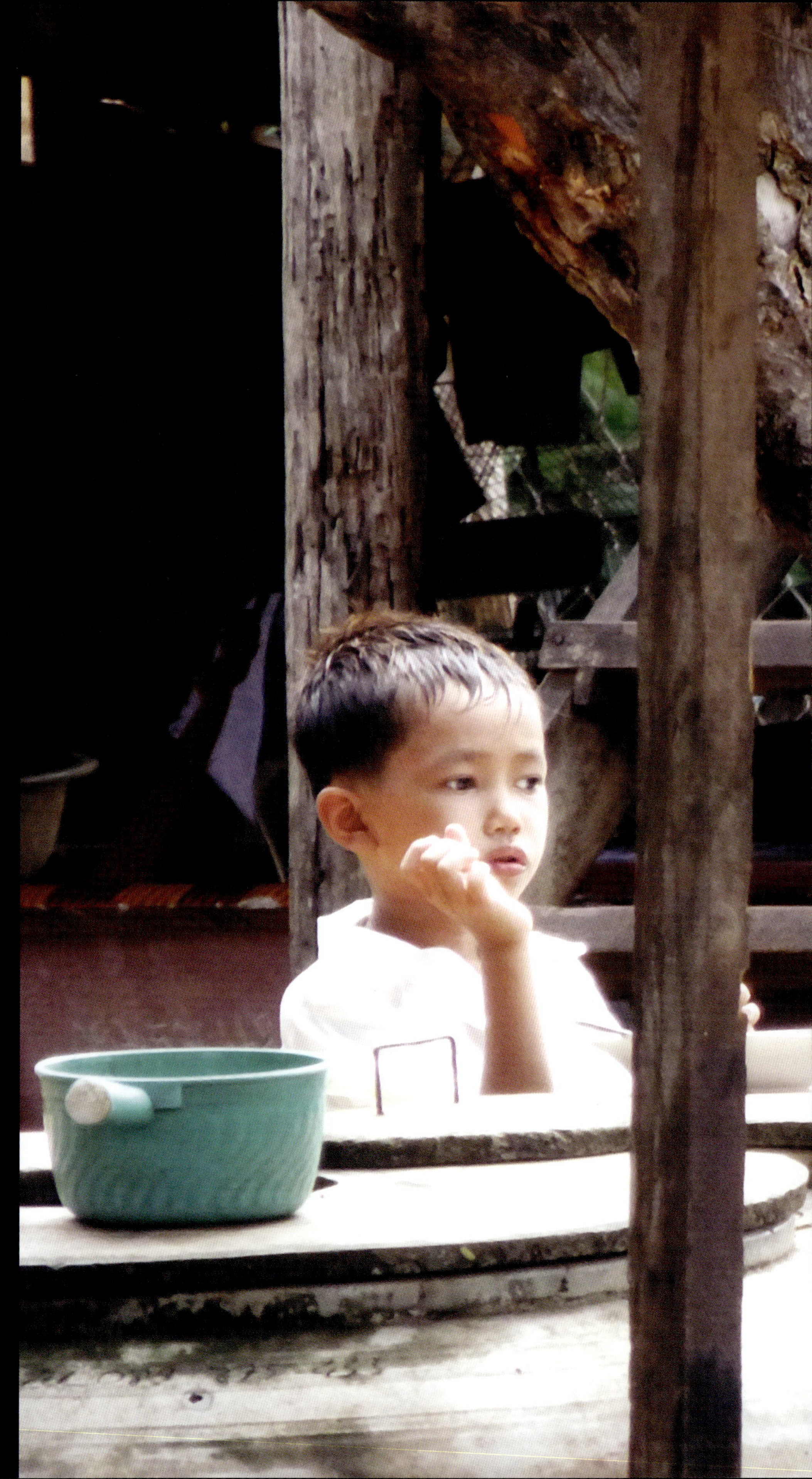

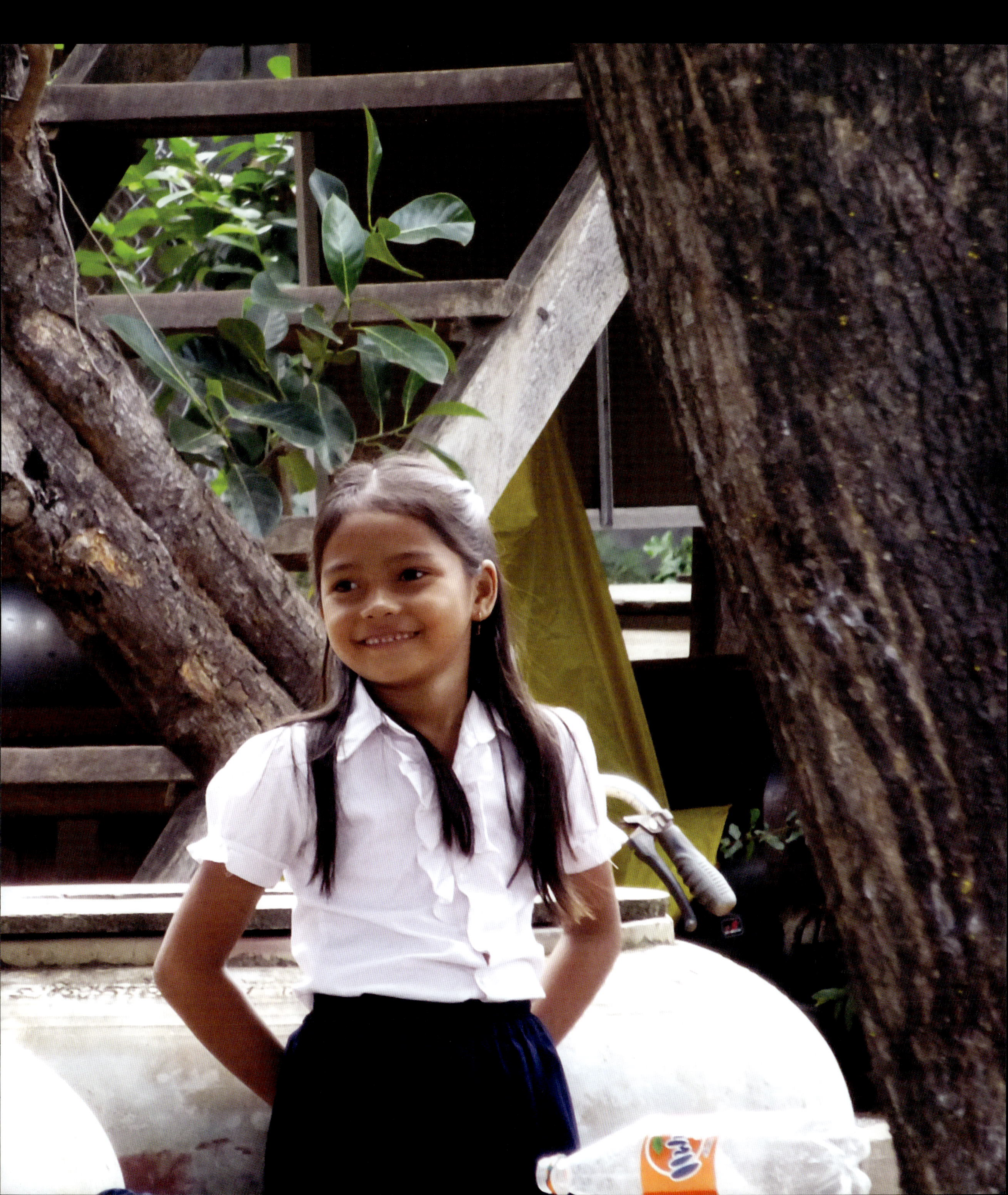

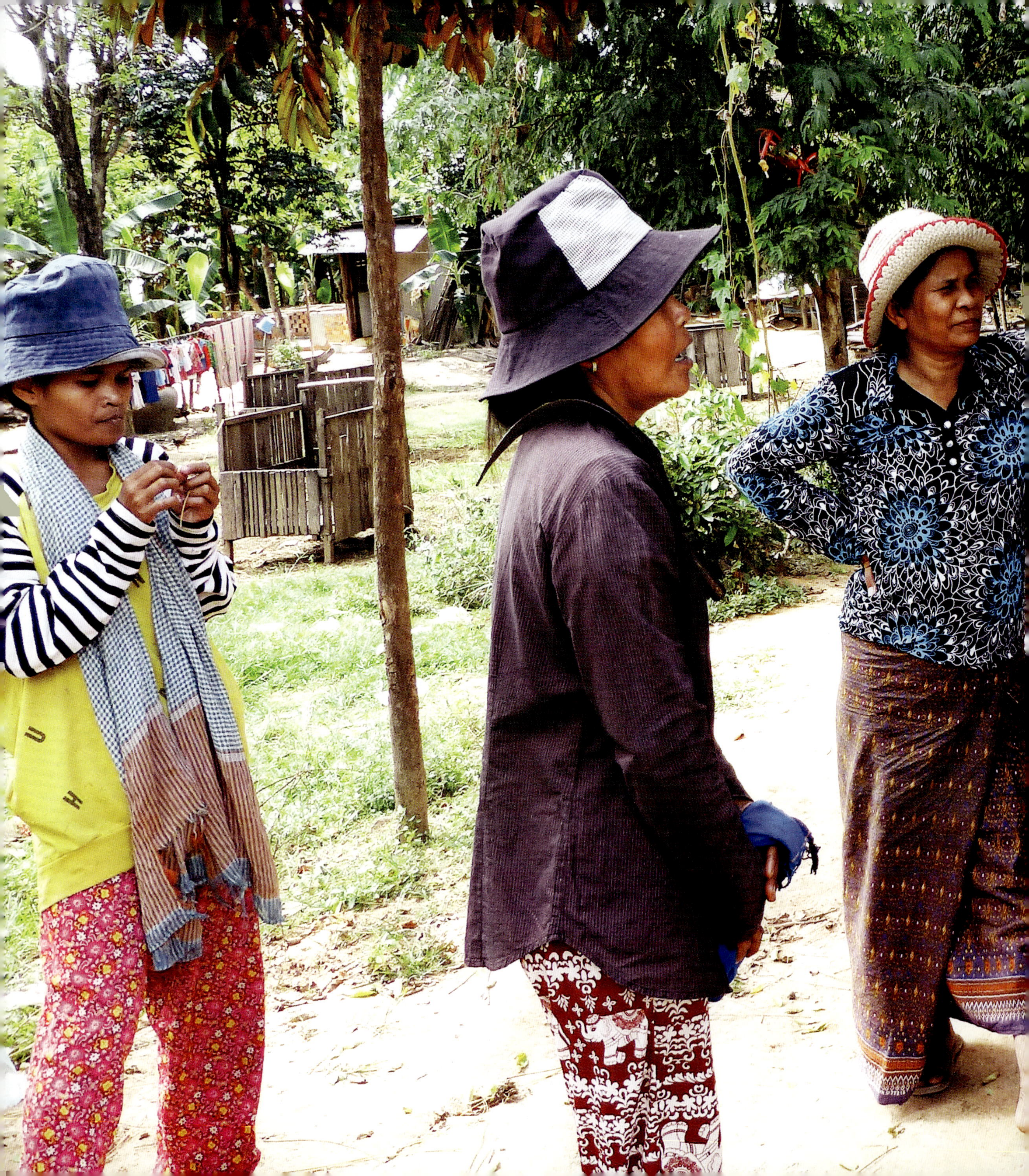

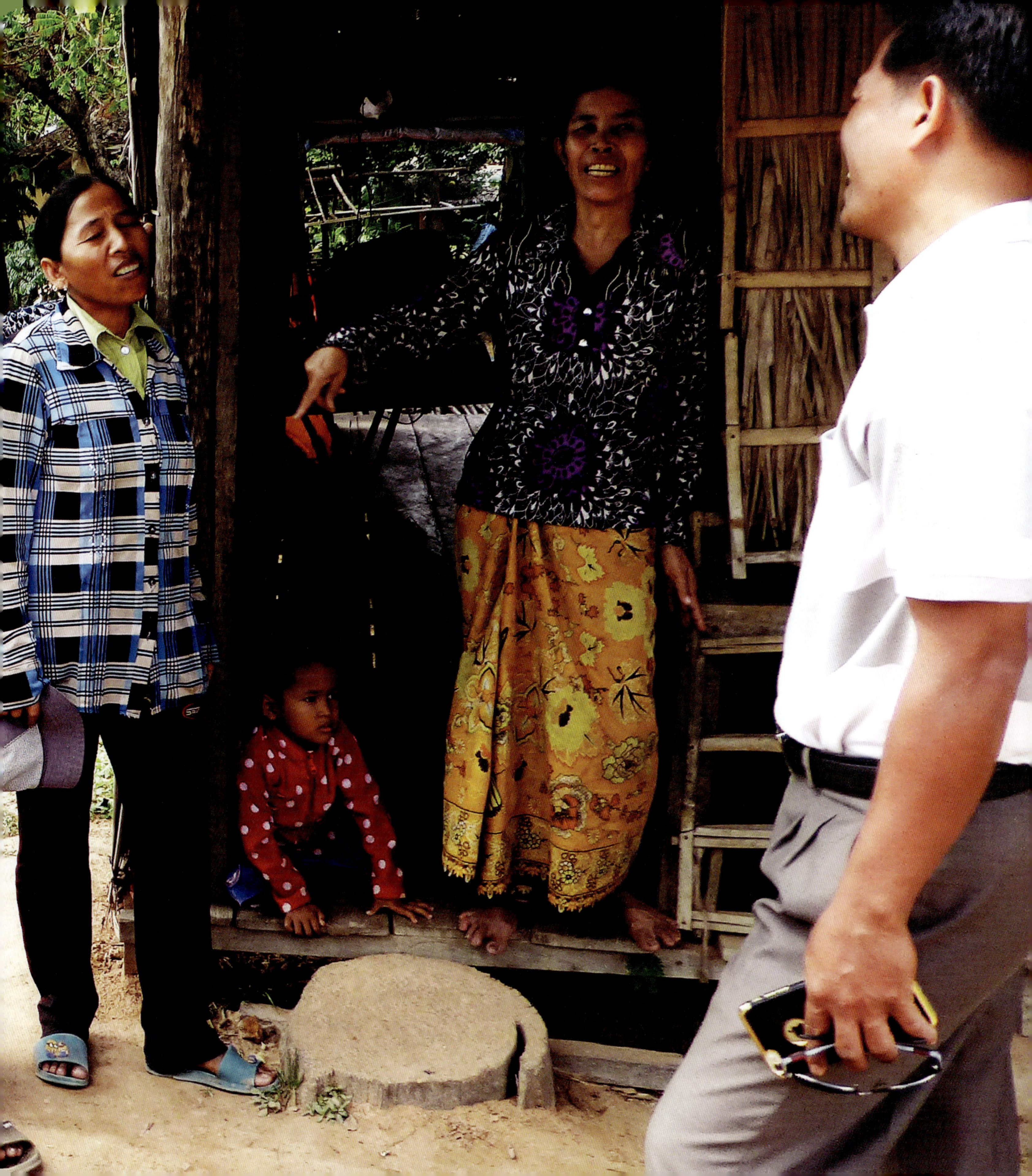

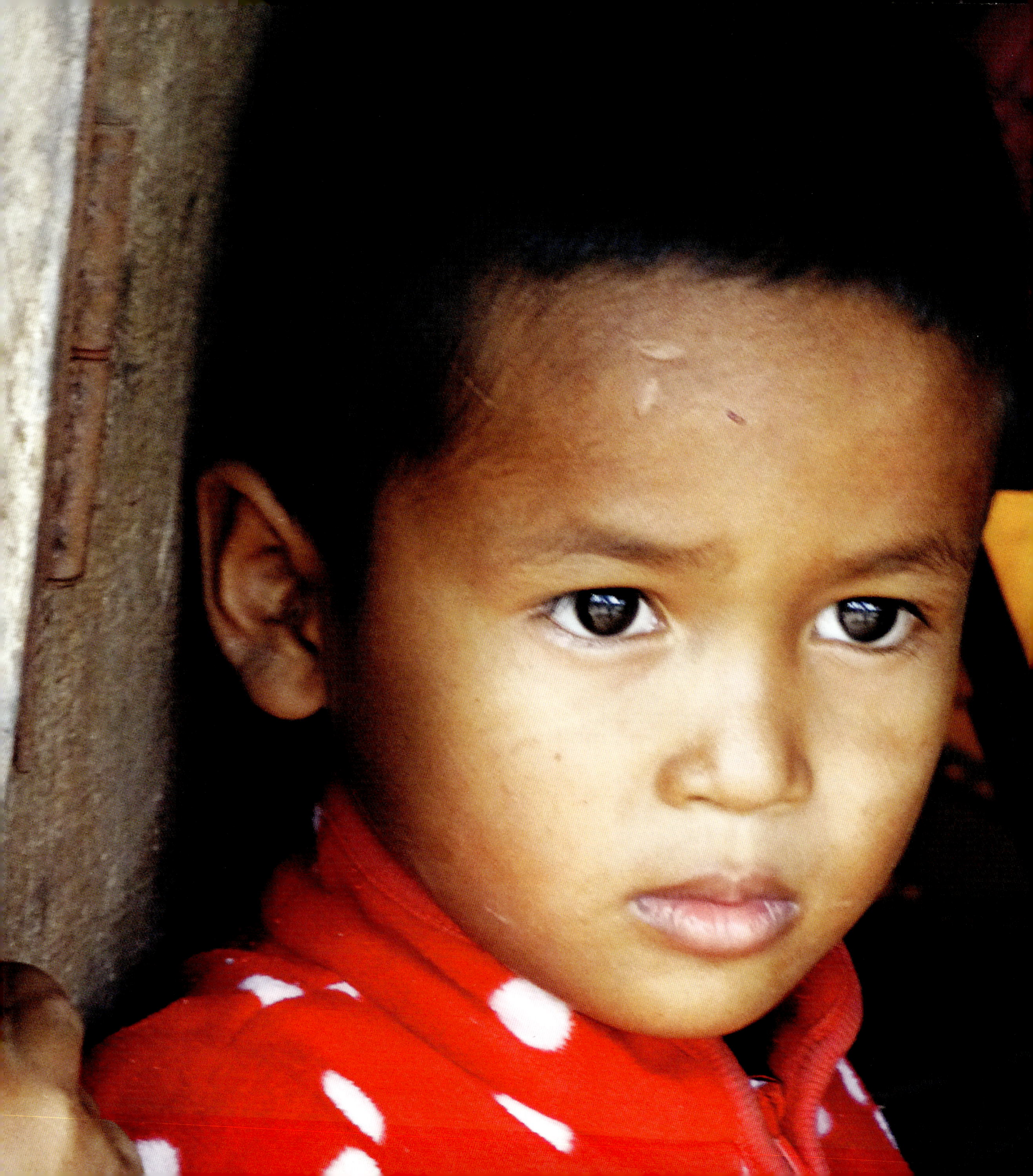

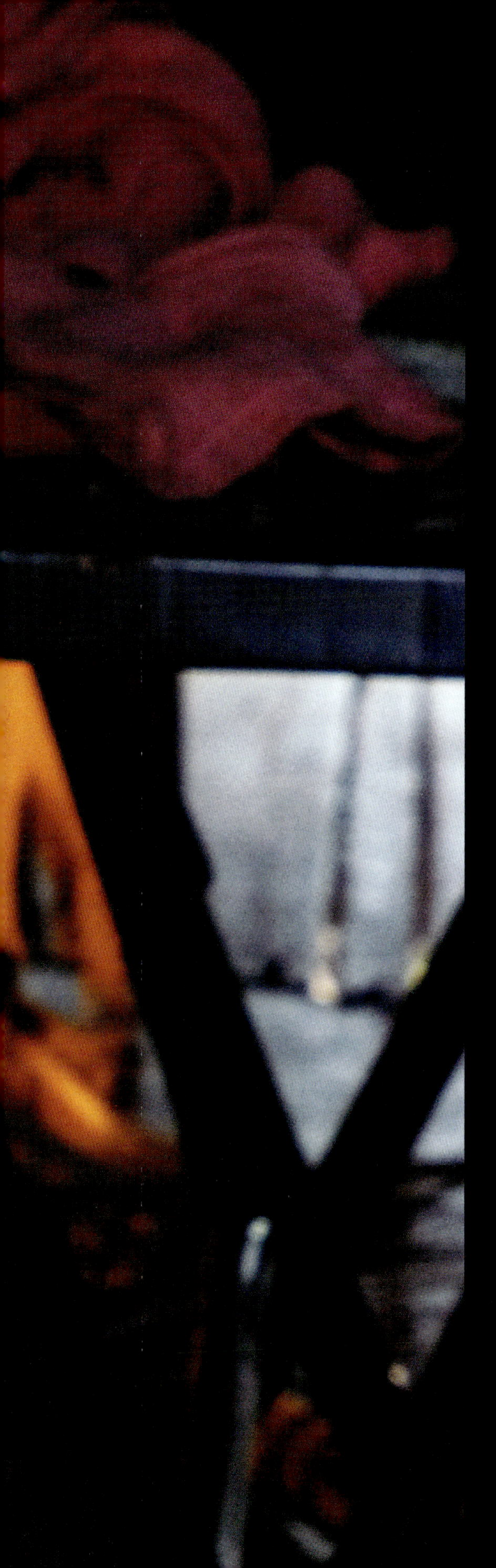

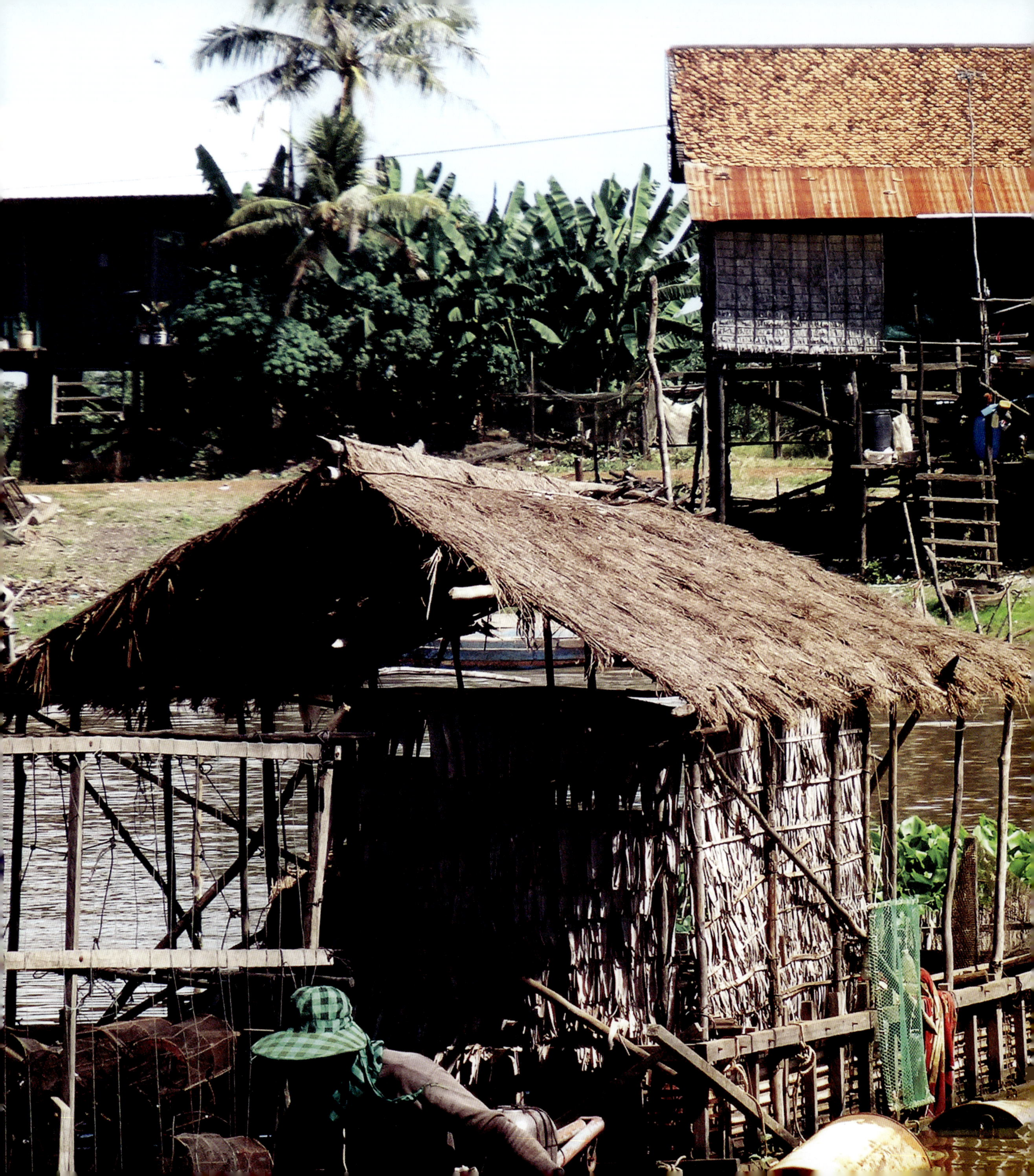

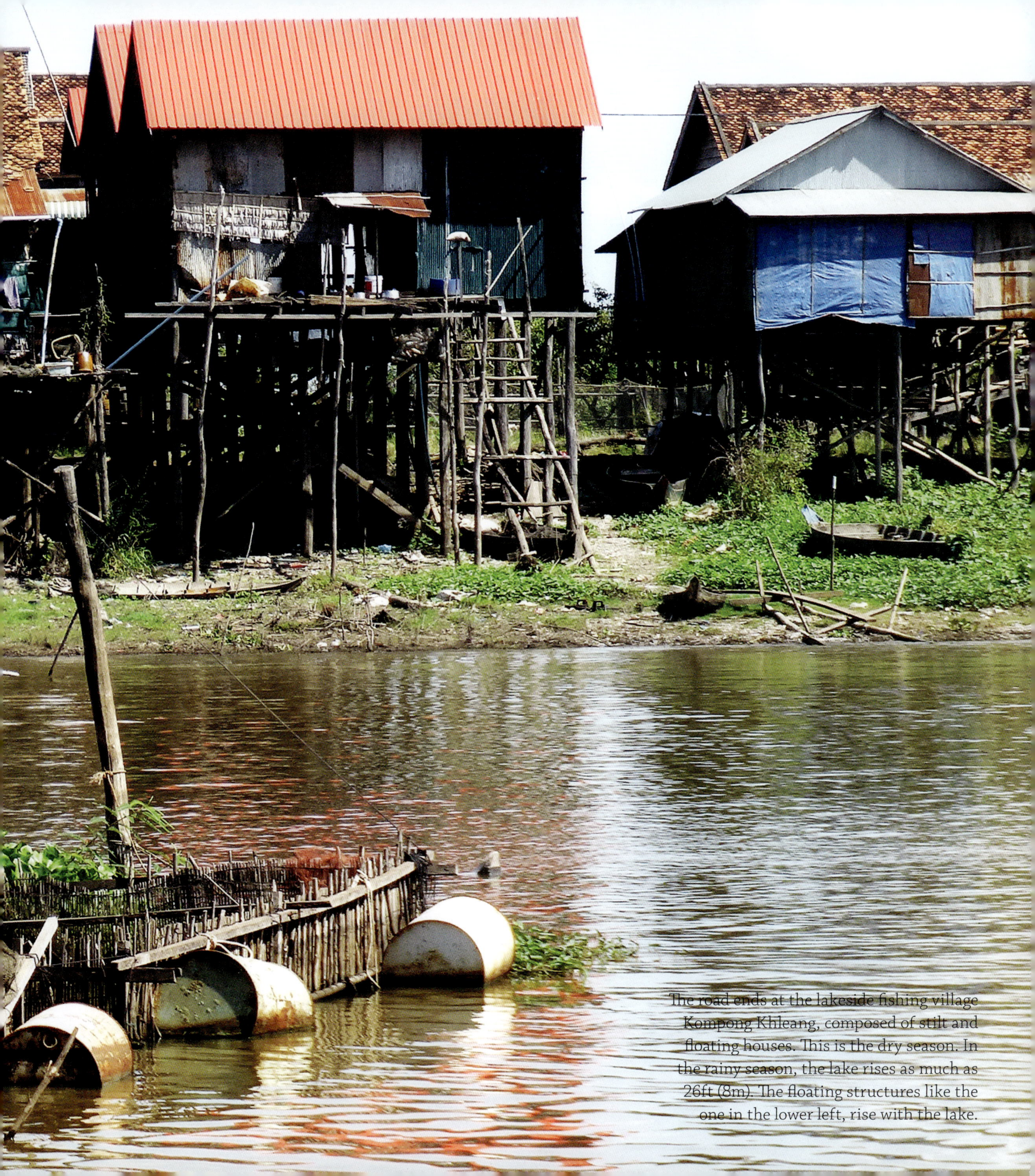

The road ends at the lakeside fishing village Kompong Khleang, composed of stilt and floating houses. This is the dry season. In the rainy season, the lake rises as much as 26ft (8m). The floating structures like the one in the lower left, rise with the lake.

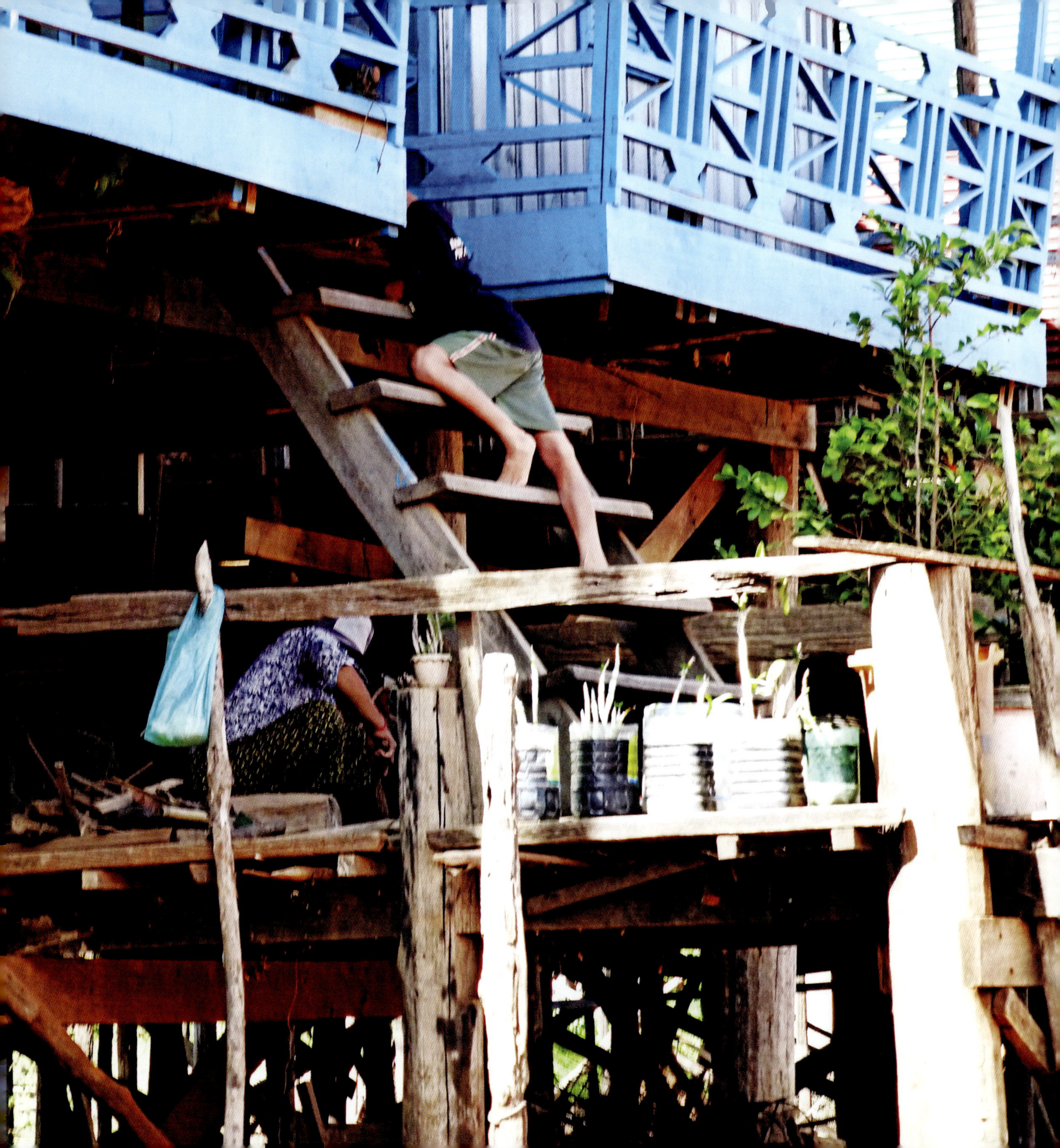

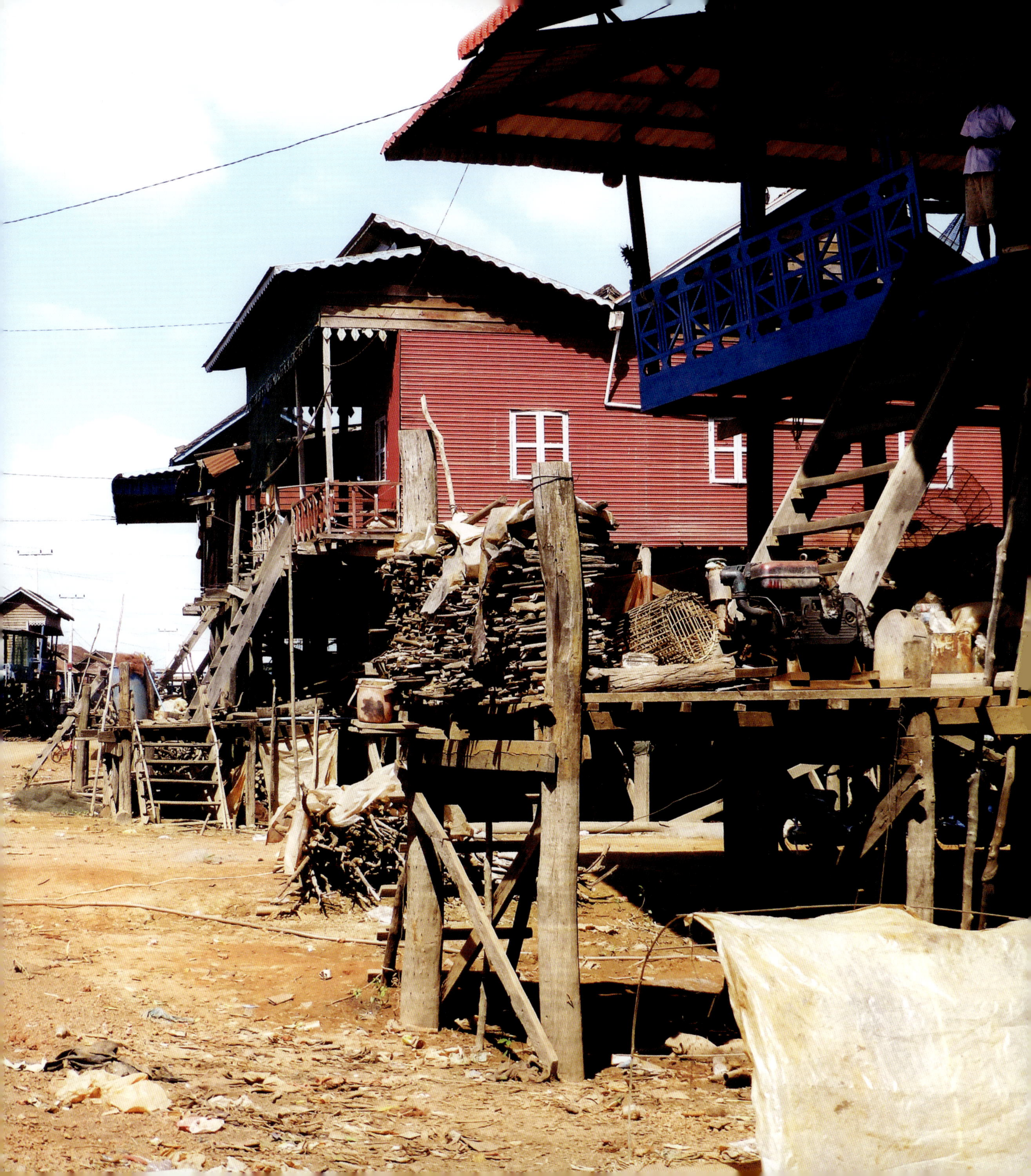

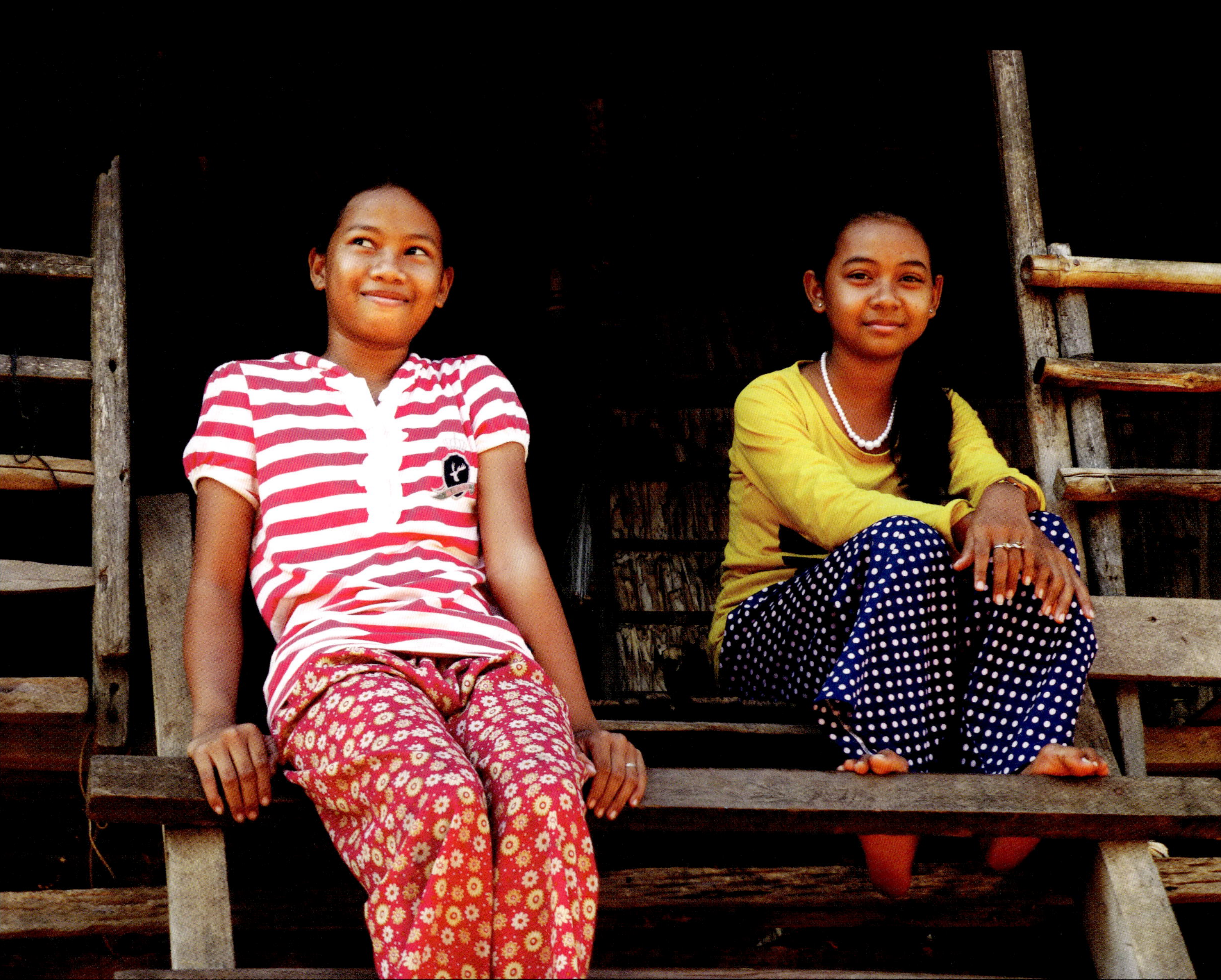

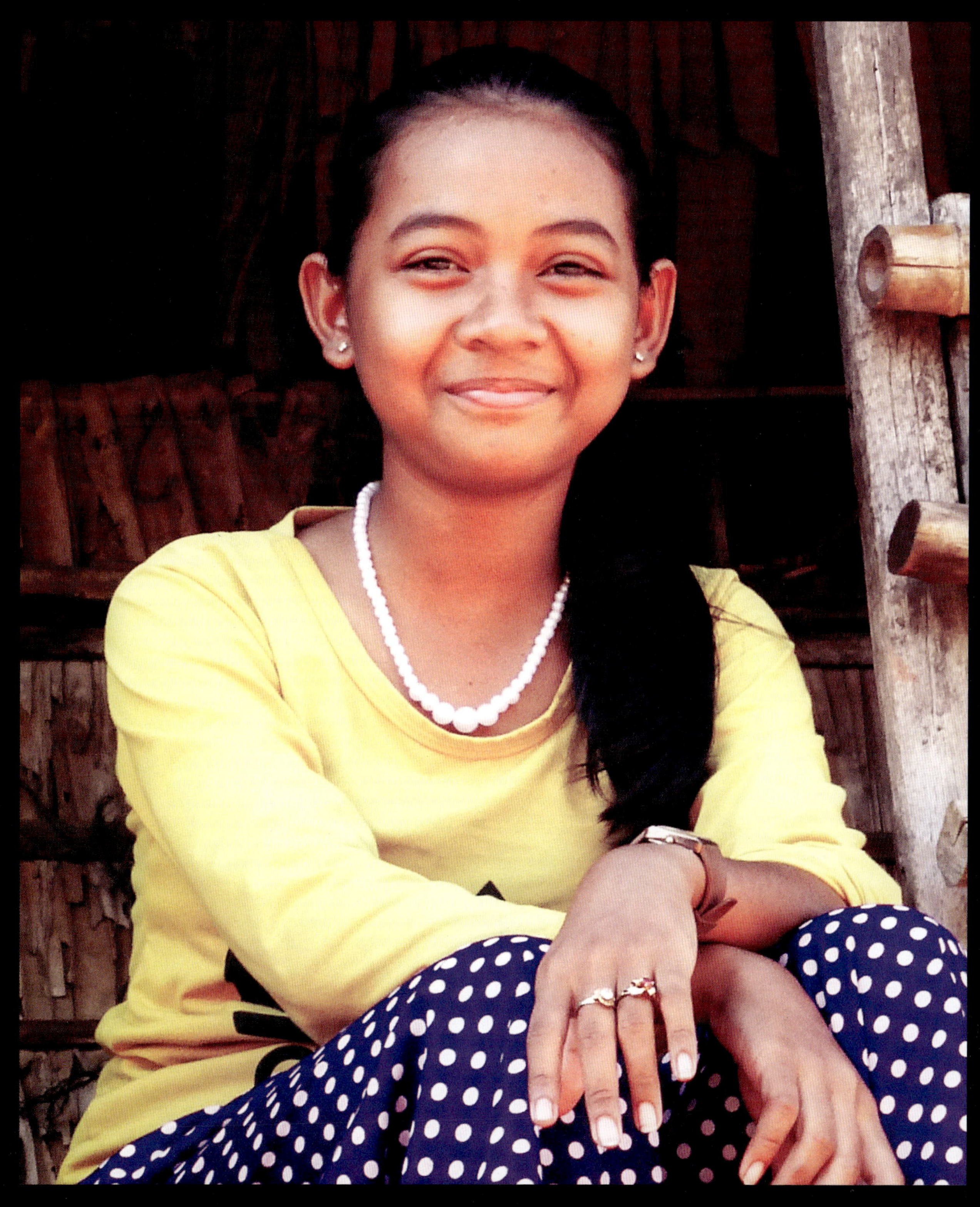

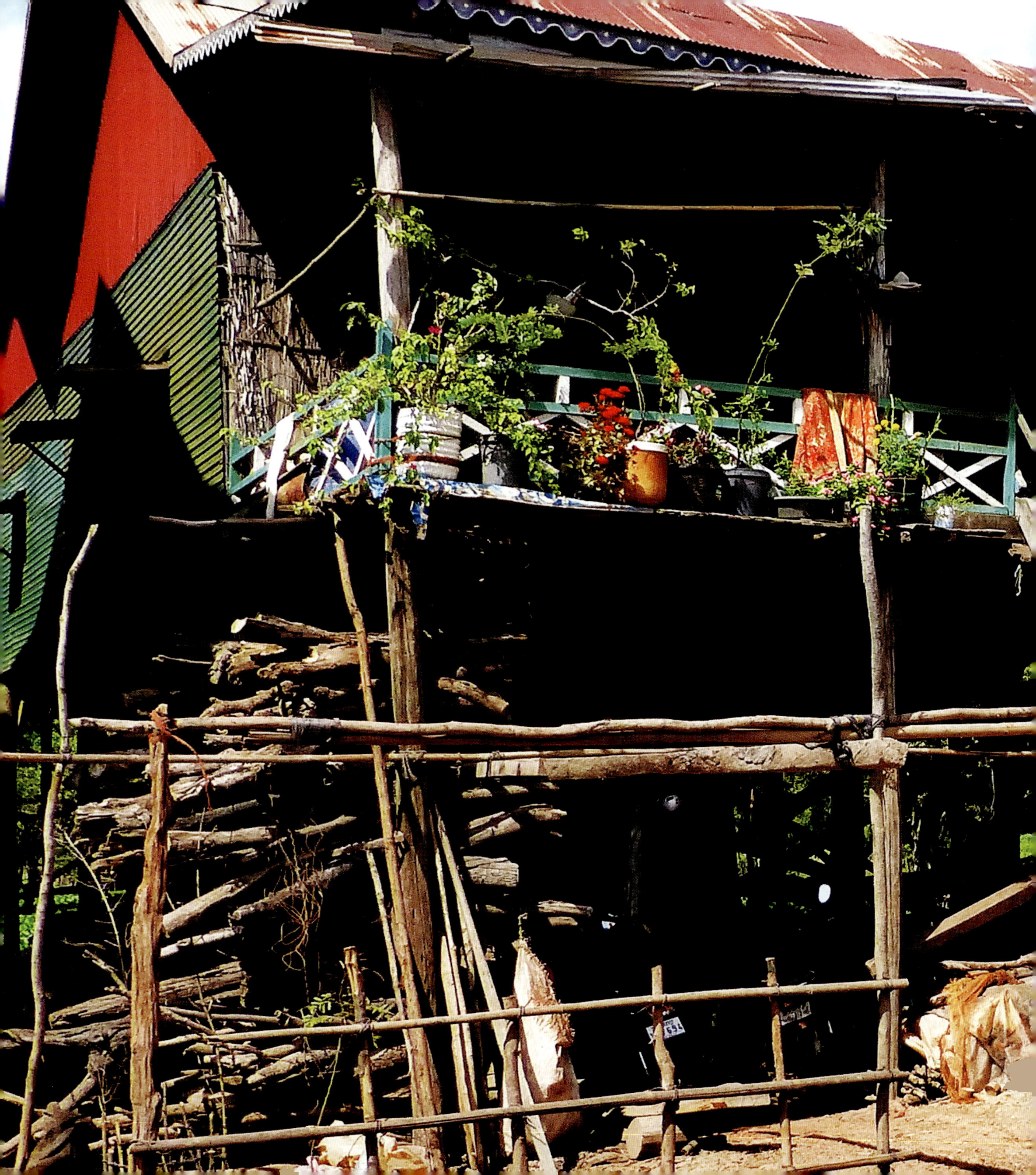

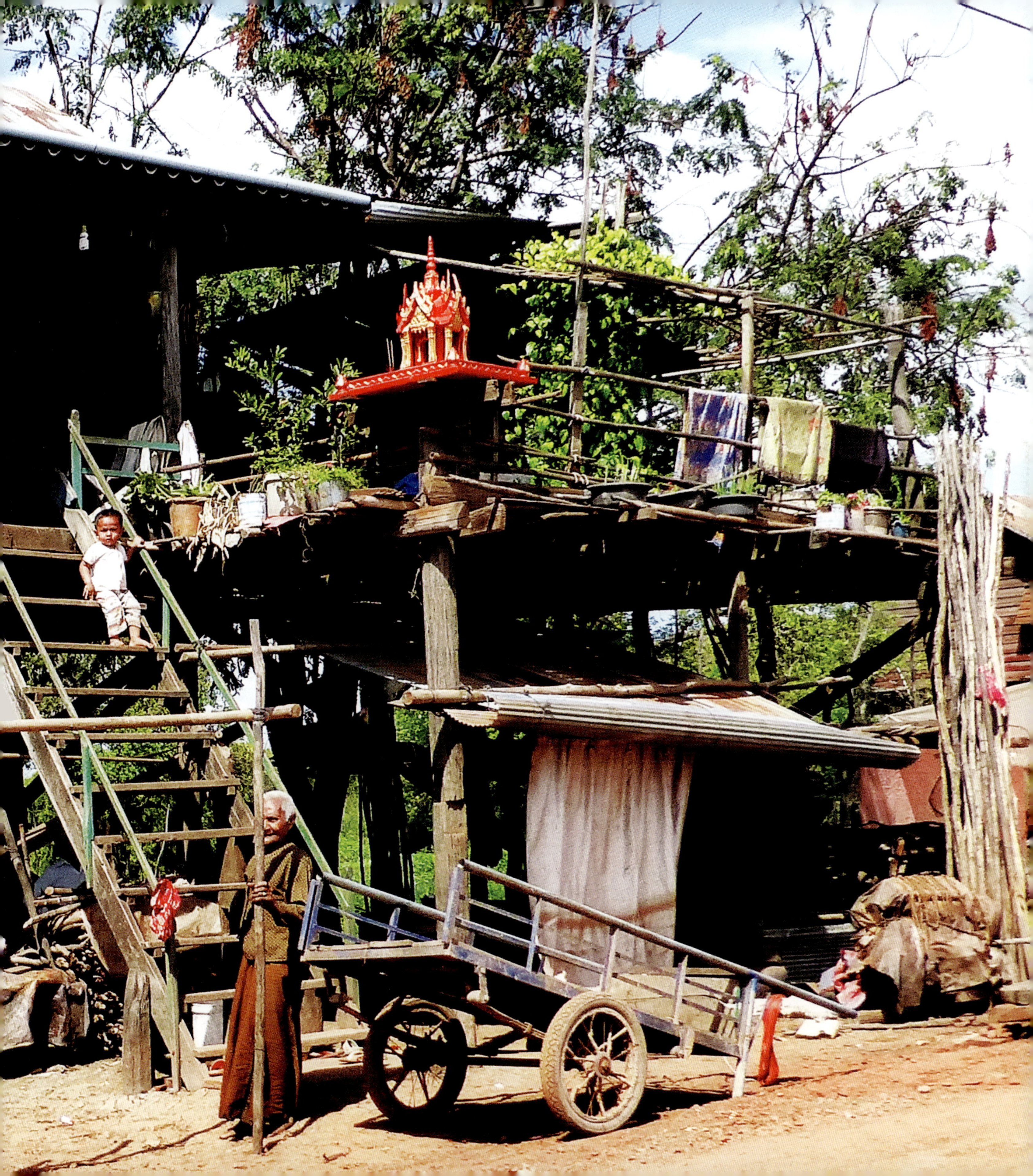

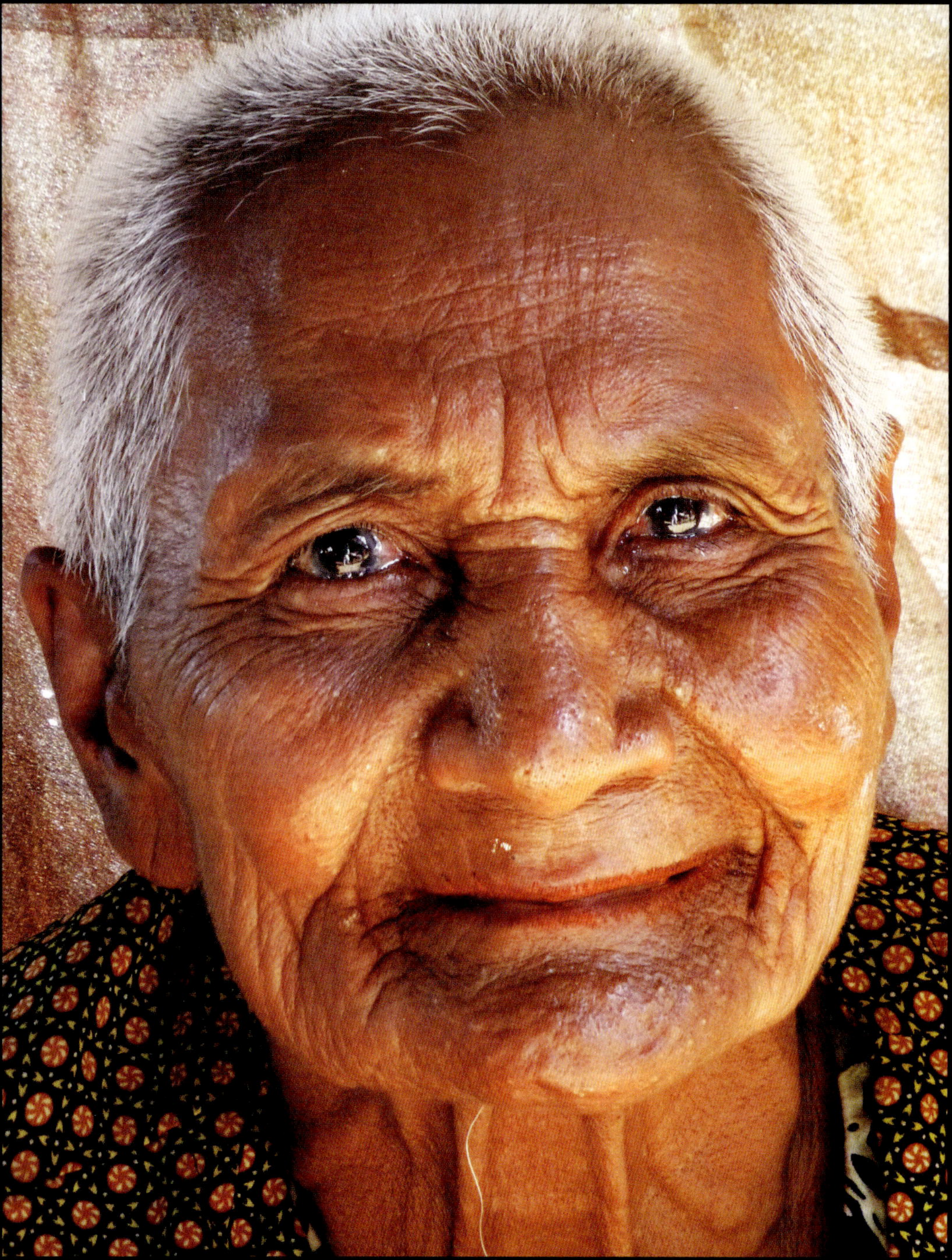

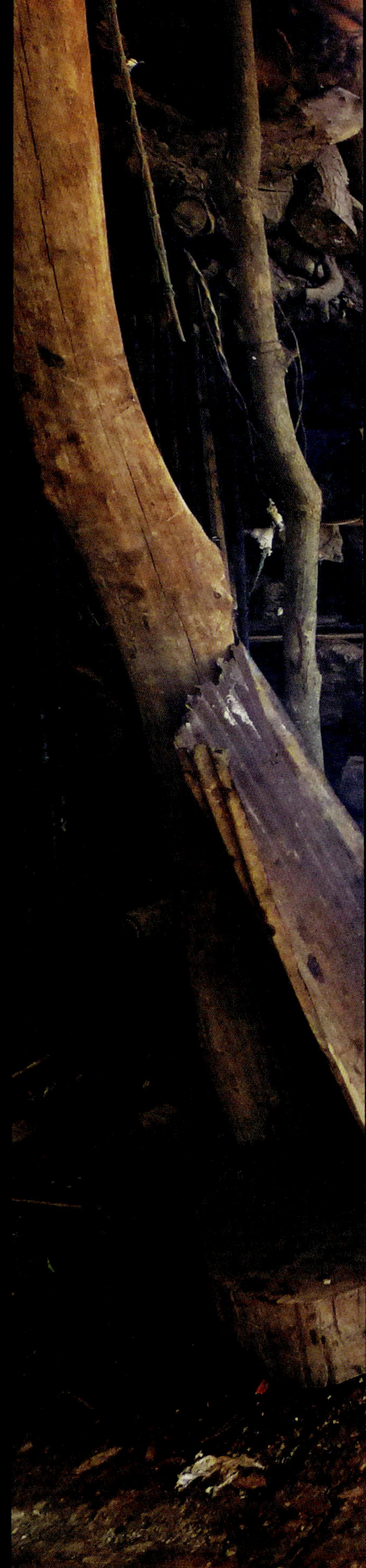

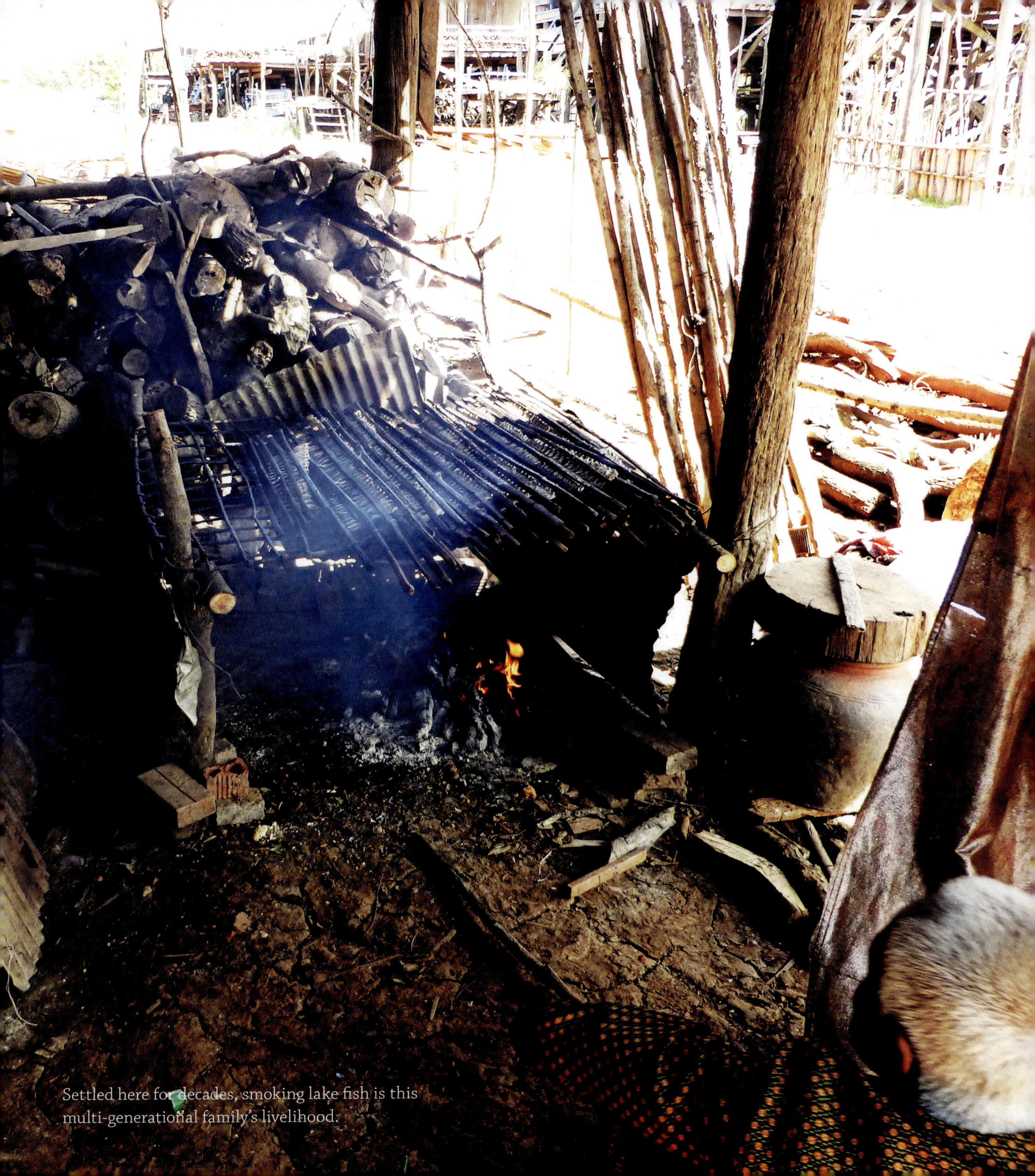

Settled here for decades, smoking lake fish is this multi-generational family's livelihood.

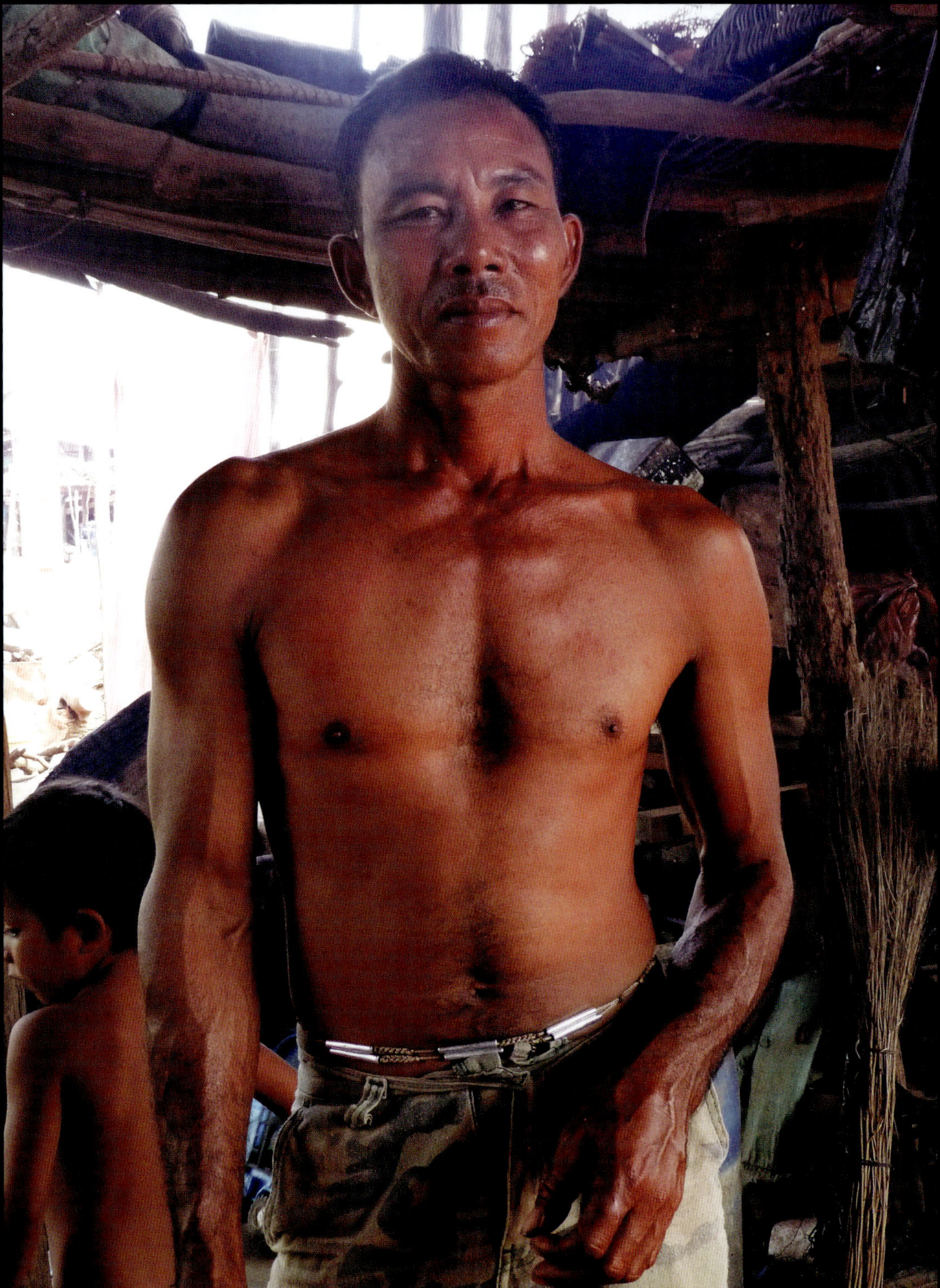

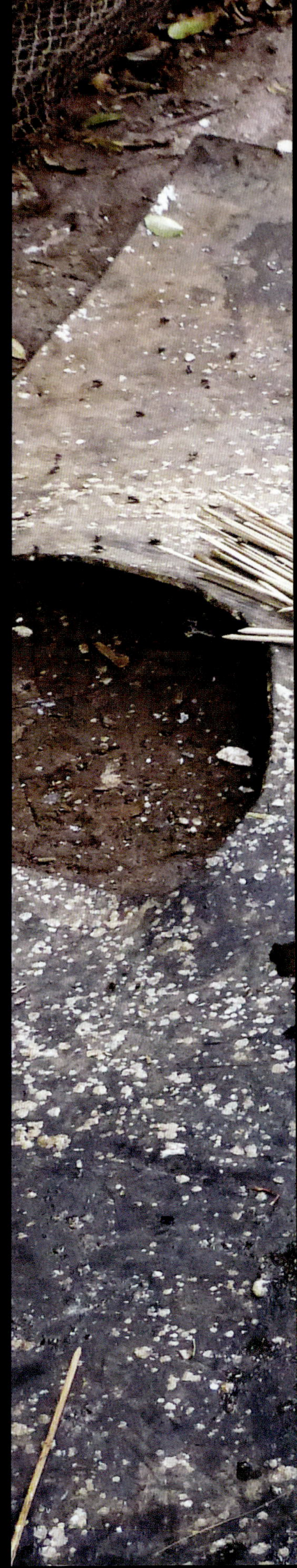

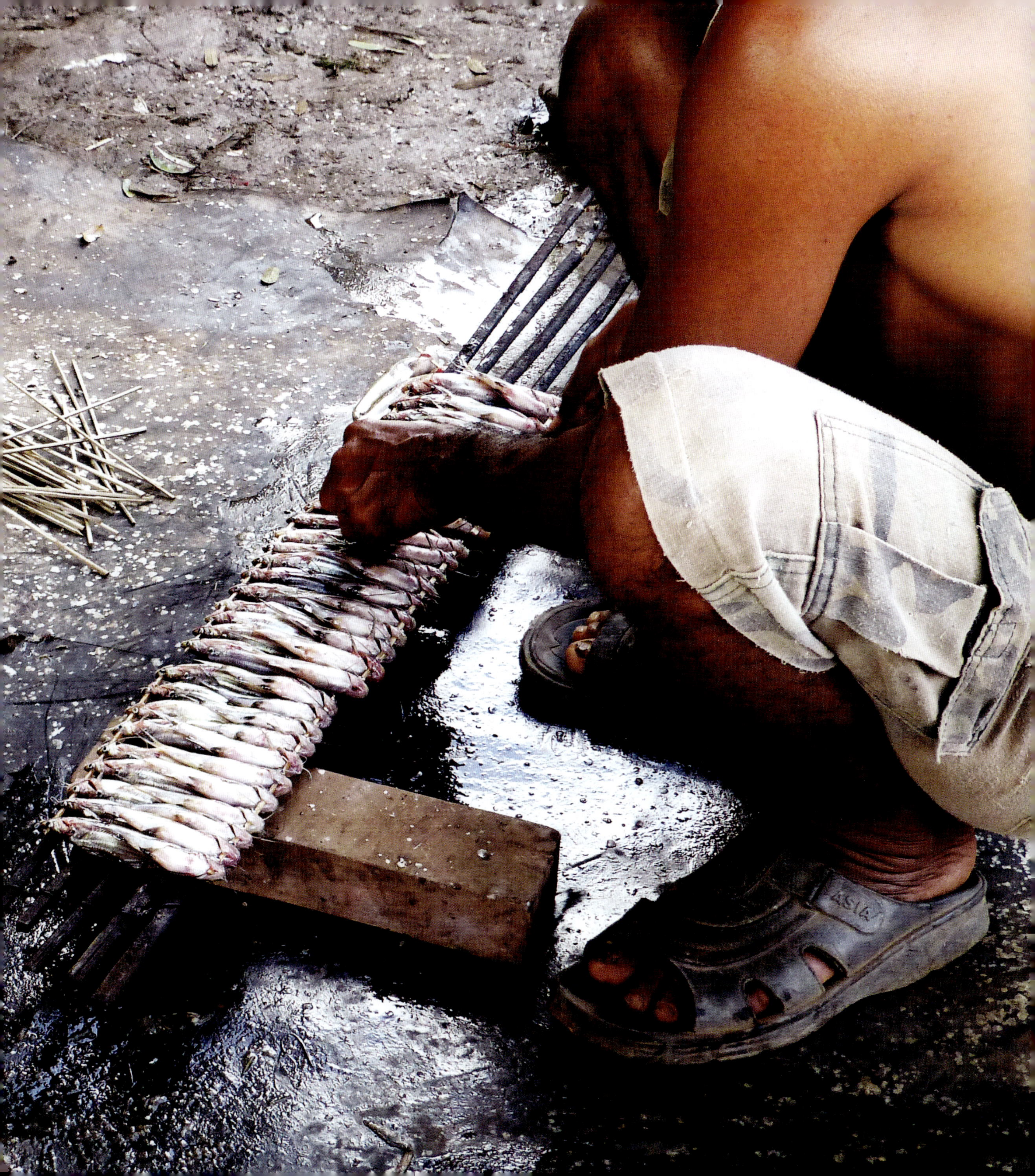
ASIA

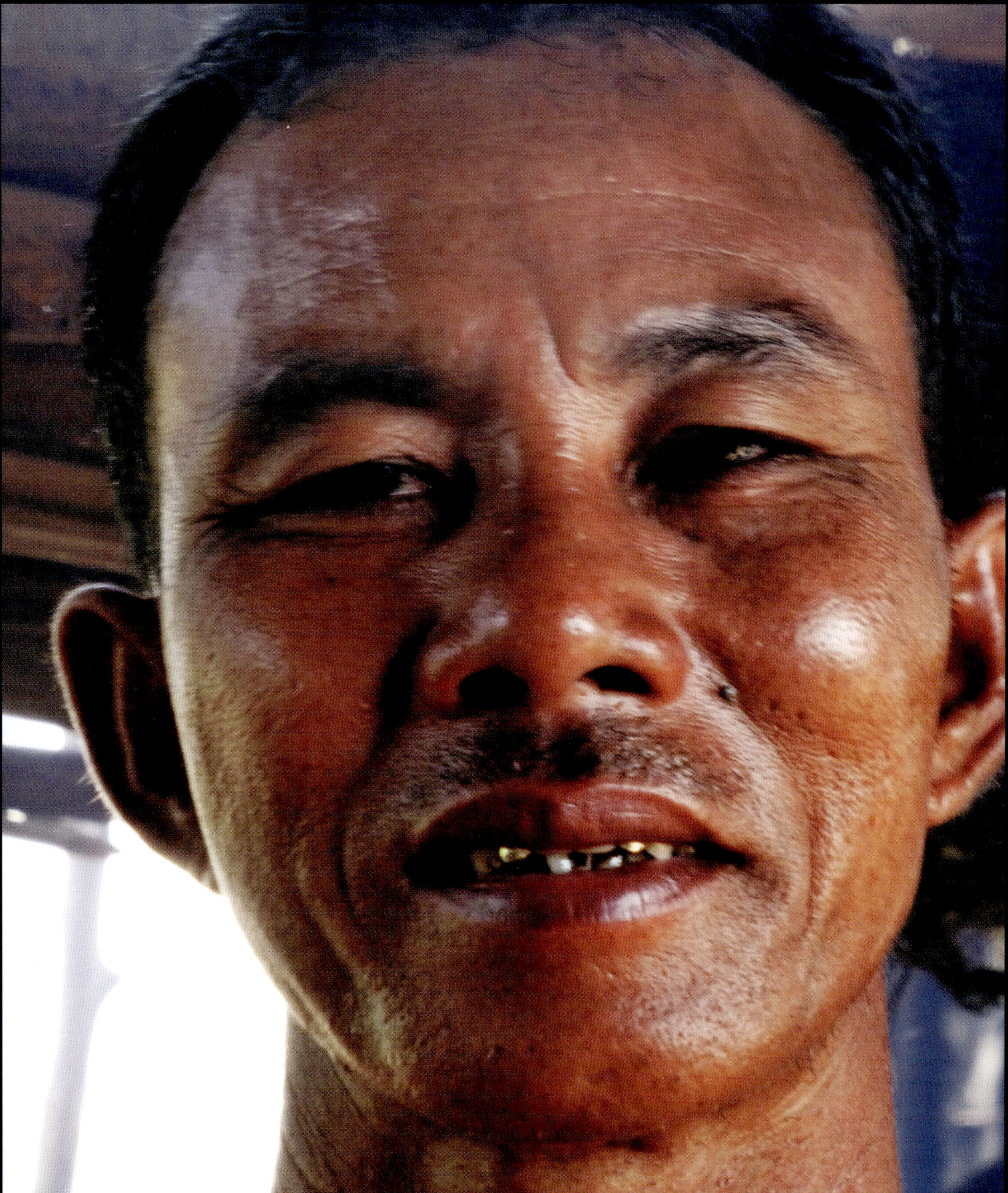

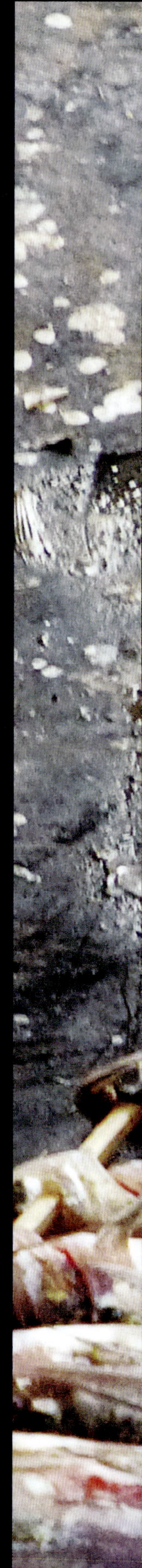

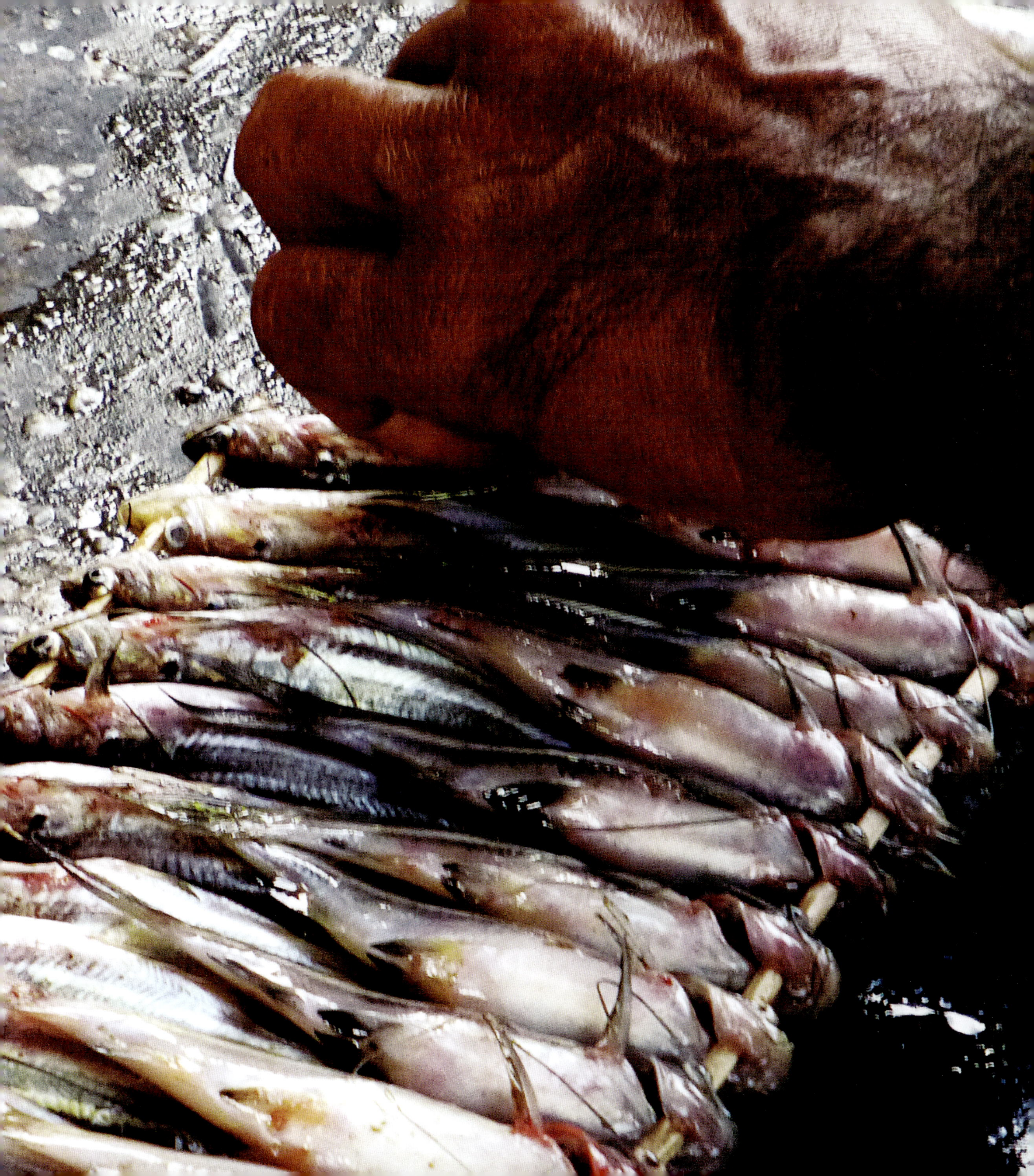

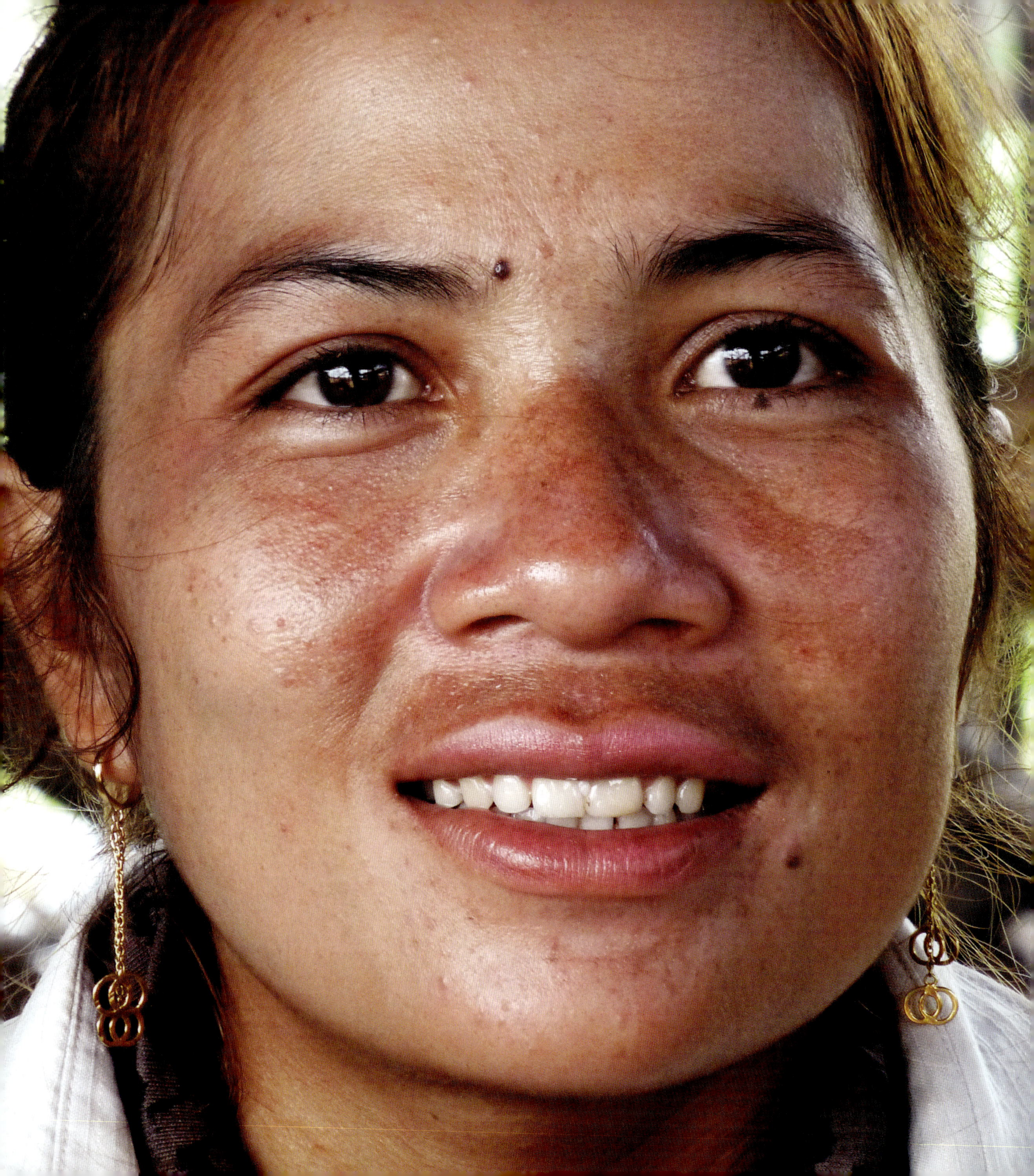

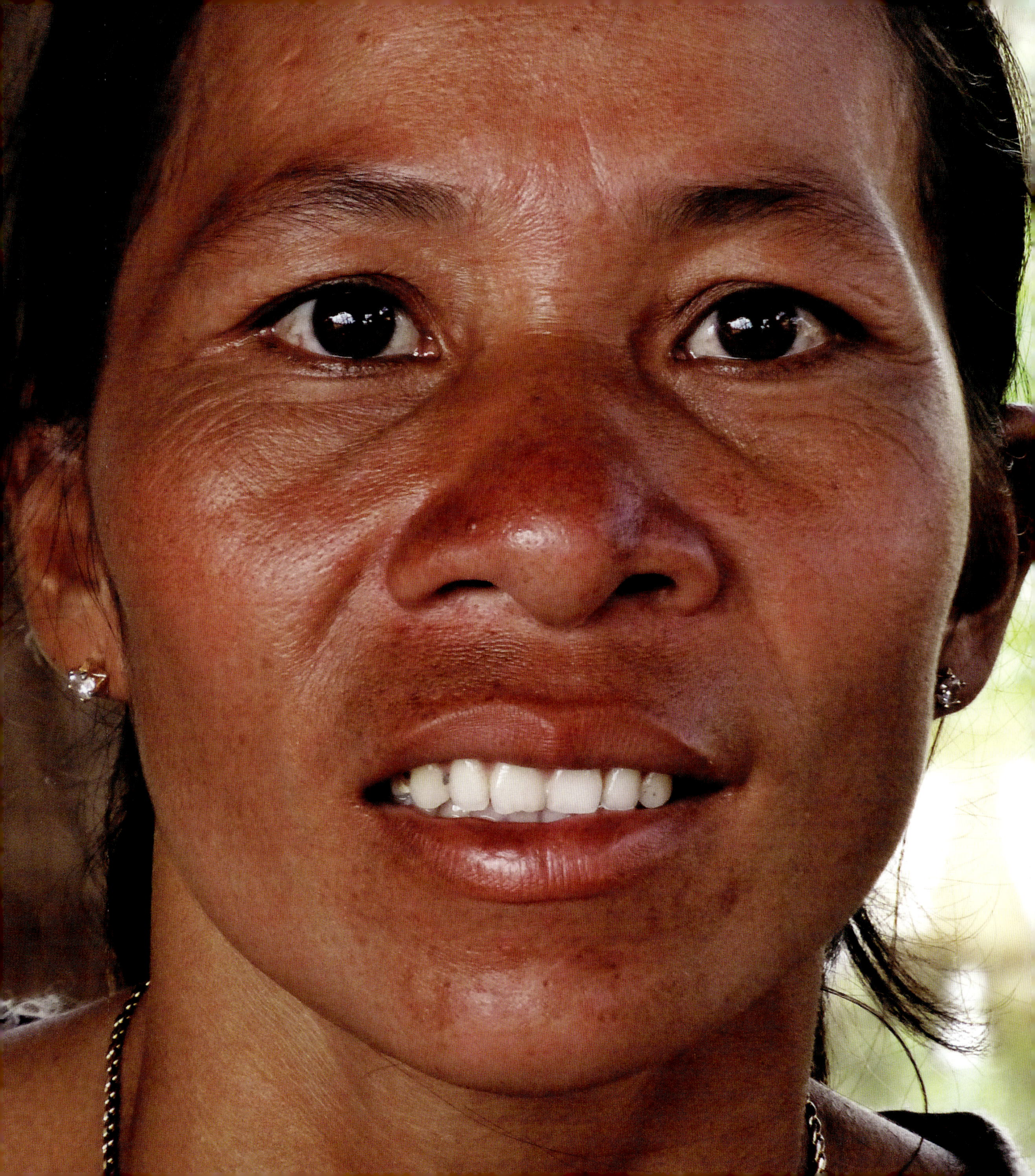

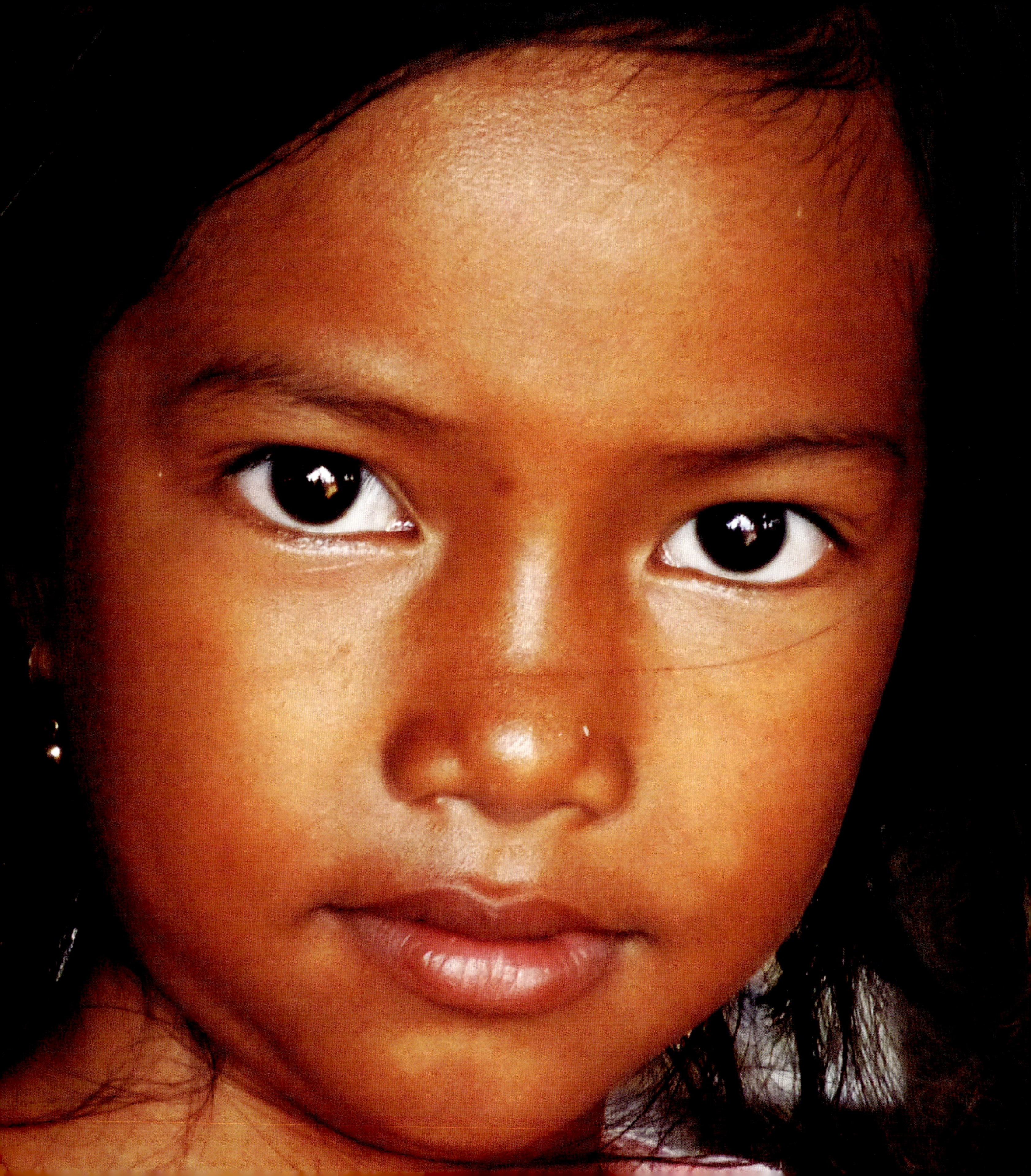

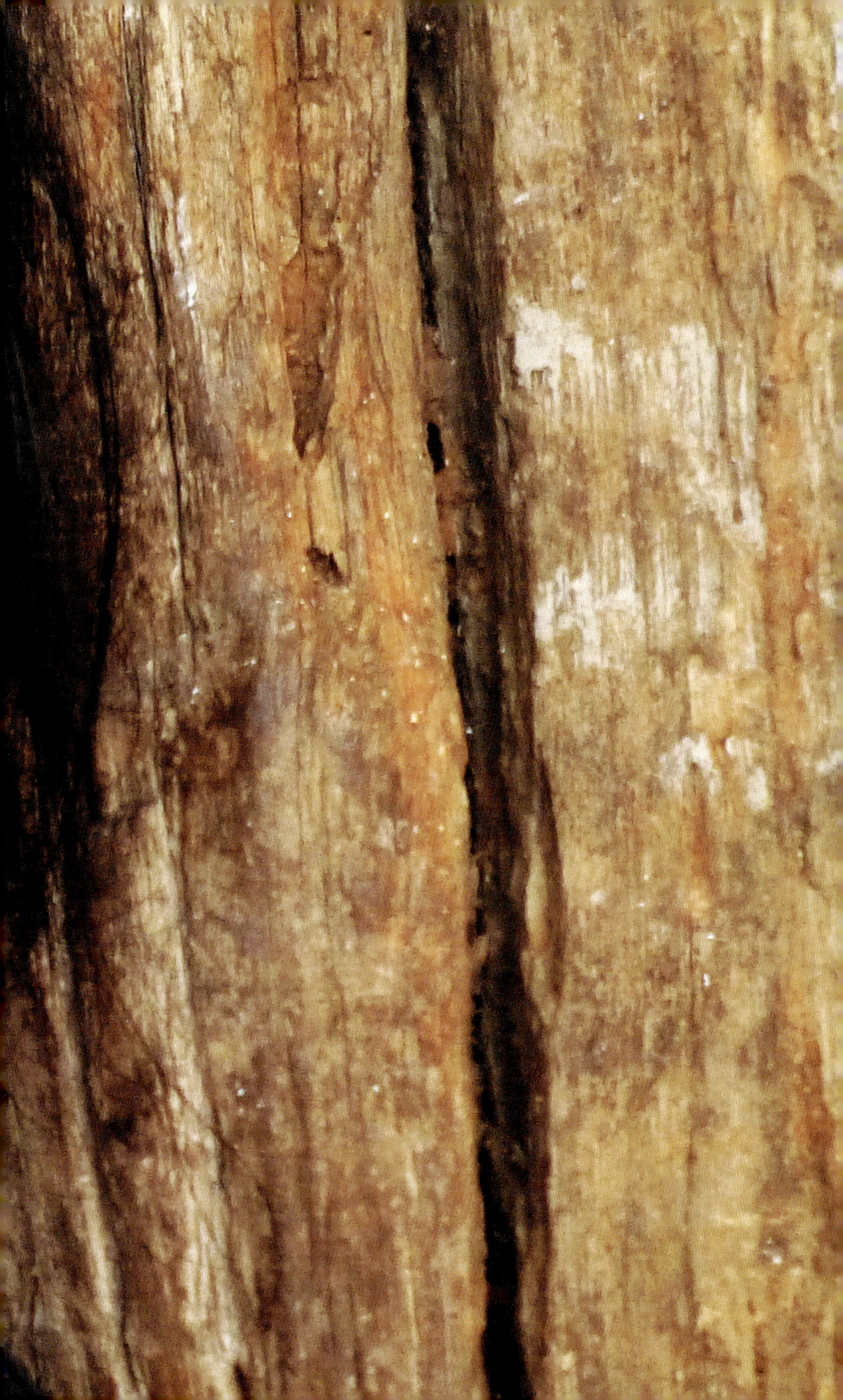

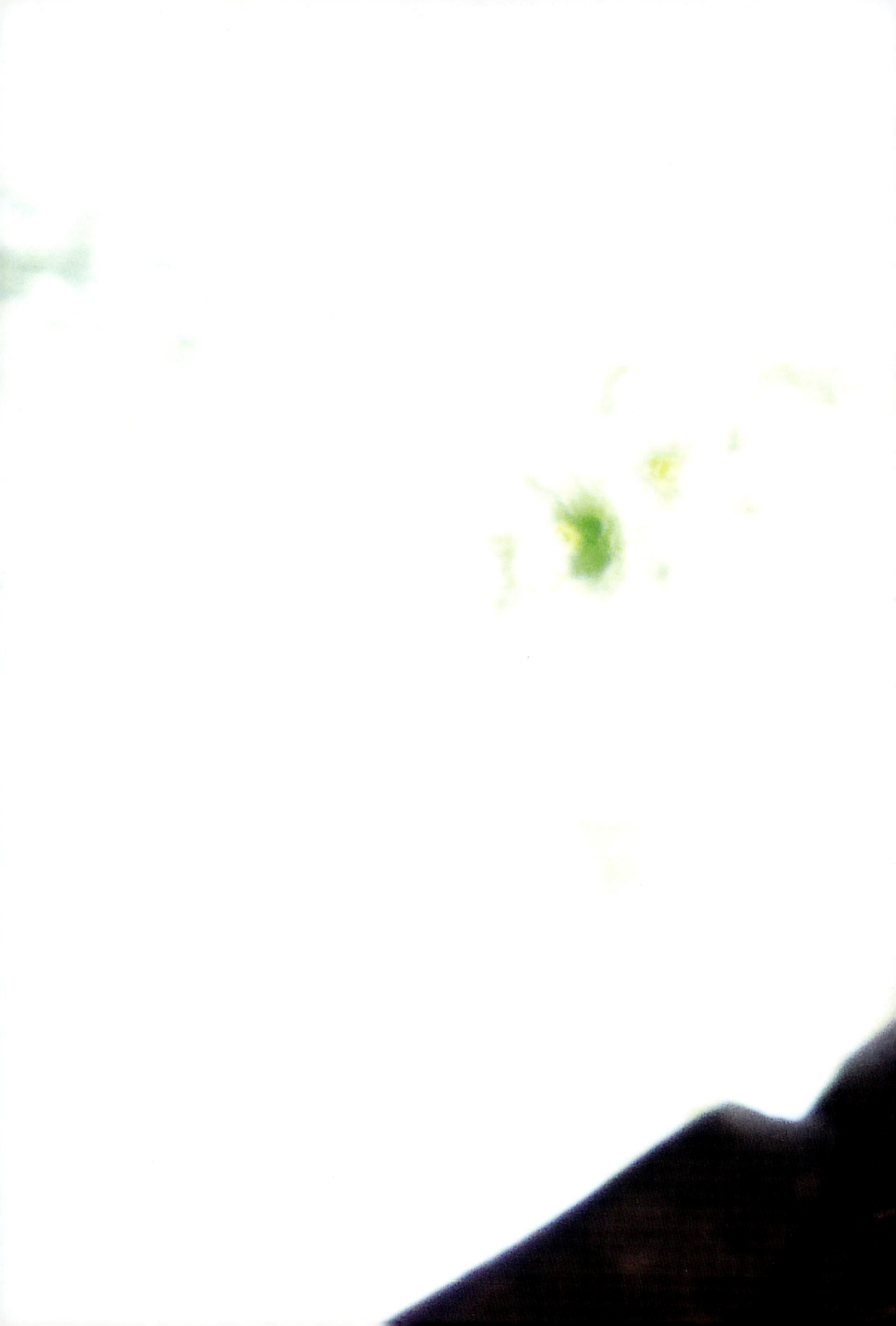

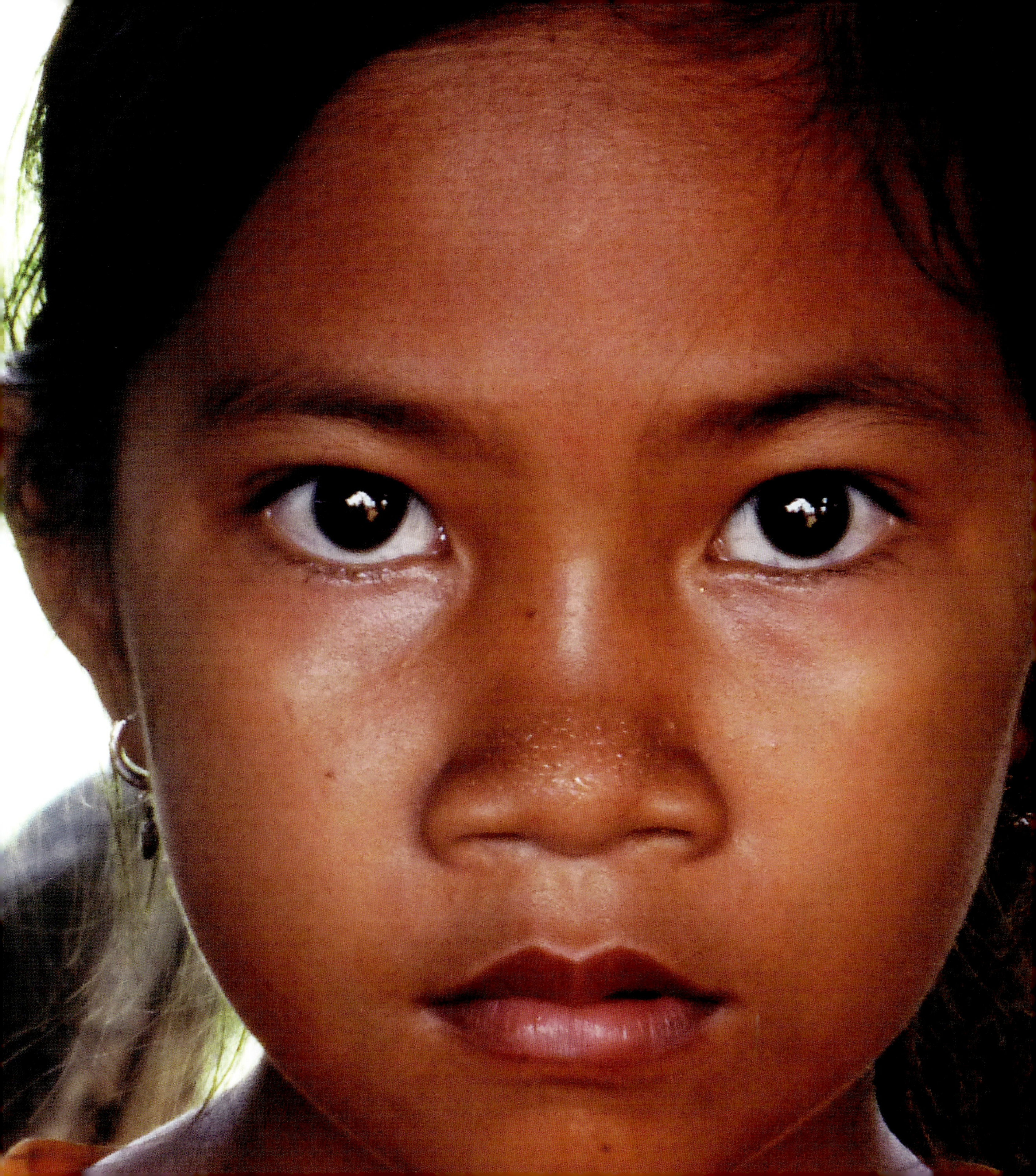

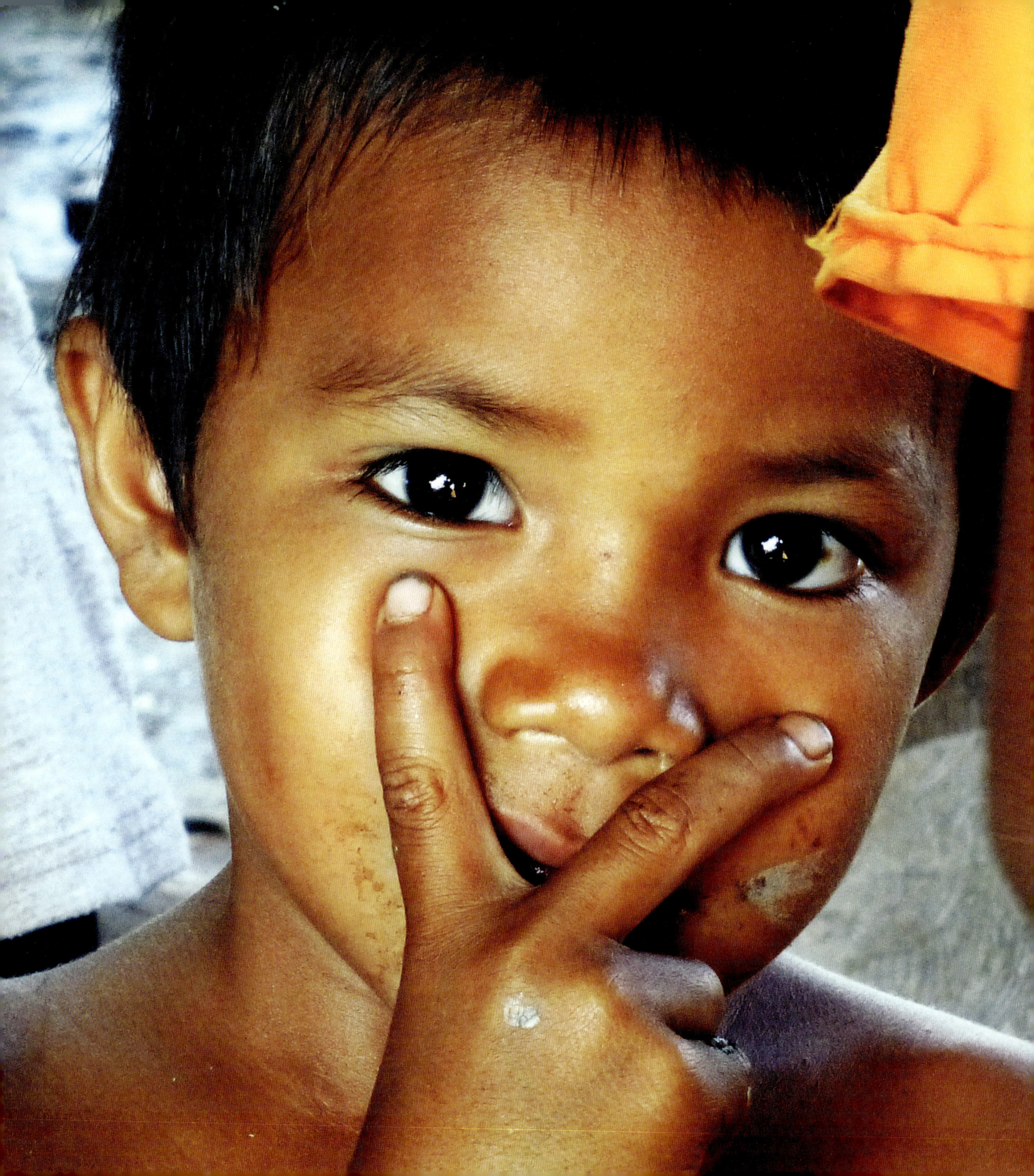

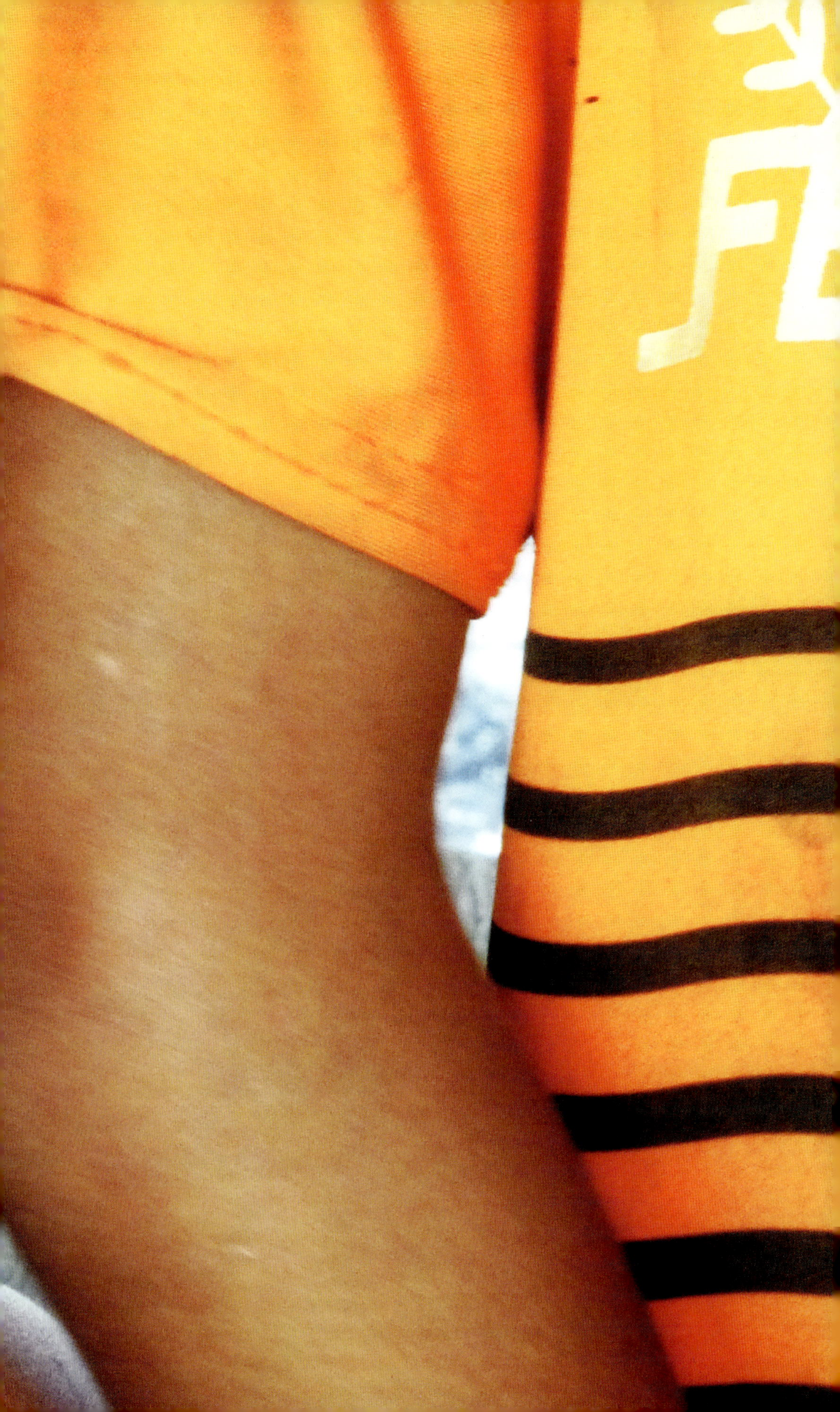

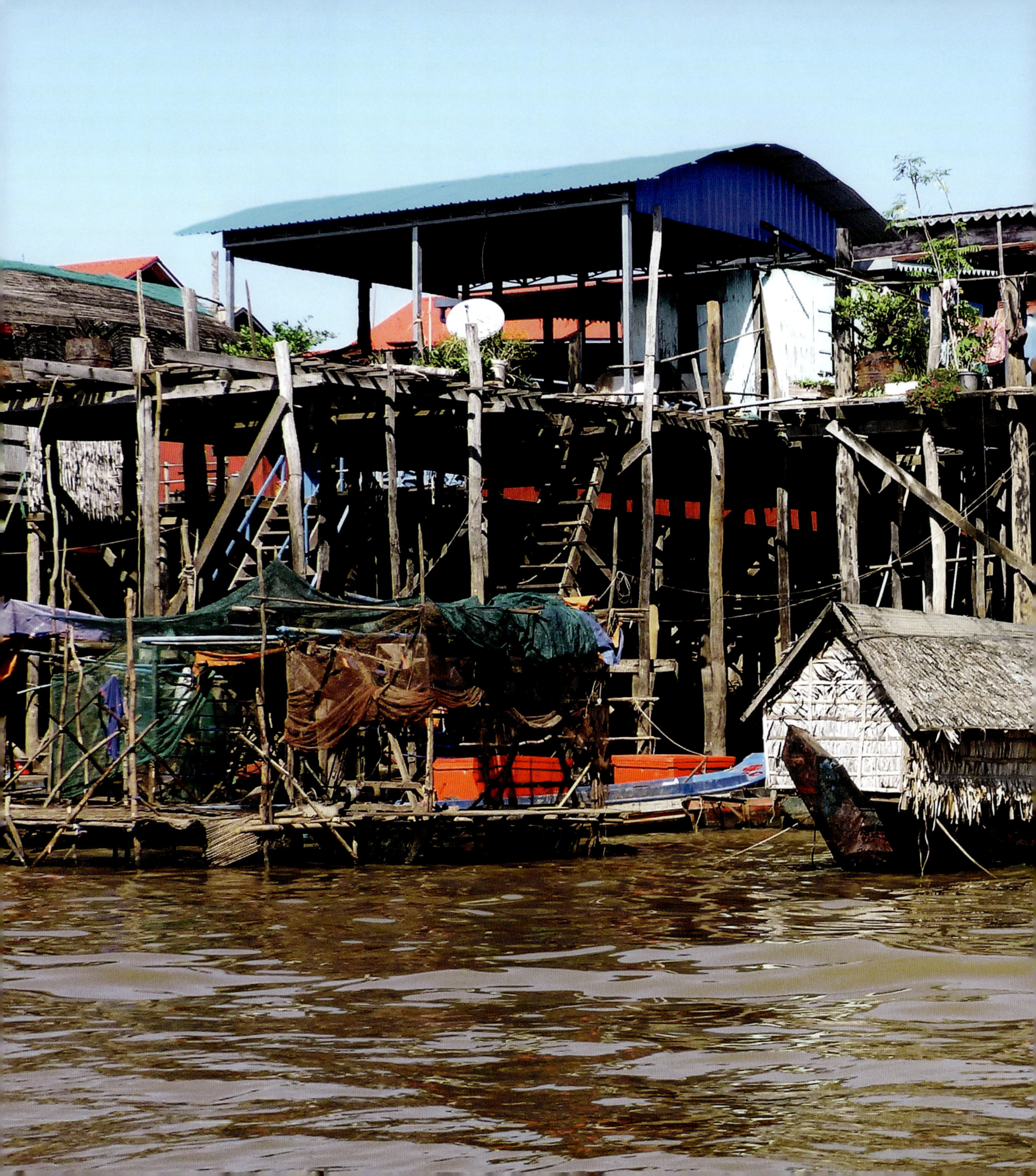

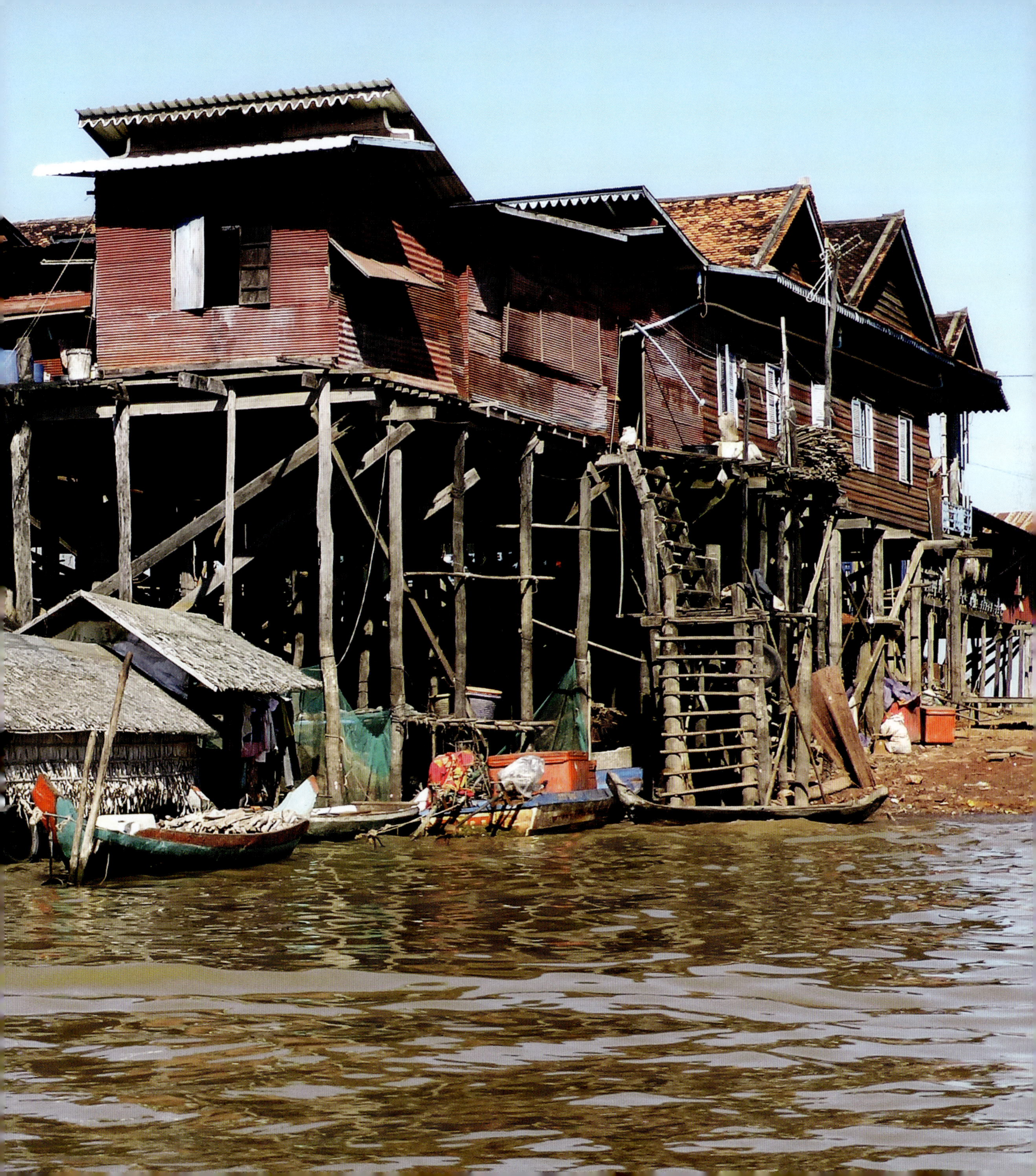

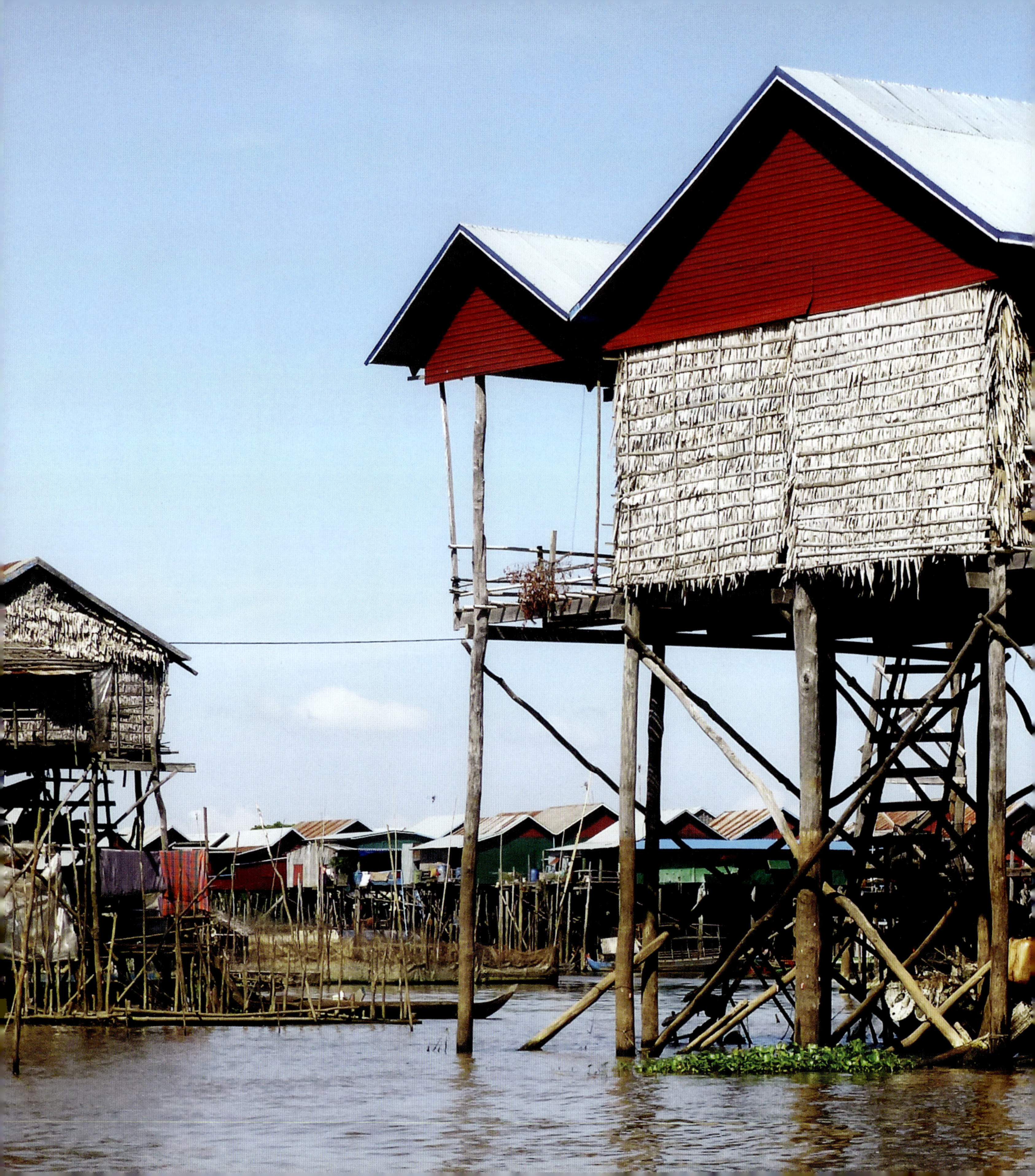

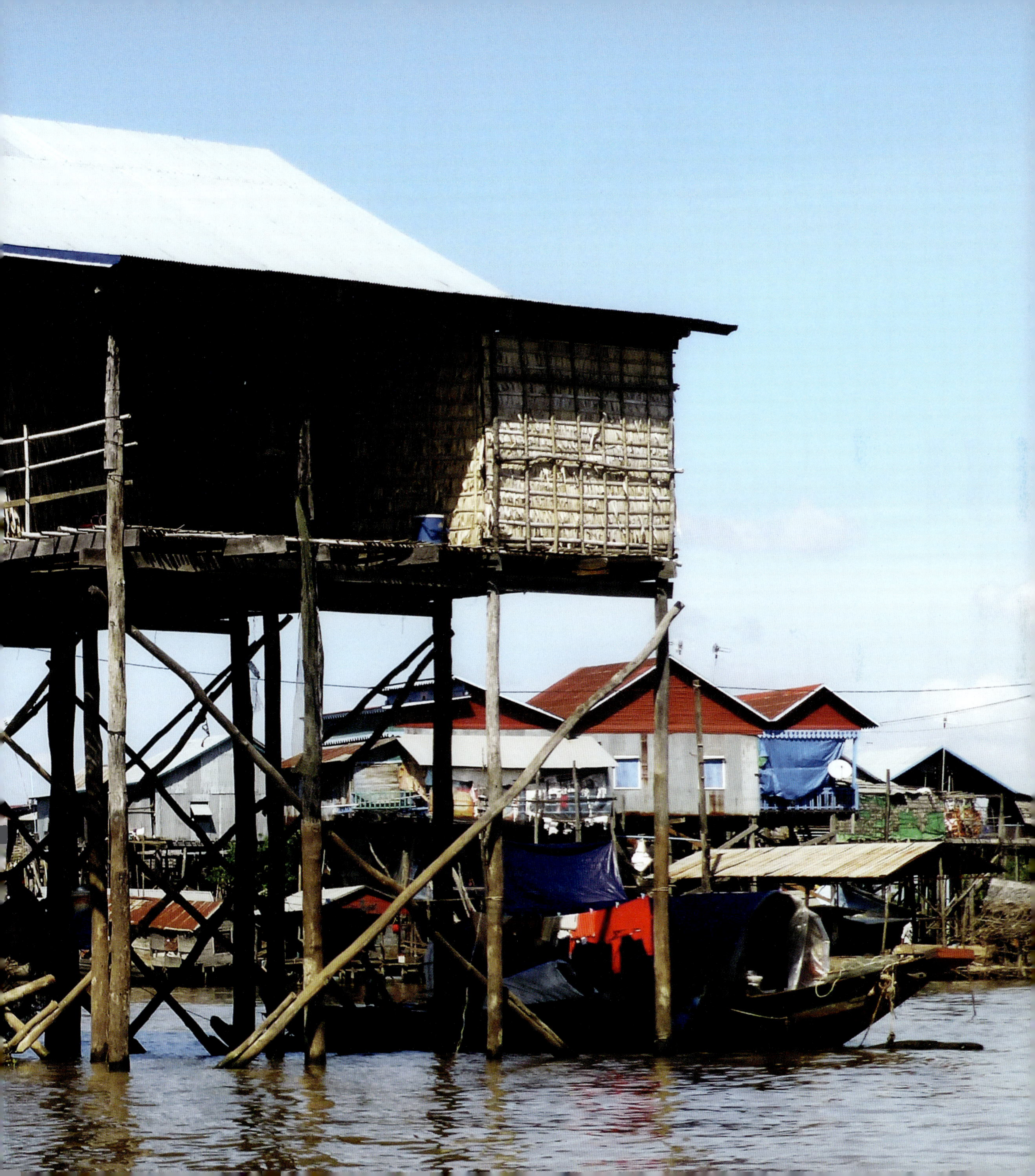

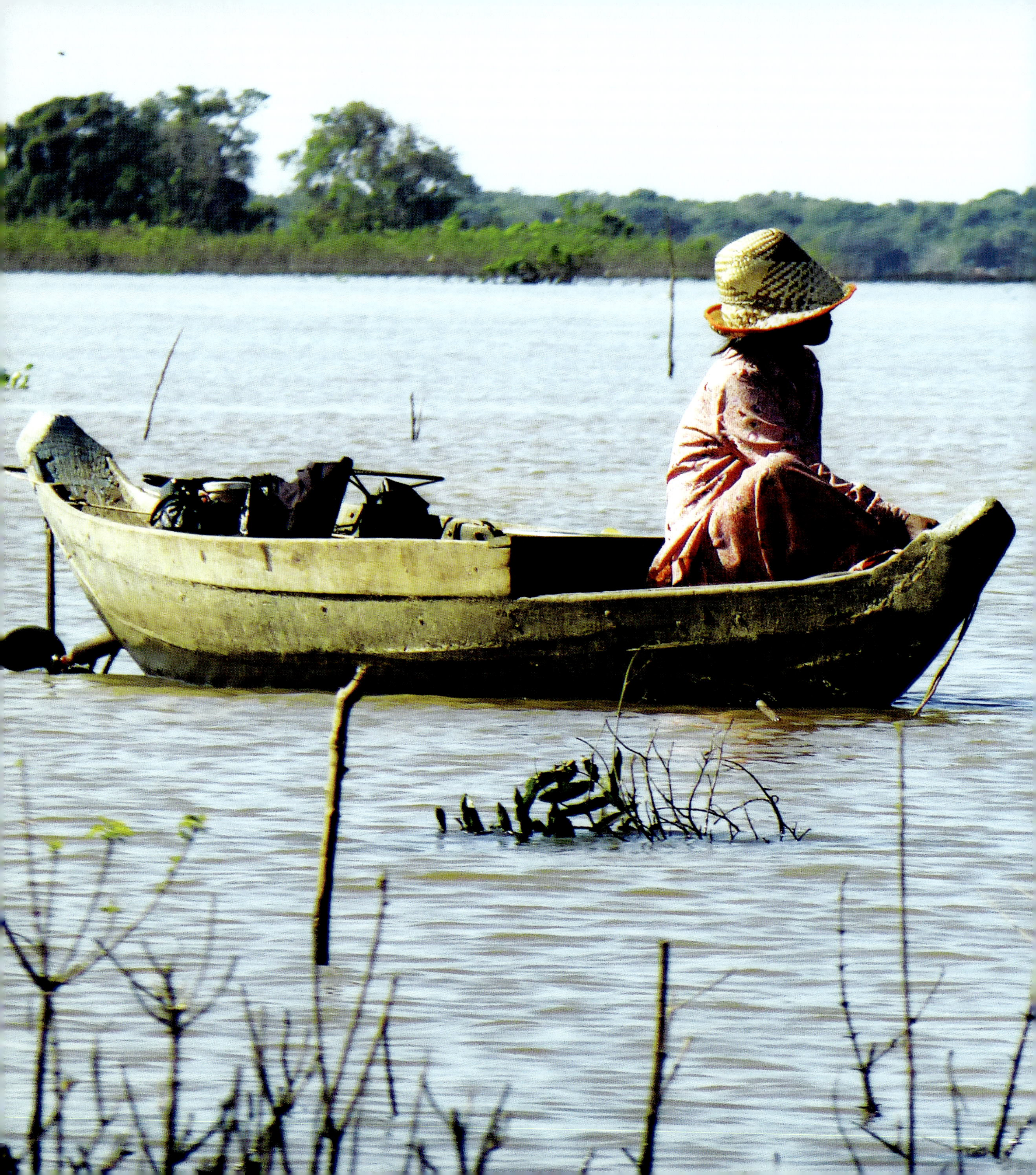

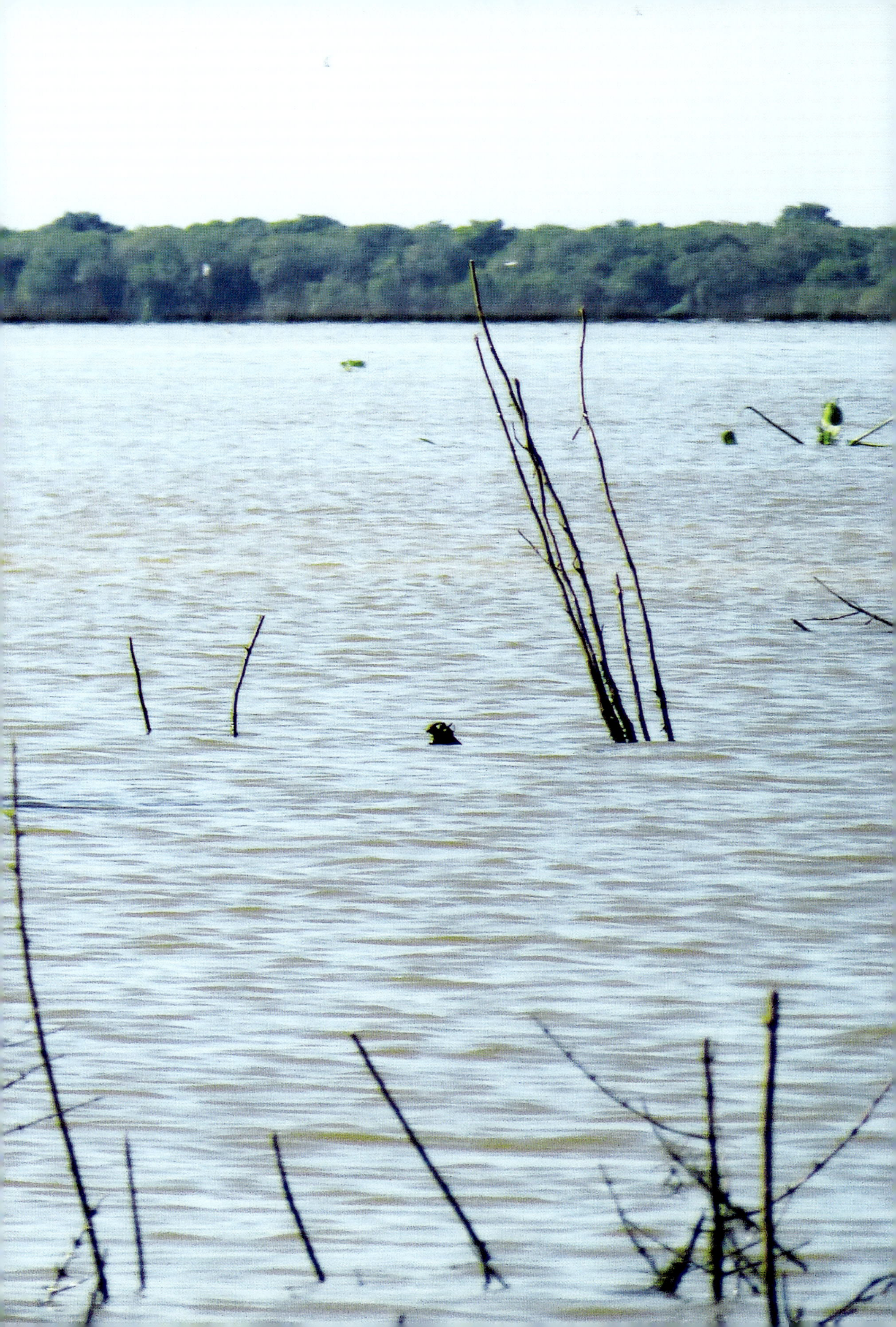

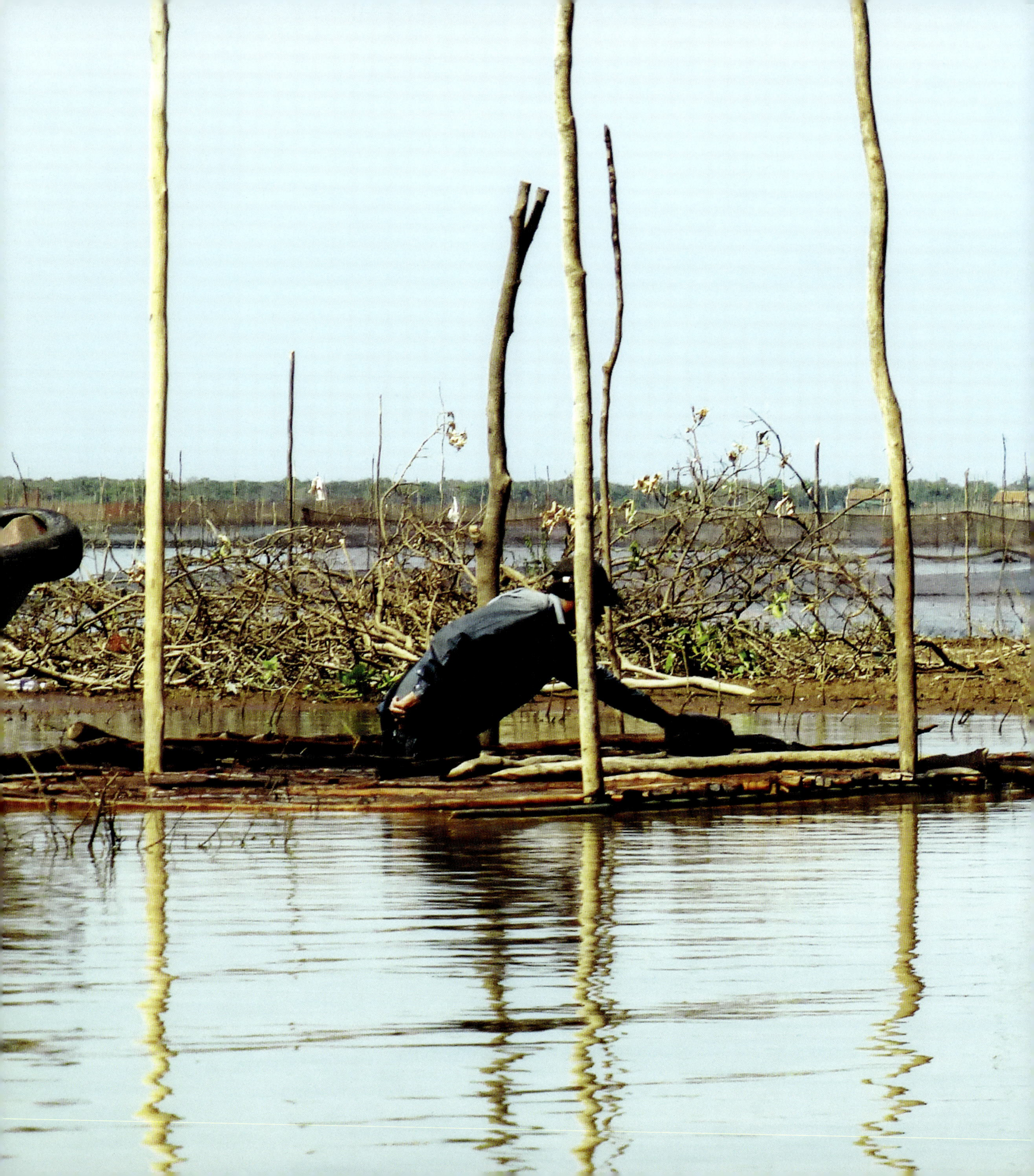

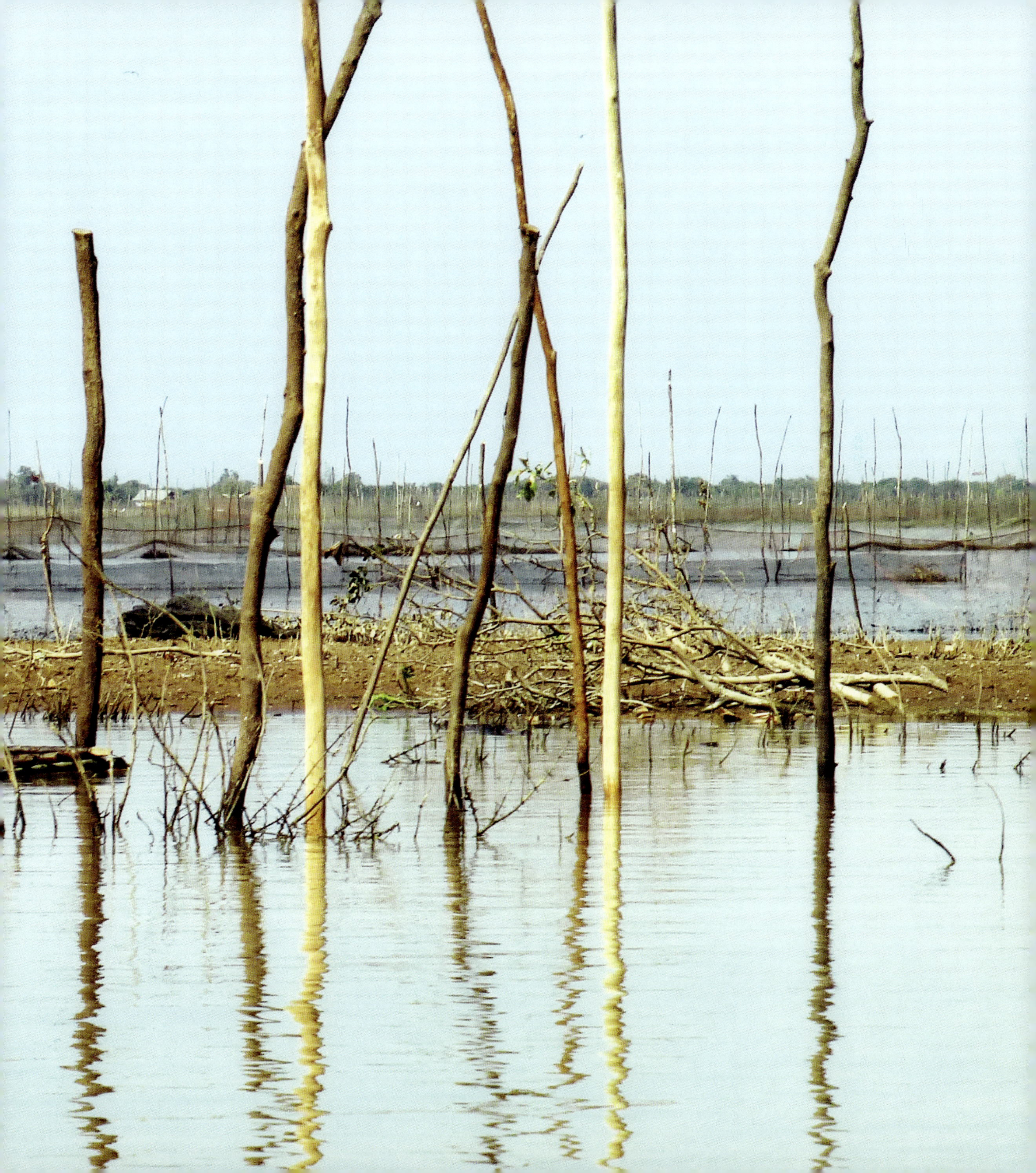

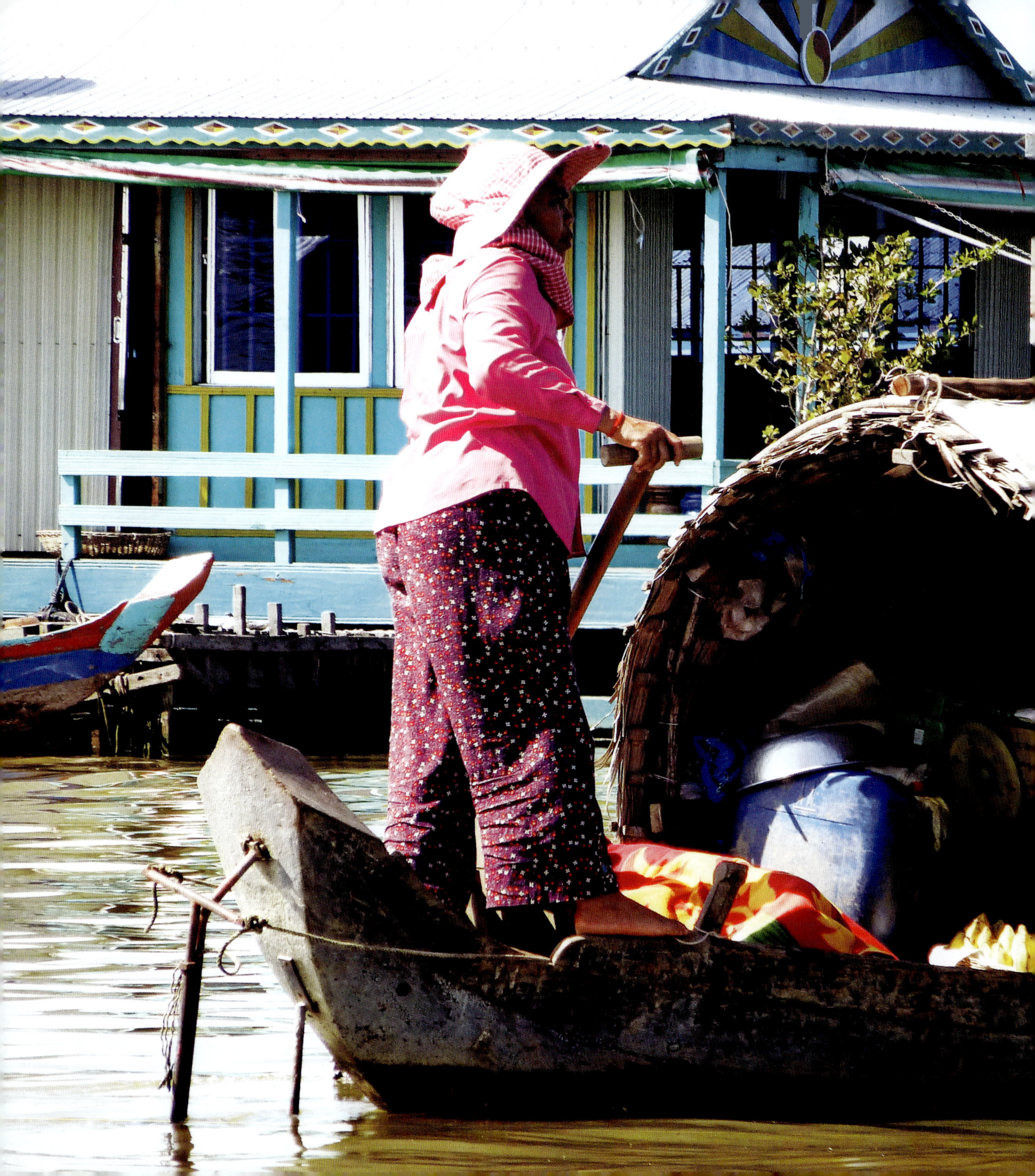

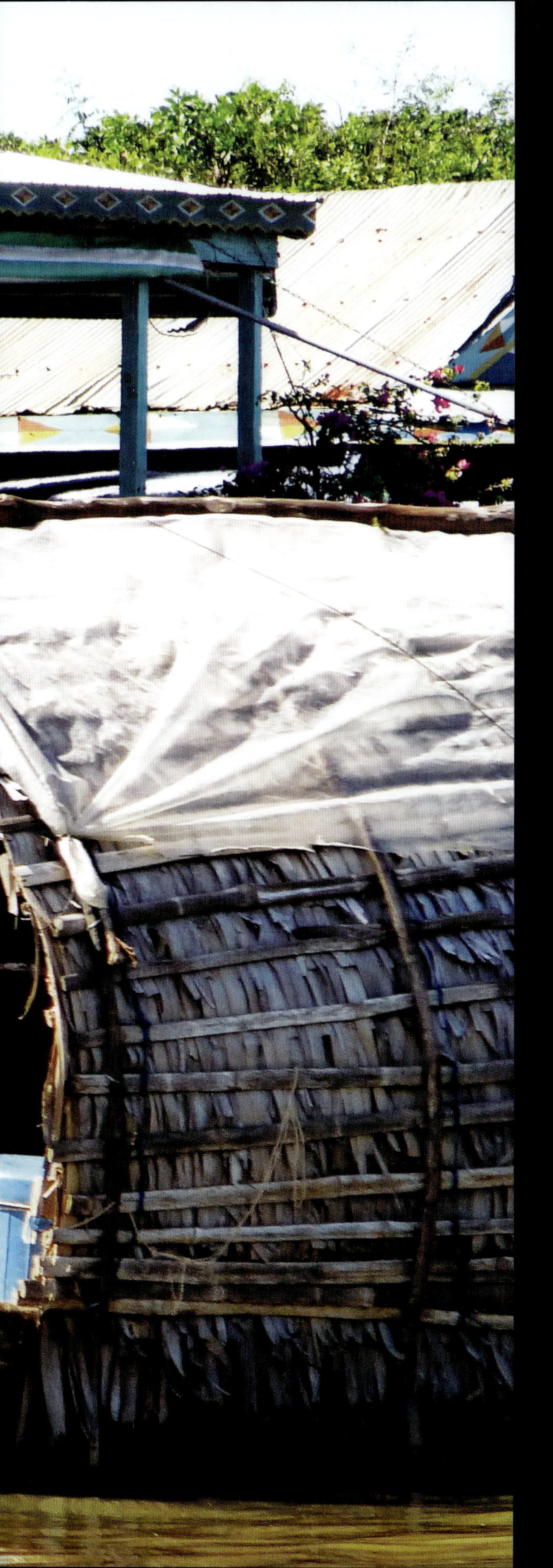

The floating village Chong Prol

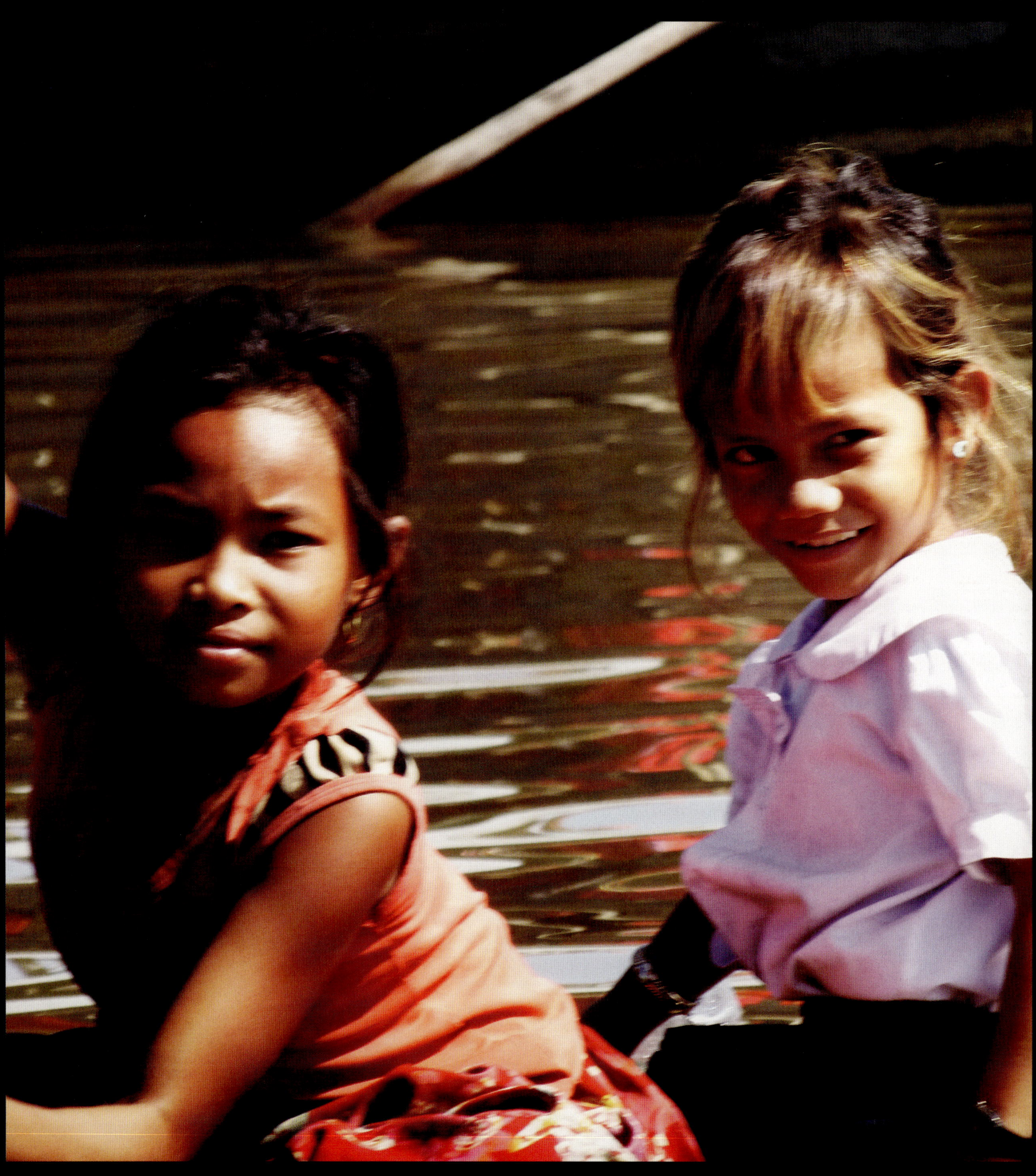

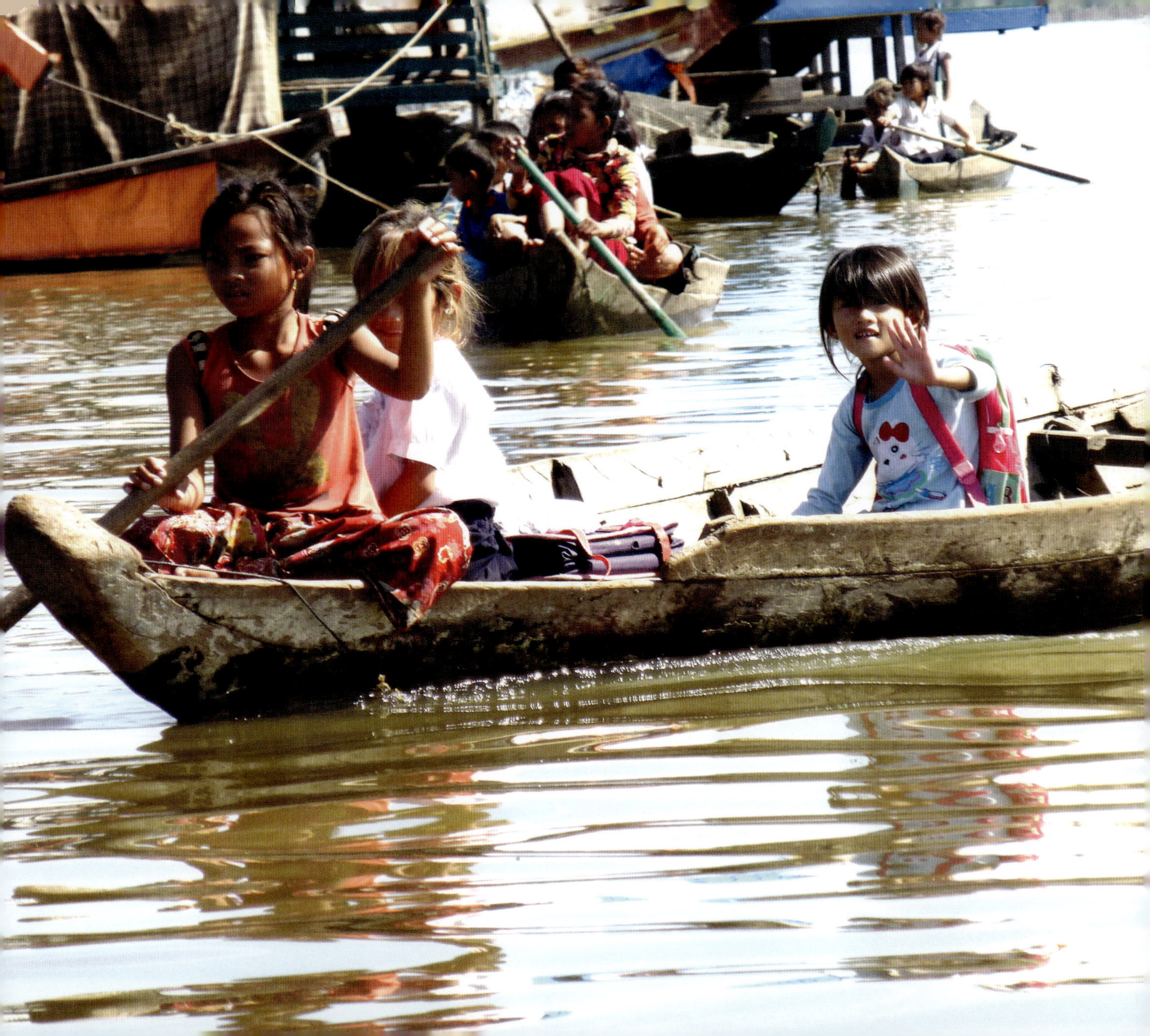

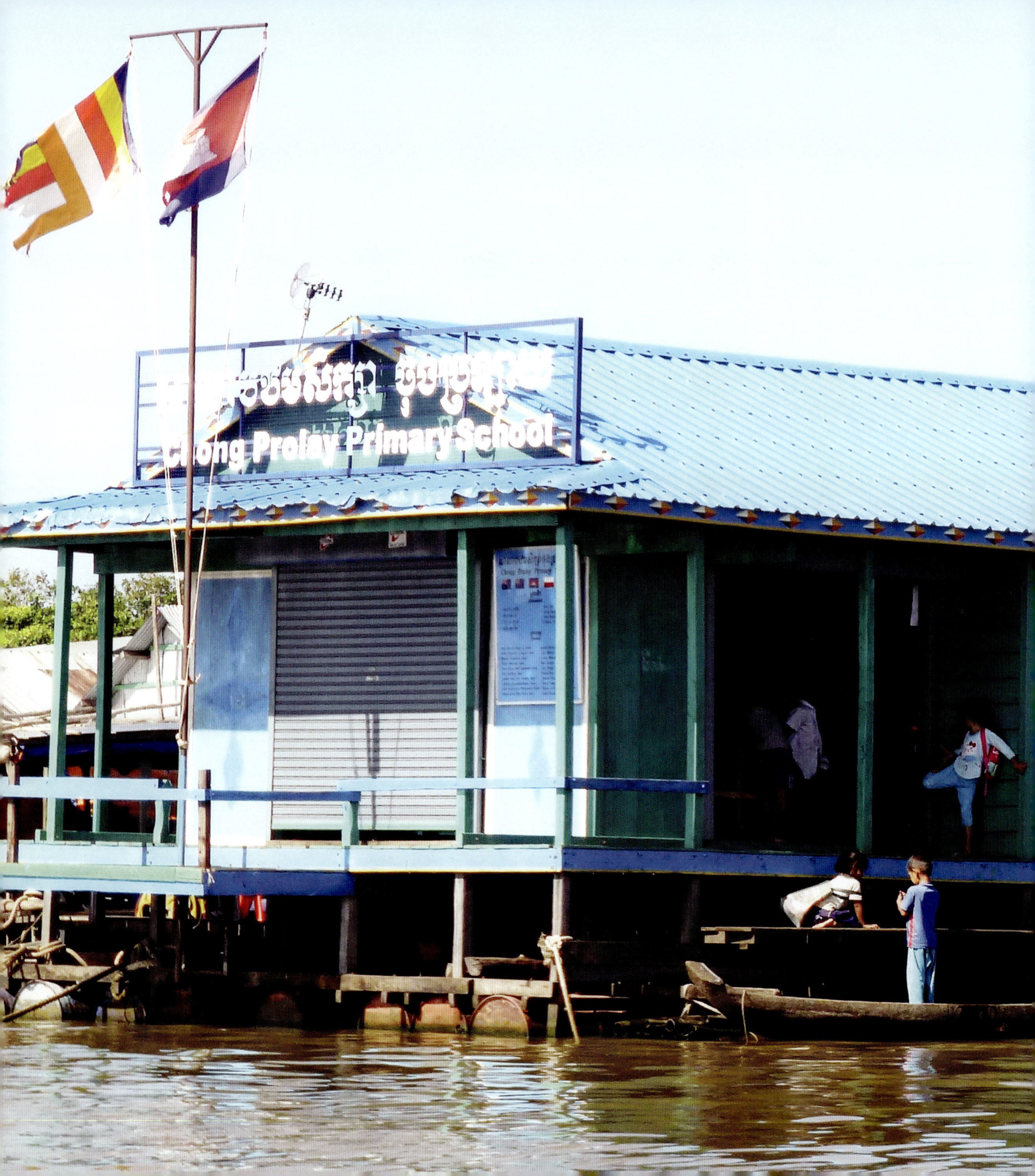
Prolay Primary School

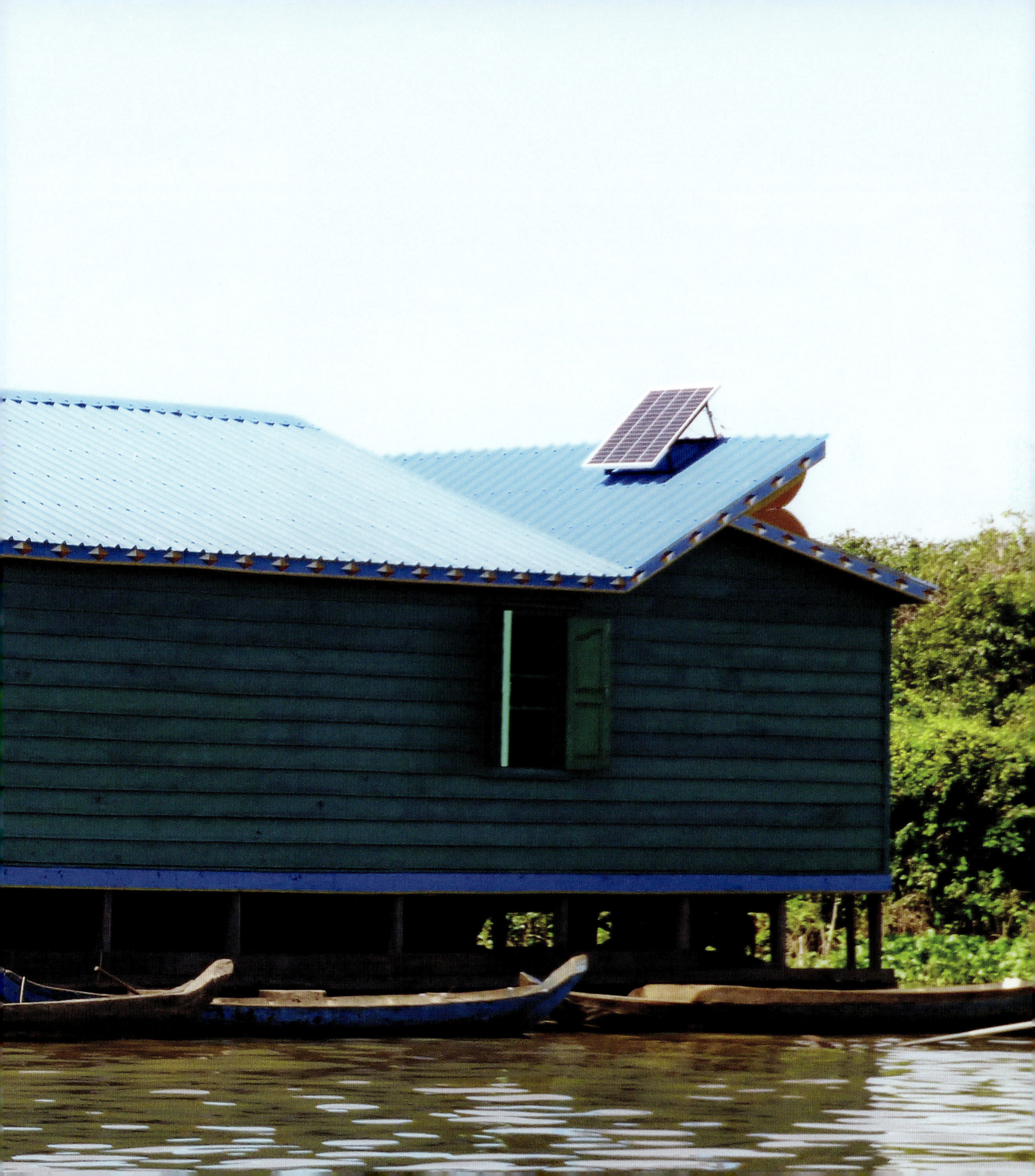

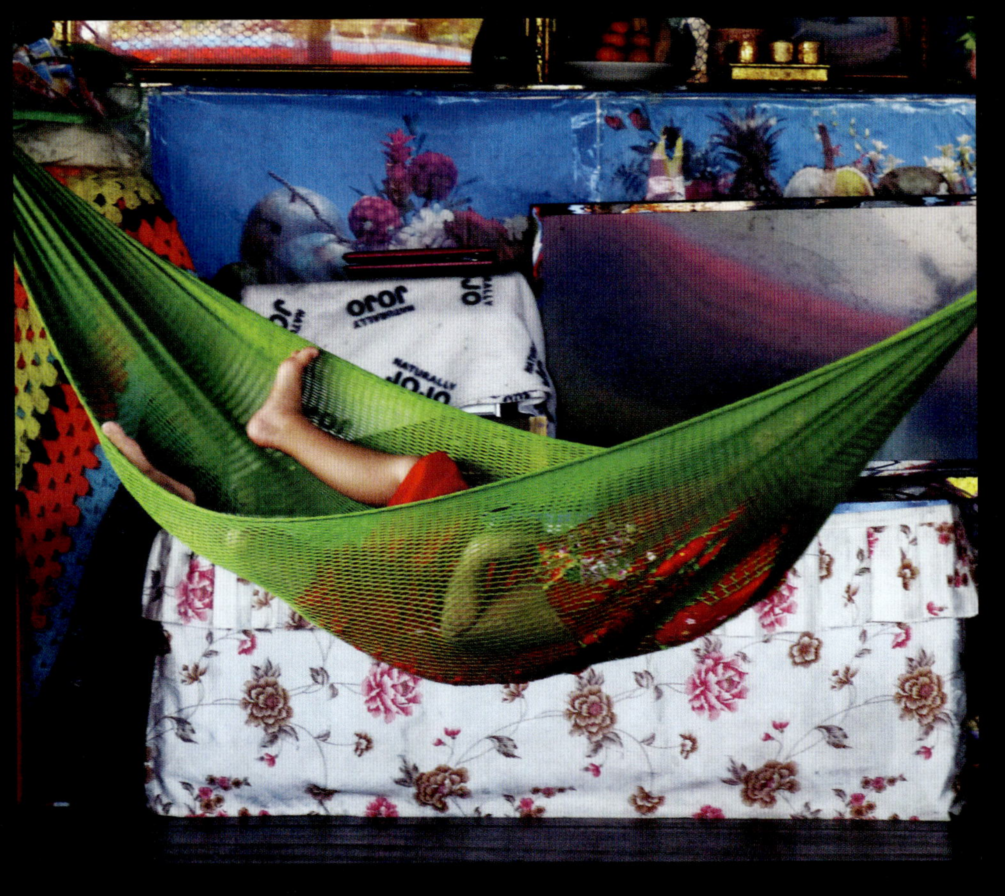

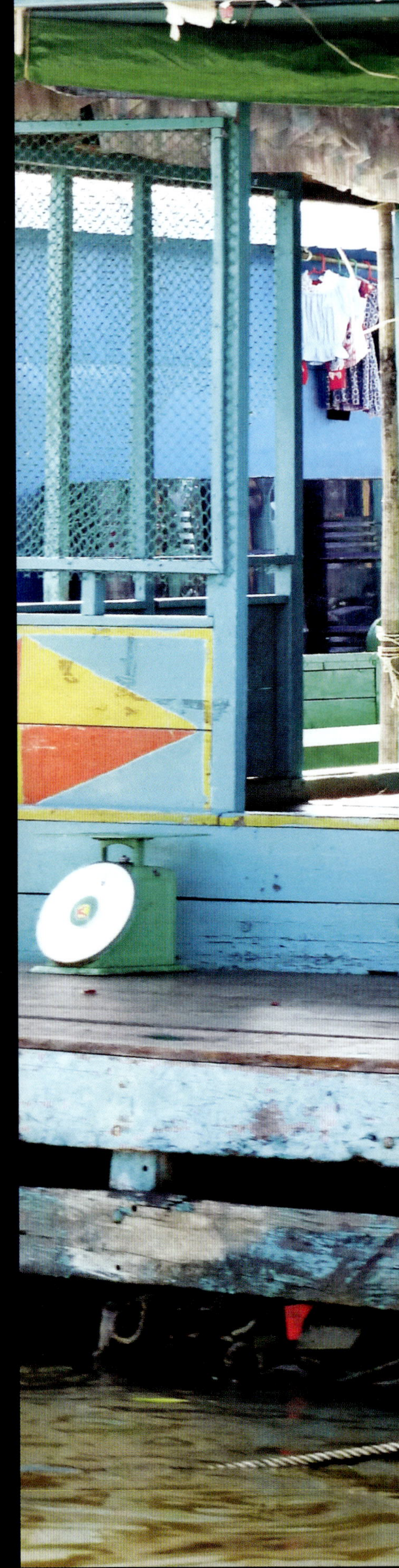

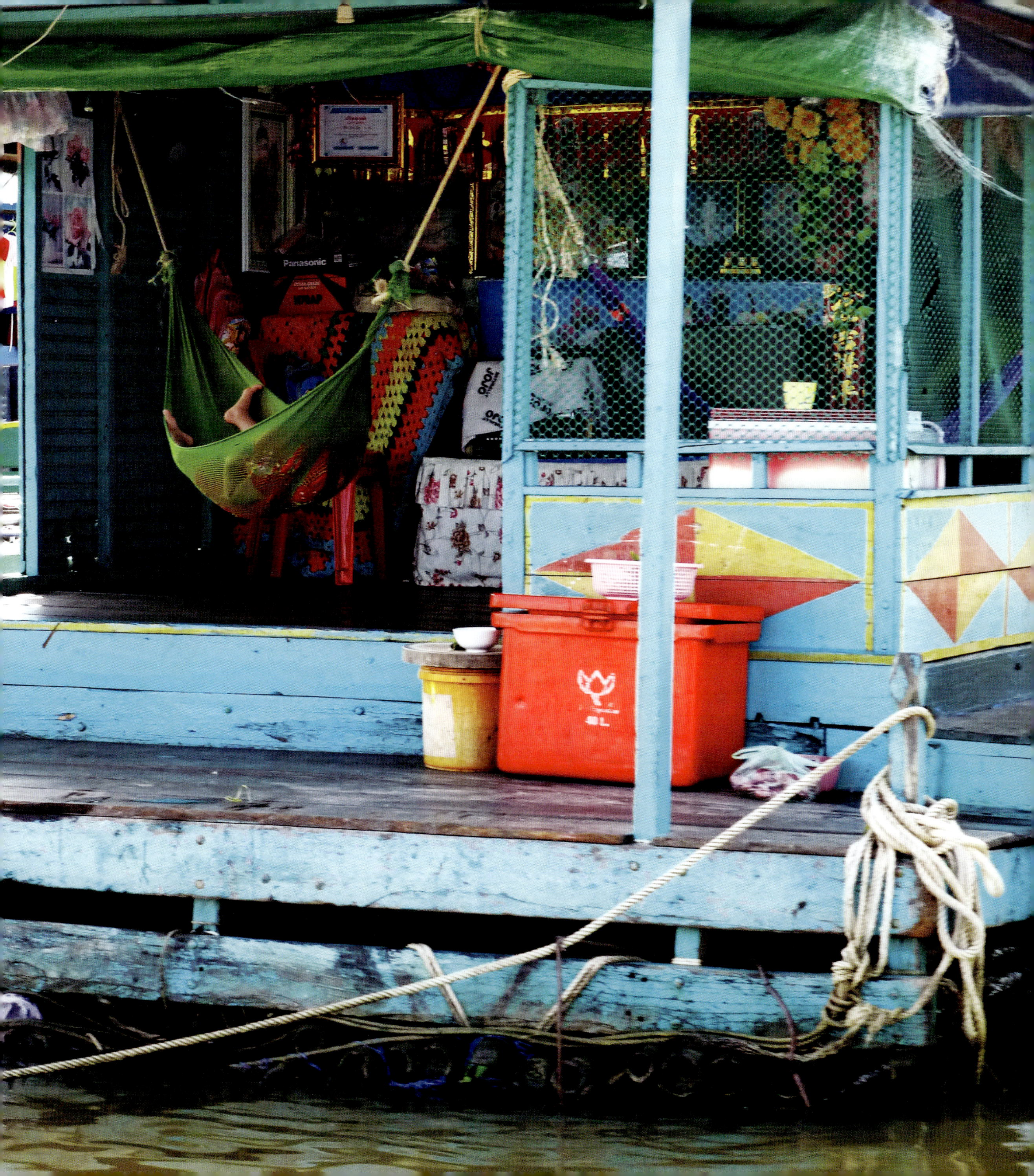
Panasonic

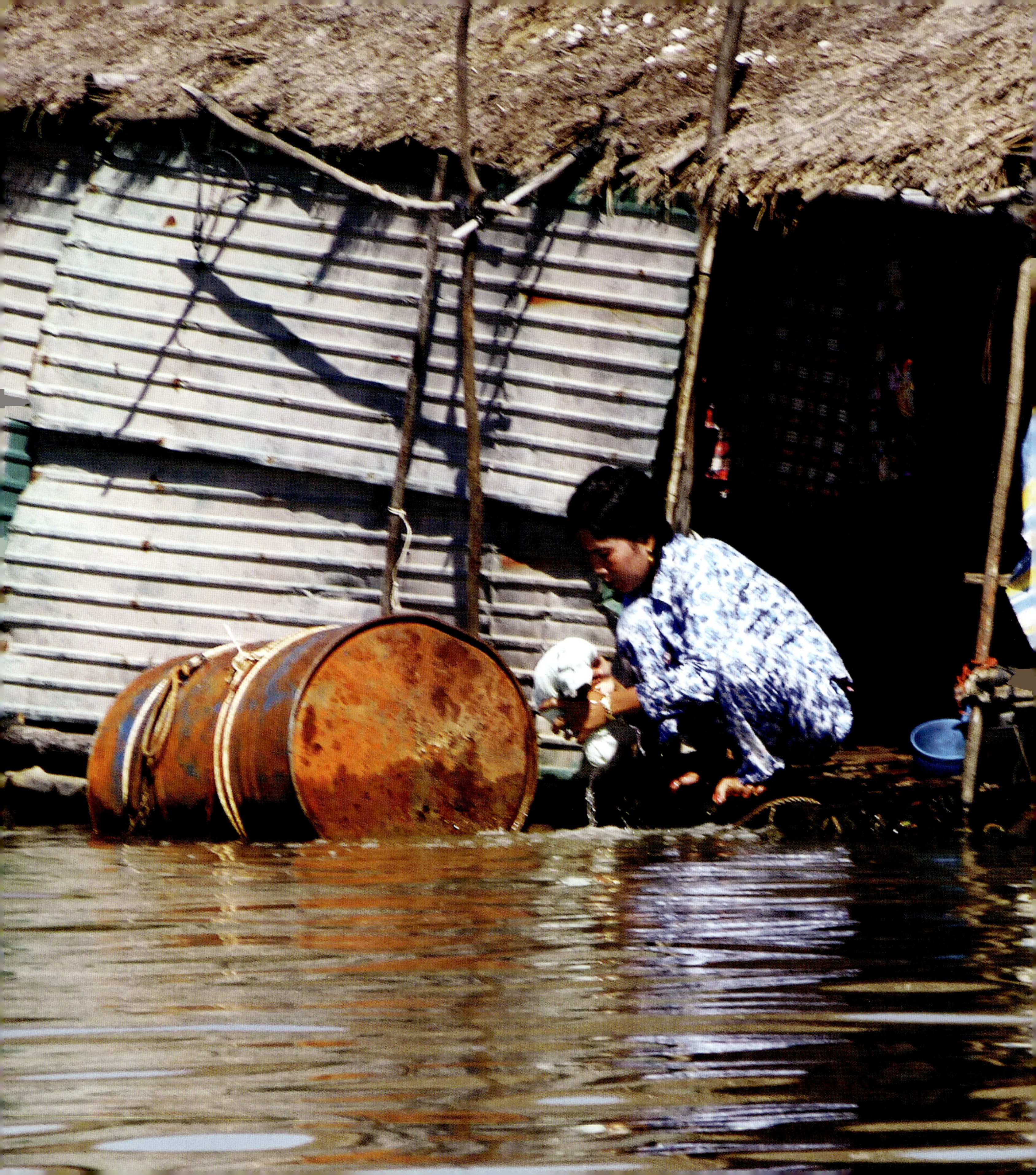

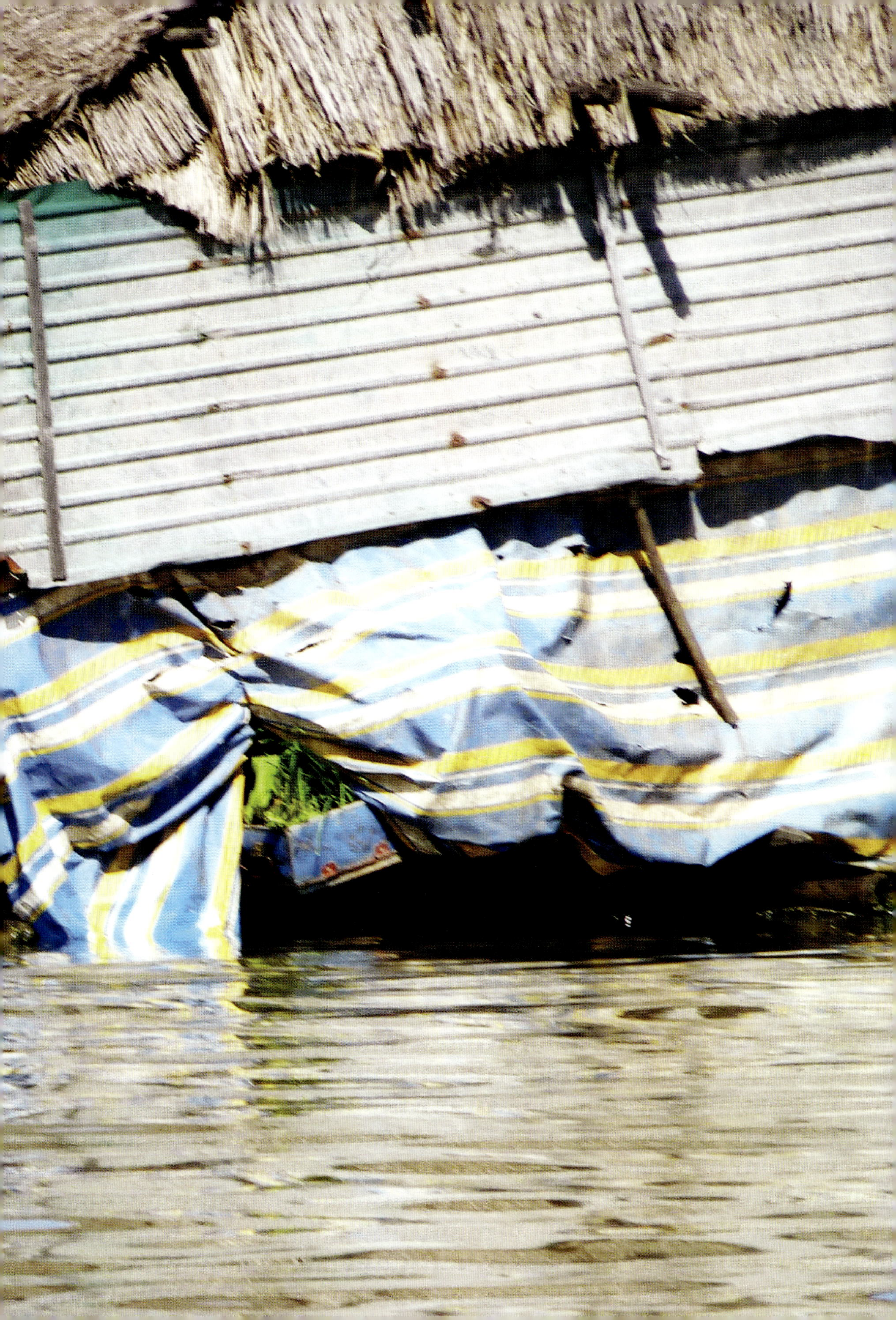

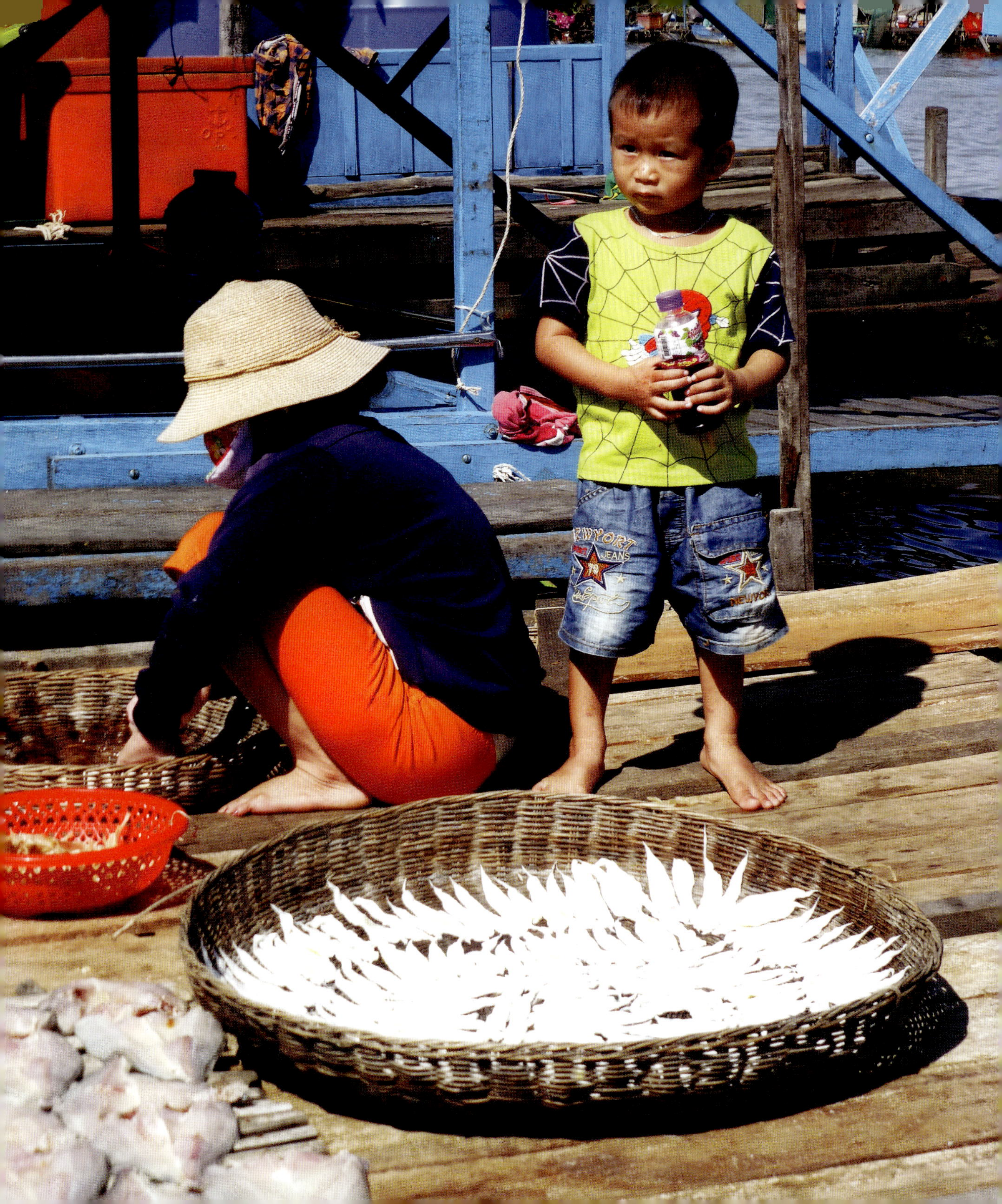
JEANS

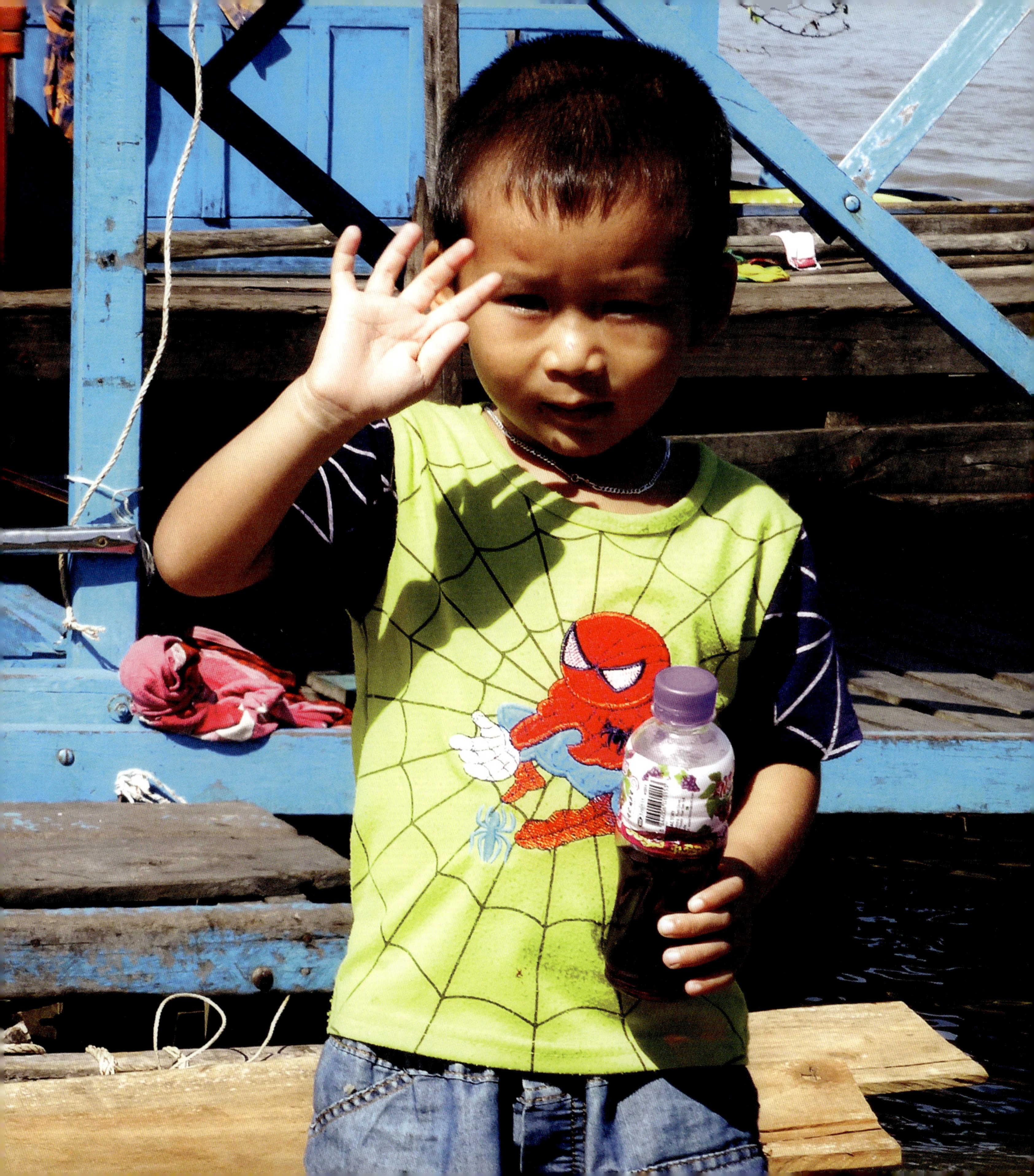

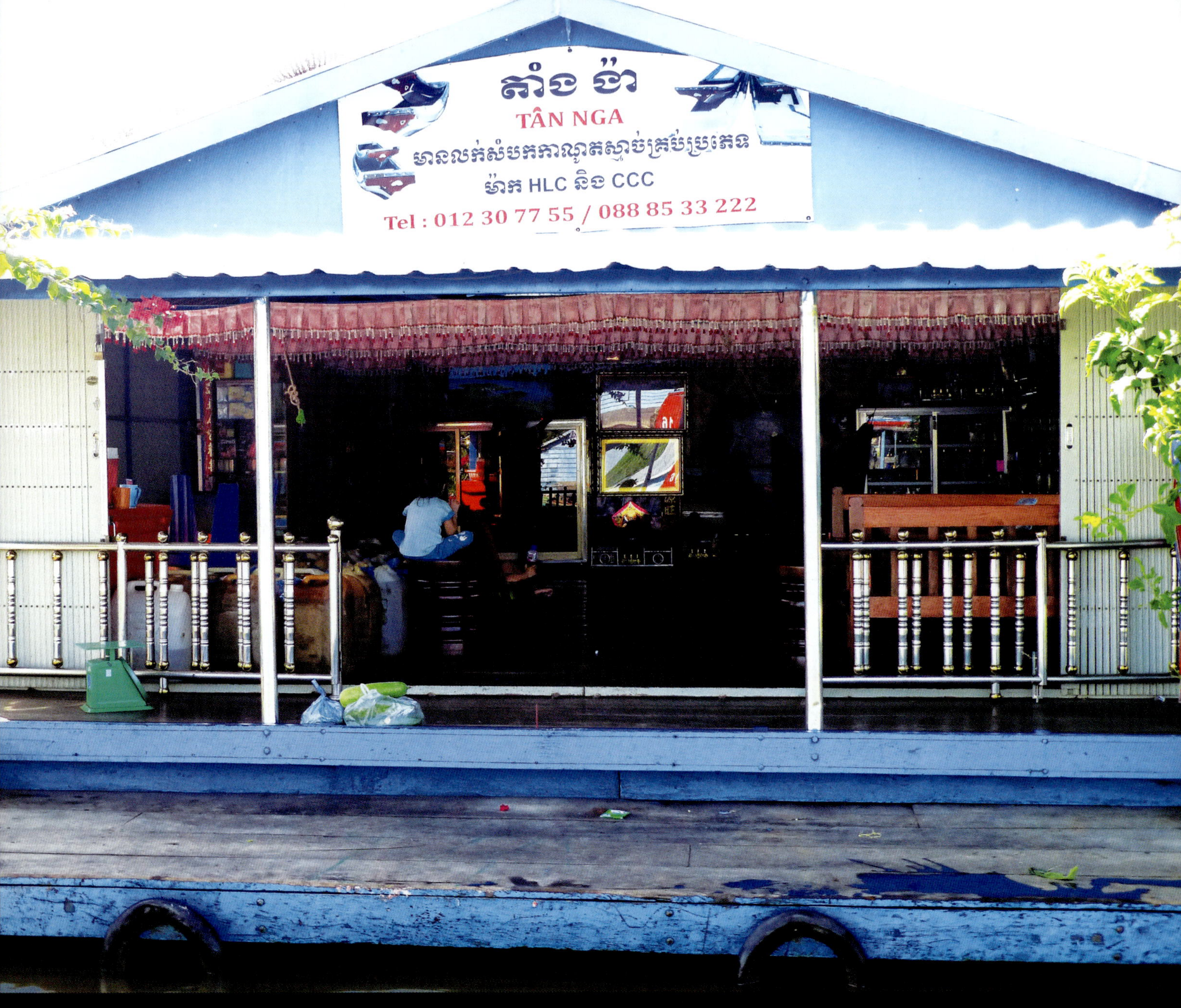

តាំង ង៉ា
TÂN NGA
ម៉ាក HLC និង CCC
Tel : 012 30 77 55 / 088 85 33 222

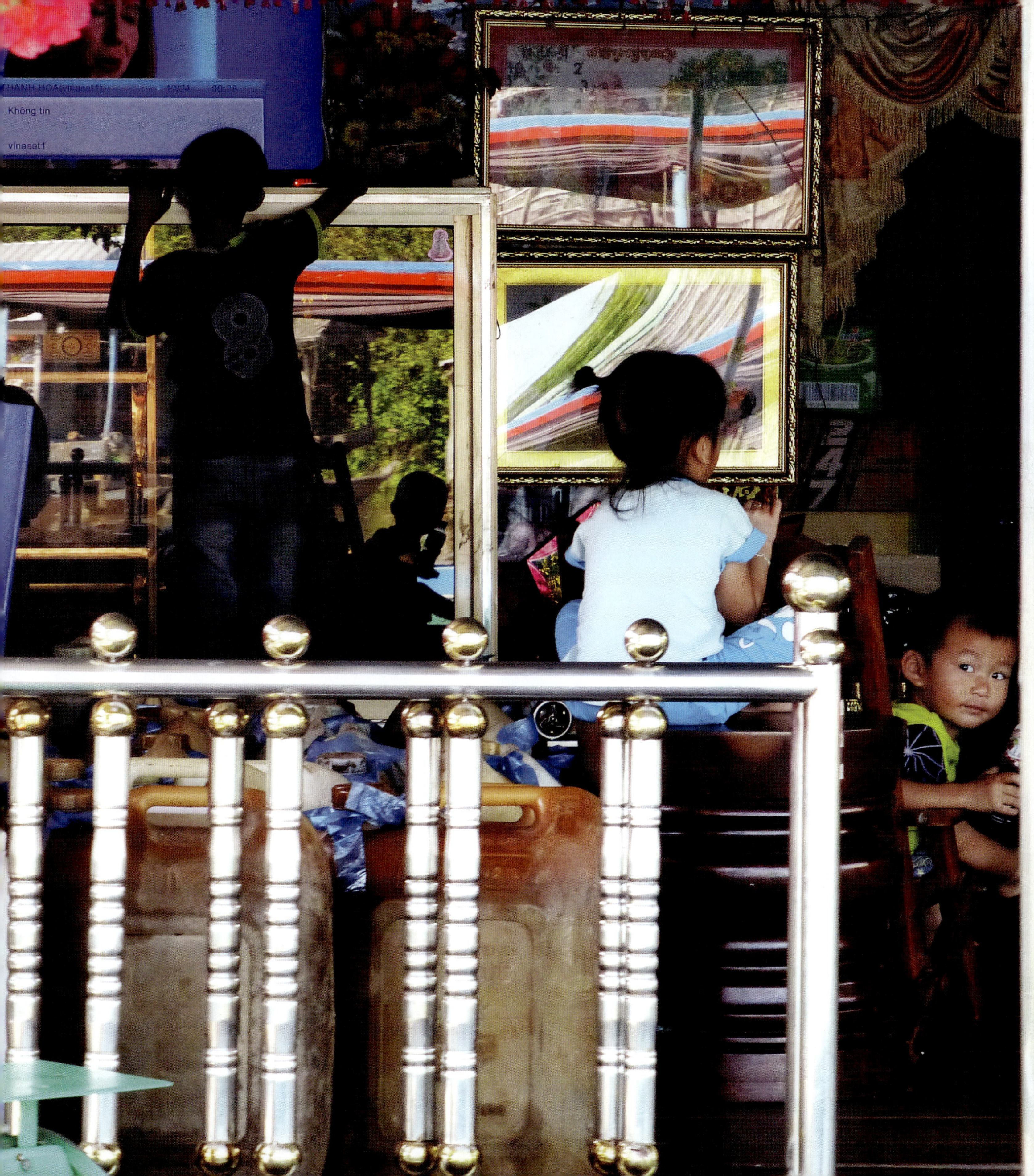
THANH HOA(vinasat1)
Không tin
vinasat1

FIVE

In the Mekong Delta Vietnam

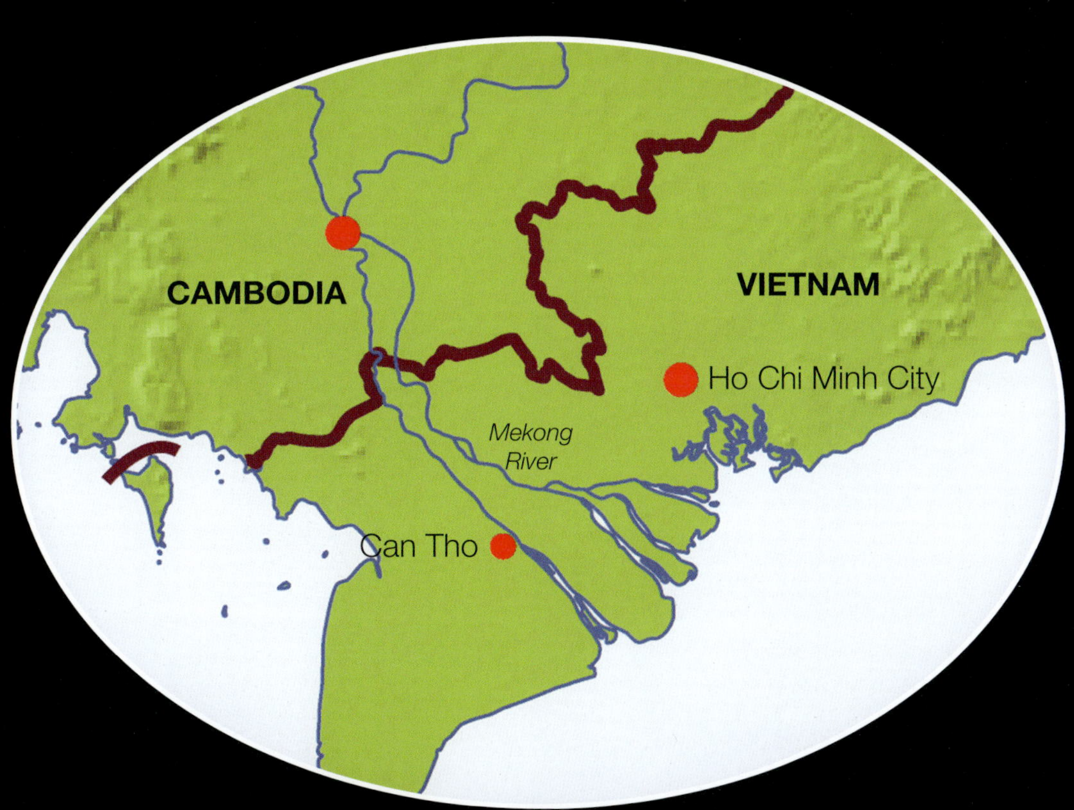

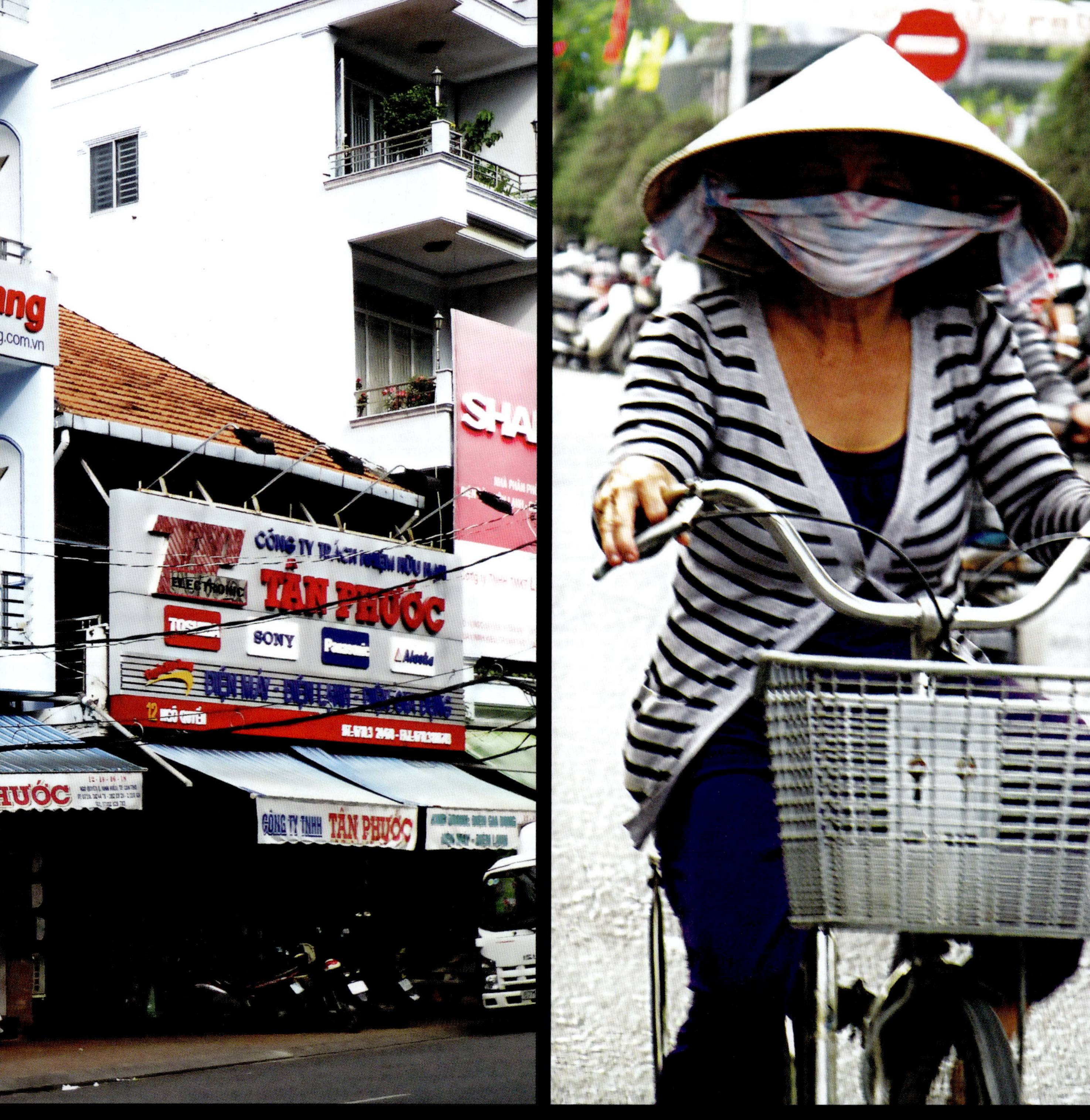

Can Tho, Vietnam's 4th largest city. A commercial hub for the Mekong Delta.

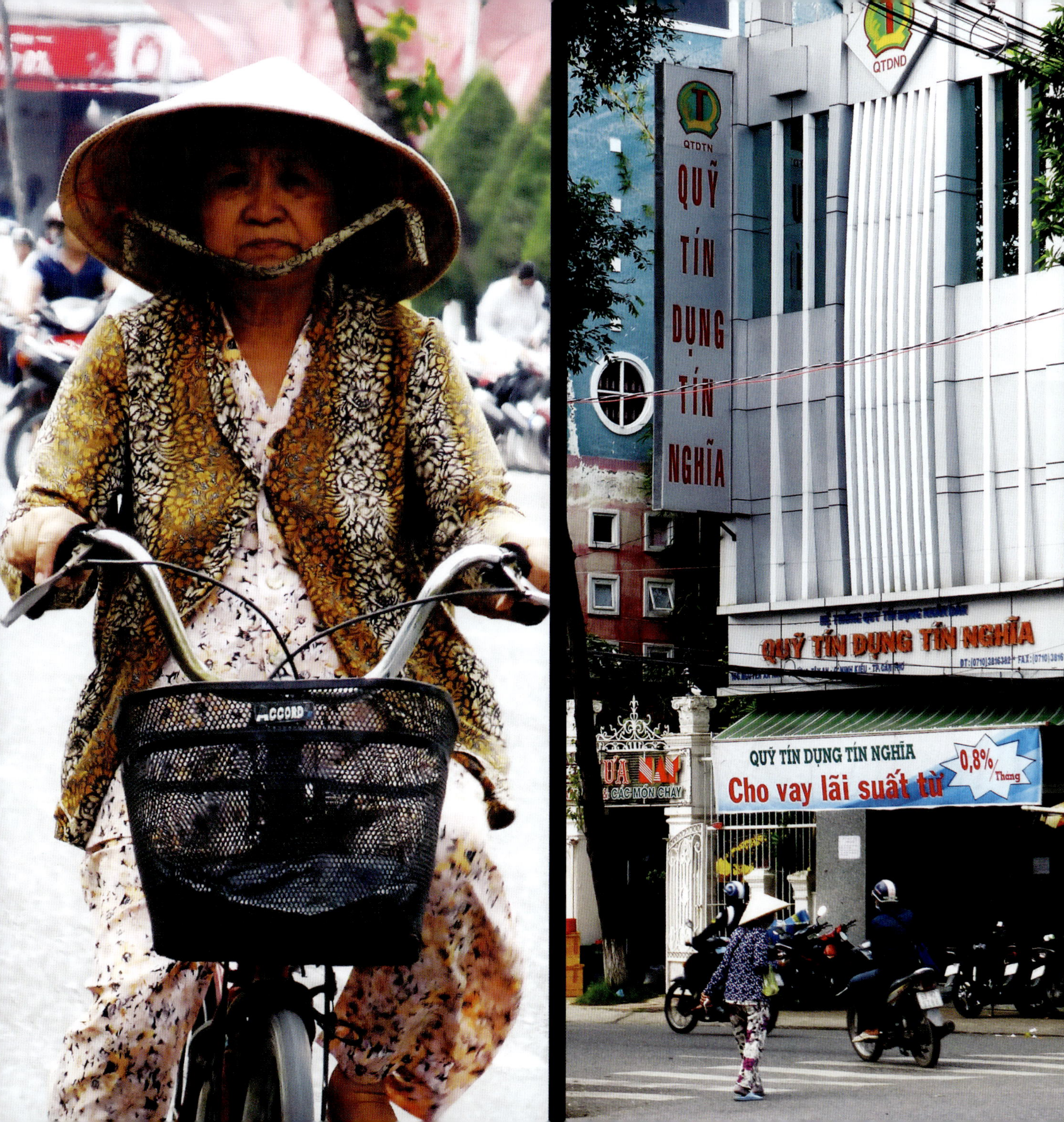
ACCORD
QTDND
QTDTN
QUỸ TÍN DỤNG TÍN NGHĨA
QUỸ TÍN DỤNG TÍN NGHĨA
QUỸ TÍN DỤNG TÍN NGHĨA
Cho vay lãi suất từ
0,8% Tháng
CÁC MÓN CHAY

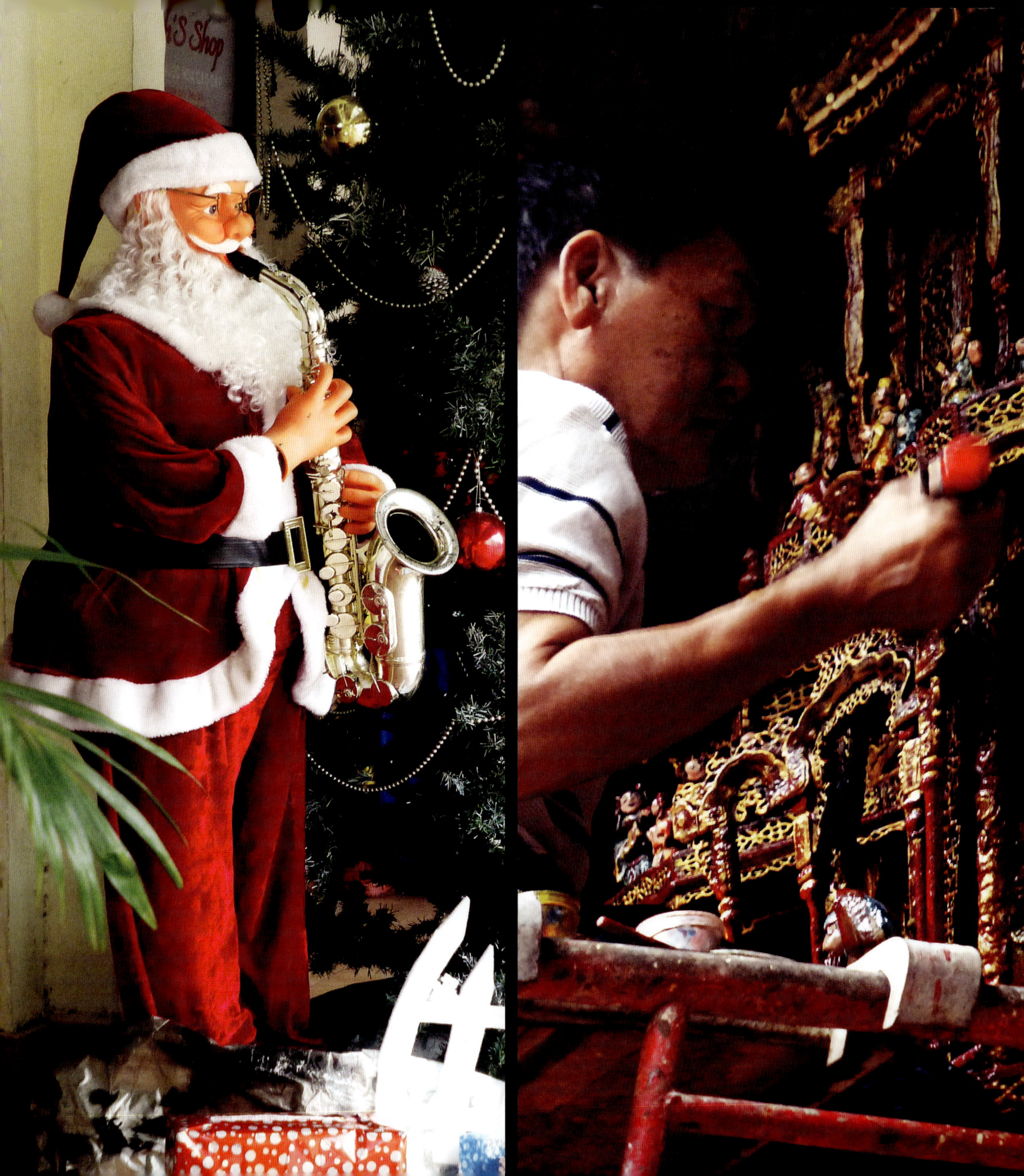

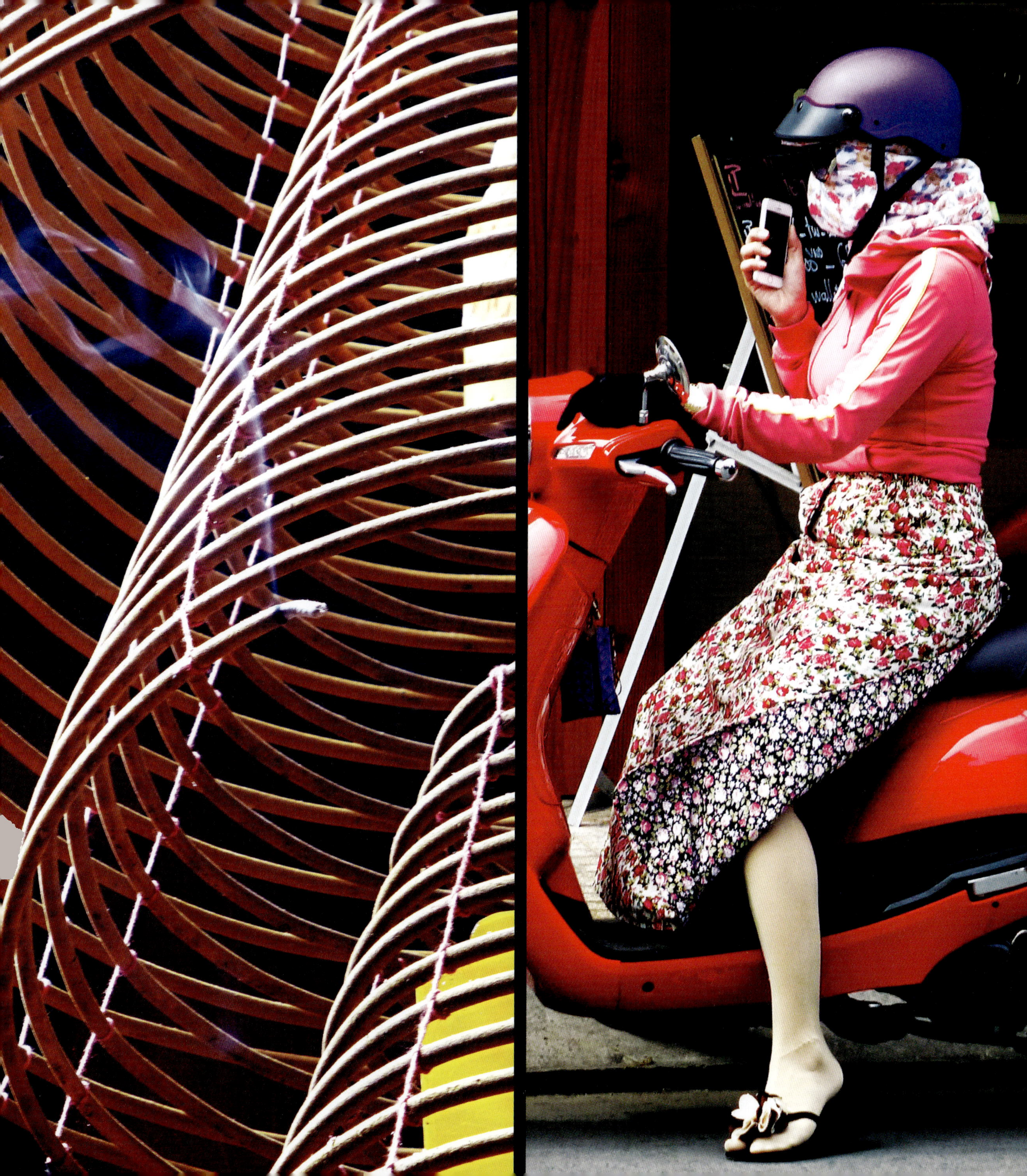

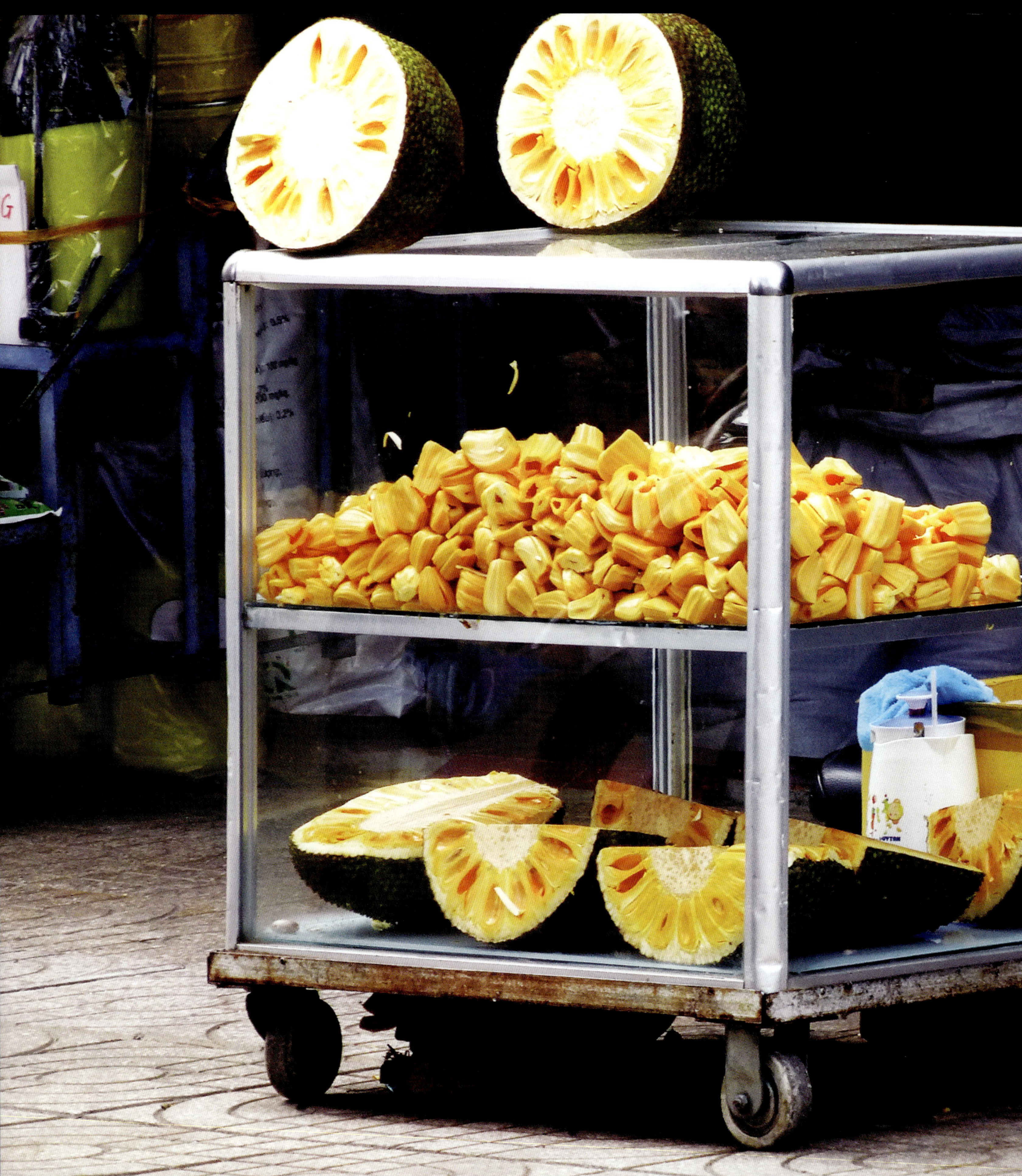

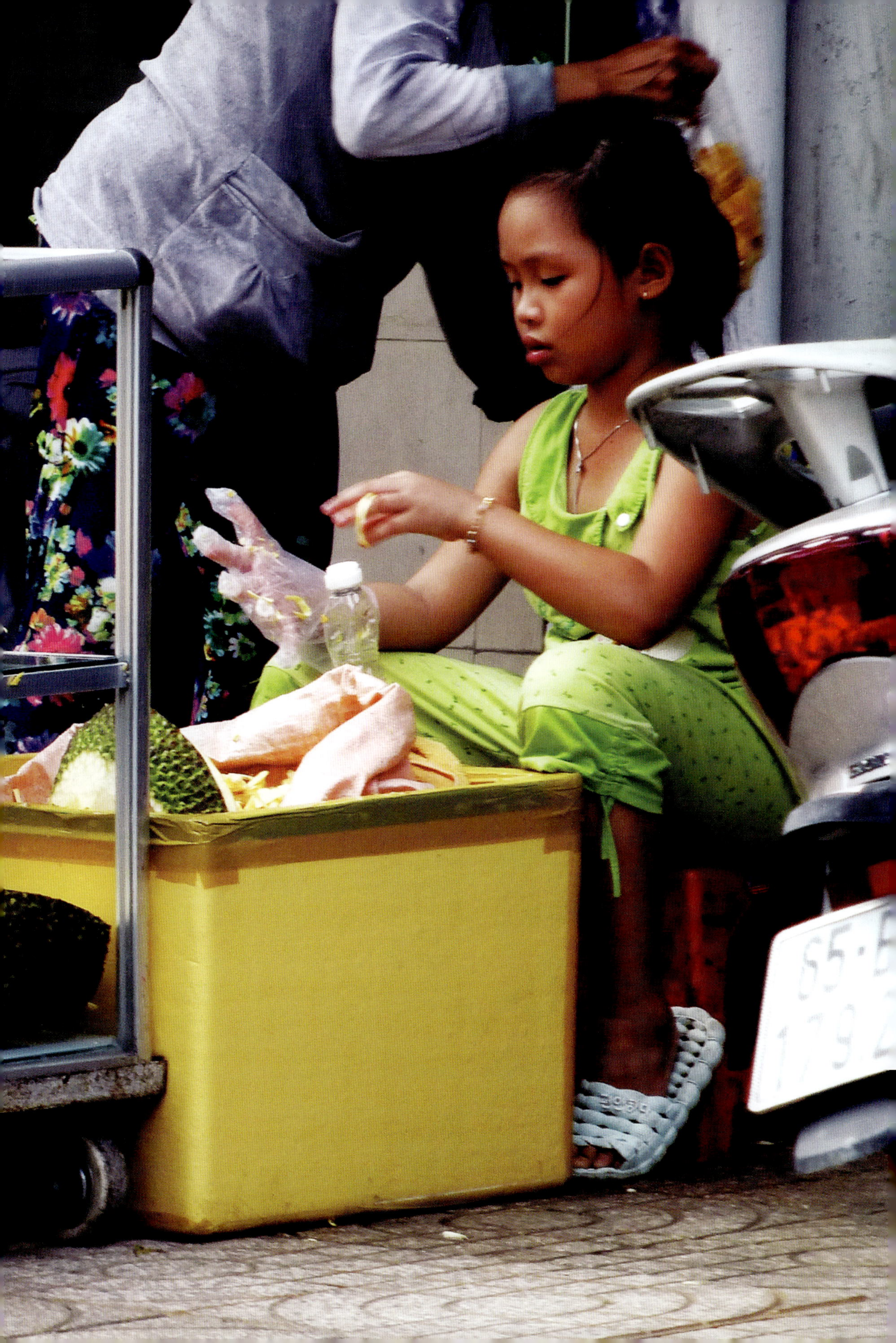

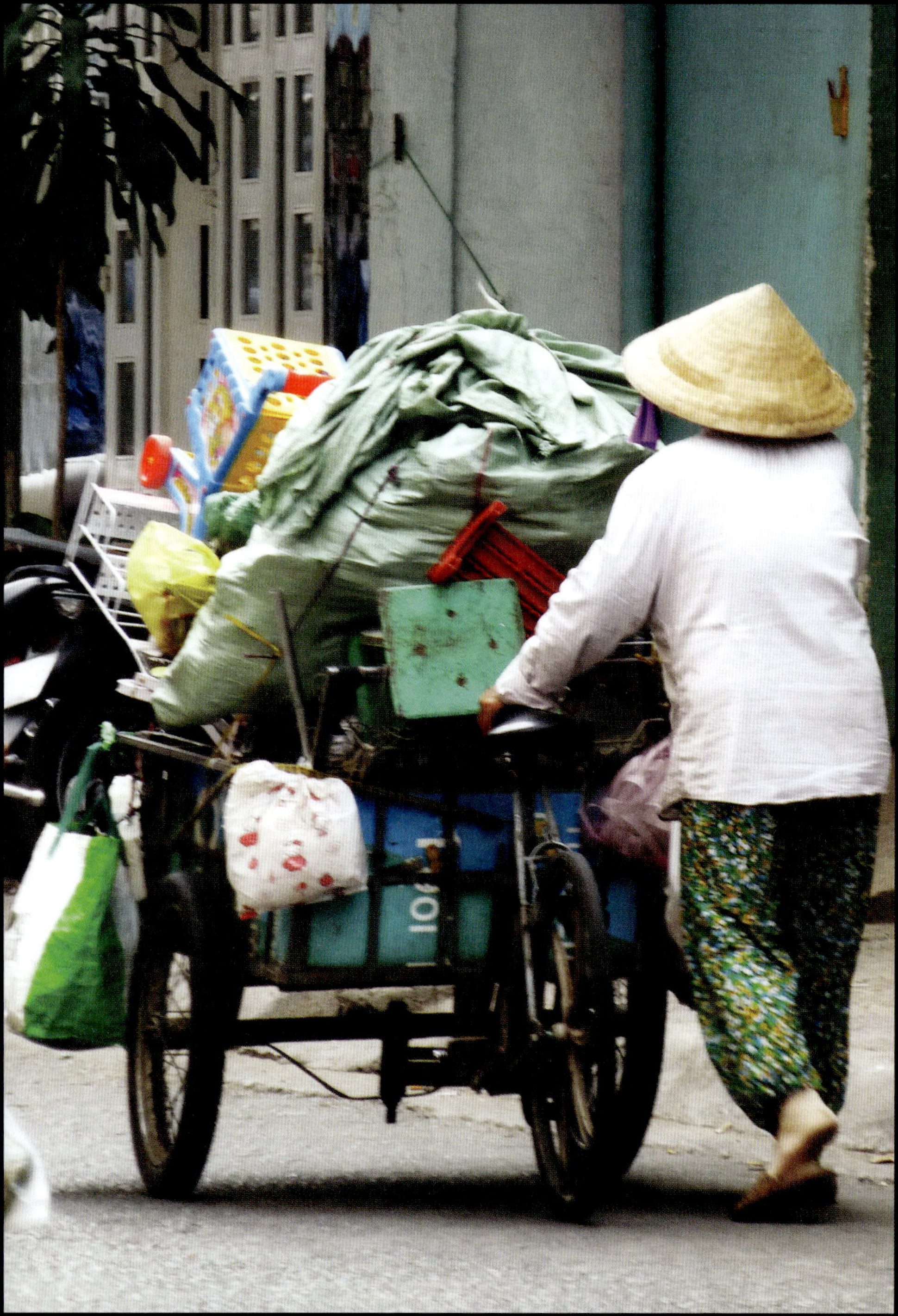

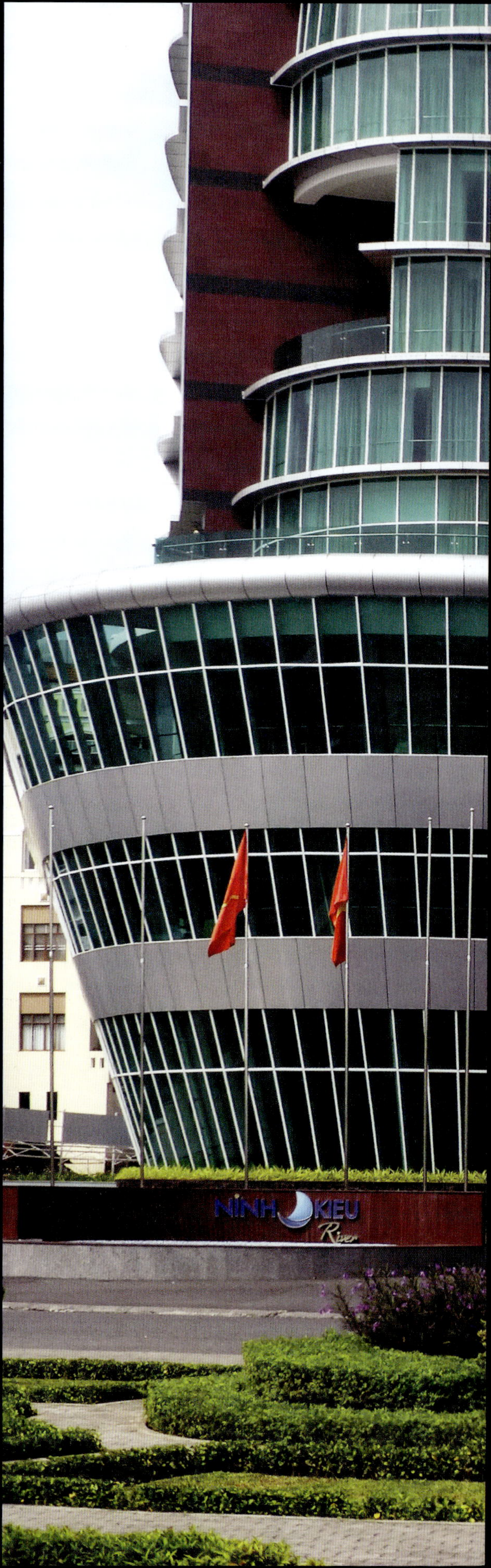

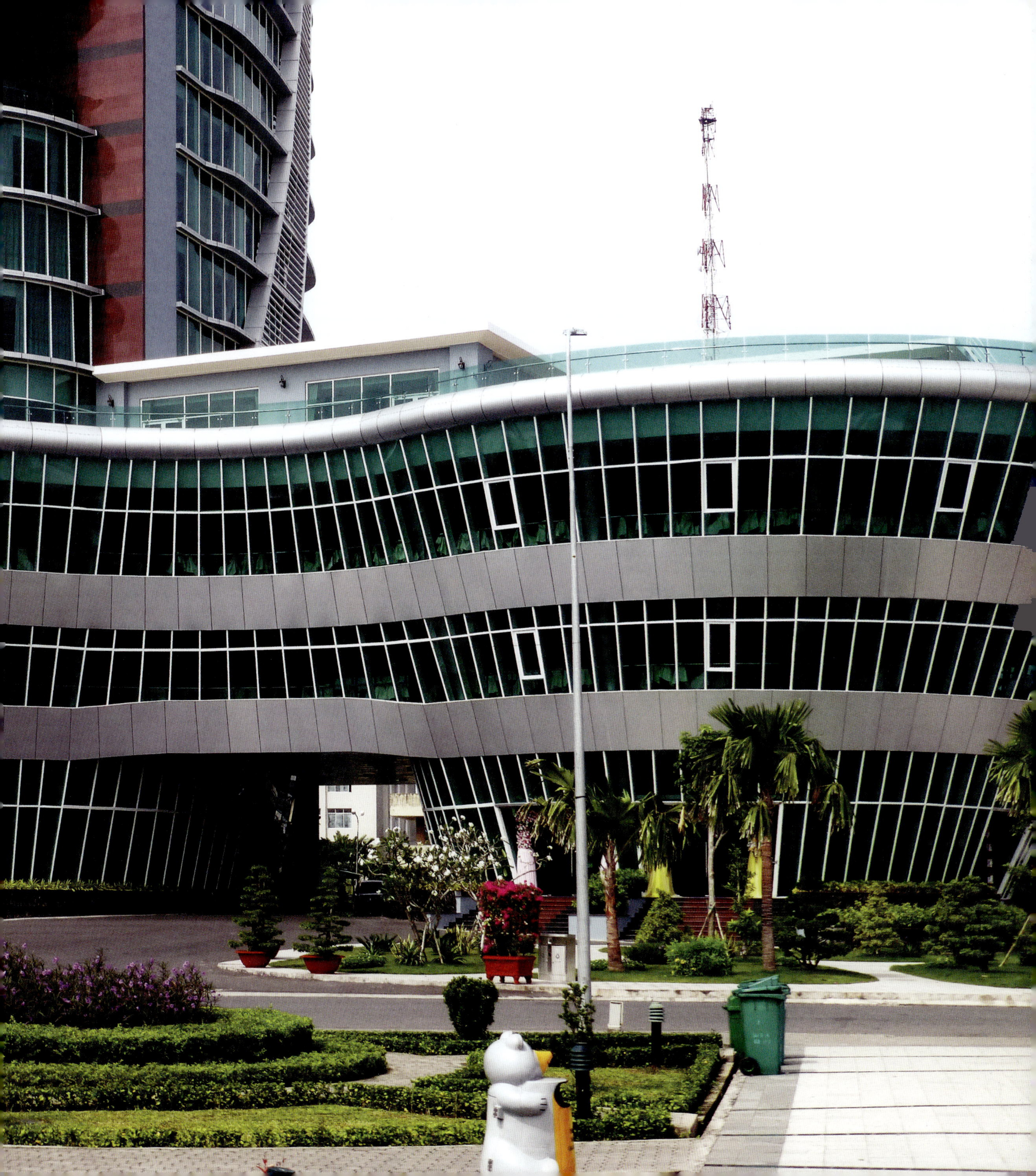

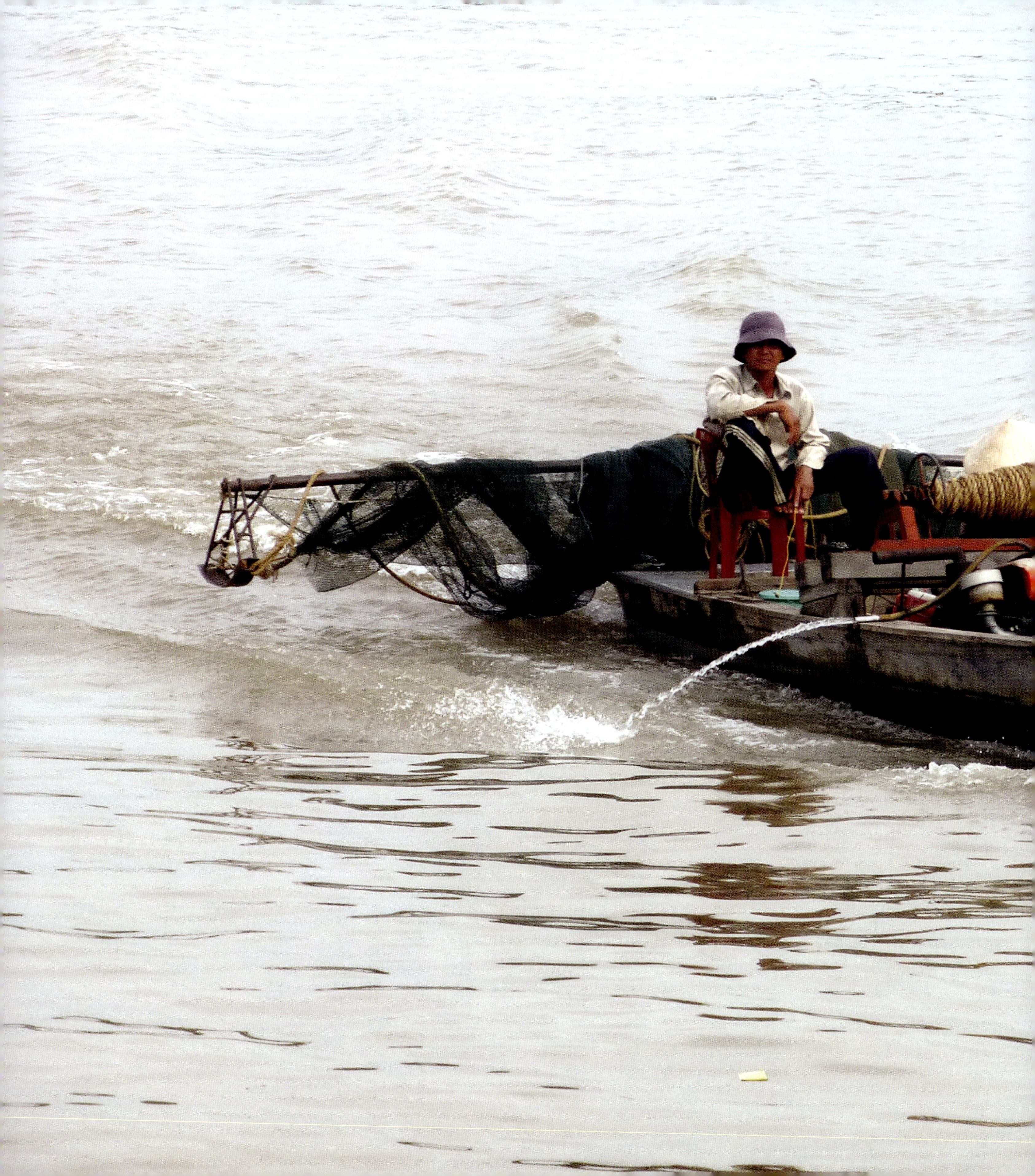

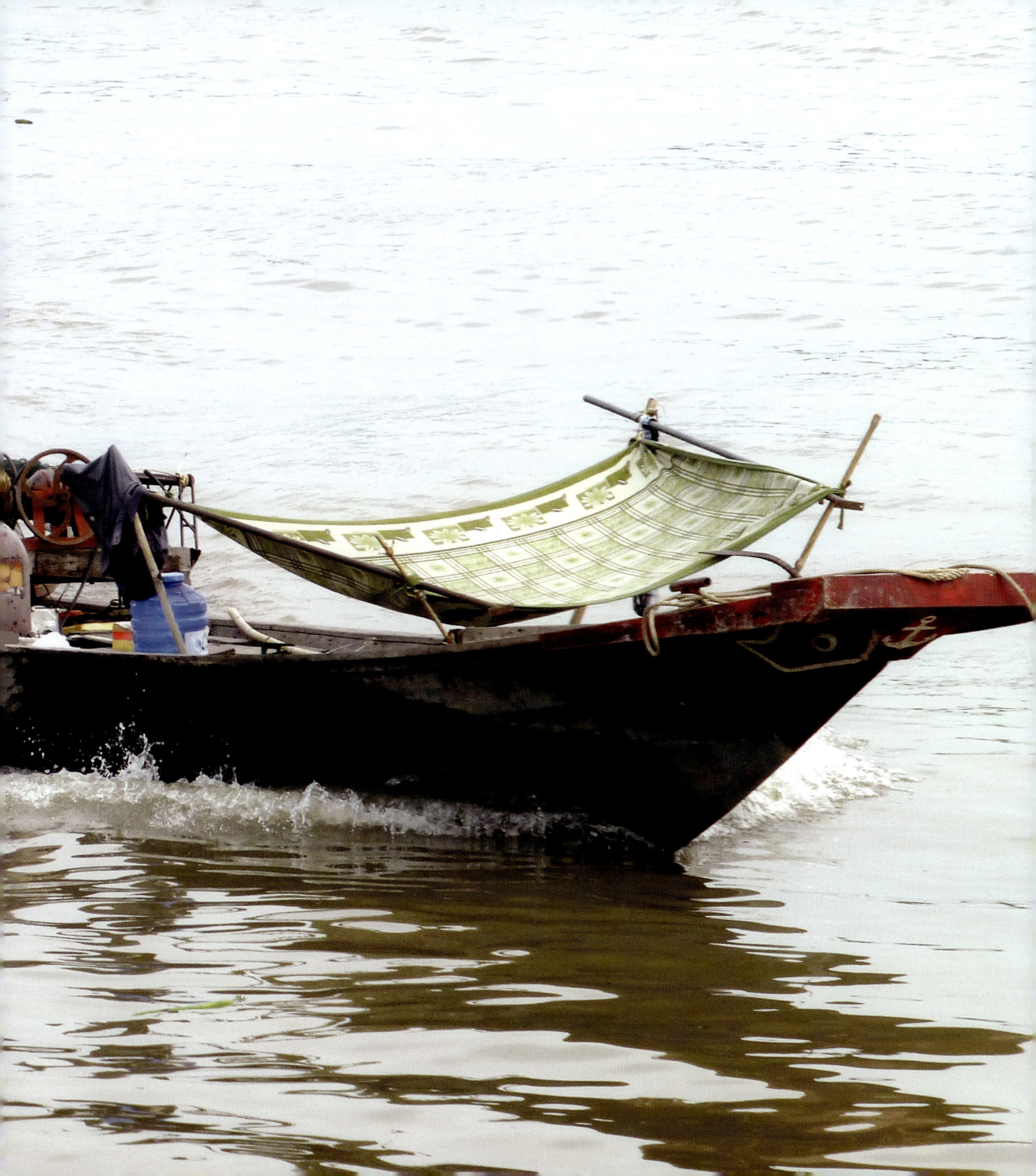

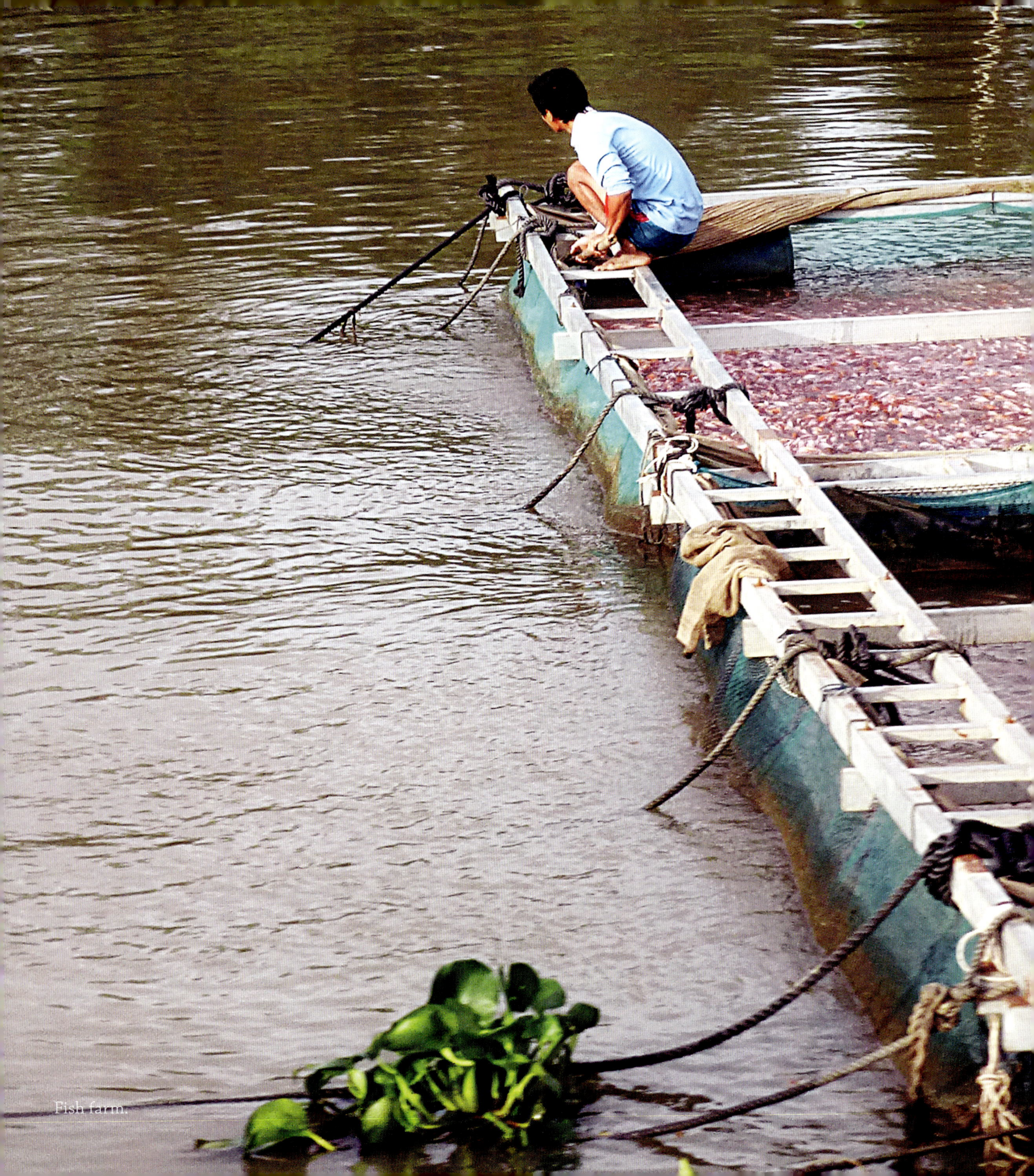
Fish farm.

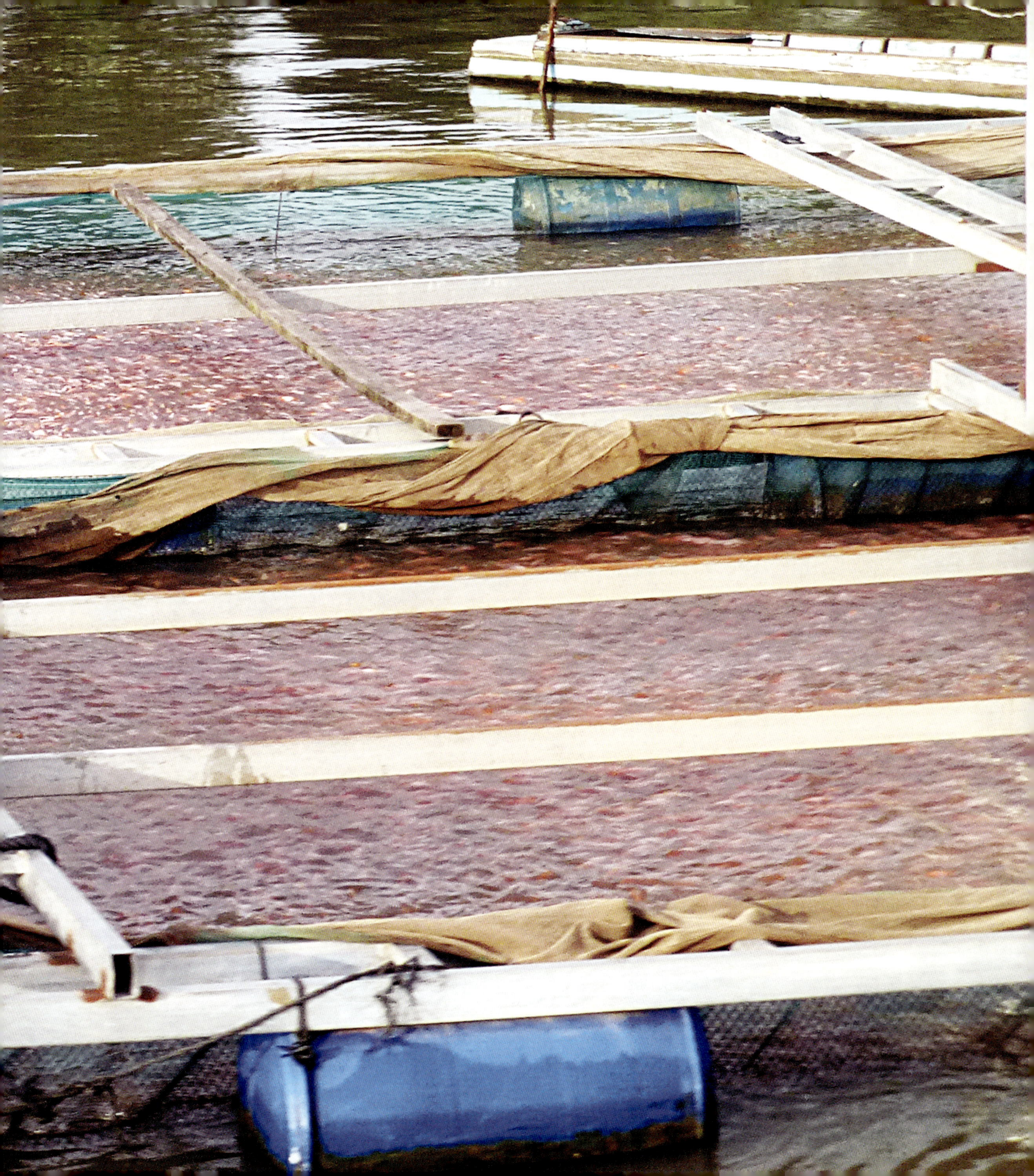

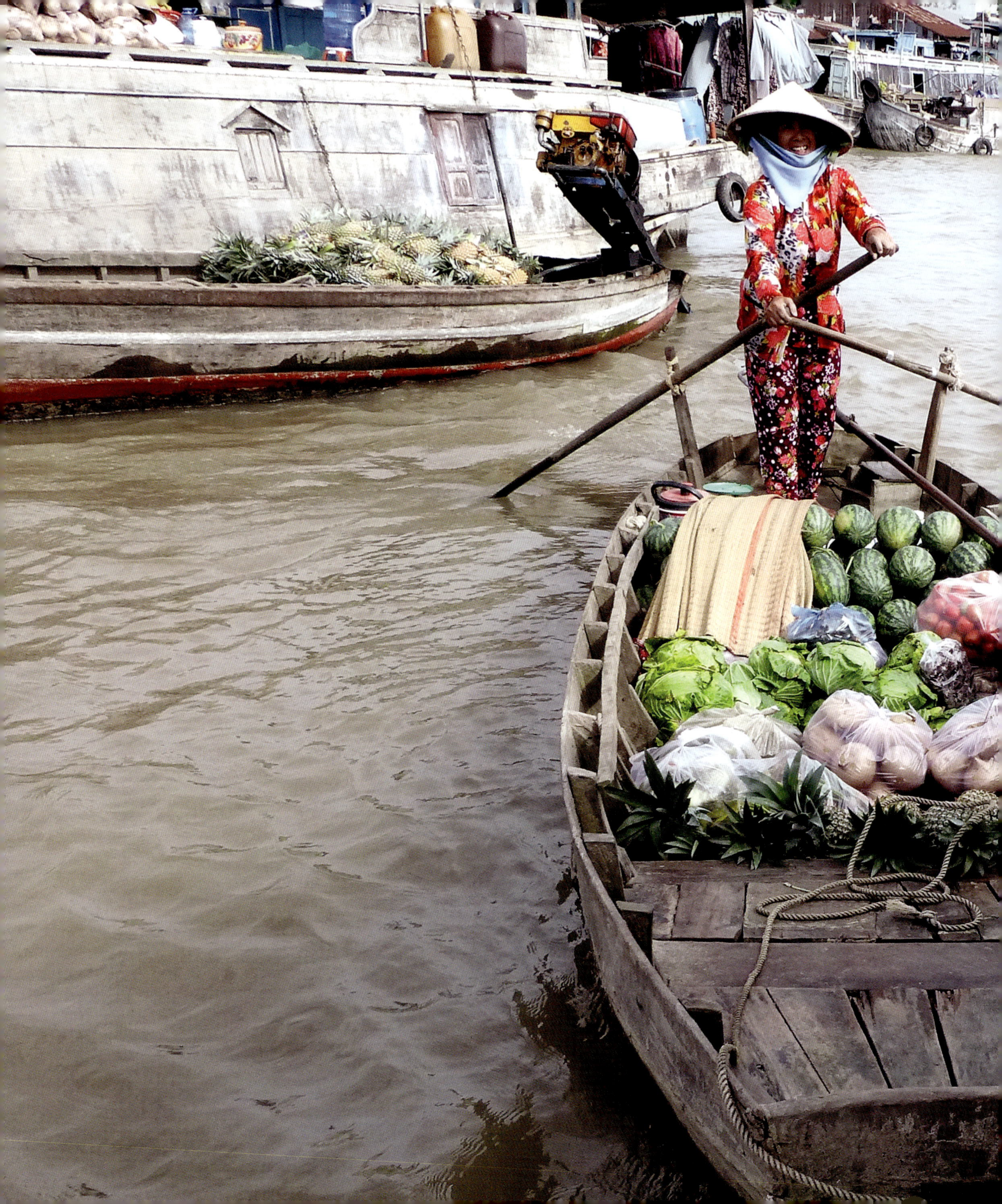

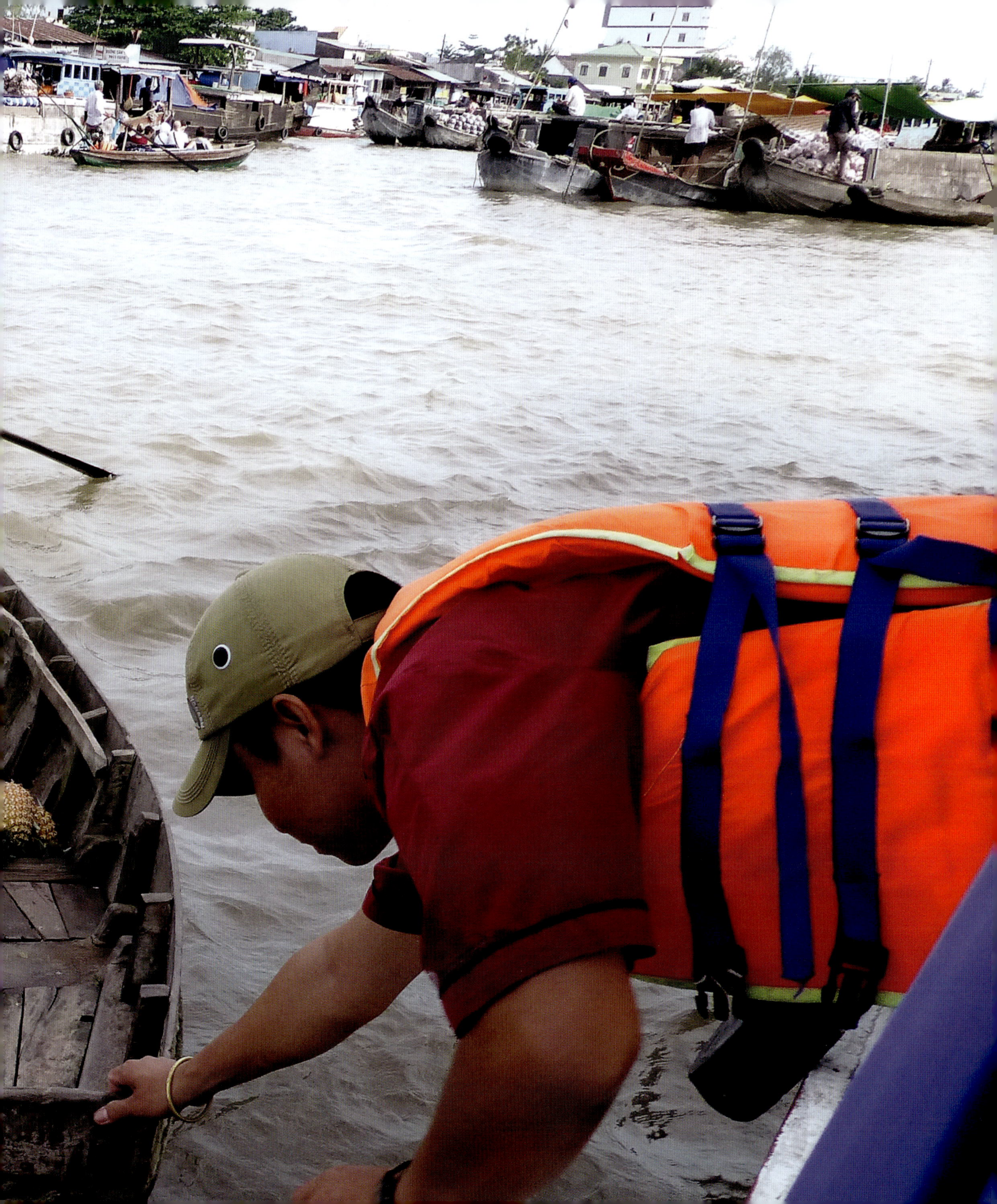

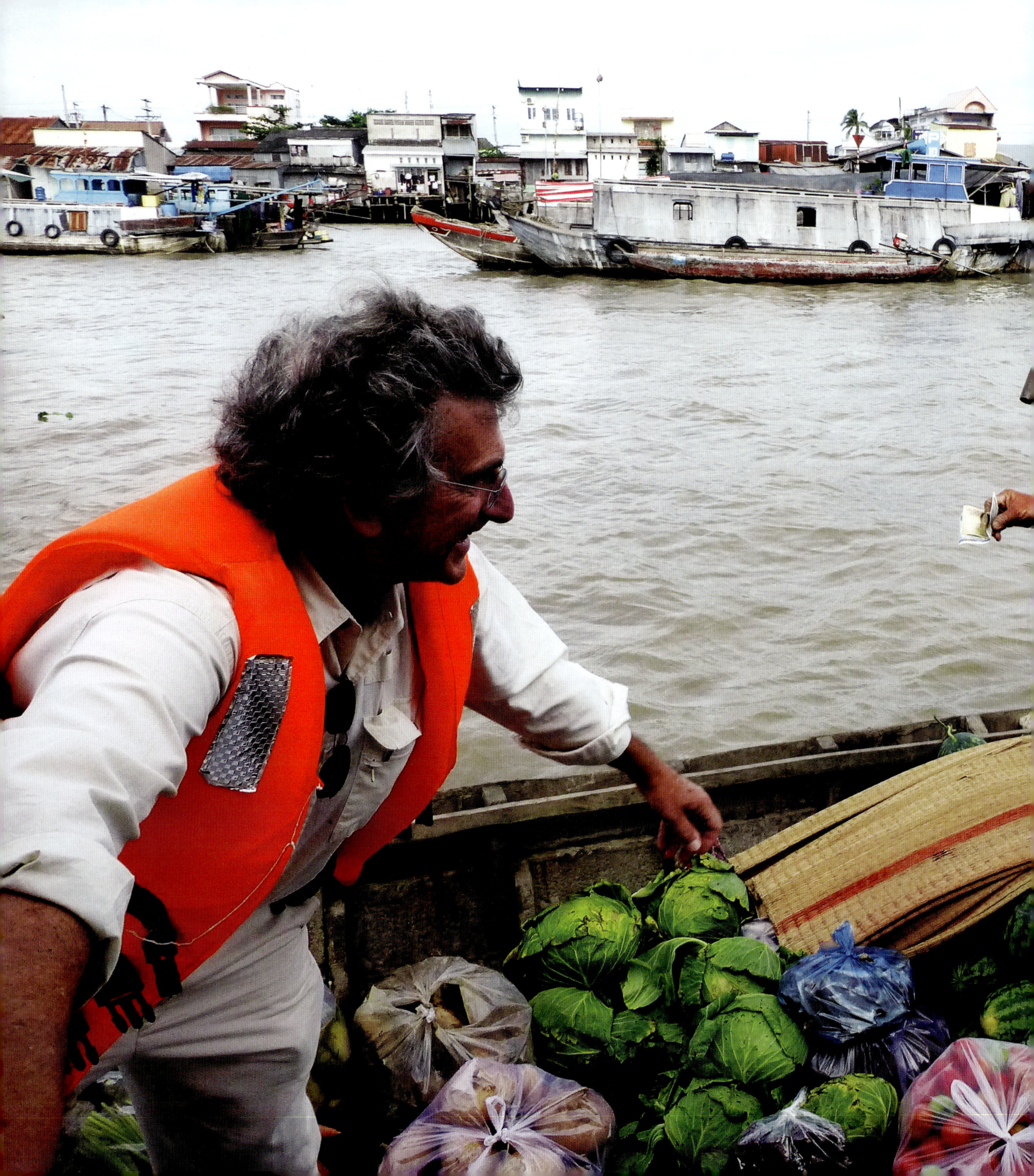

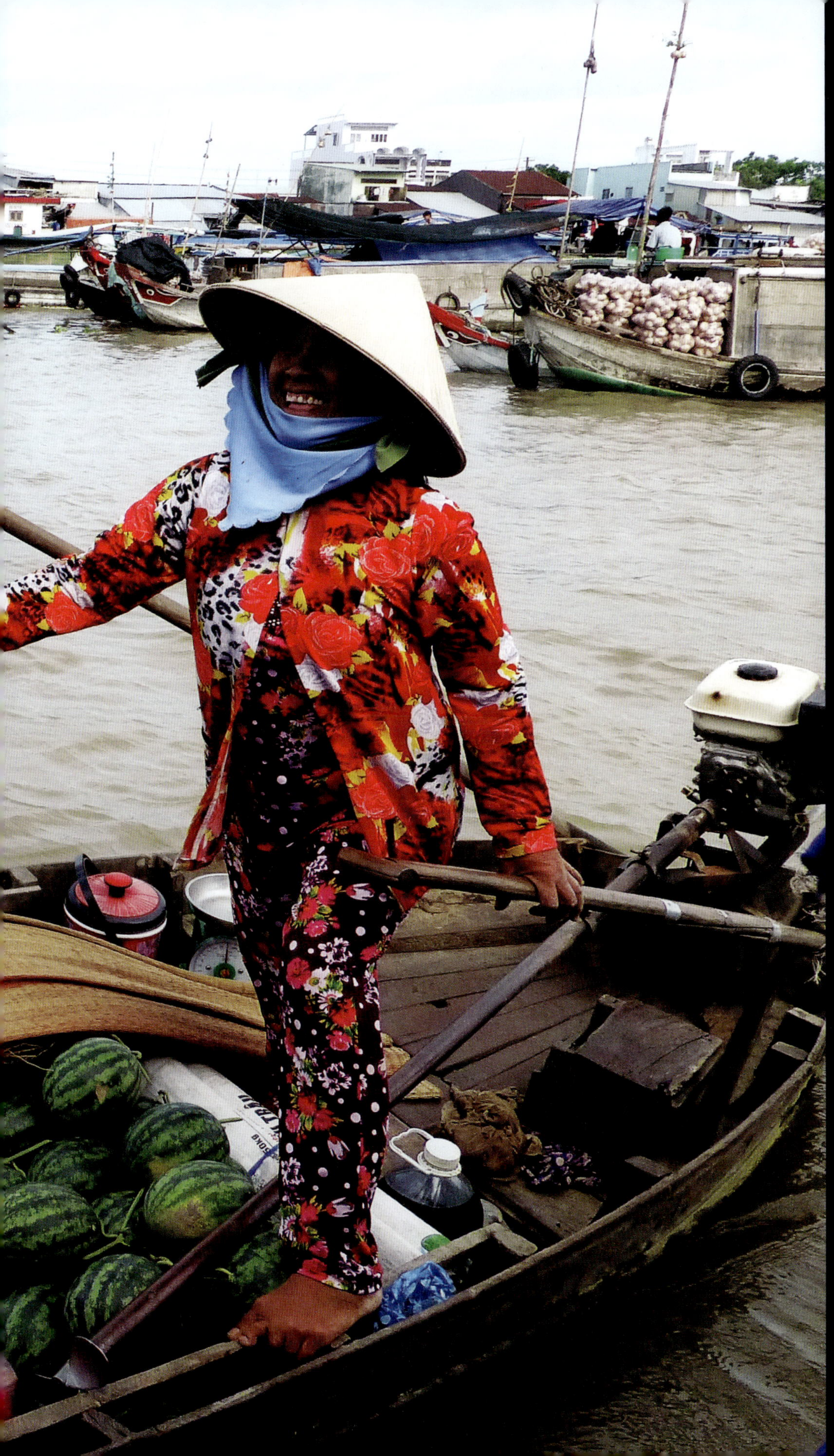

The author shopping at the floating and riverside markets.

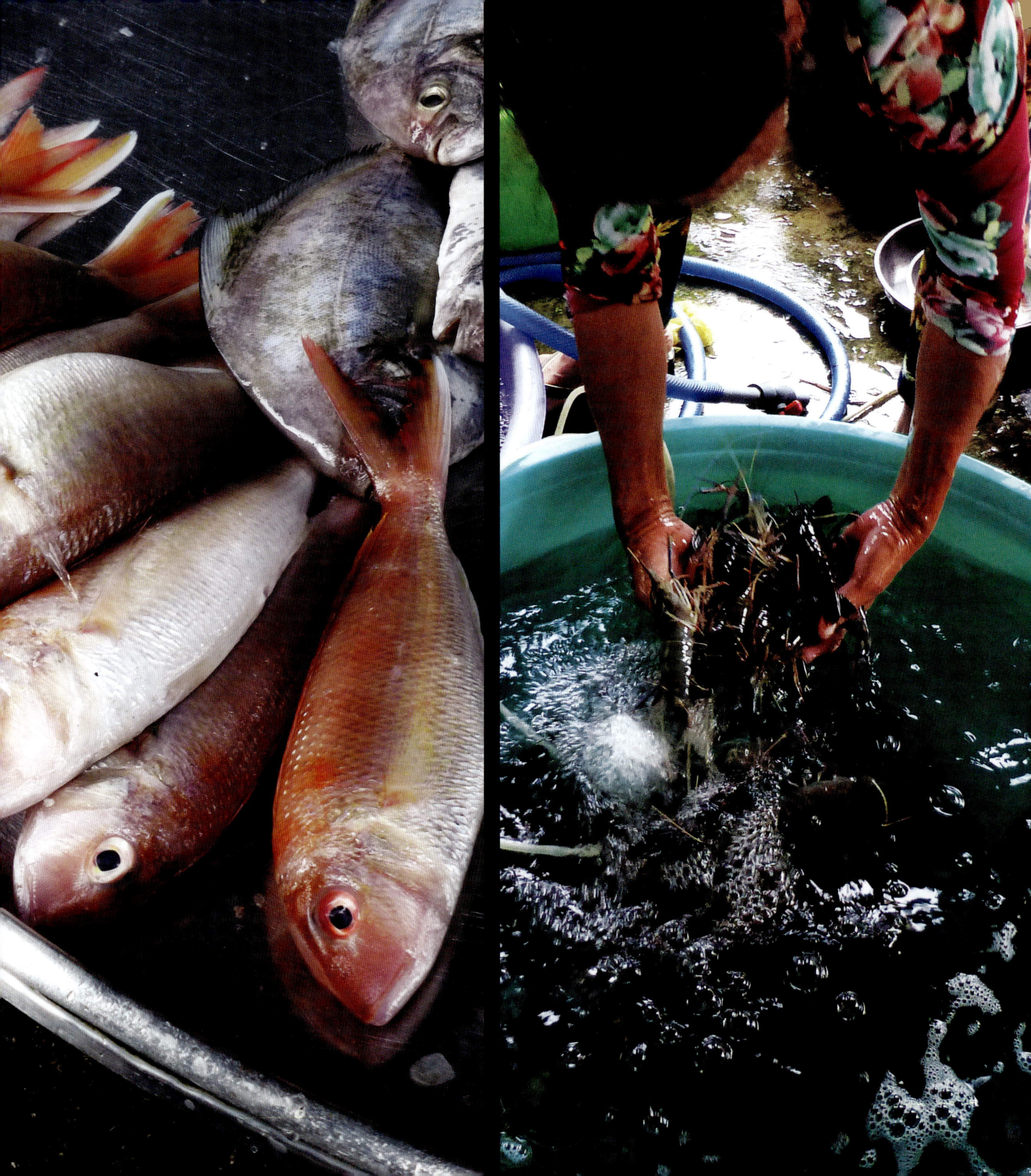

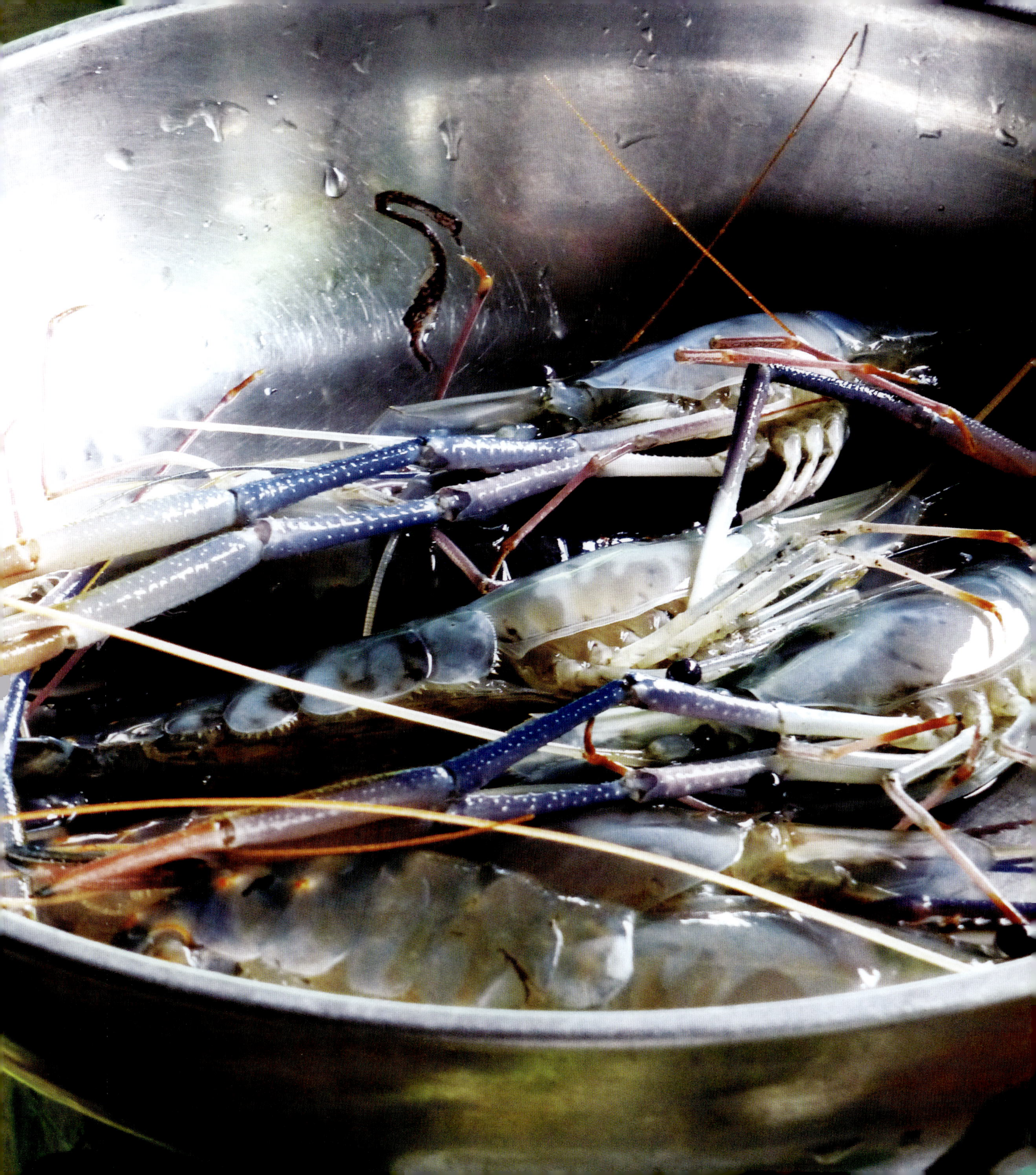

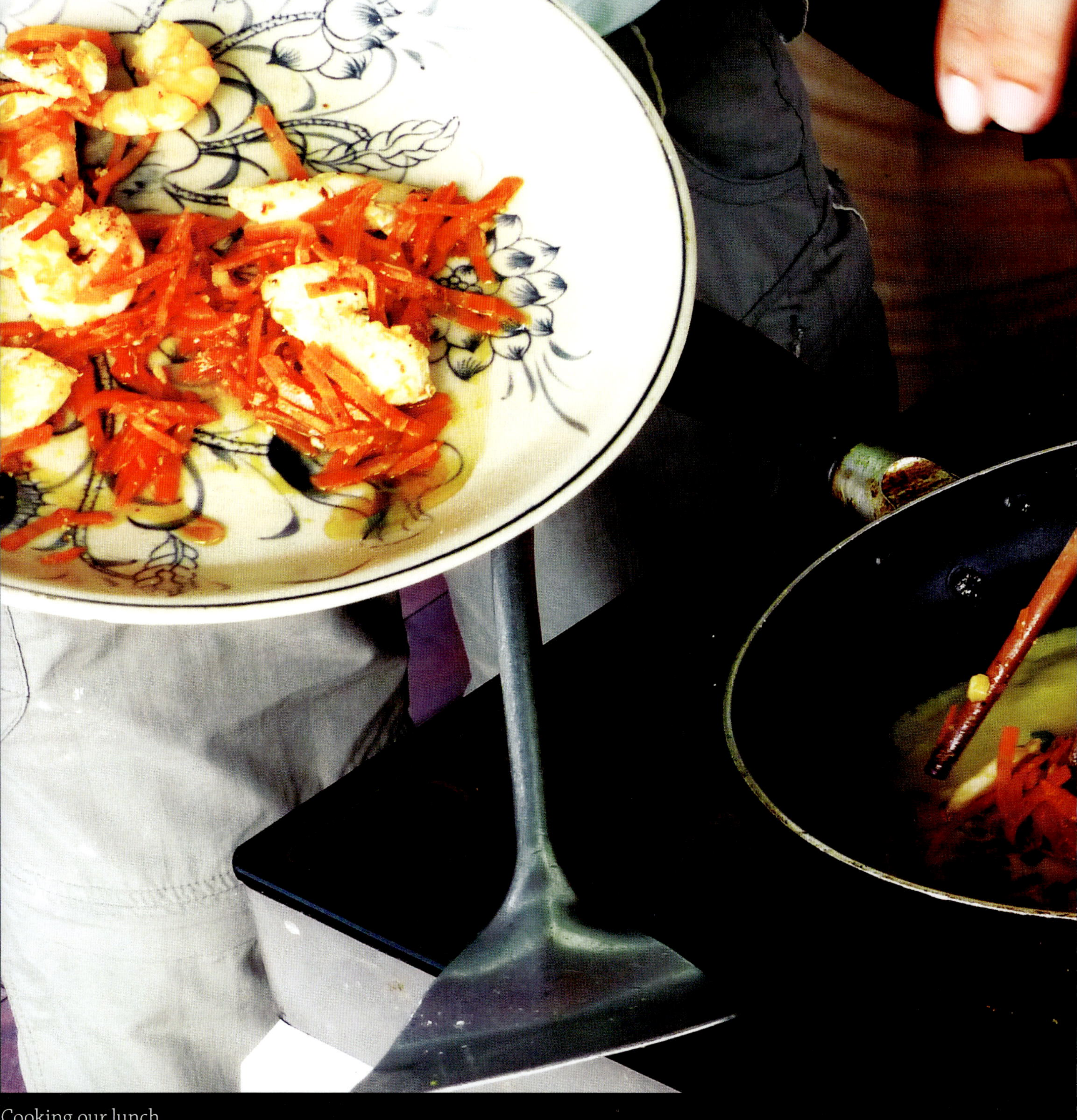

Cooking our lunch.

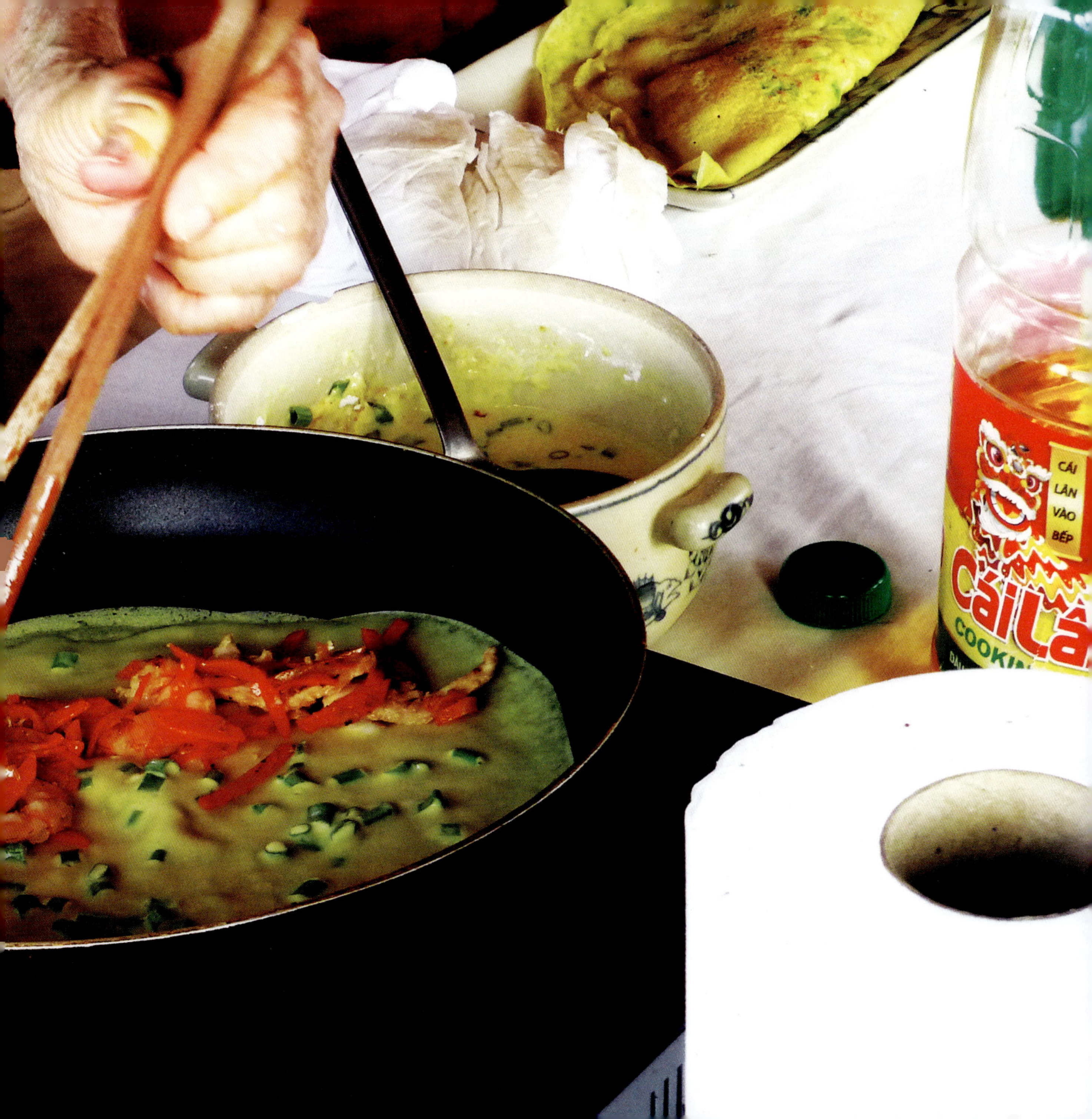
CÁI
LÂN
VÀO
BẾP

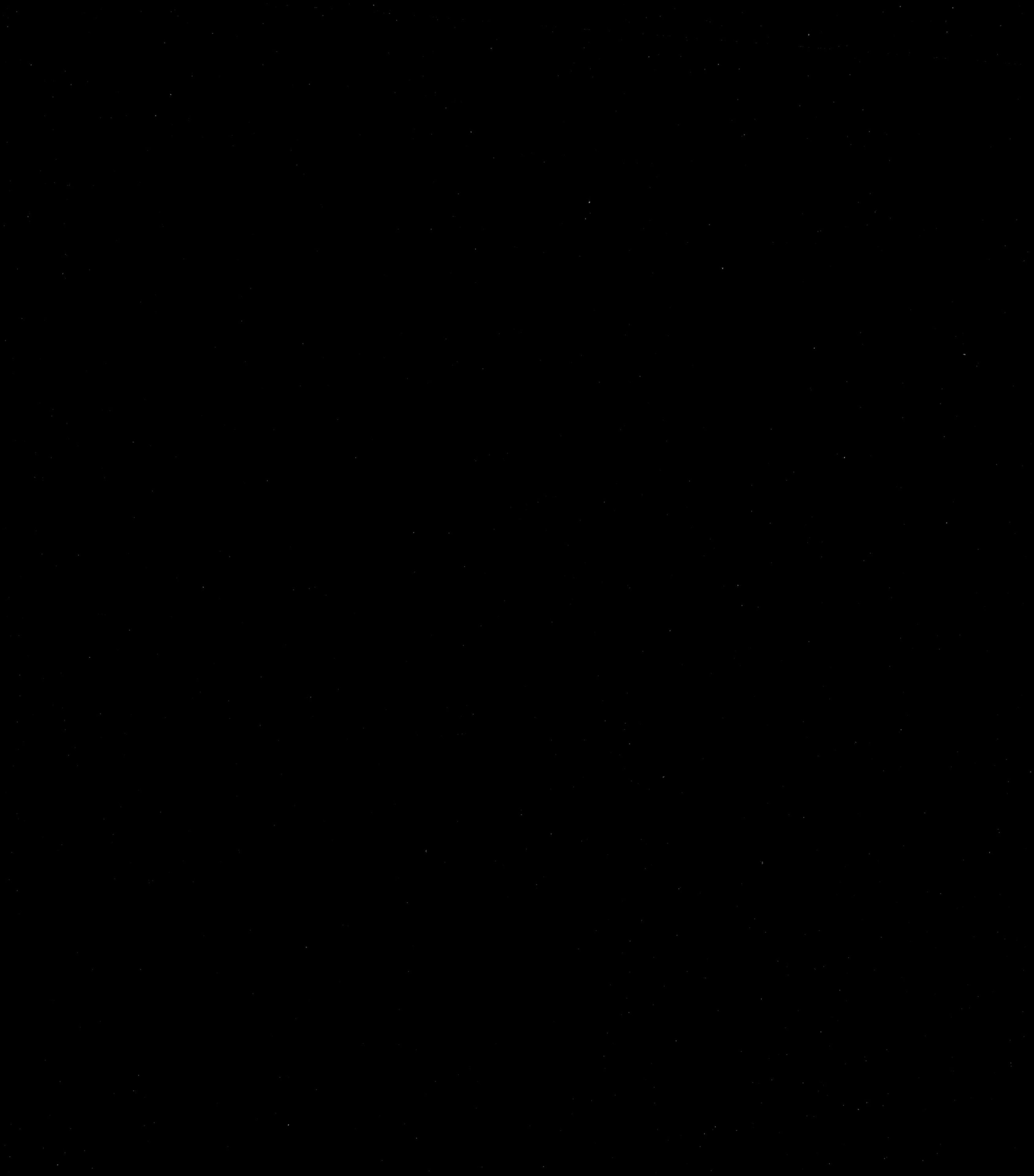

Fish are plentiful.
Produce is abundant.
Food is fresh.

This bountiful imagery
belies the reality.

The overwhelming majority of rural inhabitants struggle to emerge from a centuries-old existence. Healthy air, water and living conditions represent distant dreams.

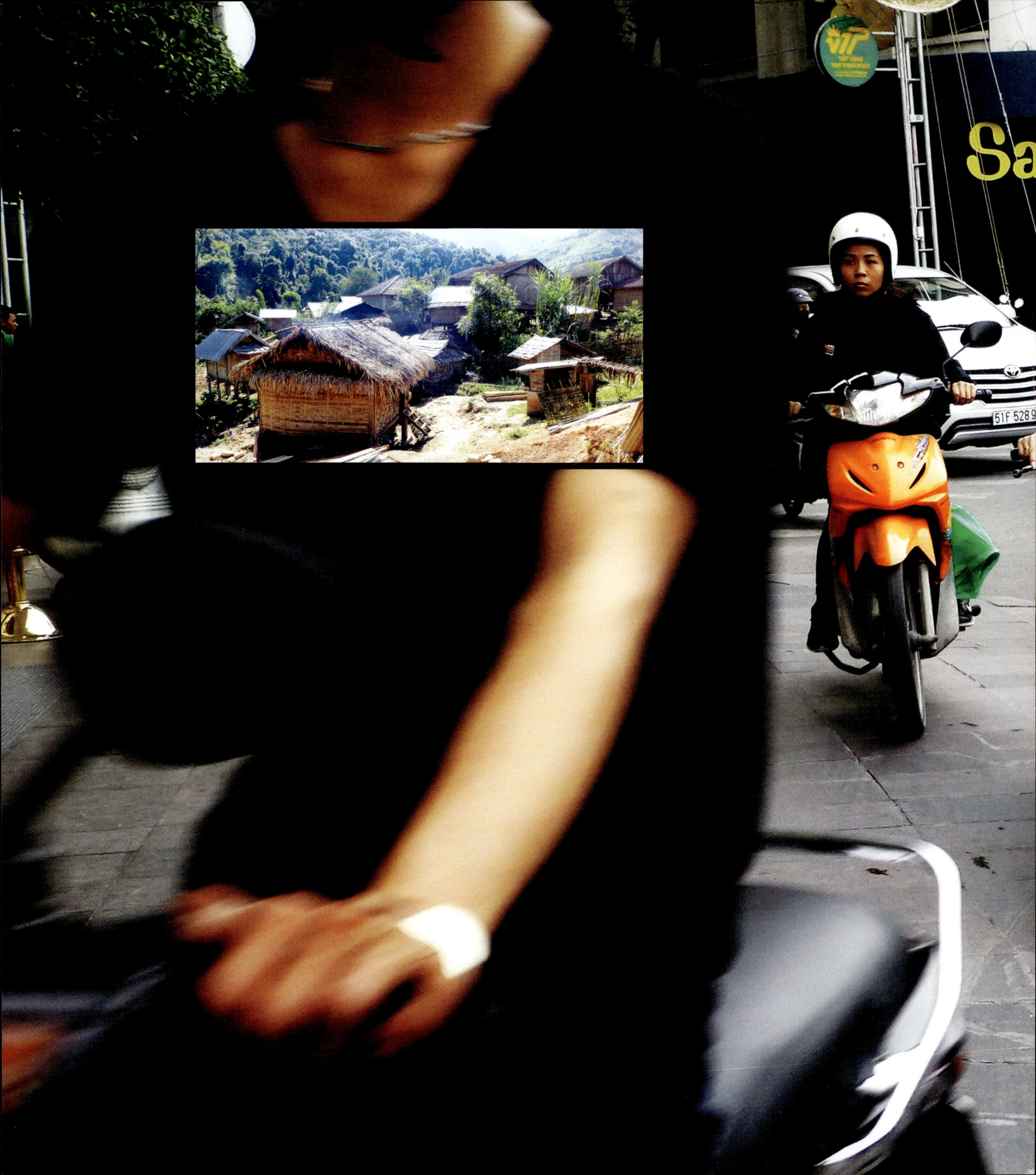

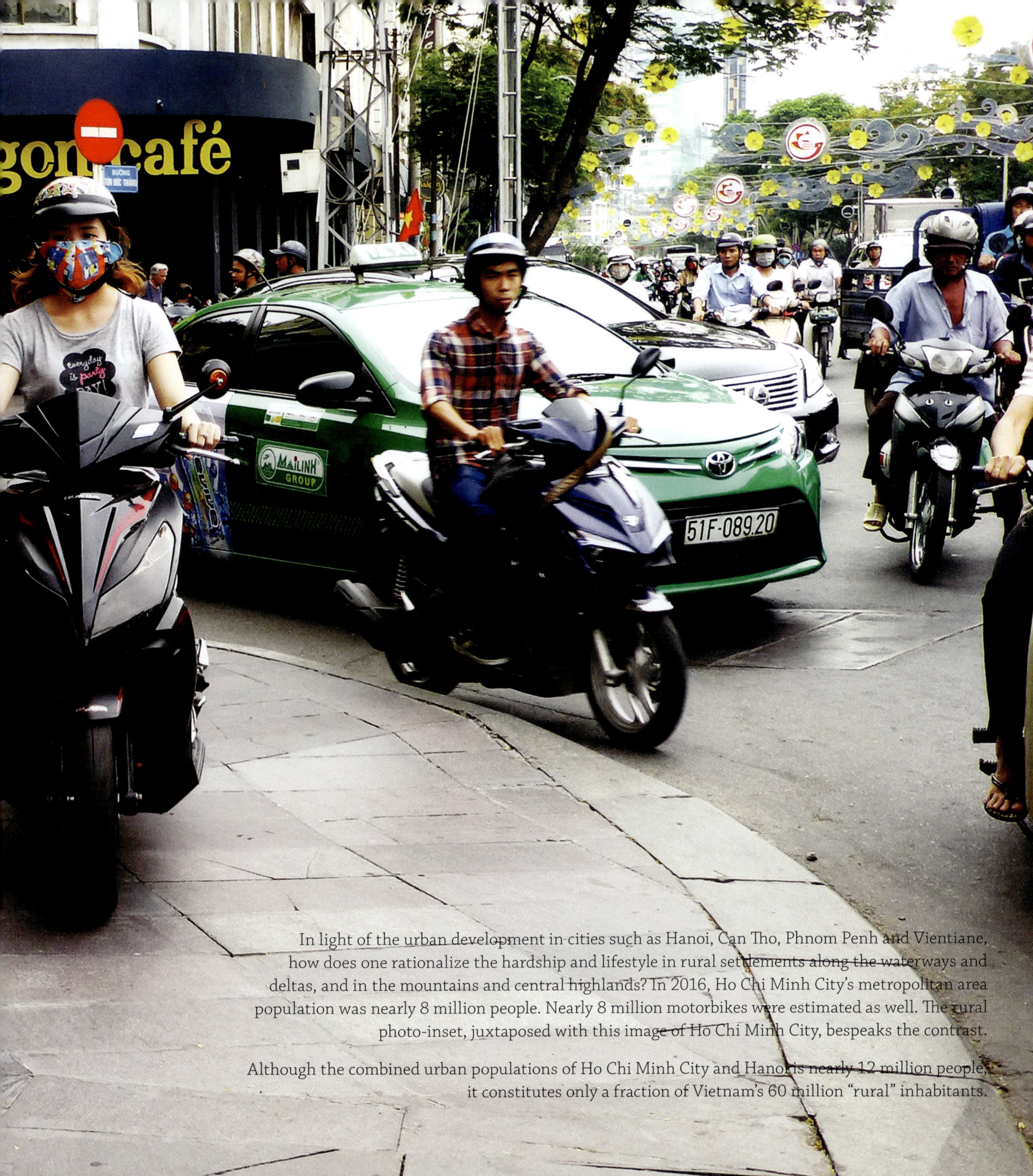

In light of the urban development in cities such as Hanoi, Can Tho, Phnom Penh and Vientiane, how does one rationalize the hardship and lifestyle in rural settlements along the waterways and deltas, and in the mountains and central highlands? In 2016, Ho Chi Minh City's metropolitan area population was nearly 8 million people. Nearly 8 million motorbikes were estimated as well. The rural photo-inset, juxtaposed with this image of Ho Chi Minh City, bespeaks the contrast.

Although the combined urban populations of Ho Chi Minh City and Hanoi is nearly 12 million people, it constitutes only a fraction of Vietnam's 60 million "rural" inhabitants.

In 2016, it was estimated that approximately 77.5 million people in Vietnam, Laos and Cambodia lived in rural areas, 67% of their combined 115 million population. An estimated 18 million were ethnic minorities, most of whom lived off the land and water. However this is not limited to minority groups. A significant portion of the rural majority live off the land and water as well. In just the eight provinces of Cambodia's Tonlé Sap Lake basin, approximately 2 million people subsist on the lake's resources or wetlands. The Kompong Khleang stilt village alone houses an estimated 10,000 majority Khmer. The numbers are staggering.

It is hard to reconcile the gap in living conditions and lifestyle between the cities and these rural villages and hamlets; modernization efforts versus economic, educational and healthcare isolation. Yet the spirit of humanity and personal expression is ever present, transcending the struggle; revealed in decoration, handcraft, color and pattern; in plantings and flowers and the articulation of tradition, family and geniality. Change will come from the children, feet rooted in the land and waters from which they live, yet eager to explore, learn and reach forward: adapting, modifying, re-using, utilizing whatever means possible to enhance their future. Resourcefulness and resilience frame the perspective, a lens to the past and a window to the future.

From the roadside villages and shoreline hamlets to the populous cities, Vietnam, Laos and Cambodia offer many contrasts for reflection – much to learn and to cause concern – especially that these contrasts still exist in this 21st century.

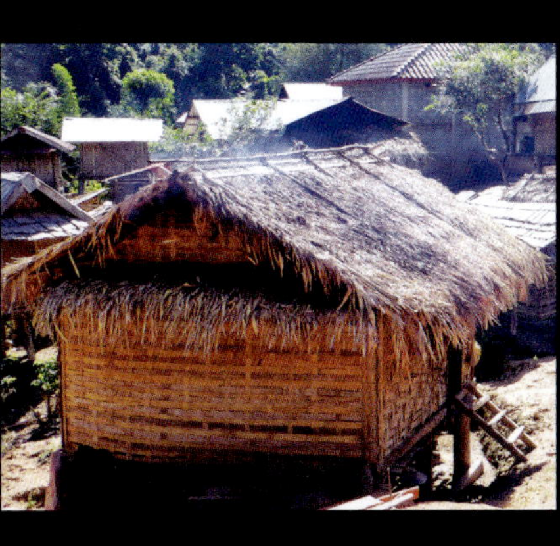
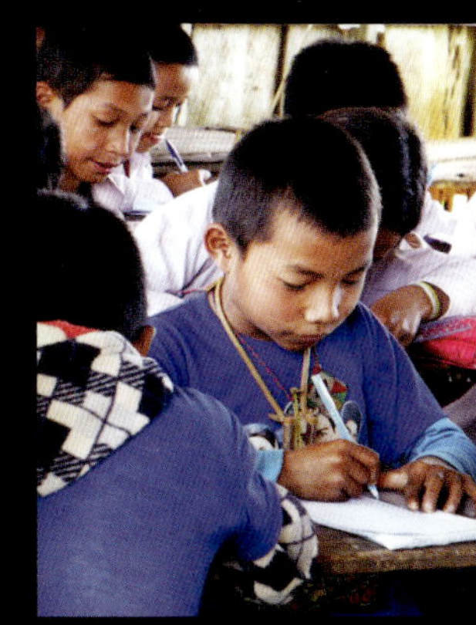
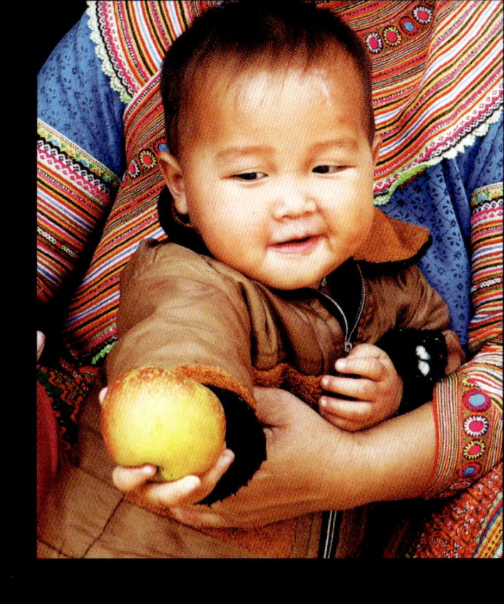
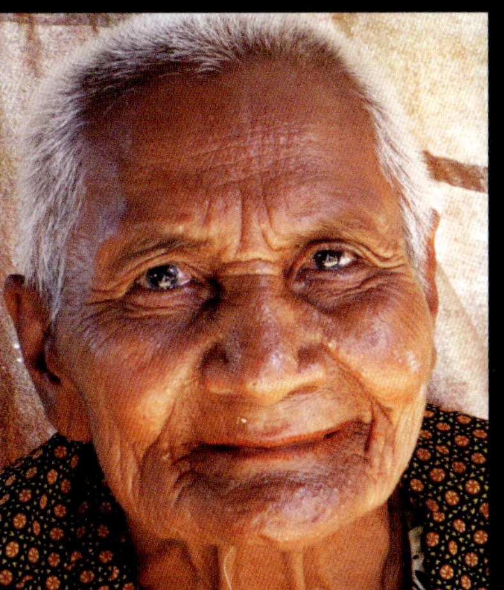
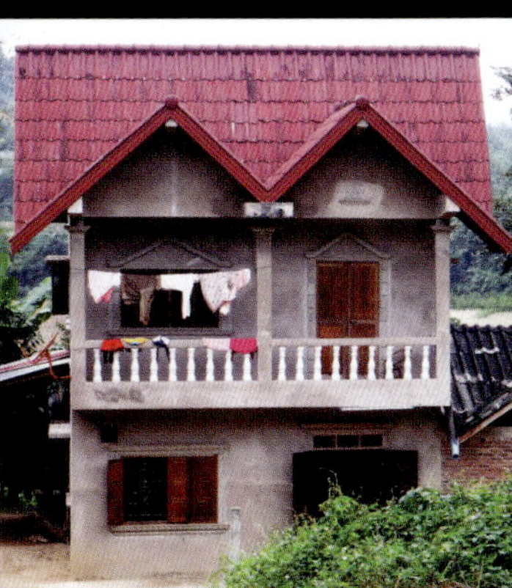
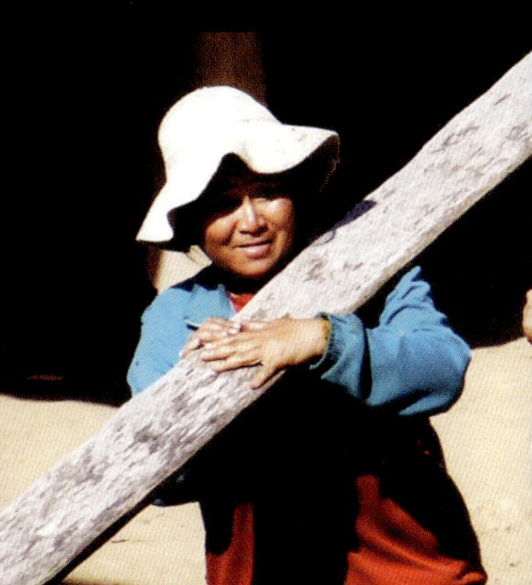

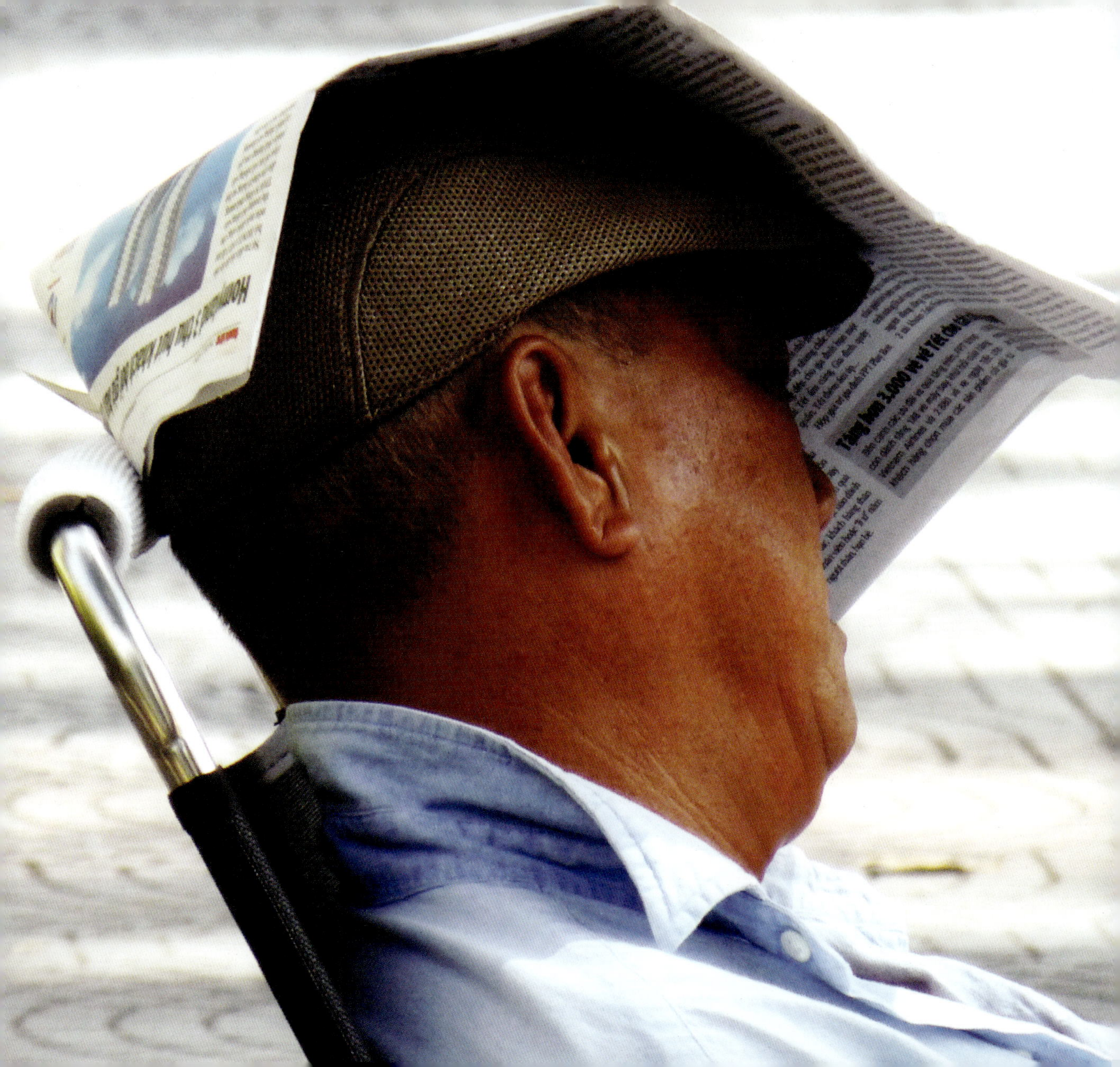

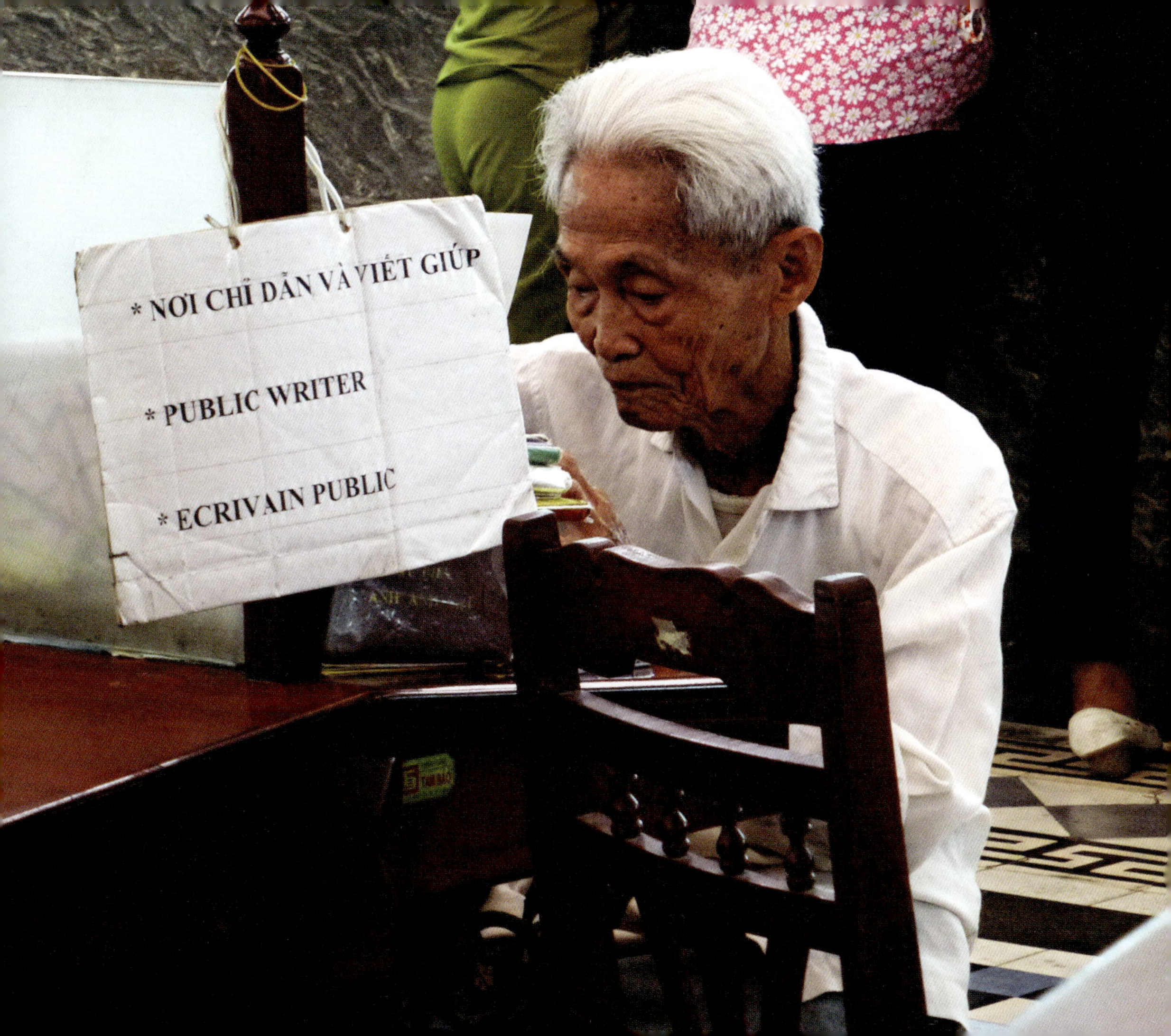
* NƠI CHỈ DẪN VÀ VIẾT GIÚP
* PUBLIC WRITER
* ECRIVAIN PUBLIC

SIX

Notes

Page x:
The United Nations Conference On Trade And Development's Least Developed Countries Report (LDC) 2017 uses the following criteria to determine LDC status, reviewed every three years by the United Nations Economic and Social Council:

- Per capita income (gross national income per capita)
- Human assets (indicators of nutrition, health, school enrolment and literacy)
- Economic vulnerability (indicators of natural and trade-related shocks, physical and economic exposure to shocks, and smallness and remoteness).

In 2017, that list contains 47 countries: Afghanistan, Angola, Bangladesh, Benin, Bhutan, Burkina Faso, Burundi, Cambodia, the Central African Republic, Chad, the Comoros, the Democratic Republic of the Congo, Djibouti, Eritrea, Ethiopia, the Gambia, Guinea, Guinea-Bissau, Haiti, Kiribati, the Lao People's Democratic Republic, Lesotho, Liberia, Madagascar, Malawi, Mali, Mauritania, Mozambique, Myanmar, Nepal, the Niger, Rwanda, Sao Tome and Principe, Senegal, Sierra Leone, Solomon Islands, Somalia, South Sudan, the Sudan, Timor-Leste, Togo, Tuvalu, Uganda, the United Republic of Tanzania, Vanuatu, Yemen and Zambia. Source: United Nations publication Sales No E.17.II.D.6 e-ISBN 978-92-1-362256-8 ISSN 0257-7550

Page 13:
According to the Vietnamese Embassy in the UK referencing the 2000 population statistics, "Vietnam is a multi-nationality country with 54 ethnic groups. The Viet (Kinh) people account for 87% of the country's population and mainly inhabit the Red River delta, the central coastal delta, the Mekong delta and major cities. The other 53 ethnic minority groups, totaling over 8 million people, are scattered over mountain areas (covering two-thirds of the country's territory) spreading from the North to the South." Source: http://www.vietnamembassy.org.uk/population.html

In 2009, the ethnic minorities comprised approximately 14% of Vietnam's population. Source: United Nations Population Fund in Vietnam: UN Apartment Building, 1st Floor, 2E Van Phuc, Hanoi, Viet Nam.

Page 49:
The population of Hanoi in 2016 was estimated at 3.79 million in the United Nations The World's Cities in 2016 – Data Booklet, United Nations, Department of Economic and Social Affairs, Population Division (2016), (ST/ESA/SER.A/392).

Page 61:
The Lao PDR's terminology for diverse populations introduced in the 1991 Constitution is "ethnic groups". The 47 official ethno-linguistic groups designated for the 1995 census were increased to 49 ethnic by the Lao Front for National Construction (LFNC) and contain more than 160 subgroups. Sources: The Lao People's Democratic Republic: Northern Region Sustainable Livelihoods Development Project, Indigenous Peoples Development Plan Document Stage: Final Project Number: 35297 August 2006, prepared by the Government of Lao People's Democratic Republic for the Asian Development Bank (ADB) and The Embassy of the Lao People's Democratic Republic to the United States of America (http://www.laoembassy.com/laosusefulinformation.pdf).

Source for the data compilation by Province: Lao Health Master Planning Study: Progress Report 1, Lao People's Democratic Republic, 2001, Appendix 6 and according to Minority Rights Group International, London, UK, the Laotian population in 2007 was 65% Buddhist, 32.9% animist. (http://minorityrights.org/country/laos)

Page 233:
On January 6, 2016, Thanh Nien News, the internet news site of the Thanh Nien Newspaper (published in Ho Chi Minh City) reported that "Ho Chi Minh City now has 7.43 million motorbikes, putting serious pressure on its transport infrastructure, local media reported, citing the Department of Transport. Compared to 2011, the number of new bikes registered in the city has increased by around 2 million, according to a Tuoi Tre report. There are also more than 1 million motorbikes brought in by migrants from other places, bringing the total count to 8.5 million, the highest in the country. HCMC has a population of around 8 million." Source: http://www.thanhniennews.com/society/ho-chi-minh-city-now-has-74-million-motorbikes-and-counting-57787.html

Page 234:
Population statistics were derived from data available from Enterprise Surveys, The World Bank Group, 2121 Pennsylvania Avenue, NW, Washington DC, 20433 USA, www.enterprisesurveys.org and IECONOMICS INC, New York, www.tradingeconomics.com.

Tonlé Sap Lake basin information was sourced from The Tonlé Sap Basin Strategy, April 2005, Asian Development Bank, Mandaluyong City, 1550 Metro Manila, Philippines, Publication Stock No. 050105. The population of Kompong Khleang is estimated from http://citypopulation.info/php/cambodia-admin.php?adm2id=171104 sourced from the National Institute of Statistics of Cambodia and from The Food and Agriculture Organization (FAO), an agency of the United Nations.

SEVEN

Acknowledgements

After the release of ***Buildings Are for People: Human Ecological Design*** in 2016 (Libri Publishing UK), my wife and I took a trip to Vietnam, Laos and Cambodia to visit and learn about the ethnic group settlements in the mountain highlands and river deltas. No book was intended. Our goal was to meet people and to explore their environs. It was an eye-opening experience that made us reflect on life's values, human adaptability and the incredible contrasts between rural and city life in this region of the world. It also brought to the forefront the conflicts between self-sufficiency, sustainability and pollution. The warmth of the people we met, their adaptability and spirit are what inspired this book. We came home with more than 10,000 photographs and a lot to ponder.

I wish to thank the guides that we met in each locale, for their patience with our incessant inquisitiveness, their translation skills, their rapport with the people we met and their willingness to share.

A special thank you to Paula Luria Caplan, my wife, whose edits and insights as an urban planner were indispensable, and who was herself a magnet to those we met.

I would like to thank Libri Publishing for even considering publishing a photojournalistic essay of this nature, let alone its publishing, and to Celia Cozens of Libri Publishing and her team for their incredible effort to publish ***Contrasts 21c*** in such a short timeframe.

Most of all, I wish to thank the numerous people in Vietnam, Laos and Cambodia that welcomed us into their lives, however briefly.

Photography Credits

The photographs in Contrasts 21c: Vietnam, Laos and Cambodia were taken by the author © 2018 Bill Caplan from November 2016 through January 2017 except for the small photographs inset in the lower right corner on pages 109 and 113 and the photograph spanning pages 224 and 225 which were taken by Paula Luria Caplan, © 2018 Paula Luria Caplan.

Maps

The maps on page xii and at the beginning of each chapter are not to scale. They have been adapted by the author from the ***Blank relief map of Indochina*** of April 4, 2014 by NordNordWest, released for use under Creative Commons by-sa-3.0 de [CC BY-SA 3.0 de (https://creativecommons.org/licenses/by-sa/3.0/de/deed.en)], via Wikimedia Commons, available at https://commons.wikimedia.org/wiki/File:Indochina_blank_relief_map.svg. The maps as adapted by the author are also available for use under the Creative Commons license and are available for free usage with credit to NordNordWest, the license https://creativecommons.org/licenses/by-sa/3.0/de/legalcode, the work's title ***Blank relief map of Indochina***, as adapted by Bill Caplan and by identifying the use of the work in any other adaptation. You are free: to share – to copy, distribute and transmit the work, and to remix – to adapt the work. You must attribute the work in the manner specified by the author or licensor (but not in any way that suggests that they endorse you or your use of the work). If you alter, transform, or build upon this work, you may distribute the resulting work only under the same or similar license to this one.